DOLLARS
AND SENSE

PROBLEM SOLVING STRATEGIES
IN CONSUMER MATHEMATICS

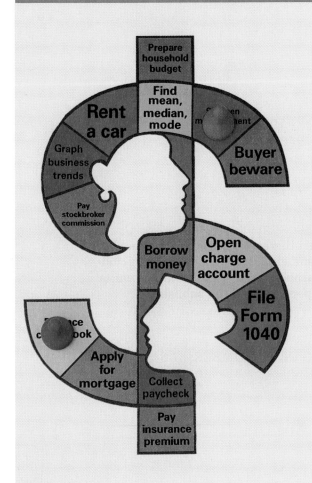

ROBERT K. GERVER

RICHARD J. SGROI

North Shore High School
Long Island, New York

MO10AA
PUBLISHED BY
SOUTH-WESTERN PUBLISHING CO.
CINCINNATI   WEST CHICAGO, IL   CARROLLTON, TX   LIVERMORE, CA

Copyright ©1989
by South-Western Publishing Co.
Cincinnati, Ohio

Teacher Consultants
Andrewdelle R. Hensley
Mathematics Teacher
Deerfield Beach High School
Deerfield Beach, Florida

Robert A. Francis, Chairman
Mathematics Department
Ross S. Sterling High School
Baytown, Texas

ISBN: 0-538-60000-4
LIBRARY OF CONGRESS CATALOG CARD NUMBER: 87-63548

23456789 D 654321098
Printed in the United States of America

PREFACE

TO THE STUDENT

Often mathematics and business teachers hear students ask, "When am I ever going to use this?" Perhaps you too have asked your teacher, "How will this help me in real life?" *Dollars and Sense — Problem-Solving Strategies in Consumer Mathematics* has the answer to both of these important questions.

Mathematics skills will play an important role throughout your life. Many decisions will require accurate problem-solving skills and computational skills. *Dollars and Sense — Problem-Solving Strategies in Consumer Mathematics* will help you to improve these skills while giving you an inside look into your role as a consumer in American society. Equipped with these skills, you will have the capability of becoming an educated consumer as well as a responsible young adult.

TO THE TEACHER

Dollars and Sense is an innovative approach to consumer mathematics that represents twelve years of teaching and field testing at the high school level. The *Dollars and Sense* package was designed to meet the needs of both the student and teacher. Since all students are not the same, *Dollars and Sense* provides many opportunities for students to sharpen their skills in different ways. These include an abundance of textbook problems, manipulative activities, computer activities, and field work. Combinations of these features can be used to review, reinforce, enrich, and reteach.

OBJECTIVES

The main objective of *Dollars and Sense* is to help students become mathematically literate and self-confident. Through the use of *Dollars and Sense,* you should be able to provide your students with a comprehensive, motivating consumer mathematics curriculum. *Dollars and Sense* will help your students improve their mathematics problem-solving skills in a consumer-oriented framework.

SPECIAL FEATURES

Dollars and Sense combines some unique features with traditionally successful ones. Instructional strategies are included to develop the use of the calculator as a problem-solving tool. Independent activities give students an opportunity to see how mathematics is used in real life. Manipulative activities allow students to discover mathematics and consumer concepts through a hands-on approach. User-friendly software allows students to supplement text material with personal computer interaction. Updatable problems, consumer resources, and a yearly newsletter offer you the ability to keep abreast of changes in consumer legislation and trends. *Dollars and Sense* also includes a chapter-by-chapter listing of key terms, a glossary, and chapter review problems.

A comprehensive teacher's annotated edition is an indispensible tool in the *Dollars and Sense* package. The *Teacher's Annotated Edition* includes lesson objectives, discussion points, and solutions to all problems.

MEET THE AUTHORS

Robert Gerver and Richard Sgroi are colleagues in the Mathematics Department at North Shore High School, Glen Head, New York. They are also doctoral candidates in the mathematics education Ph.D. program at New York University, where Mr. Sgroi is a research assistant working under a National Science Foundation Grant, "K-6 Supplementary Materials for a Technological Society." Mr. Gerver is currently serving a three-year term as a member of the New York State Regents Competency Test Committee.

The authors have taught high school consumer mathematics since 1973. In addition, Mr. Gerver and Mr. Sgroi have taught mathematics and math education at State University of New York, Long Island University, Adelphi University, Dowling College, and BOCES III Institute for Gifted and Talented Students. They have spoken at numerous national, regional, and local math conferences. Articles by Mr. Gerver and Mr. Sgroi have appeared in *The Mathematics Teacher, The Arithmetic Teacher, Games* Magazine, *Curriculum Review, The New York State Math Teacher's Journal,* and *The Balance Sheet.*

Their text-workbook, SOUND FOUNDATIONS: A Practical Mathematics Simulation, is published by South-Western Publishing Co.

CONTENTS

TOPIC 1

LET THE BUYER PREPARE

Just what is a consumer? A **consumer** is anyone who buys goods or services. **Goods** are any items for sale. **Services** are tasks that other people do for you, such as repair work or handling your telephone calls. Long ago, people made many of the things they needed and wanted. They knew the quality of what they produced. Now we are mainly consumers of goods and services provided by others. These goods and services are sold by individuals and companies that compete for our business. You need a great deal of information to make wise buying decisions. For instance, you need to know how long a product will last, whether the seller will repair or replace it if something goes wrong, how much it costs, and what size or amount you need.

CHAPTER *1*

LET THE BUYER BEWARE

SECTION 1 • TYPES OF WARRANTIES

Industry today has the technology to create everything from lipstick to lasers. Some products are manufactured with more care than others. For instance, how long should a television last? You would probably like it to last forever. Modern technology might be able to produce a television that would last a very, very long time. However, the cost of inventing and producing such a set would be high. Instead, television makers manufacture sets that will probably last a limited amount of time. This is called **planned obsolescence.**

You should not expect goods to last forever, but you do have a right to expect them to last a reasonable amount of time. If a television you bought last week stopped working, you would certainly return it. But what if the set was two years old when it stopped working? Would you still be entitled to have the set repaired free of charge? What if you accidently dropped a brand new television set while carrying it home? Should the manufacturer pay for necessary repairs?

A good way to answer these questions is to think about the manufacturer's guarantee, or **warranty,** of the product. All products are sold with a warranty. A warranty is a guarantee of a product's performance. Warranties protect consumers against defective products. There are four types of warranties.

- **Implied warranty.** This is an unwritten guarantee that a product will do what it is supposed to do. *Every* product carries this type of warranty. A light bulb must provide light; a pencil must write.

- **Express warranty.** This is a written guarantee covering specific conditions of the warranty. It lists the specific parts that are guaranteed, the length of the warranty, and any labor charges for warranty repairs.

- **Full warranty.** This is a written guarantee covering repairs or replacement of the entire product or certain parts of the product for a specified time.

- **Limited warranty.** This written guarantee covers only certain parts of the product for specified lengths of time. If a limited warranty covers only parts, the customer is required to return the product to the factory for repair and pay for handling fees and labor costs.

You should always find out what type of warranty a major purchase has. It often may be wise to pay a little more for a product and receive a better warranty. That way, you are protected if anything goes wrong with the product.

Indeed, you should always be careful when you shop, especially when you are making major purchases. The Latin phrase **caveat emptor** (let the buyer beware) has become a battle cry for consumers. You can be a careful shopper by comparing prices and warranties when possible. You should also notice the conditions of the sale. Know what your rights as a consumer are — and are not.

- Murray bought a six-dollar container of antifreeze for his car. The product was defective. It froze and cracked his car's engine. The manufacturer agreed to replace the antifreeze, but Murray now needs a new engine as well. Who is responsible for the cost of the engine?

- A magazine offered Janice $100,000 to take a picture of a famous rock musician. She took the picture and brought her film to a camera store to be developed. The store ruined the negatives and could not print the picture. The store owners gave Janice a new roll of film, but do they have to pay her the $100,000?

Sellers cannot afford to take responsibility for all the damages that are the result or consequence of defective goods and services. These damages are called **consequential damages.** Many products carry a **disclaimer** that informs the customer of the limits of the seller's responsibility. For example, the roll of film or the container of antifreeze might have been labeled "Not responsible for consequential damages." It is important to read labels and warranties carefully before purchasing a product or service.

Skills and Strategies

Once you have purchased the product, you should determine the **expiration date,** or last day of coverage, of your warranty. The calendar in Figure 1.1 will help you determine the length of a warranty's coverage.

JAN	1	2	3	4	5	6	7	8	9	10	11	12	13	14	15	16	17	18	19	20	21	22	23	24	25	26	27	28	29	30	31
FEB	1	2	3	4	5	6	7	8	9	10	11	12	13	14	15	16	17	18	19	20	21	22	23	24	25	26	27	28*			
MAR	1	2	3	4	5	6	7	8	9	10	11	12	13	14	15	16	17	18	19	20	21	22	23	24	25	26	27	28	29	30	31
APR	1	2	3	4	5	6	7	8	9	10	11	12	13	14	15	16	17	18	19	20	21	22	23	24	25	26	27	28	29	30	
MAY	1	2	3	4	5	6	7	8	9	10	11	12	13	14	15	16	17	18	19	20	21	22	23	24	25	26	27	28	29	30	31
JUN	1	2	3	4	5	6	7	8	9	10	11	12	13	14	15	16	17	18	19	20	21	22	23	24	25	26	27	28	29	30	
JUL	1	2	3	4	5	6	7	8	9	10	11	12	13	14	15	16	17	18	19	20	21	22	23	24	25	26	27	28	29	30	31
AUG	1	2	3	4	5	6	7	8	9	10	11	12	13	14	15	16	17	18	19	20	21	22	23	24	25	26	27	28	29	30	31
SEP	1	2	3	4	5	6	7	8	9	10	11	12	13	14	15	16	17	18	19	20	21	22	23	24	25	26	27	28	29	30	
OCT	1	2	3	4	5	6	7	8	9	10	11	12	13	14	15	16	17	18	19	20	21	22	23	24	25	26	27	28	29	30	31
NOV	1	2	3	4	5	6	7	8	9	10	11	12	13	14	15	16	17	18	19	20	21	22	23	24	25	26	27	28	29	30	
DEC	1	2	3	4	5	6	7	8	9	10	11	12	13	14	15	16	17	18	19	20	21	22	23	24	25	26	27	28	29	30	31

*Except leap year, when there are 29 days.

Figure 1.1 Calendar Showing the Number of Days in Each Month

To find the expiration date of a warranty, subtract the date of purchase from the number of days in that month. Use the calendar in Figure 1.1 to help you. The difference gives you the number of days covered by the warranty in the month of purchase. Then add the number of days in the next month. Continue this process until you have included the full length of time specified by the warranty.

Here you will learn how to find the expiration dates of warranties. You will also see how warranties are important in many consumer situations.

1. Marty Safran bought a stereo radio on July 24. It was guaranteed for 30 days. What is the expiration date of the warranty?

    Solution: Use Figure 1.1.

31	number of days in July
− 24	date of purchase
7	number of days in July that are covered by warranty

30	length of warranty in days
− 7	number of days in July that are covered by warranty
23	number of days in August that are covered by warranty

    The expiration date of the warranty is August 23.

2. Sandra's new electronic keyboard carries a 60-day full warranty and a 1-year warranty for parts. She bought the keyboard on April 17. When does the full warranty expire?

Solution:

$$
\begin{array}{rl}
30 & \text{number of days in April} \\
-\ 17 & \text{date of purchase} \\
\hline
13 & \text{number of days in April that are under warranty}
\end{array}
$$

$$
\begin{array}{rl}
13 & \text{number of days in April that are under warranty} \\
+\ 31 & \text{number of days in May} \\
\hline
44 & \text{number of days in April and May that are covered}
\end{array}
$$

$$
\begin{array}{rl}
60 & \text{length of warranty in days} \\
-\ 44 & \text{number of days in April and May that are covered} \\
\hline
16 & \text{number of days in June that are covered}
\end{array}
$$

The full warranty expires on June 16.

Problems

Use the calendar in Figure 1.1, page 4, to complete Problems 1–10.

1. On May 10, Steve Rozales noticed that there were 30 days left on the warranty for his videocassette recorder. What is the expiration date of the warranty?

✓ **2.** Akira bought a new car on July 30. It came with a 1-year warranty. On May 27 of the following year, Akira noticed that his car's air conditioning was not working. Had the warranty expired by May 27? Explain your answer.

3. A local department store offers a 60-day full warranty on all goods in addition to the manufacturer's warranty. Stan bought a microwave oven on June 8. When does the store's warranty on the oven expire?

✓ **4.** Janine has 94 days left on the warranty on her electric guitar. It is September 23. When does her warranty expire?

5. The Squeaky-Klean Dishwasher Company gives limited warranties for 60 days on all of its dishwashers. Nina bought a dishwasher on June 26. It stopped working on August 18. Was the product still under warranty when it broke?

✓ **6.** On December 1, Ruth Fanelli bought a food processor that came with a 30-day money-back guarantee. If after 30 days, she wasn't completely satisfied, she could return the product for a full refund. What is the latest date she can return the food processor?

7. Many automobile carburetors are guaranteed for 30 days. If you purchase such a carburetor on December 18, will it still be under warranty on January 18?

✓ **8.** Barbara purchased a radio on May 17. It was a gift for her brother, Robert, whose birthday is May 30. The store manager agreed to begin the 60-day exchange period on Robert's birthday instead of the date of purchase. When is the last day Robert can exchange the radio?

9. Linda bought an air conditioner at an end-of-summer sale on September 8. It was warranted for 200 days. She didn't use the air conditioner during the fall and winter. On a hot spring day she turned it on, and it didn't work. She took the air conditioner in to be repaired the next day, May 27. The dealer told her that her warranty had expired. Was he correct?

10. Rose bought a telephone on August 10. The phone came with a 90-day warranty. On what date does the warranty expire?

SECTION 2 ● THE SALES RECEIPT

Saul was shopping at his favorite hobby store to buy materials for a new model plane. He bought five jars of paint ($1.15 each), two jars of sealer ($2.25 each), and three different sizes of balsa wood ($2.45, $3.10, $4.85). The store clerk added Saul's purchases on a cash register and told him the total was $26.03. Saul was surprised that it was so high, but he paid the bill. When he got home, he added the prices and realized that he had been overcharged. He had to return to the store for a refund.

How could Saul have avoided a second trip to the store? He could have added the prices of the products before he brought them to the counter. That would have been difficult, unless he had been carrying a calculator with him. A simpler approach would have been to estimate the total cost of his goods. **Estimation** is a technique used to determine whether your answers are reasonable. Saul could easily have done the following estimation in his head:

5 jars of paint	about $1.00 each =	$5.00
2 jars of sealer	about $2.50 each =	$5.00
balsa wood	about $3.00	$3.00
balsa wood	about $3.00	$3.00
balsa wood	about $5.00	$5.00
	estimated total cost $21.00	

Because he needed only a rough estimate, Saul would not have had to estimate sales tax. Even this rough estimate would have alerted him to the fact that the total of $26.03 was not reasonable. He could then have checked the sales receipt for accuracy. A **sales receipt** is a paper record of a transaction. Every consumer is entitled to get a sales receipt with each purchase.

Figure 1.2 Receipts

Look at the receipts in Figure 1.2. Notice that both the handwritten and computerized receipts include a list of the goods and services purchased. A wise consumer will use a receipt to make sure that the charges are the same as the agreed prices. Costly mistakes can be made by clerks and complicated machines.

To inspect a sales receipt, first check each item. Make sure that you have been charged the price you expected to pay. If you bought more than one of the same item, check to see that you were charged for the right number of items. Saul found out that the clerk had charged him for eight jars of paint instead of five.

Next, you should check the **subtotal** on the receipt. The subtotal is the **sum** of the goods and services purchased. The subtotal does not include sales tax. You should add the prices of your purchases to find the sum.

You should save your sales receipts as proof of purchase for warranty purposes. A copy of the sales receipt must also be submitted if you claim a rebate from a manufacturer. A **rebate** is a partial refund of the purchase price sent to the buyer by the manufacturer. Many companies offer rebates to increase sales.

Skills and Strategies

Here you will see how an alert consumer can use a sales receipt to check the total cost of goods purchased. Read each example carefully.

1.   Allison bought the following items at the Buymore Department Store. What should the subtotal on her receipt be?

    a pair of earrings, $9.95
    a pair of jeans, $35.00
    a business suit, $142.50

    Solution: Only one of each item was purchased. Therefore, the subtotal is the sum of the prices of the three items. When numbers containing decimal points are added, the decimal points must be lined up vertically.

    $$
    \begin{array}{r}
    \$ \quad 9.95 \\
    35.00 \\
    +\ 142.50 \\
    \hline
    \$187.45
    \end{array}
    $$

    A decimal point can be written to the right of any whole number. Here, zeros are inserted after the decimal point as placeholders.

    subtotal

Shoppers usually do not carry pencil and paper with them. It is often impractical to do computations by hand in an aisle of a store. A calculator is an essential tool for today's consumer. It computes quickly and accurately when used correctly. You can "speak" to your calculator by pressing certain keys in a particular order. This is called a **calculator keystroke sequence.** All new calculator keystroke sequences should begin with the pressing of the AC (all clear) key. This key removes the digits from the display and shows a zero. The following calculator sequence can be used to solve the problem.

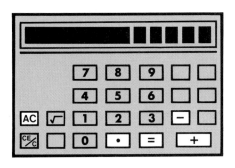

AC 9.95 + 35 + 142.50 =

The number 187.45 should appear in the display. Allison's subtotal should be $187.45.

2. Erik bought a portable radio for $34.79, including tax. How much change should he receive from a $50 bill?

Solution: You must remember to line up the decimals and then subtract. The answer to a subtraction problem is called the **difference.**

$50.00   amount Erik gave the cashier
− 34.79   cost of the radio
$15.21   Erik's change (the difference)

Erik should receive $15.21 in change.

You could also use this sequence of calculator keystrokes to solve the problem:

AC 50.00 − 34.79 =

The number 15.21 should appear in the display. Erik's change should be $15.21.

3. Ted made these purchases at Grail's Hardware Store. Find the correct subtotal.

GRAIL'S HARDWARE STORE			
Quantity	Item	Unit Price	Amount
3	Hammers	$2.95	
5	Light Bulbs	.75	
1	Ladder	37.95	
2	Garbage Cans	9.00	
		Subtotal	

Solution: Find the amount spent on each item. To do this, multiply the number of items purchased by the price of the item. The answer to a multiplication problem is called a **product.**

The following calculator keystroke sequence can be used to solve this problem.

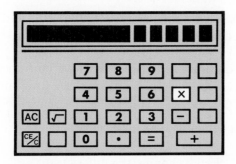

AC   3 × 2.95 =   The amount spent on hammers
$\underbrace{}_{\text{quantity}}$ $\underbrace{}_{\text{unit price}}$ ($8.85) should appear in the display.

AC   5 × 0.75 =   The amount spent on light bulbs
$\underbrace{}_{\text{quantity}}$ $\underbrace{}_{\text{unit price}}$ ($3.75) should appear in the display.

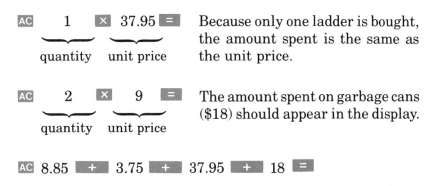

Because only one ladder is bought, the amount spent is the same as the unit price.

The amount spent on garbage cans ($18) should appear in the display.

AC 8.85 + 3.75 + 37.95 + 18 =

The correct subtotal ($68.55) should appear in the display.

A *single* keystroke sequence can be used to find Ted's subtotal. It uses the calculator's **memory** to store (remember or save) the individual amounts. The memory stores numbers for you. The sequence uses the keys you used above, and three new keys.

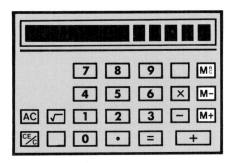

This is a two-function key:
    Pressed *once* it becomes MR
    Pressed *twice* it becomes MC

This key *recalls* or displays the number currently in the memory.

This key *clears* the calculator memory.

This key *adds* the number in the display to the number stored in the memory.

This key *subtracts* the number in the display from the number in the memory.

Ted's subtotal can be found by using the keystroke sequence at the top of the next page. Enter the sequence on your calculator. Notice the way that the sequence finds the same answer you got by adding the amounts separately.

AC 3 × 2.95 = M+ 5 × 0.75 = M+ 37.95 M+

2 × 9 = M+ M⁻

4. Millie bought two gallons of antifreeze that cost $4.99 each. She received a rebate coupon good for $1.50 off each gallon purchased. What is the final cost of the antifreeze?

Solution:

$4.99	price of each gallon of antifreeze
× 2	number of gallons
$9.98	total cost

$1.50	amount of rebate coupon
× 2	number of gallons
$3.00	total rebate

$9.98	total cost
− 3.00	total rebate
$6.98	final cost

The following keystroke sequence could be used to find the final cost of the antifreeze:

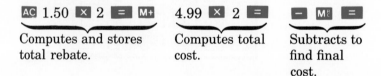

| Computes and stores total rebate. | Computes total cost. | Subtracts to find final cost. |

Problems

1. **a.** 69.38 + 1.12 + 6.3 =
   b. 15.38 + 1.15 =
   c. 16.3 + 5.1 =
   d. 18.8 + 15.13 =
   e. 9 + 4.1 + 16.33 =
   f. Find the sum of 6 and 7.2.

2. **a.** 15.19 − 6.13 =
   b. 213.1 − 4.2 =
   c. 163.004 − 4.1 =
   d. 38.12 − 2.04 =
   e. 17.9 − 6.12 =
   f. 180 − 12.3 =

3. **a.** $69.13 \times 4.1 =$
   b. $12.1 \times 6 =$
   c. $12.1 \times .06 =$
   d. $5 \times 19.3 =$
   e. $16 \times 3.1 \times 4.8 =$
   f. Find the product of 16.2 and 8.9.

✓ **4.** **a.** Estimate the product of 10.2 and 6.7.
   b. Write the calculator keystroke sequence that you would use to find the product of 10.2 and 6.7.

   c. Find the product of 10.2 and 6.7.

5. **a.** Estimate the sum of 5.7 and 12.9.
   b. Write the calculator keystroke sequence that you would use to find the sum of 5.7 and 12.9.

   c. Find the sum of 5.7 and 12.9.

6. **a.** Estimate the difference between 7.4 and 3.3.
   b. Write the calculator keystroke sequence that you would use to find the difference between 7.4 and 3.3.

   c. Find the difference between 7.4 and 3.3.

7. Lindsey bought eight SuperCell batteries for her radio. The batteries cost $2.95 for a package of two batteries. She received a rebate slip good for 50¢ off each package of two batteries. What is her final cost for the batteries?

✓ **8.** Find the subtotal of Karl's shopping list below.

   wheelchair, $342.50
   cane, $5.00
   portable ramp, $187.95

9. Nancy is buying equipment for the Glen Oaks girls' softball team. She purchases a dozen softballs ($4.75 each) and three bats ($9.35 each).

   a.   What is the total amount of her purchase?
   b.   How much change should she receive from a $100 bill?

10.   The computerized cash register at the One Note Music Store has broken down. Phil is purchasing 1 gross (a gross = 144 units) of guitar picks. The picks sell for 13 cents each. The cashier fills in Phil's receipt by hand. The receipt lists a subtotal of $19.72. Is the subtotal correct?

✓ **11.**   Find the amount spent for each item from the U-Repair Auto Supplies Shop.
   a.   4 ball joints at $29.95 each
   b.   2 front shock absorbers at $10.90 each
   c.   2 rear shock absorbers at $12 each
   d.   1 idler arm at $38.50
   e.   What is the subtotal for the above items?

12.   The Alpine Diner has its Pay What You Weigh Special every Tuesday afternoon. On that day, lunch costs 1 cent for each pound of the customer's weight. The Bethpage family eats at the diner and are weighed as follows: Lars (211 pounds); Nina (103 pounds); Neil (121 pounds); Art (163 pounds); Linda (119 pounds).
   a.   How much will the Bethpage family pay for lunch?
   b.   What will be their change from a ten-dollar bill?

✓ **13.**   Find the missing amounts and the subtotal.

ROSEANN'S JEANS			
LAKE SUCCESS MALL			
Quantity	Description	Unit Price	Amount
3	Jeans	$19.99	**a.**
2	Belts	5.00	**b.**
1	Jacket	94.95	**c.**
		Subtotal	**d.**

14. Jose found a mistake on his receipt from Barbara's Beepers. Find the mistake, and correct the amount.

Quantity	Item	Unit Price	Amount
	BARBARA'S BEEPERS		
	Miami, Florida		
	"Jeepers, Creepers—Buy Our Beepers!"		
3	Superphones	$68.88	$206.64
2	Walkie-Talkies	17.00	34.00
10	Batteries	.99	99.00

15. Pizza Cove is ordering ingredients for next week's menu. There is a mistake on the order form. Find the mistake, the correct amount, and the subtotal.

Quantity	Ingredients	Unit Price	Amount
	PIZZA COVE		
3 cans	Tomato Sauce	$9.00	$ 27.00
120 lb	Flour	.90	180.00
1 lb	Yeast	3.50	3.50
60 lb	Mozzarella Cheese	1.18	70.80
		Subtotal	$281.30

SECTION 3 ● DISCOUNTS AND PERCENTS

Each of the photos shows a common situation in which you will encounter **percents.** There are many others as well. For example, a salesperson at your favorite store might tell you that prices are 40% below regular price. You need to understand percents before you can compute how much you will save on your purchase.

Percents are also used in newspapers and magazines. For example, you might read that "55% of Monroe County residents support Senator Harris's plan to decrease the sales tax by 2%." A working knowledge of percents will help you understand the statement.

Skills and Strategies

Percent literally means "per hundred." The symbol for percent is %. A percent can also be represented as a fraction whose denominator is 100. Percents are also commonly written as decimals. For example, 35% literally means "35 per 100." It can also be written as $\frac{35}{100}$, thirty-five hundredths, or .35. Look at the following list.

6% means 6 per 100, and can be written as $\frac{6}{100}$, six-hundredths, or .06.
2.5% means 2.5 per 100, and can be written as $\frac{25}{100}$, .25 hundredth, or .025.
100% means 100 per 100, and can be written as $\frac{100}{100}$ $\left(\frac{1}{1}\right)$, one, or 1.00.
150% means 150 per 100, and can be written as $\frac{150}{100}$, one hundred fifty hundredths, or 1.50.

Suppose you read that 35% of a company's employees are female. That means that 35 out of every 100 employees are female. If 6% of the sophomore class at a college are handicapped, 6 out of every 100 sophomores are handicapped. Look at Figure 1.3. It shows you the four ways you can express a percent. All the ways of expressing a percent are **equivalent** (equal in value).

Words	Symbols	Fractions (Denominator 100)	Decimals
two percent two-hundredths	2%	$\frac{2}{100}$	.02
sixteen percent sixteen-hundredths	16%	$\frac{16}{100}$	.16
seventy percent seventy-hundredths	70%	$\frac{70}{100}$	.70
three hundred percent three hundred hundredths	300%	$\frac{300}{100}$	3.00

Figure 1.3 Percent Equivalents

It is especially important to learn how to find the **decimal equivalent** of a percent. It is usually much easier to compute a problem with a decimal than with a fraction.

Every whole number can be written with a decimal point to its right. (70 = 70. and 6 = 6.) To change a percent to its decimal equivalent, move the decimal point two places to the left and drop the % sign. Look at the following list.

$$2\% = 2.\% = .02 \qquad 35\% = 35.\% = .35$$
$$16\% = 16.\% = .16 \qquad 1\% = 1.\% = .01$$
$$50\% = 50.\% = .50 \qquad 150\% = 150.\% = 1.50$$
$$300\% = 300.\% = 3.00 \qquad 106\% = 106.\% = 1.06$$
$$.4\% = .004 \qquad 65.8\% = .658$$

You might find it easier to convert the whole number part of the percent to a fraction first. Then find the decimal equivalent of the fraction.

$$9\% = \frac{9}{100} = .09 \qquad 5\% = \frac{5}{100} = .05$$
$$90\% = \frac{90}{100} = .90 \qquad 50\% = \frac{50}{100} = .50$$
$$.9\% = \frac{.9}{100} = .009 \qquad .5\% = \frac{.5}{100} = .005$$

Here you will practice finding the decimal equivalents of percents. You will also see how this can be a useful consumer skill. Read each example carefully.

1. Find the decimal equivalent of 40%.

    Solution: First write 40% as 40.%. Then move the decimal point two places to the left and drop the % sign (.40). The decimal equivalent of 40% is .40.

2. Jenny has moved to a state where the tax rate is 4.5%. What is the decimal equivalent of 4.5%?

    Solution: Move the decimal point two places to the left and drop the % sign (.045). The decimal equivalent of 4.5% is .045.

Problems

✓ **1.**   The following chart shows several equivalent expressions.

Words	Symbols	Fractions (Denominator 100)	Decimals
sixty-three percent sixty-three hundredths	63%	$\frac{63}{100}$	.63
eight percent eight-hundredths	8%	$\frac{8}{100}$	.08

Using the preceding chart as a guide, find the missing equivalents in the chart at the top of the next page.

✓ **2.**   Find the decimal equivalent for each percent.

a.	98%	**g.**	18.8%
b.	6%	**h.**	19.23%
c.	16.2%	**i.**	7%
d.	7.25	**j.**	70%
e.	91%	**k.**	.7%
f.	9.1%	**l.**	700%

Words	Symbols	Fractions (Denominator 100)	Decimals
ten percent	**a.**	**b.**	**c.**
sixty percent	**d.**	**e.**	**f.**
twelve-hundredths	**g.**	**h.**	**i.**
nine percent	**j.**	**k.**	**l.**
forty-seven hundredths	**m.**	**n.**	**o.**

3. In 1986 the United States government took 7.15% of a worker's paycheck for Social Security. Express 7.15% as an equivalent decimal.

✓ 4. A toy store is advertising a sale in which everything is 30% to 50% off.
   a. Express 30% as an equivalent decimal.
   b. Express 50% as an equivalent decimal.
   c. During this sale, could an item be marked 44% off?
   d. During this sale, should an item be marked 22% off?

5. Lazy Teddy is having a sale on reclining chairs. Every chair in the store is on sale at 18% to 33% off the regular price.
   a. Express 18% as an equivalent decimal.
   b. Express 33% as an equivalent decimal.
   c. During this sale, should an item be marked 11% off?
   d. Two recliners, regularly $300 each, are on sale. The Relaxer is now 19% cheaper. The Sleep-Eez is 37% less. Which chair is now less expensive?

SECTION 4 • SALES TAX

Wendy was buying three pairs of socks at the Sock Emporium. Each pair cost $2.25. While waiting in line, she figured that the exact cost of the socks should be $6.75. She got the exact change ready. When she looked at the display on the register, the price wasn't $6.75; it was $7.16. Was there a mistake? When she asked the clerk, Wendy found out that she had not included sales tax in her computation. The sales tax accounted for the extra 41 cents.

Sales tax is money that state and local governments use to fund the services they provide. The **tax rate** is the amount of money per dollar that a government collects. Tax rates are expressed as percents. Tax rates vary from state to state and sometimes from city to city.

In some states, not all goods are taxed. Goods that are subject to sales tax are called **taxable items.** Goods that are not taxed are **nontaxable items.** As a consumer, you should be able to check the sales tax that is added to your purchases. You should know the sales tax rates that apply to the area where you live.

Skills and Strategies

How does one compute the sales tax on a purchase? Read each example carefully.

1. Waylan has been saving money for a bicycle. The model he wants costs $216. The tax rate in Waylan's state is 6%. How much will the sales tax on the bicycle be?

    Solution: Multiply the price by the tax rate.

    $216   price
    × .06   tax rate (expressed as a decimal equivalent)
    $ 12.96   sales tax

    The keystroke sequence at the top of the next page can be used to find the sales tax on the bicycle.

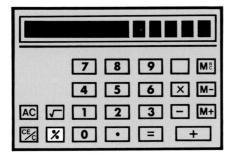

AC 216 × 6 %

The sales tax $12.96 should appear in the display.

2. Phyllis purchased an exercise bike that cost $318.99. The sales tax rate in her state is 7%. How much sales tax did she pay?

Solution: Multiply the price by the tax rate.

$318.99   price
× .07   tax rate (decimal equivalent)
$22.3293

The result of multiplying the price by the tax rate is $22.3293. That is not a possible price because it has four decimal places. The smallest denomination of United States currency is the penny. A penny is one-hundredth of a dollar. Since hundredths can be represented in two decimal places, prices must always be represented by only two decimal places. For example, 1 penny = $.01 and 78 cents = $.78.

To find the solution to the above problem, you must **round** the answer to the nearest cent. The rounded number is not exactly equal to the original number. The symbol ≈ shows an approximation. Follow these instructions to round.

Examine the digit in the third decimal place. If it is 0, 1, 2, 3, or 4, **round down.** When you round down, the number in the second decimal place stays the same. If the third-place digit is 5, 6, 7, 8, or 9, **round up.** To round up, increase the number in the second decimal place by one.

Look at the answer 22.3293. The number in the third decimal place is a 9, so you should round up the answer to 22.33. 22.3293 ≈ 22.33. Phyllis paid $22.33 in sales tax.

3. Larry bought an air conditioner that cost $428. He was charged 4% sales tax. Find the total cost of his purchase.

   Solution: First find the amount of the sales tax.

$428	price
× .04	tax rate (decimal equivalent)
$17.12	sales tax

   Then add the sales tax to the price of the purchase.

$428.00	price of the air conditioner
+ 17.12	sales tax
$445.12	total cost of purchase

   The total cost of the air conditioner was $445.12.

4. Yoko is redecorating her home. She spent $210.50 for wallpaper, $95 for paint, and $380.10 for curtains. The tax rate in her state is 6%. What was the total cost of these supplies?

   Solution: Find the subtotal.

$210.50	price of the wallpaper
95.00	price of the paint
+ 380.10	price of the curtains
$685.60	subtotal

   Next find the sales tax.

$685.60	subtotal
× .06	tax rate (decimal equivalent)
$41.136	≈ $41.14 (round up) sales tax

   Then add the sales tax to the subtotal.

$685.60	subtotal
+ 41.14	sales tax
$726.74	total cost of the supplies

   The total cost of Yoko's supplies was $726.74.

Problems

✓ **1.** Round to the nearest cent.

    a. $72.563   **d.** $8.2391

    b. $189.042   **e.** $16.423

    c. $1,920.0085   **f.** $.3819

2. Write the calculator keystroke sequence that you would use to find 6.125% of 300.

✓ **3.** **a.** Find 7% of 626. **d.** Find 11% of $242.50.

    b. Find 12% of 2,375. **e.** Find 40% of $6,100.

    c. Find 50% of 6,400,000. **f.** Find 9% of $12.38.

4. Luis bought a toaster oven that cost $35. The sales tax rate in his town is 5%. How much sales tax did Luis pay?

✓ **5.** Kennedy County imposes a 3% sales tax. How much sales tax would Alice have to pay on an item costing $1,200?

6. A snowmobile sells for $965.80. Find the total price, including 9% sales tax.

✓ **7.** Glendale and Richmond counties border each other. Glendale County residents are charged 4% sales tax; Richmond County residents are charged 6% sales tax. A Glendale dealer sells a certain sports car for $16,900. A Richmond dealer sells the same car for $15,500. The figures quoted by the dealers do not include sales tax. The sales tax charged is based on the purchaser's county of residence.
    a. What is the sales tax on the sports car at the Glendale dealership for a Glendale resident?
    b. What is the sales tax on the sports car at the Richmond dealership for a Richmond resident?
    c. What is the difference in total cost of the two cars (including tax)?

✓ **8.** In addition to the counties mentioned in Problem 6, a dealership in the county of Redhook sells the same car for $15,000, not including the county's 5% sales tax. What is the total price of the car from the Redhook dealership for a Redhook resident?

9. Complete this receipt.

Item	Quantity	Unit Price	Amount
Milk	5 gal	$1.70/gal	a.
Eggs	3 doz	.99/doz	b.
Flour	4 bags	1.50/bag	c.
Sugar	2 bags	.79/bag	d.
		Subtotal	e.
		6% tax	f.
		Total	g.

10. Artie went shopping at Benny's Bargain Basement. This was his original sales receipt.

```
                    23.85  +
                     6.00  +
                    15.00  +
                    12.50  +
                     2.65  +
                    _____
   Subtotal         60.00  ✕
   8% tax            4.80  +
                    _____
   Total            64.80  ✕
```

Artie decided to return the fifteen-dollar item. How much money should he receive as a refund?

SECTION 5 ● CATALOG SHOPPING

Have you ever been expecting a letter only to find your mailbox full of catalogs, advertisements, and letters addressed to Resident? You probably thought of it all as junk mail. Indeed, much of the mail you get from companies probably won't interest you. However, there are many reputable firms in the mail-order business. They can make shopping at home a pleasure and a benefit.

Catalog shopping can provide consumers with a number of advantages. Many catalogs specialize in a particular type of product. There are catalogs devoted to camping goods, chocolate, or electronics. In fact, there is probably a catalog for just about anything you can think of. In these catalogs you will probably find many items that you could not find in a store. Shopping by catalog is also very convenient. You don't have to go to the store; the store comes to you.

There are several advantages to ordering from a catalog. Many catalogs offer discounted prices. A well-informed shopper will know approximately what price would be charged for the catalog goods in a store. The consumer can then decide whether or not the catalog is offering a bargain. Another advantage to catalog shopping is that purchases are often not subject to sales tax. If you order from a company based in another state, you probably do not have to pay sales tax.

However, there are often extra costs involved in shopping by catalog. These costs cover the shipping and handling of your order. The charges are usually based on how much you spend or the weight of the items you order. The shipping charge may also depend on the distance of your home from the mail-order company's warehouse.

When ordering by catalog, it is important to read the instructions on the order form very carefully. Always print as neatly as possible when placing an order. Follow these steps to fill out most order forms.

1. Fill in the products you want to order. List the name of each product, its order number, and price.

2. Find the subtotal.

3. Add the sales tax, if applicable.

4. Add the shipping and handling charges to find the total cost.

Skills and Strategies

Here you will learn how to order from a catalog. Look at the catalog pages in Figure 1.4 on page 26. The chart is used to find the shipping and handling charges. Shipping and handling charges increase as the zones are farther away from the warehouse.

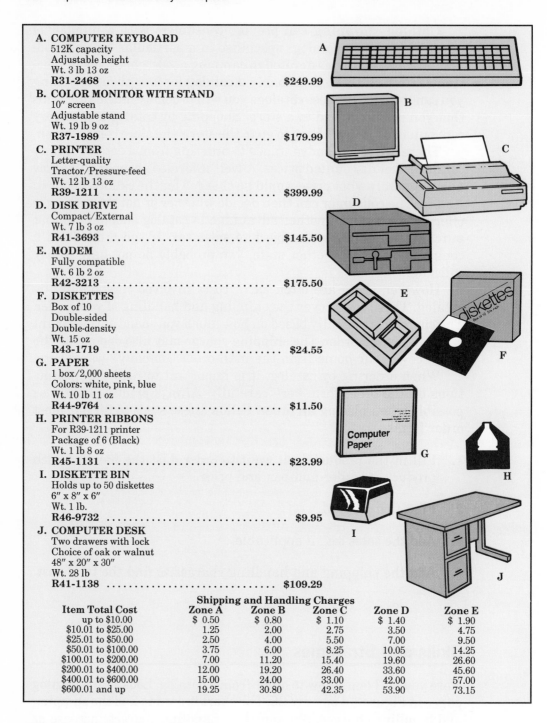

A. COMPUTER KEYBOARD
512K capacity
Adjustable height
Wt. 3 lb 13 oz
R31-2468 .... **$249.99**

B. COLOR MONITOR WITH STAND
10″ screen
Adjustable stand
Wt. 19 lb 9 oz
R37-1989 .... **$179.99**

C. PRINTER
Letter-quality
Tractor/Pressure-feed
Wt. 12 lb 13 oz
R39-1211 .... **$399.99**

D. DISK DRIVE
Compact/External
Wt. 7 lb 3 oz
R41-3693 .... **$145.50**

E. MODEM
Fully compatible
Wt. 6 lb 2 oz
R42-3213 .... **$175.50**

F. DISKETTES
Box of 10
Double-sided
Double-density
Wt. 15 oz
R43-1719 .... **$24.55**

G. PAPER
1 box/2,000 sheets
Colors: white, pink, blue
Wt. 10 lb 11 oz
R44-9764 .... **$11.50**

H. PRINTER RIBBONS
For R39-1211 printer
Package of 6 (Black)
Wt. 1 lb 8 oz
R45-1131 .... **$23.99**

I. DISKETTE BIN
Holds up to 50 diskettes
6″ x 8″ x 6″
Wt. 1 lb.
R46-9732 .... **$9.95**

J. COMPUTER DESK
Two drawers with lock
Choice of oak or walnut
48″ x 20″ x 30″
Wt. 28 lb
R41-1138 .... **$109.29**

Shipping and Handling Charges

Item Total Cost	Zone A	Zone B	Zone C	Zone D	Zone E
up to $10.00	$ 0.50	$ 0.80	$ 1.10	$ 1.40	$ 1.90
$10.01 to $25.00	1.25	2.00	2.75	3.50	4.75
$25.01 to $50.00	2.50	4.00	5.50	7.00	9.50
$50.01 to $100.00	3.75	6.00	8.25	10.05	14.25
$100.01 to $200.00	7.00	11.20	15.40	19.60	26.60
$200.01 to $400.00	12.00	19.20	26.40	33.60	45.60
$400.01 to $600.00	15.00	24.00	33.00	42.00	57.00
$600.01 and up	19.25	30.80	42.35	53.90	73.15

Figure 1.4 Page from a Catalog

1. What is the shipping and handling charge for a computer desk being sent to Zone C?

   Solution: Find the price of the computer desk in the catalog.
     Computer desk $109.29

   Use the shipping and handling chart to find the charge. The cost is between $100.01 and $200. Follow that row to the column labeled Zone C. The shipping and handling charge is $15.40.

2. Find the total cost of an order for one keyboard, one monitor, and one box of paper to be mailed to Zone B. (There is no sales tax.)

   Solution: Find and add the prices of the items.

$249.99	keyboard
179.99	monitor
+ 11.50	paper
$441.48	subtotal

   Add the shipping and handling cost.

$441.48	subtotal
+ 24.00	shipping and handling charge
$465.48	total cost of the order

Problems

Use the catalog in Figure 1.4 to help you find the solution to each problem.

✓ **1.** Find the shipping and handling charge for each amount and zone.

   a. $9.60 (Zone A)
   b. $68.87 (Zone E)
   c. $278.88 (Zone D)
   d. $22.26 (Zone B)
   e. $550 (Zone C)
   f. $401.01 (Zone B)
   g. $100 (Zone C)
   h. $100 (Zone E)
   i. $1,040 (Zone A)
   j. $601 (Zone D)

2. Arnie purchased three boxes of paper from the catalog. He lives in Zone D. What was the total cost of his order? (No sales tax was included.)

✓ **3.** The Star Connection needs 7,500 sheets of computer paper to print its Guide to the Celebrities Homes.
    a. How many boxes of paper should the company buy?
    b. What is the price of the paper without sales tax and shipping and handling charges?

4. Aileen purchased a disk drive and ten boxes of diskettes. She lives in Zone A and had to pay 4% sales tax on her purchase. What was the total cost of her order?

5. Lonette ordered four packages of printer ribbons, a modem, and a computer desk. There was no sales tax. She lives in Zone C. What was the total cost of her order?

✓ **6.** Philippe ordered one of each item listed in Figure 1.4, page 26. He lives in Zone B and does not have to pay sales tax. What was the total cost of his order?

✓ **7.** An office worker at Comp-U-Tutors is ordering 1 dozen boxes of diskettes to create training programs for students. He also wants to order enough diskette bins to hold the new diskettes.
    a. What is the cost of the diskettes?
    b. How many diskettes is he ordering?
    c. How many diskette bins will he need to store the new diskettes?
    d. What is the cost of the diskette bins he orders?
    e. What is the total price of the items he orders?
    f. What is the shipping charge to Zone B?
    g. What is the total of his order? (no sales tax)

8. Find the missing information on the order form at the top of page 29 for a customer in Zone A who must pay 5% sales tax.

9. Emily can buy printer ribbons at her local computer store for $4.85 each. She wants to decide whether to order from the catalog in Figure 1.4, page 26, instead. She needs 12 new ribbons.
    a. What is the price of 12 ribbons from the catalog?
    b. What is the price of 12 ribbons from the store?
    c. Emily lives in Zone E. What would the shipping cost of her order be?
    d. Emily would not have to pay sales tax on the catalog purchase. What would the total cost of her order be?

Item	Catalog Number	Unit Price	Quantity	Total Amount
diskettes	a.	b.	3 boxes	c.
paper	d.	e.	5 boxes	f.
keyboard	g.	h.	1	i.
diskette bin	j.	k.	2	l.

	Subtotal	m.
	Sales tax	n.
	Shipping charge	o.
	Total order	p.

   e. The sales tax rate in Emily's area is 4%. What would her total cost be at the store?

   f. Is the catalog or the store a better buy?

10. Paulo is also comparing a store and the catalog. He finds the following prices for the same products at a computer store. He wants to buy one of each product.

      diskette bin $10.95   printer $379.99
          modem $172.20   monitor $180.85

   a. Paulo lives in Zone C. What would the total cost of his catalog order be, including shipping and handling charges? (He would not have to pay sales tax on the catalog order.)

   b. The sales tax rate in Paulo's area is 8%. What would the total cost of his store purchase be?

   c. Does the store or the catalog offer a better buy?

SECTION 6 • UNDERSTANDING PRICES

Imagine that you are shopping for a new pair of sneakers. Each pair of sneakers above is exactly the same, but the prices are different. Why? To understand the way items are priced, you need to know some consumer terms.

A product is produced by a manufacturer. The manufacturer supplies all the materials and labor necessary to produce the item. The manufacturer then sells the product to a store. The store pays a **wholesale price** for the product.

The store then decides how much to charge for the item. In order to make a profit, the store charges more for the item than it paid. The price a store charges for an item is called the **retail price.** The increase from the wholesale to the retail price is called the **markup.**

There are many ways that a store can select a retail price. One way is simply to use the **manufacturer's suggested retail price,** or **list price.** This is a price that the manufacturer suggests the store use. However, the store does not have to use this price. Many stores use their own business sense to set prices, which can be higher or lower than the list price.

Consider the sneakers again. Here are some possible reasons for the price differences. Store A is using the list price, which is a markup of $8.50. Store B is a newer and more attractive store. Customers like to shop there and are willing to pay slightly more for the convenience. Store C ordered too many of that item and needed to use a lower price to attract customers.

Think of some other reasons that the prices could vary. For example, consider the merchandise you are buying. Merchandise can be sold as first-quality, irregulars (or seconds), or floor samples.

- **First-quality** goods are sold with no defects.

- **Irregular** goods may be damaged or contain defects. When selling goods marked *irregular*, the seller is letting the consumer know that something is wrong with the product.

- **Floor samples** are products that were used for demonstration or for advertising displays in stores and store windows. They are sold *as is*. A customer buying a floor sample takes home the actual product that was on display.

Usually, the defects in irregulars and floor samples are *cosmetic* — they only affect the *looks* of the product. You must make sure, however, that the irregularity does not affect the product's performance. Many sellers offer the same warranty on these products as on first-quality items.

Consider the following items that might be sold as irregulars or floor samples. Which would you be willing to purchase?

- a scratched bicycle

- a scratched record album

- a ripped blouse

- a stereo speaker with a ripped grille cloth

- a pair of jeans with an irregular inseam

- a pair of sneakers with the left tongue sewed in crooked

Another factor that affects prices is the pricing strategy that the store uses to attract customers. Some of these strategies are fair methods of business. Others can take advantage of an unprepared consumer. For example, some stores will advertise a group of products at prices lower than wholesale. These items are called **loss leaders.** The idea is that the loss leaders will attract customers to the store, who will then buy other items as well. Loss leaders are often out-of-season, discontinued, or overstocked merchandise. It is possible to get many bargains this way, but it is also possible to buy unnecessary or untimely goods.

You should also watch out for **bait-and-switch** advertising. This occurs when a store advertises an item at a discounted price. When customers ask about the item, they are encouraged to buy a higher-priced item instead. It is a good idea to know what type of product you want, so that you are not overly influenced by a persuasive salesperson.

An alert consumer can find many terrific bargains. A **discount** is a reduction in the regular price of the item. Discounts are often expressed as a percentage of the retail price. The discounted price is called the **sale price.** You will often use percents to help you determine sale prices and discount rates.

Skills and Strategies

Here you will learn how to compute sale prices using percents. Read each example and its steps carefully.

1. The Sew-Nice Sewing Machine Company sells its machines to stores at a wholesale price of $410 each. The Tenser Department Store in Miami uses a 10% price markup. What is the retail price of a sewing machine at Tenser's?

    Solution: Find the amount of the markup.

    $$\begin{array}{r} \$410 \quad \text{wholesale price} \\ \times\ .10 \quad \text{markup rate (decimal equivalent)} \\ \hline \$\ 41 \quad \text{markup} \end{array}$$

    Add the markup to the wholesale price.

    $$\begin{array}{r} \$410 \quad \text{wholesale price} \\ +\ 41 \quad \text{markup} \\ \hline \$451 \quad \text{retail price} \end{array}$$

    The retail price of a sewing machine at Tenser's is $451.

    The following calculator keystroke sequences could be used to find the markup:

    AC 410 ┃ + ┃ 10 ┃ % ┃ or AC 410 ┃ × ┃ 10 ┃ % ┃ ┃ + ┃ ┃ = ┃

    The display should read 451.

2. The Kivet Ski Shop is selling a pair of ski boots at 22% below its regular price of $260. How much does a buyer save on the boots?

Solution: Find the amount of the discount.

        $260   retail price
      × .22   discount rate (decimal equivalent)
      $57.20   discount

A customer saves $57.20 on the boots on sale.

3. The Fancy Fan Factory is having an end-of-summer clearance sale on ceiling fans. Its deluxe model has a retail price of $180. It is on sale for 15% off. What is the sale price?

Solution: First find the amount of the discount.

        $180   retail price
      × .15   discount rate (decimal equivalent)
       $27   discount

Then subtract the discount from the retail price.

        $180   retail price
      − 27   discount
       $153   sale price

The following calculator keystroke sequence can also be used to answer this problem.

`AC` 180 `×` 15 `%` `−` `=`

The sale price ($153) should appear in the display.

Problems

✓ **1.**   Find the missing information in the chart below.

Item	Wholesale Price	Markup	Retail Price
Table Saw	$280.50	$150.70	
Toaster	22.80	22.80	
Clock	9.99	12.50	
File Cabinet	15.00	28.30	
Rocking Chair	43.99		93.99
Dictionary	8.55		14.45

✓ **2.**   Find the missing information in the chart below. Round to the nearest cent, if necessary.

Item	Wholesale Price	Markup Percentage	Markup	Retail Price
Watch	$ 85.90	75	a.	b.
Radio	120.00	93	c.	d.
Television	290.90	100	e.	f.
Telephone	36.50	105	g.	h.
Camera	110.99	110	i.	j.
Bicycle	143.50	120	k.	l.

3.   Aunt Mary's Bake Shop is having a 10%-off sale on all wedding cakes ordered at least four weeks in advance. Linda and Rob order their wedding cake five weeks in advance. What is their discount on a cake that has a retail price of $95?

4.   Maria Healy is the owner of Healy's Car Dealership. Her brother bought a sports car that was originally priced at

$18,500. He received the family-member discount of 15%. The sales tax rate in the area is 6%.

   a. Find the amount of the discount.

   b. Find the sale price of the car.

   c. Find the amount of the sales tax.

   d. What was the total cost of the car?

✓ **5.** City and Town Tires purchases all of its tires from the Goodstone Rubber Company. Each X15 snow tire has a wholesale price of $38. City and Town uses a markup rate of 85%. Larry bought a set of four X15 tires during a 25%-off sale.

   a. Find the markup on one tire.

   b. Find the retail price of one tire.

   c. Find the retail price of four tires.

   d. Find the amount of the discount on four tires.

   e. What is the sale price of four tires?

   f. Find the sales tax on the purchase (8% tax rate).

   g. How much did Larry pay for the set of four tires?

SECTION 7 • WHERE TO SHOP

Where you go to buy goods depends on:

- what you are planning to buy,

- how much you are planning to spend,

- what kinds of stores are located in your area.

The importance of these factors may vary from purchase to purchase.

Where you shop can also have an effect on the price you pay. Did you ever wonder where department stores get the money to pay for their fancy carpeting, piped-in music, and elegant displays? Their prices are marked up to help pay for these extras, so you are really paying for them every time you shop in such stores. Where else can you shop?

- **Clearance centers** are places where major stores sell their damaged goods, floor samples, and overstocked items at a substantial discount.

- **Bakery thrift stores** sell bakery goods at a discount. The merchandise in these stores is there for a variety of reasons. Some items are beyond their shelf life — they are no longer considered fresh. Others are underweight or may have small defects in appearance.

- **Factory outlets** are stores located in the factory where the merchandise is produced.

Prices in these kinds of stores are lower than retail prices for several reasons:

1. There is no fancy carpeting.

2. There is no piped-in music.

3. Showrooms are not decorated.

4. There are no shipping costs.

5. Only cash is accepted — no checks or credit cards.

6. There are few salespeople.

7. The rent is low.

As you can see, consumers have many choices of what they buy and where they buy.

Skills and Strategies

Here you will learn how to read labels at a factory outlet. Then you will be able to judge the discounts found there.

Mrs. T's Appliance Outlet is a clearance center for small appliances made by one manufacturer. The discounts are determined by the length of time that an item remains on the shelf. The longer it remains, the greater the discount. Marilyn has gone to Mrs. T's looking for a telephone answering machine. The one she likes has a label that looks like the one at the top of the next page.

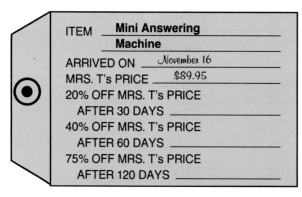

← type of merchandise

first date item was put
on the shelf for sale

← first ticketed price

← sale price with 20% off
Mrs. T's price after 30 days

← sale price with 40% off
Mrs. T's price after 60 days

← sale price with 75% off
Mrs. T's price after 120 days

1. What price would Marilyn pay for the answering machine on January 3?

   Solution: First, count the number of days between November 16 and January 3. The interval is 48 days. The answering machine's price will go down after 30 days on the shelf, after 60 days, and after 120 days. Since 48 days is a longer period of time than 30 days, and shorter than 60 days, the answering machine has been discounted once.

   To find 20% off Mrs. T's price after 30 days, use the following calculator keystroke sequence:

   AC 89.95 × 20 % − =

   The display should read 71.96. Marilyn would pay $71.96 for the answering machine.

Problems

✓ 1. Fortune's Department Store sells a certain couch for $1,150. Every few months, this couch goes on sale at 20% off. The Fortune Clearance Center sells the same couch, with slight damage, for $810.
   a. The sales tax rate at Fortune's Department Store is 6%. What is the sales tax on a couch purchased at the regular price?
   b. What is the regular price of the couch including sales tax?

   c. What is the sale price of the couch?

    d.   What is the cost of the couch on sale including sales tax?

    e.   The Fortune Clearance Center is not in the same state as the store. The sales tax rate at the clearance center is 5%. What is the price of the damaged couch with sales tax?

    f.   Which is cheaper, the couch on sale, with tax, or the damaged couch, with tax?

2. The Susan Soga company sells designer skirts to stores at a wholesale price of $16 each. The stores mark the skirts up 90%.
    a.   What is the retail price of a skirt?
    b.   During sales, the stores discount these skirts 15%. What is the sale price of one skirt?
    c.   The Susan Soga Factory Outlet sells the skirts for $24.50 each. How much lower is the price of the skirt at the factory outlet than its regular price in the store?

✓ **3.** A local merchant claims to have the lowest prices. If you find the same television for less money at another store, the merchant will refund the difference in price, plus an extra 10% of the difference. You buy a television from her for $410, and then you see an identical set in another store for $370. You decide to go back to the local merchant to get your refund. How much should she refund you?

4. Your car needs a new starter. Donny's Auto Parts sells starters for $57. The factory sells them through its catalog for $45 plus shipping. Shipping is 15 cents per pound, and the starter weighs 21 pounds. How much will you save buying directly from the factory?

✓ **5.** The Yummy Baking Corporation sells 1-pound packages of brownies to stores at a wholesale price of $1.20. The stores mark them up 70 cents. Yummy's Bakery Thrift Store sells day-old packages of brownies for 10% more than the wholesale price.
    a.   What is the thrift store price?
    b.   How much less would 1 dozen packages cost at the thrift store than in the regular stores?

Problems 6–10 refer to the factory outlet label in Figure 1.5. Round your answers to the nearest cent.

ITEM _George Ash Designer_
Jogging Suit

ARRIVED ON _April 22_

STANLEY's PRICE _$78.50_

10% OFF STANLEY's PRICE
AFTER 20 DAYS _____

15% OFF STANLEY's PRICE
AFTER 40 DAYS _____

30% OFF STANLEY's PRICE
AFTER 60 DAYS _____

Figure 1.5 Factory Outlet Label

6. What is the price of the jogging suit 23 days after April 22?

7. What is the price of the jogging suit 42 days after April 22?

8. What is the price of the jogging suit 60 days after April 22?

9. What is the price of the jogging suit on May 7?

10. What is the price of the jogging suit on July 19?

SECTION 8 ● SUPERMARKET PRICING

What do the goods on the left have in common? They are all **durable goods.** When you buy each item, you expect it to last a long time. You have already learned how warranties help protect you against goods that don't last as long as they should.

What about the goods pictured on the right? Would you expect a carton of milk to last a year? No, of course not. The goods on the right are **perishable goods.** That means that once you have used, or consumed, the item the product's life is over. You must buy a new item if you want to keep using the product.

Supermarkets specialize in selling perishable goods. Most families shop in a supermarket several times a month. Consumers probably spend more time buying perishable goods than durable goods. However, some people who are very careful when shopping at a department store are surprisingly careless when buying perishable goods. It is important to be familiar with pricing techniques in supermarkets so that you can make wise choices. There are several common supermarket features that can help you be an informed shopper there.

Unit Pricing

In many supermarkets, you will find labels on the shelf below each product. These labels will tell you what the **unit price** of the item is.

The unit price is the price for one unit (one pound, one ounce, one fluid ounce) of the product. This information allows you to compare the prices of similar products. For example, look at the two sizes of jars of spaghetti sauce below. If you look only at the prices, it is difficult to make a comparison quickly. However, the unit price label helps you quickly decide which size is a better buy.

Customer Scale

Many supermarkets offer customers the opportunity to check the weights of products before bringing them to the checkout counter. Some states require supermarkets to have **customer scales.** Many markets now use scales that have a digital display that tells you the weight of each product as a decimal.

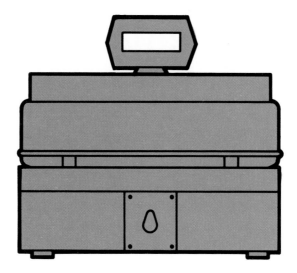

Universal Product Code

Many products now carry a symbol that looks like the picture below.

The **Universal Product Code** (UPC) is part of a system designed to speed up supermarket checkout and inventory taking. Every product brand and size has its own UPC. The number is coded into the stripes, which are read by a cashier's scanner. The scanner sends a signal to the store's computer, which assigns and displays the price of the product. It is simple for a store to change the price of a product by programming the computer.

Manufacturer's **coupons** can be found in newspapers and store circulars. They offer consumers discounts on certain products. Many coupons feature the UPC to identify the product being discounted.

Skills and Strategies

Here you will learn how to calculate problems in supermarket situations. Read each problem and its solution carefully.

1.   Emma is having a barbecue. She wants to find the price of a watermelon before checking out of the market.

Solution: Weigh the watermelon on the customer scale. The watermelon weighs 16.5 pounds. Next find the unit price per pound. The watermelon costs 16 cents per pound. Multiply to find the cost of the watermelon.

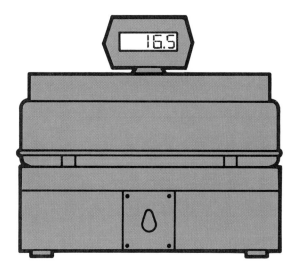

$$
\begin{array}{rl}
16.5 & \text{weight in pounds} \\
\times\ .16 & \text{cost per pound} \\
\hline
\$2.64 & \text{price of the watermelon}
\end{array}
$$

2. A 20-ounce box of cereal sells for $2.40. What should the unit price label list as the price per ounce?

    Solution: To find the price of 1 ounce, divide the total cost by the number of ounces.

    $$\text{number of ounces} \rightarrow 20\overline{)2.40} \leftarrow \text{total cost}$$

    In a division problem, the number you divide by is called the **divisor.** Here, the divisor is 20. The number being divided is called the **dividend.** The price of the cereal ($2.40) is the dividend in this problem. The answer to a division product is called a **quotient.** When dividing a decimal by a whole number, place a decimal point in the quotient, directly above the decimal point in the dividend.

    $$
    \begin{array}{r}
    . \quad \leftarrow \text{quotient} \\
    \text{divisor} \rightarrow 20\overline{)2.40} \leftarrow \text{dividend}
    \end{array}
    $$

After placing the decimal point, divide just as you would divide two whole numbers.

$$\begin{array}{r} .12 \leftarrow\text{price per ounce} \\ \text{divisor} \rightarrow 20\overline{)2.40} \leftarrow\text{dividend} \end{array}$$

The unit price of the cereal is \$.12 per ounce.

The following keystroke sequence can be used to find the cost per ounce.

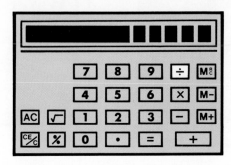

AC 2.40 ÷ 20 =

The unit price (\$.12) per ounce should appear in the display.

3. Kathryn wants to compare the cost of two brands of sugar. There are no unit price labels in this market. Three pounds of Dommy's Sugar costs \$1.29. Five pounds of Sweetina Sugar costs \$2.20. Which brand costs less per pound?

   Solution: Find the price per pound of each brand.

Dommy's	Sweetina

   $$\begin{array}{r} .43 \\ 3\overline{)1.29} \end{array} \qquad \begin{array}{r} .44 \\ 5\overline{)2.20} \end{array}$$

   Dommy's sugar is 1 cent less per pound.

4. Roberto is purchasing a box of raisin bran cereal that sells for

$1.99. He has a coupon that gives him a 35¢ discount on the cereal. How much will Roberto pay for the cereal?

Solution:

$1.99	price of the cereal
− .35	amount of the coupon
$1.64	final cost of the cereal

Roberto will pay $1.64 for the cereal.

Problems

✓ **1.** Find the missing information in the chart.

Item	Unit Price	Quantity	Total Price
Apple Juice	$ .15/fl oz	26 fl oz	**a.**
Steak	1.89/lb	4.5 lb	**b.**
Wood Shelves	1.90/ft	9 ft	**c.**
Cereal	.18/oz	24 oz	**d.**
Broccoli	.99/lb	3 lb	**e.**
Peaches	.69/lb	2.7 lb	**f.**
Tomatoes	.55/lb	4.22 lb	**g.**

2. Mary is checking the label on a package of hamburger. The meat weighs 4.1 pounds, and costs $1.19 per pound. The price on the label is $4.98. Is the price correct? If it is wrong, what is the correct price?

✓ **3.** Bill picked up a large bag of apples marked 19 pounds. He weighed the apples on the customer scale, which read 17.2 pounds. If the scale is correct, how many pounds off is the label on the bag?

4. A bag of potatoes is labeled 20 pounds.
    a. At 49 cents per pound, how much does the bag of potatoes cost?
    b. The bag is labeled incorrectly. The customer scale gives the correct weight as 16.4 pounds. How many pounds off is the label on the bag?
    c. What is the correct price of the 16.4-pound bag?
    d. By how much is a customer who pays for 20 pounds being overcharged?

✓ 5. Find the missing information in the chart below.

Item	Total Price	Quantity	Unit Price
Telephone Wire	$ 7.50	25 ft	a.
Grapes	3.24	2 lb	b.
Roast Beef	20.93	7 lb	c.
Oil	24.40	20 gal	d.
Turkey	16.02	18 lb	e.

6. A 50-foot nylon clothesline costs $7. What is the unit price of 1 foot?

7. You are going to change the oil in your new car. You need 5 quarts of oil. The 5-quart jug costs $5.95. Individual 1-quart cans cost $1.12. Which is the better buy?

✓ 8. Windshield washer fluid is on sale at two stores. At a department store a 40-fluid-ounce jug costs $1.20. At an auto parts store, a 32-fluid-ounce jug costs $1.
    a. What is the unit price per fluid ounce at the department store?
    b. What is the unit price per fluid ounce at the auto parts store?
    c. Which store offers the better deal?

9. Joe bought $65.33 worth of groceries. He then handed the cashier coupons worth

    25¢   35¢ $1   75¢   50¢

    How much of a discount will Joe receive?

10. Yvette bought $129.85 worth of groceries. She then handed the cashier coupons worth

25¢ 50¢ 50¢ $1 35¢ 15¢

What was the final cost of the groceries?

● KEY TERMS

To find the definition of any term introduced in the chapter, refer to the Glossary in the back of this book.

bait and switch	limited warranty
bakery thrift stores	list price
calculator keystroke sequence	loss leaders
catalog shopping	manufacturer's suggested
caveat emptor	retail price
clearance centers	markup
consequential damages	MC (memory clear)
consumer	memory
coupons	M+ (memory add)
customer scales	MR (memory recall)
decimal equivalent	nontaxable item
difference	percents
disclaimer	perishable good
discount	planned obsolescence
dividend	product
divisor	quotient
durable goods	rebate
equivalent	retail price
estimation	round
expiration date	round down
express warranty	round up
factory outlets	sale price
first quality	sales receipt
floor samples	sales tax
full warranty	services
goods	subtotal
implied warranty	sum
irregular	taxable items

tax rate   warranty
unit price   wholesale price
Universal Product Code (UPC)

● REVIEW PROBLEMS

1.   Rosa made the following purchases at the supermarket: shampoo ($2.49), Swiss cheese ($3.25), cereal ($1.99), three cans of soup (each can costs $.39), taco sauce ($1.19), and frozen french fries ($.79). She cut two coupons out of the store's advertisement pages. The first coupon took 35 cents off the price of the cereal, and the second coupon took 15 cents off the price of the frozen french fries. What was her bill?

2.   Kelly has a twenty-dollar bill. She wants to buy a blouse that costs $19. The sales tax rate is 8%. How much more money will she need in order to make the purchase?

     Use the following catalog entry to answer questions 3, 4, and 5.

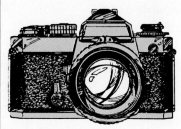

ENTIRE CAMERA OUTFIT . . . $389.99

PURCHASED SEPARATELY

Z328-9 Camera Body
        Wt. 2 lb $249.99

Z923-4 Zoom Lens
        Wt. 1.2 lb $148.90

Z371-5 Camera Case
        Wt. .5 lb $19.99

3.   How much do you save by purchasing the entire camera outfit at $389.99, rather than buying the three pieces separately?

4.   If the sales tax rate is 6%, what is the tax on the entire camera outfit?

5. If you purchase only the zoom lens and the camera case, what is your total bill including 6% sales tax?

6. The Inverse Sneaker Factory Outlet sells canvas sneakers in all colors at 30% off the list price. The list price is computed by marking up the wholesale price of $12 by 100%.
   a. What is the retail price?
   b. What is the factory outlet price?

7. Spoon Air is offering passengers who have flown over 10,000 miles a 25% discount on their next flight. Art and Sylvia have each flown over 10,000 miles on Spoon Air. How much could they save on two round-trip flights to Hawaii, which retail for $900 each?

8. The Stoneway Piano Factory sells floor-model grand pianos directly to the public at wholesale prices one day each year. On that day, what would a piano that wholesales for $7,000 cost with 8.25% sales tax?

9. The El Camino Auto Store regularly sells radial tires for $56. What would four tires cost with a 10% discount and 6% sales tax?

10. The Chin Moon Chinese Grocery sells a 6-pound bag of fortune cookies for $5.64. What is the unit price per pound of the cookies?

CHAPTER **2**

MEASUREMENT

SECTION 1 • UNITS OF LENGTH

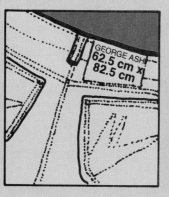

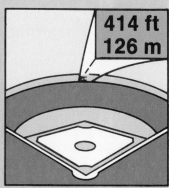

What do these pictures have in common? Each shows a situation in which it is important to know lengths and distances. Imagine you are shopping for jeans and do not know the distance from your waist to your ankles. You might have to try several pairs of jeans before finding one that fits! When you know the correct measurement, you

50

can easily find the best-fitting jeans. What are some other situations in which you use units of length? You can probably think of many. Units of length are used in hundreds of everyday activities. Being familiar with common units of length will make you a better prepared customer.

Skills and Strategies

There are two widely used systems of measurement in the world today. The United States uses the English standard system. Most other countries use the metric system. The United States is gradually using the metric system more and more. To be a well-informed consumer, you should have a working knowledge of both systems. You will use the English standard system to measure most American-made goods. Products imported from other countries are labeled in metric units.

English Standard System				Metric System			
inch	foot	yard	mile	millimeter	centimeter	**meter**	kilometer
(in)	(ft)	(yd)	(mi)	(mm)	(cm)	**(m)**	(km)

You may be familiar with the basic units of length in the English system: the inch, foot, yard, and mile. The **meter** is the basic unit of length in the metric system. A meter is about equal to the height of a kitchen table, the length of a baseball bat, or the distance from a doorknob to the floor.

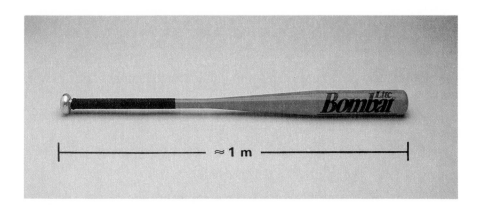

≈ 1 m

A millimeter is about equal to the thickness of a dime. A centimeter is about equal to the width of your pinkie. A kilometer is approximately $2\frac{1}{2}$ times the height of the Empire State Building.

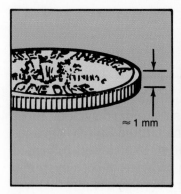 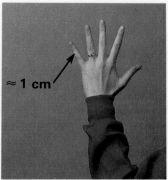 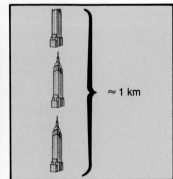

You will often need to convert from one unit of length to another. Suppose you are buying crepe paper to decorate for a party. The measurement for the length you need is in yards, but the crepe paper is sold by the foot. You will need to convert from yards to feet to find out how much to buy.

As the United States gradually changes to the metric system, you may also have to convert from one system to the other. Figure 2.1 on the next page makes converting easy, especially with a calculator. You don't have to memorize the figure, just refer to it as needed.

Here you will see how units of length are used to measure automobiles, clothing, interior design, and more. Study the following examples.

1.   Which measurement seems most reasonable for the length of a car?
     a.   4.5 mm   **b.**   4.5 cm   **c.**   4.5 km   **d.**   4.5 m

     Solution: Use the information you know to look at each answer.

     4.5 mm ≈ the thickness of a few dimes

     4.5 cm ≈ the thickness of a few pinkies

     4.5 km ≈ the combined height of several skyscrapers

     4.5 m ≈ the length of a few baseball bats

The most reasonable length for a car would be 4.5 m.

METRIC SYSTEM

There are 10 millimeters in 1 centimeter.	10 mm = 1 cm
There are 100 centimeters in 1 meter.	100 cm = 1 m
There are 1,000 meters in 1 kilometer.	1,000 m = 1 km

ENGLISH STANDARD SYSTEM

There are 12 inches in 1 foot.	12 in = 1 ft
There are 3 feet in 1 yard.	3 ft = 1 yd
There are 5,280 feet in 1 mile.	5,280 ft = 1 mi

CONVERTING FROM ENGLISH TO METRIC

1 in ≈ 2.54 cm (An inch is longer than a centimeter.)
1 ft ≈ 30 cm (A foot is longer than a centimeter.)
1 ft ≈ 0.3 m (A foot is shorter than a meter.)
1 yd ≈ 0.9 m (A yard is shorter than a meter.)
1 mi ≈ 1.6 km (A mile is longer than a kilometer.)

Figure 2.1 Conversion Chart for Measurement

2. Lauren is shopping for a new desk. The desk must fit into a space that measures 46 inches. One furniture catalog lists a desk she likes that is 4 feet long. Will this desk fit in the available space?

Solution: This problem can be solved in two ways. Lauren can change the number of feet into inches, using the information in Figure 2.1. She finds that 12 inches = 1 foot.

12	number of inches in 1 foot
× 4	the length of the desk, in feet
48	the length of the desk, in inches

No; the 48-inch desk is too long for the 46-inch space. Or, Lauren can convert the number of inches into feet.

$$\begin{array}{r} 3 \text{ ft } 10 \text{ in} \leftarrow \text{wall space, in feet} \\ 12 \overline{)46} \quad\quad \leftarrow \text{wall space, in inches} \\ \underline{36} \\ 10 \end{array}$$

No; the 3-foot, 10-inch wall space is too small for the 4-foot desk.

Notice that when you change from large units (for example, feet) to smaller units (for example, inches), you multiply. When changing from small units to larger units, you divide.

3. Jack owns a telephoto camera lens that is 270 mm long. He wants to purchase a case for the lens, but he can afford only the 28 cm case. Is this case long enough for his lens?

   Solution: Convert the 28 cm into millimeters. A centimeter is larger than a millimeter, so you must multiply using the information from page 53.

   $$
   \begin{array}{rl}
   10 & \text{number of mm in 1 cm} \\
   \times\ 28 & \text{length of case, in cm} \\
   \hline
   280 & \text{length of the case, in mm}
   \end{array}
   $$

   Yes; the 28 cm case will hold Jack's lens.

4. Debbie wants to purchase a pair of jeans imported from France. The waist measurement is given in centimeters. If Debbie's waist measures 29 inches, what size jeans should she look for?

   Solution: Look at Figure 2.1 on page 53. Notice that there are 2.54 cm in one inch. Debbie uses her calculator and the following keystroke sequence:

   AC 29 ✕ 2.54 =

   The display tells her that her 29 inch waist is 73.66 cm. She uses her rounding skills to round 73.66 to the nearest whole centimeter, which is 74 cm. Debbie should look for jeans with a 74-cm waist.

Problems

Choose the most reasonable length for each item.

✓ 1. The width of a classroom
   a. 9 m   **b.** 9 cm   **c.** 9 mm   **d.** 9 km

2. The height of a desk
   a. 1.1 cm   **b.** 1.1 m   **c.** 1.1 km   **d.** 1.1 mm

✓ **3.** The depth of a bathtub
     a. 0.5 cm   **b.** 0.5 mm   **c.** 0.5 km   **d.** 0.5 m

  4. The distance from San Francisco to Los Angeles
     a. 700 km   **b.** 700 mm   **c.** 7 m   **d.** 70 cm

  5. The height of your bedroom door
     a. 4 cm   **b.** 40 mm   **c.** 2.1 m   **d.** 30 cm

✓ **6.** The length of a guitar
     a. 7.1 m   **b.** 6.1 m   **c.** 3.1 m   **d.** 1.1 m

  7. The thickness of your math book
     a. 3 cm   **b.** 3 mm   **c.** 3 km   **d.** 0.9 m

  8. The length of a pencil
     a. 51 cm   **b.** 2 cm   **c.** 4 mm   **d.** 13 cm

  9. The length of a tennis racket
     a. 6 m   **b.** 59 cm   **c.** 17 mm   **d.** 0.5 km

10. The height of the Eiffel Tower
     a. 300 m   **b.** 3 m   **c.** 30 mm   **d.** 30 cm

Find the answer to each problem. Use Figure 2.1 on page 53 to help.

✓ **11.** A group of French students is visiting the Statue of Liberty. They read that the height of the statue is 251 feet. The students know that the Eiffel Tower is 295 meters high. They wonder which structure is taller.
     a. How high is the Statue of Liberty in meters?
     b. Which structure is taller?

12. Juan bought new tires for his truck. The tires changed the height of the truck, so he measured the truck's height with a tape measure. The truck is now 78 inches high. Will the truck fit into Juan's garage, which is 7 feet high?

13. Linda's living room window is 2.3 meters high. She found a set of curtains 180 centimeters long at a factory outlet.
     a. How high is her living-room window in centimeters?

     b. Are the curtains long enough to cover the window?

14. Which store offers a better price?
    a. Electric Town has 9 yards of telephone cord for $10.75.
    b. Phil's Phones has 10 meters of telephone cord for $10.75.
    Explain your answer.

15. Which store offers a better price?
    a. Electric Town has 9 feet of speaker wire for $1.80.
    b. Phil's Phones has 3 meters of speaker wire for $1.70.
    Explain your answer.

SECTION 2 • UNITS OF WEIGHT

≈ 4½ kg

PS 'N' DOWNS EVATOR CO.

MAX. WT. 4000 lb.
1814 kg

I.D. # 111257-30

ELEVATOR CAR CONFORMS
ALL FEDERAL SAFETY
DATE OF MANUFACTURE

What is being measured in these pictures? Each shows one aspect of measuring weight. Consider the elevator sign. Suppose you live in an apartment building and are planning to have a heavy piece of furniture delivered. You would have to know the weight of the furniture and how much weight the elevator can hold. If you did not check out these weights, you could find yourself in a very dangerous situation. Think of some other situations in which you need to know about weights.

Skills and Strategies

Like units of length, units of weight can be measured in two systems.

English Standard System			**Metric System**		
ounce	pound	ton	milligram	**gram**	kilogram
(oz)	(lb)	(t)	(mg)	**(g)**	(kg)

You may be familiar with the weights of the English standard system: ounces, pounds, and tons. The basic unit of weight in the metric system is the **gram.** A gram is about equal to the weight of a paper clip or a raisin.

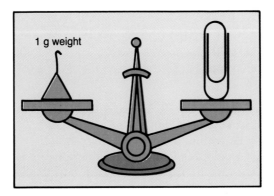

A milligram is smaller than a gram. Vitamins and pharmacy products are usually measured in milligrams. A milligram is about equal to the weight of one grain of rice. A kilogram is larger than a gram. A typical hard-cover textbook weighs about one kilogram.

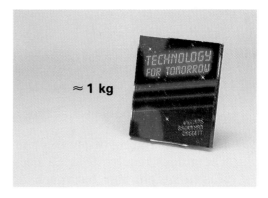

There will be many times that you need to convert from one unit to another. Imagine that you are taking a plane trip and that the airline has a luggage weight maximum of 40 kg. If your home scale measures in pounds, you will have to convert your scale reading to make sure your luggage is not overweight. Figure 2.2 gives the information you need to change from one unit to another, as well as from one system to another. It can be used for reference.

ENGLISH STANDARD SYSTEM

There are 16 ounces in 1 pound.   16 oz = 1 lb
There are 2,000 pounds in 1 ton.   2,000 lbs = 1 t

METRIC SYSTEM

There are 1,000 milligrams in 1 gram   1,000 mg = 1 g
There are 1,000 grams in 1 kilogram   1,000 g   = 1 kg

CONVERTING FROM ENGLISH TO METRIC

1 oz ≈ 28 g (An ounce is more than a gram.)
1 lb ≈ 454 g (A pound is more than a gram.)
2.2 lb ≈ 1 kg (A pound is less than a kilogram.)

Figure 2.2   Conversion Chart for Weight

Here you will see the role that units of weight play in health, nutrition, physical fitness, and more. Study the following examples.

1. Which is the most reasonable measurement for the weight of a bicycle?
    a. 12 g   **b.** 12 mg   **c.** 12 kg

    Solution: Use the information you know to look at each answer.
       12 g   ≈ the weight of 12 paper clips
       12 mg ≈ the weight of 12 grains of rice
       12 kg ≈ the weight of 12 textbooks

    The most reasonable weight for the bicycle is 12 kg.

2. Rosita is planning to go hiking in a national park this summer. The guides require that all backpacks weigh less than 6 kg. Rosita weighs her backpack and finds that it weighs 12.1 pounds. Is her backpack under the weight limit?

Solution: The 12.1 pounds can be converted to kilograms. A kilogram is more than a pound, so you will divide to find an answer. Refer to Figure 2.2, page 58, to find the information you need. From the chart you see that 2.2 lbs = 1 kg. You need to find out how many 2.2 pound weights are in Rosita's 12.1 pound backpack (12.1 ÷ 2.2). Use your calculator and the following keystroke sequence:

AC 12.1 ÷ 2.2 =

The display shows that Rosita's backpack weighs 5.5 kg. Therefore, her pack is under the 6 kg weight limit.

> Remember: when you change from small units (in this example, pounds) to larger units (in this example, kilograms) you divide.

This problem could also have been done like this:

    2.2   number of pounds in 1 kilogram
  × 6   number of kilograms in the weight limit
   13.2   number of pounds in 6 kilograms

Therefore, Rosita's backpack is under the weight limit since 13.2 pounds is greater than 12.1 pounds.

3. Some Olympic athletes are on very strict diets. They weigh their food before preparing each meal. Hiroshi is training for gymnastics competition. He plans to eat 3.5 kilograms of beef every week. It is important that he eat the same amount each day. How many kilograms of beef should he eat each day?

Solution:

$$\begin{array}{r} .5 \leftarrow \text{number of kg of beef each day} \\ 7\overline{)3.5} \leftarrow \text{number of kg of beef each week} \\ \uparrow \end{array}$$

number of days in a week

Hiroshi should eat 0.5 kilograms of beef each day.

The following calculator keystroke sequence could be used:

AC 3.5 ÷ 7 =

The display will read 0.5.

4. Janet is training for swimming competition. She is supposed to eat 0.3 kilograms of beef per day. Her scale measures in grams, so she needs to know how many grams are in 0.3 kilograms.

    Solution: Look at Figure 2.2, page 58. A gram is less than a kilogram. Janet should multiply to find an answer.

    $$
    \begin{array}{rl}
    1,000 & \text{number of grams in 1 kilogram} \\
    \times\ .3 & \text{Janet's daily allowance, in kilograms} \\
    \hline
    300.0 & \text{Janet's daily allowance, in grams}
    \end{array}
    $$

    Janet should eat 300 grams of beef each day.

    The following calculator keystroke sequence could also be used:

    AC 0.3 × 1,000 =

    The display should read 300.

Problems

Choose the most reasonable weight for each item.

✓ 1. An apple
       a. 4 lb   b. 4 oz   c. 4 t

 2. An apple
       a. 112 g   b. 112 mg   c. 112 kg

 3. A pair of sneakers
       a. 1 g   b. 1 kg   c. 1 mg

✓ 4. An infant
       a. 3.1 g   b. 3.1 kg   c. 3.1 mg

 5. A car
       a. 100 g   b. 1,000 kg   c. 100 mg

 6. A brick
       a. 2,260 kg   b. 2,260 g   c. 2,260 mg

7. An adult athlete
   a. 55 kg **b.** 55 g **c.** 55 mg

8. An aspirin tablet
   a. 200 g **b.** 200 mg **c.** 200 g

9. One grape
   a. 3 g **b.** 3 mg **c.** 3 kg

✓ 10. A key
   a. 10 g **b.** 10 mg **c.** 10 kg

Find the answer to each problem. Refer to Figure 2.2, page 58, for help.

11. Which is the better price?
    a. A 1 lb bag of potatoes for $.79
    b. A 1 kg bag of potatoes for $.79

12. Which is the better price?
    a. A 10 lb bag of dog food for $2.64
    b. A 25 kg bag of dog food for $2.75

13. The Henry Highway has a sign at its entrance that reads, "Trucks over 5 tons must use the service road."
    a. Could a 12,000 lb truck use the Henry Highway? Explain your answer.
    b. Could a 4,300 kg truck use the Henry Highway? Explain your answer.

✓ 14. Marty ordered a part for his imported car. When the part arrived, he noticed that a shipping charge of $2 per kilogram was added to his bill. He weighed the part on his scale. It weighed 198 pounds.
    a. What is the equivalent weight of the part in kilograms?

    b. How much should the shipping charges have been?

    c. He was billed $205.79 for shipping charges. Was he over-charged or undercharged? By how much?

15. Paulo is planning a rafting trip. His raft is built to carry no more than 280 kilograms. The equipment for the trip weighs 112 pounds.

   a. What is the maximum combined weight for the raft's passengers?

   b. Paulo wants to ask three friends on the trip. Their weights are: 120 lb, 110 lb, and 100 lb. Paulo weighs 125 lb. Will the raft safely hold these four passengers?

SECTION 3 • UNITS OF LIQUID MEASURE

 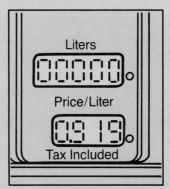 

What do the above items have in common? For one thing, they are all considered liquids. When you buy these items they are not sold by their weight. Liquids are sold by their volume, or the amount of space they take up. Many products, such as milk, oil, gasoline, shampoo, mouthwash, and paint are sold by volume, not weight. A one-liter can of soup could weigh more than a one-liter can of juice, but the volume of both cans is the same. You will frequently use units of liquid measure. You might need to compare the prices of two brands of juice, or of two different-sized bottles of the same brand. Both the English and the metric systems have common units of liquid measure.

Skills and Strategies

You may know the common units in the English system. Perhaps you have bought shampoo by the fluid ounce, sour cream by the pint, milk by the quart, and apple cider by the gallon. The **liter** is the basic metric unit of liquid measure. A liter is about the same size as a quart of milk. A milliliter is about the size of a raindrop.

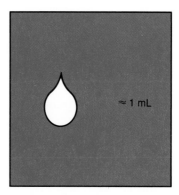

English Standard System				Metric System	
fluid ounce	pint	quart	gallon	milliliter	**liter**
(fl oz)	(pt)	(qt)	(gal)	(mL)	**(L)**

You will often need to know how to work with units of liquid measure. Suppose you are doubling or tripling a punch recipe for a large party at school. You will probably convert smaller units to larger units to make buying the ingredients easier. If you know how to measure liquids, you will have no problem. Figure 2.3 at the top of page 64 will help you to convert in both measuring systems.

Be careful! The **fluid ounce** is a unit of volume; the ounce is a measure of weight. Do not confuse the two.

In the following examples, you will see the role that units of liquid measure play in auto and home maintenance, health, and nutrition. Read each example carefully.

ENGLISH STANDARD SYSTEM

There are 16 fluid ounces in 1 pint.   16 fl oz = 1 pt

There are 2 pints in 1 quart.   2 pt   = 1 qt

There are 4 quarts in 1 gallon.   4 qt   = 1 gal

METRIC SYSTEM

There are 1,000 milliliters in 1 liter.   1,000 mL = 1 L

CONVERTING FROM ENGLISH TO METRIC

1 fl oz $\approx$ 30 mL (A fluid ounce is larger than a milliliter.)

1 qt $\approx$ 0.95 L (A quart is smaller than a liter.)

1 gal $\approx$ 3.8 L (A gallon is larger than a liter.)

Figure 2.3   Conversion Chart for Liquid Measure

1. Which is the most reasonable measure for a milk shake?
   a.   500 L   **b.**   500 mL

   Solution: Compare these numbers with measurements that you are familiar with.

   500 L $\approx$ 500 quarts of milk

   500 mL $= \frac{1}{2}$ L (you know that 1,000 mL = 1 L), which is approximately $\frac{1}{2}$ quart of milk

   The most reasonable size for the milk shake is 500 mL.

2. John wants to make a pitcher of iced tea. The package directions instruct him to add one gallon of water to the powdered mix. He has a one-pint measuring cup. He recalls that there are four quarts in a gallon and two pints in a quart. How many pints of water should John pour into the pitcher to make the gallon of iced tea?

   Solution:

   $$
   \begin{array}{rl}
   4 & \text{number of quarts in a gallon} \\
   \times\,2 & \text{number of pints in each quart} \\
   \hline
   8 & \text{number of pints in a gallon}
   \end{array}
   $$

   John needs 8 pints of water to make 1 gallon of iced tea.

3. Some juices are sold in 500 milliliter cans. These juices are also sold in 3 liter bottles. How many of the 500 milliliter cans would be equivalent to the 3 liter bottle?

Solution: Looking at Figure 2.3, page 64, you can see that 1,000 mL = 1 L

1,000	number of milliliters in one liter
× 3	size of bottle in liters
3,000	size of bottle in milliliters

Divide to find out how many 500 mL cans would make up 3,000 mL.

$$\frac{6}{500)\overline{3000}} \leftarrow \text{number of 500 mL cans}$$
$$\uparrow \quad \leftarrow \text{number of milliliters in 3 L}$$

number of milliliters in each can

Six 500 mL cans contain the same amount of juice as one 3 L bottle.

4. Certain gas stations sell gasoline by the liter. Marlene keeps a record of the number of gallons her car uses when she goes on a business trip. At the last fill-up, she added 57 liters of gasoline to her tank. How many gallons should she enter in her gasoline expense book?

Solution: Marlene uses her calculator and the information from Figure 2.3. Since a liter is less than a gallon, she divides:

AC 57 **÷** 3.8 **=**

The display tells her that the 57 liters should be entered in her expense book as 15 gallons.

Problems

Choose the most reasonable measure for each item.

✓ **1.** A bottle of shampoo
   a. .5 L   **b.** 50 L   **c.** .5 mL

  2.   A plastic jug of automobile antifreeze
       a.   4 L   **b.**   4 mL   **c.**   40 L

  3.   A bottle of eyedrops
       a.   30 mL   **b.**   30 L   **c.**   3 L

✓ **4.**   A large glass of iced tea
       a.   .8 L   **b.**   .8 mL   **c.**   8 mL

✓ **5.**   The amount of water in a full bathtub
       a.   300 mL   **b.**   3,000 mL   **c.**   300 L

  6.   A spray bottle of window cleaner
       a.   1 L   **b.**   1 mL   **c.**   .1 L

  7.   A bottle of perfume
       a.   .6 mL   **b.**   60 L   **c.**   60 mL

  8.   A jar of skin cream
       a.   2 mL   **b.**   200 mL   **c.**   2,000 mL

✓ **9.**   A bottle of mouthwash
       a.   1 L   **b.**   10 mL   **c.**   10 L

 10.   A large can of paint
       a.   4 mL   **b.**   4 L   **c.**   40 mL

Find the answer to each problem. Look at Figure 2.3, page 64, for help.

 11.   Linda is mixing photographic chemicals for the school's darkroom. One of the solutions requires 150 milliliters of water to be added to a chemical powder. The only measuring cup Linda can find is labeled in fluid ounces. How many fluid ounces does this solution require?

✓ **12.**   The Royal Ranch Club is purchasing chlorine for their pool, which uses 12 liters of chlorine each day. How many liters must the club order for the month of July, if the pool is open every day?

 13.   Barbara's dog, Mutley, is sick. Barbara was told to add 4 milliliters of medicine to Mutley's food each day for two weeks.

   a. How many bottles should she buy?

   b. How many mL of medicine will be left over after the two weeks?

14. A charcoal company recommends that one fluid ounce of lighter fluid be sprinkled on an averaged-size barbecue grill. For about how many barbecues would a 600-milliliter can of lighter fluid last?

15. Which store offers the better price?

   a. Pool Palace has 38 liters of chlorine for $76.

   b. Swim World has 10 gallons of chlorine for $76. Explain your answer.

SECTION 4 • RULERS AND TAPE MEASURES

When would you use a ruler to help you make a purchase? Often you need to make careful measurements before buying a product. Suppose you are buying wood shelves to build a bookcase. Before buying the shelves, you should measure the space where you plan to put the bookcase. Then you have to measure the shelves to make sure they are the right size. Buying carpeting, wallpaper, lumber, furniture, sod, and fabric all involve measuring lengths. There are many tools that measure length. Each tool shown in the photograph below has a specific purpose. These purposes are discussed at the top of the next page.

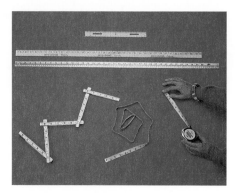

Rulers are handy for small measurements and drawing line segments. You can think of a **line segment** as a part of a line. Metersticks and yardsticks are common household items. A meterstick is slightly longer than a yardstick. Extension rulers can be helpful in places where steel tape measures are too clumsy. Tailors and clothing designers often use a special fabric tape measure. Steel tape measures come in many lengths. They can range from a few feet to 150 feet. They are used to measure long lengths, such as room sizes and window heights.

These tools are found in the home, in the school, and in the workplace. It is important that you learn how to use them.

Skills and Strategies

You can make a simple notation when reporting measurements in inches or feet: " stands for inches and ' stands for feet. For example: 17 in can be written as 17"; 25 ft can be written as 25'. Reading any measuring instrument requires a good understanding of fractions. This chapter will help you review what you know about fractions. Look at the ruler below.

Do the markings on the ruler confuse you? Could you easily locate $2\frac{5}{8}$ inches? Many people have trouble reading rulers. Let's take a closer look at the markings.

Here is a ruler that is marked in inches only.

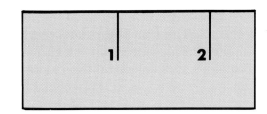

Each inch is now separated into two parts. Each part is called $\frac{1}{2}$ inch.

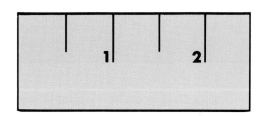

This ruler separates each inch into four parts. Each part is $\frac{1}{4}$ inch.

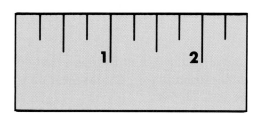

Each inch is now separated into eight parts. Each part is $\frac{1}{8}$ inch.

This ruler separates each inch into sixteen parts. Each part is $\frac{1}{16}$ inch.

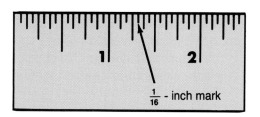

$\frac{1}{16}$ - inch mark

Rulers with inches divided into 16 parts are very common. Look at the markings on the rulers you have just seen. You can easily compare the measurements on each ruler. Look at the following sets of equivalent fractions on the rulers.

$$\frac{2}{16} = \frac{1}{8}$$ $$\frac{10}{16} = \frac{5}{8}$$

$$\frac{4}{16} = \frac{2}{8} = \frac{1}{4}$$ $$\frac{12}{16} = \frac{6}{8} = \frac{3}{4}$$

$$\frac{6}{16} = \frac{3}{8}$$ $$\frac{14}{16} = \frac{7}{8}$$

$$\frac{8}{16} = \frac{4}{8} = \frac{2}{4} = \frac{1}{2}$$ $$\frac{16}{16} = \frac{8}{8} = \frac{4}{4} = \frac{2}{2} = 1$$

Notice that $\frac{8}{16}$ can be renamed in several ways. The simplest way of renaming $\frac{8}{16}$ is $\frac{1}{2}$. Remember that the top number of a fraction is called the **numerator.** The bottom number is called the **denominator.** You don't have to look at a set of rulers to simplify a fraction. You can simplify $\frac{8}{16}$ as follows:

Find a number that divides evenly (without a remainder) into the numerator and the denominator. In this example, one possible number is 4. Divide:

$$\frac{8 \div 4 = 2}{16 \div 4 = 4}$$

Notice that $\frac{2}{4}$ can be further simplified by dividing by 2.

$$\frac{2 \div 2 = 1}{4 \div 2 = 2}$$

The fraction $\frac{1}{2}$ is $\frac{8}{16}$ expressed in the lowest (simplest) terms. Some people call this process "reducing fractions." That name is misleading because the simpler version is *equal* to the original fraction, not a smaller version of it.

You can use a calculator to check if you have correctly simplified a fraction. Remember that every fraction can be written as a division problem. The numerator is the dividend and the denominator is the divisor.

$$\tfrac{1}{2} \quad \text{means} \quad 1 \div 2 \quad \text{or} \quad 2\overline{)1}$$

Your calculator can be used to divide:

AC $1 \div 2 =$

The display should read 0.5.

The quotient 0.5 is a **decimal equivalent** of the fraction $\tfrac{1}{2}$. You can also compute a decimal equivalent for $\tfrac{8}{16}$.

AC $8 \div 16 =$

The display should read 0.5.

Two fractions are equal if they have the same decimal equivalent. Both $\tfrac{1}{2}$ and $\tfrac{8}{16}$ are equal to 0.5; therefore, they are equal.

Here you will practice measuring with a ruler. You will also see the role that measurement plays in many consumer decisions. Read each example carefully.

1. John is building a cabinet for his video equipment. The plans require $1\tfrac{3}{8}$ inch nails. John found a can of nails in his basement

and he wants to see if they are the correct size. Following this question is the actual size of one of the nails. How long is it?

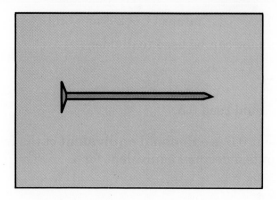

Solution: Line up the zero end of the ruler with the nail.

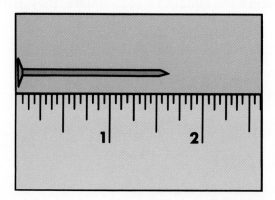

The nail is between 1 and 2 inches. Count the number of sixteenths to the right of the 1-inch mark. There are $\frac{10}{16}$. A **mixed number** contains a whole number part and a fraction part. Simplify $1\frac{10}{16}$ by dividing the numerator and the denominator of the fraction by 2.

$$\frac{10 \div 2}{16 \div 2} = \frac{5}{8} \text{ therefore } 1\frac{10}{16} = 1\frac{5}{8}$$

John cannot use the nails he found because a $1\frac{5}{8}$ inch nail is longer than a $1\frac{3}{8}$ inch nail.

2. Write $\frac{36}{48}$ in lowest terms. Check your answer.

Solution: Find numbers that the numerator and denominator can be divided by, leaving no remainder. The numbers 2, 4, 6, 8, and 12 divide evenly into the numerator and denominator. Using the largest number (12) will complete the simplification in one step.

$$\frac{36 \div 12 = 3}{48 \div 12 = 4}$$

You can check this with your calculator:

`AC` 36 `÷` 48 `=`

`AC` 3 `÷` 4 `=`

The display in both cases should read 0.75.

3. Write $\frac{7}{8}$ as an equivalent decimal.

Solution: Use your calculator and the following keystroke sequence:

`AC` 7 `÷` 8 `=`

The display should read 0.875.

4. Write $\frac{2}{3}$ as an equivalent decimal.

Solution: Use your calculator and the following keystroke sequence:

`AC` 2 `÷` 3 `=`

The display on some calculators will show 0.6666666, while other displays may read 0.6666667. Most calculators can only display 8 digits. When the solution to a problem is longer than 8 digits, some calculators round off and others do not.

Problems

✓ **1.** Use a ruler to measure the length of each line segment.

a.

b.

c.

d.

e.

2. Use a ruler to draw each of these line segments.
a. $3\frac{3}{8}''$ b. $\frac{7}{8}''$ c. $5\frac{1}{2}''$ d. $6''$ e. $2\frac{5}{16}''$

3. Write the calculator keystroke sequence that could be used to find the decimal equivalent of $\frac{7}{8}$.

✓ **4.** Write the calculator keystroke sequence that could be used to find the decimal equivalent of $\frac{8}{7}$.

5. Write the calculator keystroke sequence that could be used to find the decimal equivalent of $\frac{5}{16}$.

6. Write the calculator keystroke sequence that could be used to find the decimal equivalent of $\frac{16}{5}$.

7. Write each fraction in simplest terms. Check your answers with a calculator.
a. $\frac{15}{25}$ b. $\frac{9}{18}$ c. $\frac{36}{54}$ d. $\frac{20}{20}$ e. $\frac{12}{16}$

8. Use your calculator to find the decimal equivalent of each fraction. Copy the entire display.

a. $\frac{3}{5}$ d. $\frac{1}{2}$ g. $\frac{7}{8}$

b. $\frac{4}{16}$ e. $\frac{1}{10}$ h. $\frac{72}{648}$

c. $\frac{81}{216}$ f. $\frac{450}{500}$ i. $\frac{1350}{1800}$

9. Larry needs to replace the lock on his front door. He measures the thickness of the door as $1\frac{14}{16}$ inches. The only lock that the hardware store has in stock fits doors from 1 inch to $1\frac{3}{4}$ inches thick. Should Larry purchase this lock? Explain your answer.

10. A supermarket has two types of customer scales in the fruit and vegetable aisle. One scale shows weights in fractions and mixed numbers. The other scale electronically shows weights in decimals. Trudy measures her groceries on the fraction scale. Write the weight of each item as it would appear on the decimal scale.

   a. cantaloupe: $5\frac{3}{4}$ lb
   b. watermelon: $10\frac{5}{8}$ lb
   c. carrots: $\frac{1}{2}$ lb
   d. potatoes: $8\frac{1}{4}$ lb
   e. a sack of apples: $4\frac{3}{8}$ lb
   f. tomatoes: $2\frac{7}{8}$ lb

SECTION 5 ● PERIMETER OF POLYGONS

Suppose you wanted to enclose a garden with a small fence. How would you know the amount of fencing needed? You would measure the distance around the area you wanted to enclose. If your garden had straight sides, the fence around it would form a polygon. A **polygon** is a closed figure with straight sides. There are many other situations in which a consumer measures polygons; for example, putting molding around a room, stringing holiday lights around a window or doorway, and making a picture frame.

Skills and Strategies

All of these shapes are polygons:

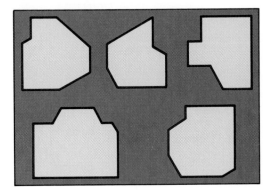

The following figures are not polygons.

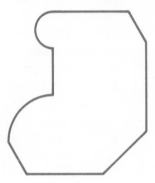

This figure has some sides that are not straight.

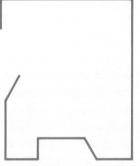

This figure is not closed. Notice the gap in the shape.

You may recognize some of these common polygons.

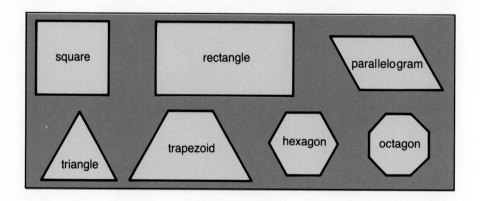

The distance around a polygon is called its **perimeter.** To decide how much fencing to buy, you need to know the perimeter of the garden. The perimeter of any polygon can be found by adding the lengths of its sides.

Read each example carefully.

1. Find the perimeter of this triangle:

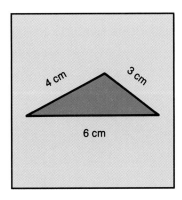

Solution: Add the lengths of the sides.

$$\left.\begin{array}{r} 3 \\ 4 \\ + 6 \end{array}\right\} \text{lengths of sides}$$

13   perimeter

The perimeter is 13 cm.

2. Find the perimeter of this rectangle:

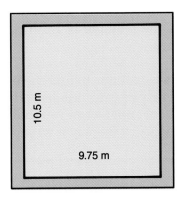

Solution: Recall that opposite sides of a rectangle are equal. Add the lengths of the sides.

$$
\left.\begin{array}{r}
9.75 \\
9.75 \\
10.50 \\
+\ 10.50
\end{array}\right\} \text{lengths of sides}
$$

$$
\overline{40.50 \text{ m}} \quad \text{perimeter}
$$

The perimeter is 40.5 m.

3. Find the perimeter of this triangle:

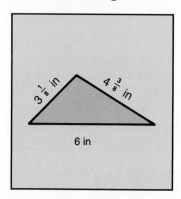

Solution: Add the lengths of the sides. Line up the whole numbers and the fractions vertically:

$$
\left.\begin{array}{r}
3\ \big|\ \frac{1}{8} \\
4\ \big|\ \frac{3}{8} \\
+\ 6\ \big|
\end{array}\right\} \text{The common denominator is 8.}
$$

$$
\overline{3 + 4 + 6\ \big|\ \tfrac{1}{8} + \tfrac{3}{8}} \quad \text{Add the numerators only.}
$$

$$
13\ \big|\ \tfrac{4}{8}
$$

The perimeter of the triangle is $13\frac{4}{8}$ inches. This can be simplified to $13\frac{1}{2}$ inches.

You can also use a calculator to find the perimeter, but there is always the possibility of your accidentally pressing the wrong keys. The calculator cannot warn you that you have pressed the incorrect key; it will just display a wrong answer.

It's a good idea to estimate your answer before using the calculator.

Estimate the answer to Problem 3 before you use the calculator.

$3\frac{1}{8}$
$4\frac{3}{8}$
$+ 6$

Examine the whole number parts only. The sum is 13. Since the sum of the fraction is small in relation to the sum of the whole numbers, the answer can be estimated to be close to 13.

Now, use the calculator.

The M+ and M$^{R}_{c}$ keys will be very important. Look back to page 11 for an explanation of how these keys function.

Try this keystroke sequence:

AC 3 M+ 4 M+ 6 M+ 1 ÷ 8 M+ 3 ÷ 8 M+ M⁻

The whole numbers are being added here.

The fractions are being expressed as decimals, and then added together.

The display should read 13.5. As you can see, certain problems involving fractions are easier to do by hand than with a calculator. Notice also that the display seems reasonable when compared with your estimate of 13.

4. Use the calculator to find the perimeter of the following trapezoid. Express the answer as a fraction.

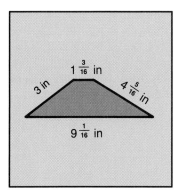

Solution: First estimate the answer by adding the whole-number parts of the mixed numbers.

$$9 + 4 + 1 + 3 = 17$$

The answer will be close to 17.

Now, use the following keystroke sequence:

[AC] 9 [M+] 4 [M+] 1 [M+] 3 [M+]

1 [÷] 16 [M+] 5 [÷] 16 [M+] 3 [÷] 16 [M+] [M◌]

This display should read 17.5625. Notice that the answer seems reasonable when compared with your estimate of 17. To express this decimal as a mixed number, you will need to use the common denominator 16, and the following keystroke sequence:

[AC] 17.5625 [−] 17 [=] [×] 16 [=]

The whole number part is being subtracted here.   Multiply by the common denominator.

The display should read 9. This is the numerator when 17.5625 is expressed as a mixed number with denominator 16.

$$17.5625 = 17\frac{9}{16}$$

Do you think that the calculator saved you time in solving this problem?

5. Rename the fractions $\frac{5}{8}$, $\frac{1}{4}$, and $\frac{1}{2}$ with the common denominator of 16.

Solution:

$\dfrac{5 \times 2}{8 \times 2} = \dfrac{10}{16}$ The numerator and denominator must be multiplied by the same number.

$\dfrac{1 \times 4}{4 \times 4} = \dfrac{4}{16}$

$\dfrac{1 \times 8}{2 \times 8} = \dfrac{8}{16}$

6. Write the fractions $\frac{11}{8}, \frac{25}{4}$ as mixed numbers.

Solution:

An **improper fraction** is one in which the numerator is greater than, or equal to, the denominator. Look at these improper fractions: $\frac{17}{5}, \frac{9}{9}, \frac{252}{8}, \frac{200}{199}, \frac{12}{3}$

Improper fractions can be written as mixed numbers by dividing and using the remainder as a numerator:

$$\frac{11}{8} \qquad\qquad\qquad \frac{25}{4}$$

$$8\overline{)11} \;\; {}^{1\,r\,3} \qquad\qquad 4\overline{)25} \;\; {}^{6\,r\,1}$$
$$\underline{\;\;8\;\;} \qquad\qquad\qquad \underline{\;\;24\;\;}$$
$$3 \qquad\qquad\qquad\qquad 1$$

$$\frac{11}{8} = 1\frac{3}{8} \qquad\qquad \frac{25}{4} = 6\frac{1}{4}$$

7. Find the perimeter of the following triangle:

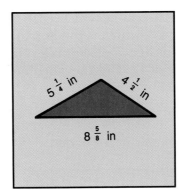

Solution: Line up the mixed numbers. Use 17 as an estimate.

$8\frac{5}{8}$
$5\frac{1}{4}$
$+\; 4\frac{1}{2}$

You will need a common denominator. Use any number that is divisible by each of the given denominators. Your work will be easier if you use the **lowest common denominator.**

Use the lowest common denominator to rename each fraction as shown at the top of the next page.

Rename each fraction using the common denominator

$\frac{5}{8} \times \frac{1}{1} = \frac{5}{8}$ therefore $8\frac{5}{8} = 8\frac{5}{8}$

$\frac{1}{4} \times \frac{2}{2} = \frac{2}{8}$ therefore $5\frac{1}{4} = 5\frac{2}{8}$

$\frac{1}{2} \times \frac{4}{4} = \frac{4}{8}$ therefore $4\frac{1}{2} = 4\frac{4}{8}$

$$17\frac{11}{8}$$

The improper fraction $\frac{11}{8}$ must be changed to a mixed number $17\frac{11}{8} = 17 + \frac{11}{8} = 17 + 1\frac{3}{8} = 18\frac{3}{8}$

The perimeter of the triangle is $18\frac{3}{8}$ in.

The following calculator keystroke sequence can also be used:

[AC] 8 [M+] 5 [M+] 4 [M+] 5 [÷] 8 [M+] 1 [÷]

4 [M+] 1 [÷] 2 [M+] [M∺]

The display should read 18.375. You can use your calculator to verify that $18\frac{3}{8} = 18.375$ by subtracting 18, then multiplying by 8. The display shows 3, which is the numerator of $\frac{3}{8}$. So, 18.375 $= 18\frac{3}{8}$. Notice that the display seems reasonable when compared with your estimate of 17. Did the calculator save you time in solving this problem?

8. Use the calculator to find the perimeter of the following polygon. Express the answer as a fraction.

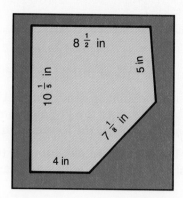

Solution: Use 34 as an estimate. Choose a common denominator. In this example, 40 is a common denominator. If you are unable to find a common denominator easily, use the product of the given denominators. In this example, 80 could also be used as a common denominator. Use the following keystroke sequence:

[AC] 4 [M+] 5 [M+] 7 [M+] 8 [M+] 10 [M+] 1 [÷] 8 [M+] 1 [÷]

2 [M+] 1 [÷] 5 [M+] [M≡]

The display should read 34.825. The answer 34.825 can be expressed as a mixed number using the denominator 40 and the following keystroke sequence:

34.825 [−] 34 [=] [×] 40 [=]
↑
This is already in the display

The display should read 33. This is the numerator when 34.825 is expressed as a mixed number with denominator 40.

$$18.825 = 18\frac{33}{40} \text{ in}$$

Problems

✓ **1.** Rename the fractions.

a. $\frac{1}{2} = \frac{?}{8}$ **g.** $\frac{7}{8} = \frac{?}{16}$

b. $\frac{3}{4} = \frac{?}{16}$ **h.** $\frac{5}{8} = \frac{?}{32}$

c. $\frac{1}{3} = \frac{?}{6}$ **i.** $\frac{3}{7} = \frac{?}{21}$

d. $\frac{2}{5} = \frac{?}{15}$ **j.** $\frac{1}{4} = \frac{?}{100}$

e. $\frac{4}{8} = \frac{?}{16}$ **k.** $\frac{1}{3} = \frac{?}{12}$

f. $\frac{3}{8} = \frac{?}{16}$ **l.** $\frac{3}{5} = \frac{?}{20}$

✓ **2.** Change the mixed numbers to improper fractions.

a. $7\frac{1}{2}$ **f.** $2\frac{3}{8}$

b. $3\frac{1}{8}$ **g.** $6\frac{5}{6}$

c. $9\frac{1}{16}$ **h.** $9\frac{1}{5}$

d. $12\frac{1}{3}$ **i.** $11\frac{1}{6}$

e. $4\frac{3}{4}$ **j.** $5\frac{5}{7}$

✓ **3.** Change the improper fractions to mixed numbers.

a. $\frac{15}{4}$ **f.** $\frac{12}{5}$

b. $\frac{19}{5}$ **g.** $\frac{21}{4}$

c. $\frac{17}{8}$ **h.** $\frac{50}{6}$

d. $\frac{22}{3}$ **i.** $\frac{18}{8}$

e. $\frac{18}{6}$ **j.** $\frac{40}{7}$

4. Find the perimeter of the polygons.

a.

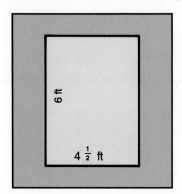

6 ft

$4\frac{1}{2}$ ft

b.

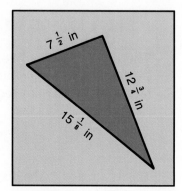

$7\frac{1}{2}$ in

$12\frac{3}{4}$ in

$15\frac{1}{8}$ in

c.

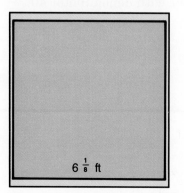

$6\frac{1}{8}$ ft

d.

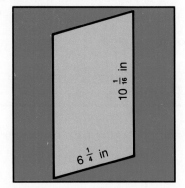

$10\frac{1}{6}$ in

$6\frac{1}{4}$ in

✓ **5.** A rectangular kitchen measures $15\frac{1}{2}$ feet by $9\frac{3}{4}$ feet. New floor molding is going to be installed around the floor. How many feet of molding will be needed?

6. Tina would like to fence her garden. The garden is a rectangle, $10\frac{1}{2}$ feet by 12 feet. The price of the fencing is \$24 a foot.
   a. What is the perimeter of the garden?
   b. How much would the fence cost before sales tax?

    c.   The sales tax rate is 6 percent. What would the tax be on this purchase?

    d.   What would the total cost be including tax?

✓ **7.** Stan is replacing the tiles around the walls of his swimming pool. The tiles are sold in 2-foot lengths for $9 each. Stan's pool measures 75 feet by 25 feet.

    a.   What is the perimeter of the pool?

    b.   How many tiles must Stan buy?

    c.   What will the tiles cost with 4 percent sales tax?

8. Eve is making a wooden picture frame in her shop class. The picture measures $13\frac{1}{8}$ inches by $11\frac{1}{2}$ inches.

    a.   What is the perimeter of the picture?

    b.   Would 4 feet of picture-framing wood be enough for the frame?

✓ **9.** A square has a perimeter of 140 meters. How long is each side?

10. A rectangle has a perimeter of 70 feet. Its length is 19 feet. What is its width?

SECTION 6 • CIRCUMFERENCE

Many consumer purchases involve circular objects. For example, suppose you are buying a bicycle. The tires will come in many different sizes. How do you tell which size bike you should buy? Only one size will be the best for you. Or you could need plumbing supplies or electrical wire, some of which are also circular.

    In this chapter, you will learn the names of several parts related to circles. You will also learn a rule that will help you find the distance around a circle.

Skills and Strategies

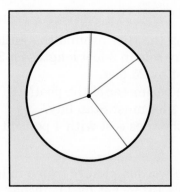

This is a **circle**. Each circle has only one center. The green line is a radius. A **radius** is a line segment that connects the center to any part of the circle. The plural of radius is **radii**. Many radii can be drawn in any circle. The blue lines are also radii. All radii in the same circle have the same length.

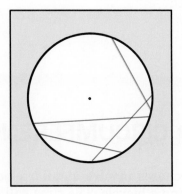

The red line in this circle is called a chord. A **chord** is any line segment that connects two different points on a circle. A circle has many chords. The green lines are other chords for the same circle.

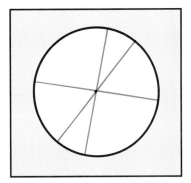

The longest chord of any circle is its diameter. The **diameter** connects two points on a circle and passes through the center. The blue line is one diameter of the circle above. The red lines are also diameters. For any given circle, many diameters can be drawn.

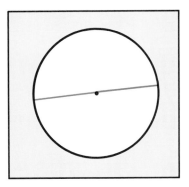

Notice that the diameter above is made up of two radii. The length of any diameter is equal to twice the length of a radius.

Circles are not polygons. Therefore, you cannot find the "perimeter" of a circle. The distance around a circle is called the **circumference**. For any circle, the circumference is a little more than the length of three diameters.

The circles below are marked in lengths equal to the diameter of the circle. You can see that it takes a little more than three diameter lengths to go around the circle. The diameter lengths are shown in red. You can check this by measuring any circle with a tape measure.

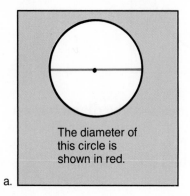

The diameter of this circle is shown in red.

a.

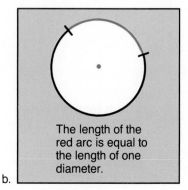

The length of the red arc is equal to the length of one diameter.

b.

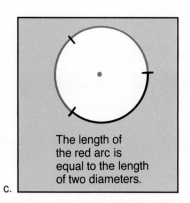

The length of the red arc is equal to the length of two diameters.

c.

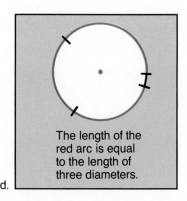

The length of the red arc is equal to the length of three diameters.

d.

The circumference of any circle is approximately 3.14 diameters (or $\frac{22}{7}$ diameters). You may remember that the nonrepeating, nonterminating decimal that is about equal to 3.14 can be represented by the Greek letter π (pi). You may also recall the formula:

$$C = \pi \times d$$

This formula can be used to compute the circumference of any circle, if you know the diameter. See letter "e" on the next page.

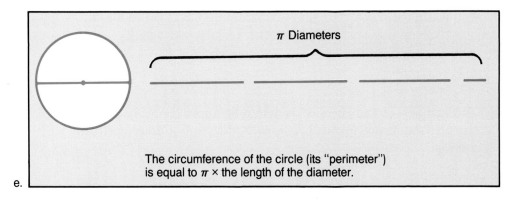

π Diameters

The circumference of the circle (its "perimeter")
is equal to π × the length of the diameter.

e.

Here you will practice finding the circumference of circles. You will also see how knowledge of circles can help you in many consumer purchases, from garden fences to bicycles.

1. Find the circumference of a circle that has a diameter of 12 feet.

   Solution: Use the formula C = π × d

   ```
   3.14   π
   × 12   diameter (d)
   37.68  circumference
   ```

   The circumference of the circle is 37.68 feet.

2. Find the diameter of a circle that has a radius of 4 inches.

   Solution: The length of a diameter is equal to the length of two radii.

   ```
   4   radius
   × 2
   8   length of diameter
   ```

   The diameter is 8 inches long.

3. Find the circumference of a circle with a radius of 5 m.

   Solution: To find the circumference, you must first find the diameter. Find the length of two radii.

   ```
   5    radius
   × 2
   10   diameter
   ```

You could estimate your answer by using 3 as a value for π.

π ≈ 3
C = π × d
C ≈ 3 × d
C ≈ 3 × 10

You can expect the circumference to be approximately 30. Use the circumference formula C = π × d to find a more accurate answer.

  3.14   π
× 10   diameter
31.40 circumference

The circumference is 31.4 m.

Some calculators feature a π key. This key can display π to several decimal places.

Remember: π is *approximately* 3.14. It is really a nonrepeating, nonterminating decimal.

The following calculator keystroke sequences could be used to solve Problem 3.

AC 10 ☒ 3.14 ▭

The display should read 31.4

OR

AC 10 ☒ π ▭

The display should read 31.515927

Problems

Use π = 3.14 where necessary.

1. Find the diameter of a circle that has a radius of 6.5 m.

✓ **2.** What is the radius of a circle if its diameter is 37 yards?

3. Find the radius of a circle if its diameter is 15.7 m.

✓ **4.** Write a calculator keystroke sequence that could be used to find the circumference of a circle having a diameter of 8 meters.

5. Find the circumference of a circle that has a diameter of 10 inches.

6. Find the circumference of a circle that has a diameter of 12.3 meters.

✓ **7.** Write a calculator keystroke sequence that could be used to find the circumference of a circle that has a radius of 20 inches.

8. Find the circumference of a circle that has a radius of 8 feet.

9. Find the circumference of a circle that has a radius of 4.6 meters.

✓ **10.** What is the circumference of this circle?

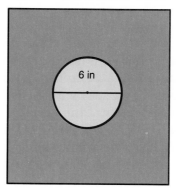

11.   What is the circumference of this circle?

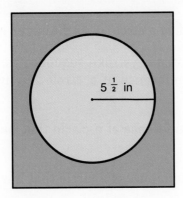

$5 \frac{1}{2}$ in

12.   What is the radius of this circle?

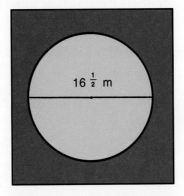

$16 \frac{1}{2}$ m

13.   Henry sells jewelry at a local flea market. He hangs a curtain around his rectangular table so he can store supplies underneath. The table is 40 inches by 30 inches.
   a.   What is the perimeter of the table?
   b.   Henry sometimes uses a circular table with a 50-inch diameter. What is the circumference of this table?
   c.   Would the curtain that Henry uses for the rectangular table fit around the circular table?

14.   Last year, Sarah cut a circular plot out of her lawn to plant flowers. The plot was 10 feet in diameter. Sarah put a fence around it. This year, she plans to increase the garden's diameter by 2 feet.

    a. What is the circumference of the smaller garden?

    b. What will be the circumference of the new, widened garden?

    c. How many feet of extra fencing will Sarah have to purchase to enclose the new garden?

15. **a.** A bicycle wheel has a diameter of 28 inches. Find the circumference using $\frac{22}{7}$ for π.

    b. Find the circumference using 3.14 for π.

    c. Why are the two answers for the circumference not the same?

SECTION 7 • AREA

Arlene wants to plant sod in a rectangular space in front of her home. What information does she need before she starts? She needs to know how much space the lawn covers, so she can decide how much sod to buy. She is more concerned with the space *inside* the rectangle than the distance *around* it. You know that the distance around a polygon is its perimeter. The amount of space inside a flat, closed figure is called its **area**.

There are many other situations in which you will need to know the area of a given shape. Think of times when you need to cover a flat surface. Wallpapering, carpeting, and painting all require area measurements.

Remember, in some situations you need to find the distance around a shape. For these problems, you will have to find the perimeter or circumference. In other situations, you want to find the amount of space inside a shape. Then you need to find an area.

Skills and Strategies

Examine the following rectangle.

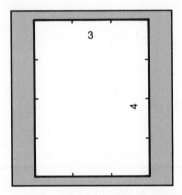

The sides are 3 units and 4 units long. The word **unit** is used as a general name for one of any measurement, such as 1 inch, 1 yard, or 1 meter.

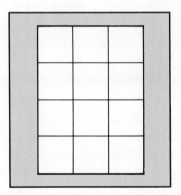

Notice that the 3-unit by 4-unit rectangle is made up of 12 squares. Since the squares measure 1 unit by 1 unit, each is called 1 **square unit**. The area of this rectangle is 12 square units.

To find the area of any rectangle, multiply the length by the width. The answer will always be in square units.

area of rectangle = length × width
$$A = L \times W$$

To find the area of any circle, use the formula $A = \pi \times r^2$; "r^2" is the same as "$r \times r$."

area of a circle = pi × radius²
$$A = \pi \times r^2$$

Here you will learn how area is used in many consumer purchases, from floor tiles to wallpaper. Read each example carefully.

1. Find the area of this rectangle.

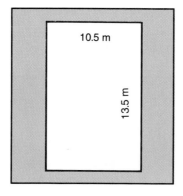

10.5 m

13.5 m

Solution: Use the formula $A = L \times W$. Multiply the length by the width.

$$\begin{array}{ll} 13.5 & \text{length, in meters} \\ \underline{\times\ 10.5} & \text{width, in meters} \\ 141.75 & \text{area, in square meters} \end{array}$$

The area is 141.75 square meters.

Remember, area is always reported in square units.

Here the units are **square meters**. Square meters can be written as m². **Square centimeters** can be written as cm².

2.   Find the area of a circle that has a radius of 8 units.

Solution: Use the formula $A = \pi \times r^2$.

Remember, $r^2 = r \times r$

$8 \times 8 = 64$ (r^2)

$$\begin{array}{rl} 3.14 & \pi \\ \times\ 64 & r^2 \\ \hline 200.96 & \text{area of the circle, in square units} \end{array}$$

The area of the circle is 200.96 square units.

3.   Find the area of a rectangle that has a length of $\frac{3}{4}$ inch and a width of $\frac{1}{2}$ inch.

Solution: Draw a diagram.

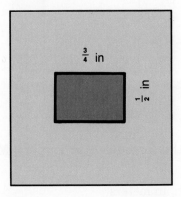

To multiply fractions, first find the product of the numerators then find the product of the denominators.

$$\frac{3}{4} \times \frac{1}{2} = \frac{3 \times 1}{4 \times 2} = \frac{3}{8}$$

The area is $\frac{3}{8}$ square inch (sq in).

The following keystroke sequence can also be used to find the area of the $\frac{3}{4}$ inch by $\frac{1}{2}$ inch rectangle:

AC   3 ÷ 4   ×   1 ÷ 2 =

This computes the decimal equivalent of $\frac{3}{4}$.   This computes the decimal equivalent of $\frac{1}{2}$.

The display should read 0.375.

If you want to express the answer as a fraction, use this keystroke:

AC 4 × 2 × .375 =

This finds the product of the denominators.
This is the denominator of the answer.

$0.375 = \frac{3}{8}$

The display should read 3.
This is the numerator.

4. Find the product of $\frac{3}{5}$ and $\frac{20}{21}$.

   Solution:

   $$\frac{3}{5} \times \frac{20}{21} = \frac{60}{105}$$

   The fraction $\frac{60}{105}$ can be expressed as $\frac{4}{7}$ in simplest form. Make your work easier by simplifying before you multiply.

   $$\frac{3}{\cancel{5}} \times \frac{\cancel{20}^{4}}{21} \qquad \text{divide numerator and denominator by 5.}$$

   $$\frac{\cancel{3}}{\cancel{5}} \times \frac{\cancel{20}^{4}}{\cancel{21}_{7}} \qquad \text{divide numerator and denominator by 3.}$$

   $$\frac{1}{1} \times \frac{4}{7} = \frac{4}{7} \qquad \text{multiply the fractions.}$$

5. Find the area of a rectangle that measures $1\frac{1}{2}$ by $2\frac{1}{3}$.

   Solution:

   $$\frac{3}{2} \times \frac{7}{3} \qquad \text{rename the mixed numbers as improper fractions.}$$

   $$\frac{\cancel{3}}{2} \times \frac{7}{\cancel{3}_{1}} = \frac{7}{2} \qquad \text{simplify and multiply.}$$

   $$\frac{7}{2} = 3\frac{1}{2}$$

6.   Wallpaper is sold in standard rolls $1\frac{3}{4}$ feet wide. Each strip cut from a roll must reach from the floor to the ceiling. How many strips would you need to cover a wall that is $12\frac{1}{4}$ feet wide?

Solution: This problem can be stated in another way: how many times does $1\frac{3}{4}$ go into $12\frac{1}{4}$?

$12\frac{1}{4} \div 1\frac{3}{4}$ set up division problem.

$\frac{49}{4} \div \frac{7}{4}$ rename as improper fractions.

$\frac{49}{4} \times \frac{4}{7}$ write as a multiplication example, using the reciprocal of the second fraction (the divisor).

$\frac{\overset{1}{\cancel{49}}}{\cancel{4}} \times \frac{\cancel{4}^{1}}{\cancel{7}} = 7$ simplify and multiply.

You will need 7 strips of wallpaper.

The following calculator keystroke sequence can be used after the mixed numbers have been renamed as improper fractions:

AC 4 ÷ 4 M+	49 ÷ 7	÷ Mʀ =
Denominators are divided, quotient is stored in memory.	Numerators are divided.	Numerator quotient is divided by denominator quotient.

The display should read 7.

7.   A jeweler has $48\frac{9}{16}$ inches of solid gold chain. It is important for the jeweler to measure accurately, because gold is very expensive. How much chain is left after $25\frac{1}{2}$ inches are cut off to make a necklace?

Solution: You must subtract $25\frac{1}{2}$ from $48\frac{9}{16}$. An estimate can be found by subtracting 25 from 48. The estimate is 23.

$$
\begin{array}{r}
48\frac{9}{16} \\
- 25\frac{1}{2} \\
\end{array}
$$

$$
\begin{array}{r}
48\frac{9}{16} \\
- 25\frac{8}{16} \\
\hline
23\frac{1}{16} \\
\end{array}
$$ rename using the common denominator 16.

There are $23\frac{1}{16}$ inches of chain left. This answer is reasonable when compared with your estimate of 23.

8. Suppose that the jeweler from Problem 7 cut $25\frac{3}{4}$ inches from the $48\frac{9}{16}$ inch chain. How much chain would be left?

Solution: Set up the subtraction problem.

$$48\tfrac{9}{16}$$
$$-\ 25\tfrac{3}{4}$$

$$48\tfrac{9}{16}$$
$$-\ 25\tfrac{12}{16}$$ rename using the common denominator 16.

Notice that $\frac{12}{16}$ is too large to be subtracted from $\frac{9}{16}$.

$$47\ +\ 1\tfrac{9}{16}$$ rename $48\tfrac{9}{16}$ as $47\ +\ 1\tfrac{9}{16}$.
$$-\ 25\tfrac{12}{16}$$
$$\overline{22\tfrac{13}{16}}$$

$$47\tfrac{25}{16}$$ rename $1\tfrac{9}{16}$ as an improper fraction.
$$-\ 25\tfrac{12}{16}$$ subtract.
$$\overline{22\tfrac{13}{16}}$$

There are $22\frac{13}{16}$ inches of chain left.
The following calculator keystroke sequence could also be used:

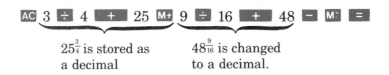

$25\frac{3}{4}$ is stored as $48\frac{9}{16}$ is changed
a decimal.   to a decimal.

The display should read 22.8125. This can be converted to a fraction using the technique from page 97.

Problems

1. Find the answer to each problem.

a. $5\frac{1}{8}$
    $-\ 3\frac{1}{16}$

b. $15\frac{3}{4}$
    $-\ 9\frac{1}{2}$

c. $13\frac{1}{2}$
    $-\ 4\frac{3}{8}$

d. $104\frac{1}{2}$
    $-\ 12\frac{3}{4}$

e. $60\frac{7}{8}$
    $-\ 9\frac{5}{16}$

f. $12\frac{1}{3}$
    $-\ 9\frac{1}{2}$

✓ **2.**   Find the product.

    a. $5\frac{1}{4} \times \frac{1}{3} =$ **d.** $4\frac{1}{8} \times 1\frac{1}{2} =$

    b. $8\frac{3}{4} \times \frac{2}{9} =$ **e.** $1\frac{1}{7} \times 3\frac{1}{2} =$

    c. $15\frac{1}{2} \times 6 =$ **f.** $5\frac{1}{5} \times 2\frac{1}{2} =$

✓ **3.**   Find the quotient.

    a. $1\frac{1}{2} \div \frac{3}{4} =$ **d.** $18\frac{1}{3} \div 1\frac{5}{6} =$

    b. $2\frac{3}{16} \div 1\frac{1}{4} =$ **e.** $20 \div 1\frac{7}{8} =$

    c. $11\frac{1}{3} \div 2\frac{5}{6} =$ **f.** $4\frac{3}{4} \div \frac{4}{5} =$

4.   Write a calculator keystroke sequence that could be used to find the area of a rectangle that measures 16 inches by $8\frac{1}{2}$ inches.

✓ **5.**   Find the area of each rectangle.

    a.   **b.**

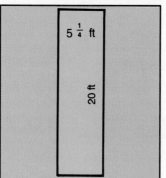
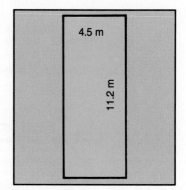

6.   Find the area of each circle. Use $\pi = 3.14$.

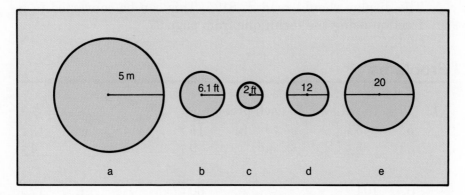

✓ **7.** What is the area of a square with sides measuring $12\frac{1}{2}$ feet?

8. A circle has a radius of 6 meters.
   a. Draw a picture and label the radius.
   b. What is the area of the circle?
   c. What is the length of the diameter?
   d. What is a good estimate for the circumference of this circle?
   e. What is the circumference of this circle?

9. Find the area of this circle.

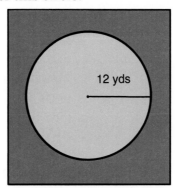

12 yds

✓ **10.** Find the area of a circle that has a diameter of 10 feet.

11. John has a rectangular garden that measures 20 feet by 30 feet.
   a. What is the area of the garden?
   b. John wants to put new sod down. Sod costs $0.32 per square foot. How much would John need to spend on sod?

12. Marta is planning to have the front of her property landscaped. Her front yard measures 40 feet by 45 feet. She plans to put down sod over the entire yard, except for a circular flowerbed in the middle. The flowerbed has a radius of 10 feet.
   a. What is the area of the entire yard?
   b. What is the area of the flowerbed?
   c. How much sod will Marta need to cover the entire yard, but not the flowerbed?

✓ **13.** Diane is having a new diving board installed for her pool. The board is $18\frac{1}{4}$ feet long, and $8\frac{3}{4}$ feet must extend over the pool. How many feet will go over the *ground*?

14. How many strips of wallpaper $1\frac{7}{8}$ feet wide would be needed to cover a wall that is $20\frac{5}{8}$ feet wide? (See page 98.)

15. How many strips of wallpaper $1\frac{7}{8}$ feet wide would be needed to cover a wall that is 21 feet wide? (Hint: Use your answer from No. 14, or refer back to the page reference for No. 14.)

● KEY TERMS

To find the definition of any term introduced in the chapter, refer to the Glossary in the back of this book.

area	lowest common denominator
center	meter
chord	mixed number
circle	numerator
circumference	perimeter
decimal equivalent	polygon
denominator	radii
diameter	radius
fluid ounce	square centimeter (cm²)
gram	square meter (m²)
improper fraction	square unit
line segment	unit
liter	

● REVIEW PROBLEMS

1. Laura wants to put fancy wood molding around a window in her bedroom. The window is $48\frac{1}{4}$ inches high and $32\frac{1}{2}$ inches wide. What is the perimeter of the window?

2. How many $\frac{1}{4}$ pound hamburgers can be made from $5\frac{3}{4}$ pounds of meat?

3. A rectangular kitchen countertop measures 63 cm by 142 cm. What is the area of the countertop?

4. Floor tiles cost $1.10 per square foot. How much would it cost to tile a room that measures 12 feet by 18 feet?

5. Find the perimeter of this room:

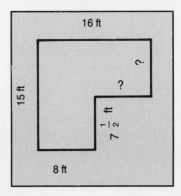

6. Felicia's town is putting a circular fence around the Veterans' Memorial. The diameter of the piece of land to be enclosed measures 15.5 feet. How many feet of fencing are needed to enclose this area?

7. When Jack's extension ladder is closed, it measures $15\frac{1}{4}$ feet long. When the ladder is fully extended, it measures $27\frac{3}{8}$ feet long. What is the length of the extension?

8. Dwight weighs 195 pounds. What is his approximate weight in kilograms? (Round to the nearest kilogram.)

9. Mr. Abrams owns a rectangular piece of property that is $30\frac{1}{2}$ feet by 20 feet. If he purchases the adjoining rectangular lot, which measures $12\frac{1}{4}$ feet by 16 feet, what would the total area of his property be?

10. Moe's Movers have three sizes of packing crates. The small size is $3\frac{1}{2}$ feet high; the medium size is $5\frac{1}{4}$ feet high; and the large size is $8\frac{5}{8}$ feet high. The movers stack the boxes as tightly as possible so they don't shift during the move. If the inside of the van is 15 feet high, which of the following combinations would fit?
    a. 1 small crate on top of a large crate
    b. 4 small crates on top of one another
    c. 2 small crates on top of a medium crate
    d. 1 small on a medium on a large

1. Go to a library and find the address of the Federal Trade Commission (FTC) in Washington, DC. Write a letter asking them for pamphlets and information about warranties.

2. Go to three different stores (department, supermarket, pharmacy, stationery, electronics, shoe store, for example). Find out their specific policy for refunds, returns, and exchanges.

3. Go to a local food store. Find an item that is sold in at least three different sizes. Make a chart listing the item, the three sizes, the unit price of each size, and the total cost of each size.

4. Cut out 20 coupons for supermarket items from a newspaper. Paste them vertically on a wall chart. Visit a local supermarket and find out the price of each item for which you have a coupon. (Make sure that you price the size stated on the coupon.) List these prices in a column next to each coupon. Find the sum of the regular cost of the 20 items. In a third column, list the price you would pay for each item if you used each coupon. Find the sum of these lower prices. Show how much you could save if you used the 20 coupons.

5. Make a list of 20 supermarket items that are available in nationally advertised brands. Include the size of each item. Visit two local supermarkets and find the price of each item in both supermarkets. Find the total cost of the 20 items sold in each supermarket. Prepare a wall chart displaying the information you found. Include the name and address of each supermarket.

6. Make a list of 20 supermarket items that are available in a nationally advertised brand and a store's own label. Include the size of each item. Be sure each nationally advertised item is available in the same size container as the store's own brand. Prepare a wall chart displaying the item, size, and price for the nationally advertised brand, and for the store's own label. Find the sum of each column of prices. Find the difference between the two columns.

UNITS OF LIQUID MEASURE

In Chapter 2 you learned about units of measurement in the English standard and metric systems. It is difficult to get a sense of length, weight, or volume from a photograph. Look at these two containers:

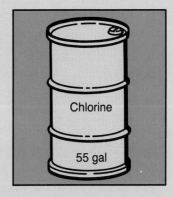

These pictures can be misleading. This manipulative activity will help you and your classmates become familiar with units of liquid measure.

Directions: Gather ten empty containers from products that are sold by their volume. For example,

- milk
- anti-freeze
- oil
- bleach

Wash out each container. Do not remove the labels. Mount each empty container onto a piece of wood or plastic. Identify the metric or English size of each container by printing a sign in front of each item. Submit this project for display in the classroom.

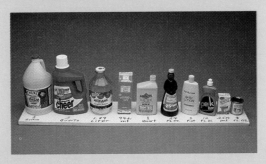

ESTIMATION

In Chapters 1 and 2, you learned strategies that could help you become a smart shopper, and your buying skills were sharpened after working through those chapters.

This computer application will strengthen your ability to estimate amounts of money. Estimation is a method of approximating a result without performing the exact computation. A shopper must be a good estimator. Consider these two situations:

1. You are at home making up a shopping list, and you need to estimate the amount of money you must take to the store.

2. You are at a store without a shopping list. You must estimate the total cost of the items you select to make sure you have enough money to pay for them.

Directions: This is your chance to see how well you can estimate the price of some picnic supplies and some supermarket and music store items using the computer. Follow the start-up procedures for your computer which are found in Appendix A. Select Topic 1 titled *Estimation* from the Main Menu. Follow the instructions on your computer screen to complete the following charts. Do not write in this book. Put your answers on a piece of paper.

Picnic Supplies			
Item	Actual Price	Your First Estimate	Computer Estimate
Paper plates	$2.95	$3	$3
Paper cups	2.39	2.50	2.50
Plastic utensils	1.79	a.	b.
Meat	13.52	c.	d.
Pickles	2.95	e.	f.
TOTAL	g.	h.	i.

Supermarket Items

Item	Actual Price	Your First Estimate	Computer Estimate
Juice	$ 1.69	a.	b.
Watermelon	2.20	c.	d.
Cheese	4.49	e.	f.
Bread	1.35	g.	h.
Shampoo	3.99	i	j.
Macaroni	.79	k.	l.
Turkey	11.93	m.	n.
TOTAL	o.	p.	q.

Music Store Items

Item	Actual Price	Your First Estimate	Computer Estimate
Album	$10.99	a.	b.
Compact disc	15.79	c.	d.
Cassette	6.29	e.	f.
Poster	4.30	g.	h.
TOTAL	i.	j	k.

TOPIC *2*

TRAVEL AND TOURISM

Travel is a part of our way of life. People commute to jobs that are considerable distance from their homes. Some students even travel many miles to school. Stores and businesses are clustered in central locations. As our sprawling communities and shopping areas continue to grow, the need for a way to get around becomes even more critical. You probably recognize the need to have convenient transportation readily available. Young people are often willing to work hard to buy a car. Many young men and women want the independence that a car can give. Besides traveling to school, work, or shops, many Americans travel by car, bus, train, or plane when they take vacations. Becoming well-informed before you buy a car or take a vacation could make travel a more enjoyable experience.

CHAPTER 3

THE AUTOMOBILE

SECTION 1 • CLASSIFIED ADS

One afternoon, a friend from school tells you about a job as a part-time salesclerk at the shopping mall. You decide to apply for the job because you think you can earn money to save for college. You have one problem, however: no car! To travel to and from the shopping mall, you need a car of your own. What should you do? You know that you cannot afford to buy a brand-new car, so you consider buying a used car. You recall that your cousin bought a fabulous car from someone who advertised a used car for sale in the **classified** section of the newspaper. You get the paper and begin to look at the different **classified ads** for used cars. But what do all the abbreviations mean?

TRI-COUNTY Jeep/ Eagle 771-1222.

BUICK '76—Skylark 2 dr hatchback, runs & looks good. $650. 876-3415 after 6pm

BUICK '79—LeSabre Limited, 4 dr, auto, ps/pb, AM/FM stereo radio, mint cond. Asking $1950. 683-8215

BUICK '80—Regal Ltd. Okla. car, no rust, clean, 3.8 liter engine, good cond, air, am/fm, $2300. 791-3562

BUICK–81 LeSabre, 4 dr. 307 V8, air, auto, power, real clean, 81,000 mi, $2700. 231-4678

BUICK '81—Regal Ltd. V-6. 66,500 miles. Excellent condition. $3595. Call 863-0536

BUICK '81—Regal AM/FM, air, ps, pb, cruise. 83,000 mi. $2500-best offer. Call 451-6385

BUICK '81—Skylark Limited, 4dr, ps/pb, cruise, am/fm, tilt, no rust. excellent cond. $1800 677-0237

CAD '82: Cimmarron. Good condition. Sacrifice, $2700. 831-7418

CAD '84—Eldorado, fully equipt, midnight blue, cloth int, 60K mi, asking $10,900/offer 331-0386

CAD '84—ElDorado. Loaded. Immaculate. 49,000 miles. $11,995. Call 831-0699

CAD '87—Sedan deville, executives personal car. very low mi, loaded. Desert frost/matching interior a bargain at $17,900 call 248-1532

CADILLAC '75—Coupe DeVille. Fully equipt, good cond. & good tires. Call 984-1800.

CADILLAC '76—Eldorado Cpe, white, w/red leather, new Michelin tires, under 49,000 miles. 891-5355.

CADILLAC '78—In good cond. Must sell. $3500 or best offer. Call 761-8346

Used-car advertisements are written in a language all their own. You can learn how to translate the "shorthand" in these ads by becoming familiar with these expressions:

ac	air conditioning
AM/FM	AM/FM radio
auto	automatic transmission
cruise	cruise control
cyl	cylinders
dr	doors
p/ant	power antenna
pb	power brakes
p/locks	power door locks

p/mirrors	power mirrors
p/seats	power seats
ps	power steering
pw	power windows
spd	speeds (for transmissions)
standard	standard transmission
sunrf	sunroof
ww	whitewall tires

A car that has many of the features from this list might be referred to in an ad as *loaded*. Words such as *mint* and *immaculate* are often used to describe cars in excellent condition. Sometimes a classified ad will include information about the number of miles the car has been driven. *Lo mi* means the car has low mileage, and the letter *K* is used to represent thousands of miles (for example, 49 K = 49,000 miles).

The price is usually given in the advertisement. *Neg* means that the price is negotiable; in other words, the seller is willing to bargain with you. *Firm* means that the owner is unwilling to change the price. *Sacrifice* means that the seller believes that the price is lower than the car's worth.

By knowing what these expressions and terms mean, you will be able to skim the classified ads and focus on the ones that describe the used car that would be best for you.

Skills and Strategies

Here you will learn some of the steps that may be involved when buying or selling a car. Examine each example carefully.

1. In some states new and used cars are subject to sales tax. Kerry purchased a used car for $1,700. The tax rate in his state is $8\frac{1}{4}\%$ How much sales tax did he pay?

Solution:

$$
\begin{array}{rl}
\$1,700 & \text{price of car} \\
\times\ .0825 & \text{sales tax rate (decimal equivalent)} \\
\hline
\$140.25 & \text{sales tax}
\end{array}
$$

Kerry paid $140.25 in sales tax.

2. One year later, Kerry decides to sell his car. He wants to put this ad in the newspaper:

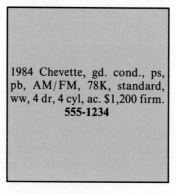

1984 Chevette, gd. cond., ps, pb, AM/FM, 78K, standard, ww, 4 dr, 4 cyl, ac. $1,200 firm.
555-1234

The cost of a classified ad is determined by its length. Kerry's newspaper charges these rates:

$18.00 for the first two lines
$8.75 for each additional line

How much will the newspaper charge Kerry to print his ad?

Solution: There are four lines in Kerry's ad.

$18.00	cost of the first two lines

$ 8.75	cost of one additional line
× 2	number of additional lines
$17.50	cost of two additional lines

$18.00	cost of the first two lines
+17.50	cost of two additional lines
$35.50	total cost

The newspaper will charge Kerry $35.50 to print his ad.

Problems

1. The *North Shore News* charges $9.50 for a two-line classified ad. Each additional line costs $6. How much does a five-line advertisement cost?

✓**2.** The *Antique Auto News* charges $40 for a three-line classified ad. Each additional line costs $7.50. For an extra $20, a seller can include a photo in the ad. How much would a four-line ad with a photograph cost?

3. The *Hammonton Citizen* gives senior citizens a 10% discount on classified ads. Carla Johnson, a senior citizen, is selling her car and wants to take out a classified ad. The ad is three lines long. The paper regularly charges $6.50 per line.
   a. What is the regular price of the ad?
   b. How much money does Carla Johnson save because of the discount?
   c. What price does Carla Johnson pay for this ad?

✓ 4. Sandy placed this ad in the *Hot Rod Journal:*

> 1972 Camaro Rally Sport, ps, pb, ac, AM/FM, 8 cyl, ww, p/seats, p/ant, garaged, $7,200. (512) 555-1234

Hot Rod Journal charges $8.75 per line plus a service fee of $5. How much did Sandy's ad cost?

5. The *Bayside Bugle* charges by the word to run classified ads. The newspaper charges $10 for the first 20 words and 12 cents for each additional word. How much would a 30-word classified ad cost?

6. The *Monthly Motor Guide* charges $12 for a two-line classified ad. Each additional line costs $7. How much does a five-line classified ad cost?

✓ 7. The *Southern Auto Guide* charges $27.50 to print a photograph with a classified ad. A four-line classified ad costs $26, and each additional line costs $5.50. How much would a ten-line advertisement with a photograph cost?

8. The *Amityville American* charges $13 for a two-line classified ad and $4.75 for each additional line. Tyrone wants to place an ad that is five lines long. How much will his ad cost?

✓ **9.** The *Evening Sun* charges for each word printed in a classified ad. The paper charges $12.25 for the first 25 words and 15 cents for each additional word. How much would a 32-word classified ad cost?

10. The *Good Ole Times* magazine charges for classified ads by the column inch. A column inch is as wide as one column, and it is 1 inch high. The cost is $14 per column inch. How much would the *Good Ole Times* charge a customer to print a $2\frac{1}{2}$-inch classified ad?

SECTION 2 • USING STATISTICS

Laura is planning to purchase her first car. She decides that she wants a 1981 Trans Am, and she looks in the classified section of her newspaper. How does she know which prices are reasonable?

Jason plans to sell his 1983 Dodge pickup truck. How does he know what price he should charge?

The price of a used car obviously depends on its condition. A reasonable price for a particular car, however, can be determined by examining the prices of similar cars listed in the classified ads.

Over a period of time, Laura should gather prices of many 1981 Trans Am cars from the newspaper to determine what would be a fair price for the car she wants. Jason should follow the same procedure for setting a price for his 1983 Dodge pickup.

Before long, Laura and Jason will each have compiled a list of advertised prices. They will then be able to use a branch of mathematics call **statistics** to help analyze the **data** or the numbers they gather, and figure out a fair price.

Suppose that both Jason and Laura have recorded the prices they found in the newspaper. Now examine how each one would use statistics.

Skills and Strategies

Here you will learn how to use statistics to determine reasonable prices.

1. Jason made the following list of 1983 Dodge truck prices that he found in the newspaper:

   $2,655
   $1,800
   $3,700
   $1,995
   $2,450
   $2,700

   What is a reasonable selling price for Jason's pickup truck?

   Solution: To determine a reasonable price, Jason could find the mean of the six prices. The **mean** is the arithmetic average of a collection of data. The mean must fall between the highest price and the lowest price. (You can use this fact to estimate that your result is correct.) Jason computes the mean by first adding up the prices, or data.

$$
\left.\begin{array}{r}
\$\ 2,655 \\
1,800 \\
3,700 \\
1,995 \\
2,450 \\
+\ 2,700 \\
\end{array}\right\} \text{data}
$$

$$
\overline{\$15,300} \quad \text{sum}
$$

Then he divides the sum by the number of prices.

$$\text{number of pieces of data} \rightarrow 6 \overline{\smash{)}\ 15{,}300} \quad \begin{array}{l} \leftarrow \text{mean (average price of one truck)} \\ \leftarrow \text{sum} \end{array}$$

This problem could also be solved using a calculator. Remember that the mean must fall between the lowest price ($1,800) and the highest price ($3,700).

AC 2,655 **+** 1,800 **+** 3,700 **+** 1,995 **+**
2,450 **+** 2,700 **=** **÷** 6 **=**

The mean ($2,550) should appear in the display. In this case, the mean is a reasonable price for Jason's truck. Depending on the condition of his truck, Jason could raise or lower this price.

2. Laura wants to find a reasonable purchase price for the 1981 Trans Am that she plans to buy. She looks in the classified ads and finds seven cars that interest her. Their listed prices are:

$ 600
$ 400
$ 500
$ 650
$ 800
$ 450
$6,400

Based on the data, what is a reasonable price for Laura to pay for her car?

Solution: Laura finds that the mean is $1,400. She does not think, however, that the mean approximates any of the prices well.

The mean may not always be a practical representation of the data for all purposes. The mean is drastically affected by the presence of extreme (very high or very low) numbers. Notice that $6,400 is an extreme price when compared with the other six prices.

Based on the data she has gathered, Laura should use the median to find a reasonable price. When values are arranged in numerical order, the **median** is a value at which there is an equal number of values below and above.

Laura arranges the prices in numerical order.

400   450   500   600   650   800   6,400

She then pairs up the numbers as follows, starting with the outside numbers:

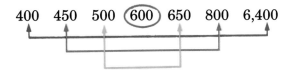

The median is the *middle* piece of data. Notice that the median price, $600, is a more reasonable price than the mean, which is $1,400. Depending on the condition of the car Laura wants to buy, the seller could raise or lower the price.

3. Find the median for the following set of scores:
    7, 6, 3, 1, 2, 5, 8, 10

Solution:

    1, 2, 3, 5, 6, 7, 8, 10   Arrange the numbers in numerical order.

    1, 2, 3, 5, 6, 7, 8, 10   Pair the numbers.

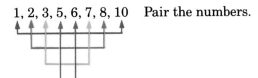

Notice that there is no middle score because there is an even number (eight) of scores. The median is found by averaging the two innermost scores.

    5 + 6 = 11

$$\begin{array}{r} 5.5 \\ 2\overline{)11.0} \end{array}$$

The median is 5.5.

4. A new-car dealer is rearranging her showroom. She wants to attract more customers, so she plans to put a car painted in a popular color in the window. Here is a listing of her sales over the past year.

Car Color	Number Sold
Red	101
White	78
Black	20
Blue	172
Yellow	95
Green	112
Tan	112

What is the most popular car color?

Solution: The list shows the colors chosen by the buyers of the 690 cars sold during the past year. The color chosen most often was blue. In statistics, the piece of data that occurs most often is called the **mode**. In this example, the mode color is blue, so the dealer should put a blue car in the showroom window.

REMEMBER: The **mean** is the arithmetic average. The **median** is the middle piece of data. The **mode** is the most frequently occurring piece of data.

Problems

✓ **1.** Find the mean of each of the sets of data.
   a. 7, 12, 1, 7, 6, 5, 11
   b. 85, 105, 95, 90, 115
   c. 10, 14, 16, 16, 8, 9, 11, 12, 3

✓ **2.** Find the mean and the median of each of the sets of data:
  a. 10, 8, 7, 5, 9, 10, 7
  b. 45, 50, 40, 35, 75
  c. 15, 11, 11, 16, 16, 9

✓ **3.** Find the mean, the median, and the mode of each of the sets of data:
  a. 40, 15, 5, 40, 20
  b. 4, 8, 6, 14, 2, 2

4. Fred wants to sell his grandfather's 1932 antique Ford. He begins to set his price by looking at ads for antique Fords in the newspaper. He finds these five prices:
  $4,600 $9,000 $8,000 $6,000 $6,000
  What is the mean price of the five cars?

5. The Dyna-Sound Car Stereo Company installed these sound systems last month:

System	Number Sold
AM radio	3
AM/FM radio	2
AM/FM stereo radio	49
AM/FM stereo cassette system	39
Compact disc player	12

  a. What was the mode system installed?
  b. How many sound systems did Dyna-Sound install last month?

✓ **6.** Five students at North Shore High School are saving up to buy their first cars. They all have after-school jobs, and their weekly salaries are listed below.
  Pat, $70
  Nancy, $60
  Kim, $80
  Raul, $90
  Ruth, $265

    a. What is their mean weekly salary?

    b. What is the median salary?

    c. Which number do you think is a better representative of the data, the mean or the median? Explain your answer.

7. Roseann is selling her 1971 Mustang. She wants to include a photo of her car along with her classified ad. Three publications give her prices for ads with photographs:

Lake Success Shopsaver, $19.50

Floral Park Bulletin, $11.50

Glen Oaks News Saver, $8.90

    a. What is the mean price of the three photo advertisements?

    b. Roseann is considering placing photo ads in each of the two newspapers with the lower prices. What would be the total cost of the two ads?

    c. How much more would Roseann pay for the two lower-priced ads together than for one ad in the *Lake Success Shopsaver?*

8. There were seven advertisements for antique Chevrolets in last week's *Orange Grove News.* The prices of the seven ads were $19, $16, $7, $14, $10.50, $14, and $14.

    a. What was the mean price of these seven classified ads?

    b. What was the median price?

    c. What was the mode price?

✓ **9.** The *Daily Times* charges $17 for a four-line classified ad. What is the average cost per line?

10. Elliot has cut out four classified ads for cars that interest him most. He plans to buy a car soon, and he wants to get a general idea about the prices for the kinds of cars he is considering. The prices of the cars in the ads are $1,750, $2,400, $2,200, and $1,450.

    a. What is the mean price of these four cars?

    b. What is the median price?

    c. Elliot has saved $1,995 for a car. To be able to buy the $2,400 car or one the same price at the end of three weeks, what is the average amount of money that he would have to save each week?

SECTION 3 • PROBABILITY: THE BASIS OF INSURANCE

As soon as Helene got her driver's license, she bought a used car. She pays $700 per year to insure the car. This amount is called her annual **premium.**

If Helene becomes involved in a car accident, the insurance company might have to pay thousands of dollars to cover damages. Have you ever wondered how an insurance company can promise to cover drivers for much more money than the drivers pay in annual premiums? Or why the insurance companies don't go bankrupt?

The answers to your questions start with the fact that not all drivers who pay premiums get into accidents. Many drivers never receive any money from an insurance company. The insurance companies must collect enough money to pay for the damages claimed by people they insure. It would be disastrous for an insurance company if *all* the people insured by the company got into accidents regularly. What are the chances of this happening? Insurance companies are very interested in the answer to this question.

In mathematics, the study of chance is called **probability.** All insurance rates are based on probability. Before you can understand how insurance companies set rates, you need to learn about probability.

Skills and Strategies

A hat contains three marbles: one red, one white, and one blue. If one marble is going to be picked at **random** (without looking into the hat), there are three possible **outcomes**, or **events:**

- The red marble will be chosen.

- The white marble will be chosen.

- The blue marble will be chosen.

Since the chance of selecting a red, a white, or a blue marble is the same, we say that the outcomes are **equally likely.**

Suppose that a hat contains 1 red, 1 white, and 98 blue marbles. If one marble is going to be picked at random, there are three possible outcomes: red, white, or blue. Because there is more of a chance that a blue marble will be selected, these outcomes are *not* equally likely.

The probability of an event occurring can be expressed as a ratio. A **ratio** is a comparison of two numbers. Ratios can be expressed as fractions. Study these problems.

1. Last Saturday, Galveston Motors held a special sale of new cars. The names of the 20 people who bought new cars that day were entered in a contest. Each name was written on a separate slip of paper and placed in a hat. The winner will be randomly chosen by picking one name from the hat next week. Bryan bought a car on that special Saturday. What is the probability of his winning the contest?

    Solution: The probability of Bryan winning can be expressed by the following ratio:

    $\dfrac{1}{20}$ number of slips of paper with Bryan's name
    total number of slips of paper

    The probability of Bryan winning the contest is $\frac{1}{20}$.

2. There are three green marbles, five blue marbles, and eight red marbles in a container. One marble will be selected at random. What is the probability that a blue marble will be selected?

    Solution: Before setting up the fraction, you must figure out how many marbles are in the container.

    $$\begin{array}{rl} 3 & \text{green marbles} \\ 5 & \text{blue marbles} \\ +\ 8 & \text{red marbles} \\ \hline 16 & \text{total marbles} \end{array}$$

    There are 16 marbles in the container.

    $\dfrac{5}{16}$ blue marbles
    total marbles

    The probability that a blue marble will be selected is $\frac{5}{16}$.

3. In Example 2, what is the probability of *not* selecting a blue marble?

    Solution:

    $\dfrac{11}{16}$ number of marbles that are *not* blue
    total marbles

The probability of *not* selecting a blue marble is $\frac{11}{16}$.

The **sample space** of an experiment is a set of every possible outcome of that experiment. If all the events in a given sample space are equally likely, the probability of an event can be expressed as the ratio:

number of ways the event could occur
―――――――――――――――――――――――
total number of possible occurrences

---

4. Often you will hear people talking about the **odds** of something happening. The ratio used to express the odds of an event is different from the one used for probabilities.

The odds of an event occurring can be expressed as the ratio:

number of ways the event could occur
―――――――――――――――――――――――
number of ways the event could not occur

Examine this problem.

An urn contains seven red, three white, and ten blue marbles. One marble will be drawn at random. What are the odds that a red marble will be picked?

Solution: Before setting up the odds, you must know how many marbles are in the urn.

```
   7   red marbles
   3   white marbles
+ 10   blue marbles
  20   total marbles
```

Then the odds would be the ratio of red marbles to the number of white plus blue marbles:

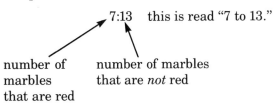

7:13   this is read "7 to 13."

number of   number of marbles
marbles   that are *not* red
that are red

The odds on selecting a red marble are 7:13. Notice that the *probability* of selecting a red marble is $\frac{7}{20}$.

5. Alvarez has selected several options for the new car he plans to purchase. He still has to decide on the transmission and engine types. How many different engine and transmission combinations are available?

Solution: Alvarez uses a **tree diagram** to list all the possibilities:

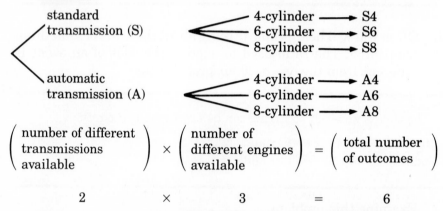

$$\begin{pmatrix} \text{number of different} \\ \text{transmissions} \\ \text{available} \end{pmatrix} \times \begin{pmatrix} \text{number of} \\ \text{different engines} \\ \text{available} \end{pmatrix} = \begin{pmatrix} \text{total number} \\ \text{of outcomes} \end{pmatrix}$$

$$2 \qquad \times \qquad 3 \qquad = \qquad 6$$

Notice that there are six different transmission/engine combinations. The set of these six different outcomes {S4, S6, S8, A4, A6, A8} is the sample space of the problem. Alvarez can choose from six different transmission/engine combinations.

The Fundamental Counting Principle of Probability

If the first step of a two-step experiment can occur in x ways, and for each of the x ways, a second step can occur in y ways, the total number of outcomes in the sample space is x times y.

---

6. You can extend the fundamental counting principle to a multi-step tree diagram, although it may not be practical to draw a tree diagram for very large experiments. The fundamental counting principle, however, can be used without tree diagrams. Read through the following example.

A certain state issues license plate numbers that have three digits followed by two letters. The state wants to know whether there are enough license plates for all the registered car owners. How many different license plates can this state make?

Solution:

Keep in mind that there are 26 letters in the alphabet and 10 digits (0, 1, 2, 3, 4, 5, 6, 7, 8, 9).

10	×	10	×	10	×	26	×	26
↑		↑		↑		↑		↑

number of digits that could occupy first position	number of digits that could occupy second position	number of digits that could occupy third position	number of letters that could occupy fourth position	number of letters that could occupy fifth position

Use the calculator and the following keystroke sequence:

AC 10 × 10 × 10 × 26 × 26 =

The display should read 676,000.

The state can manufacture 676,000 different license plates.

Notice that the order of the characters is important.

The plates on the previous page are different, even though they use the same characters. An arrangement in which order is important is called a **permutation.** These license plates are two of the many different permutations of the characters 2, 6, 0, R, S.

7. A sports car manufacturing company is testing the steering and handling of its newest model. The firm wants to see how passengers of different weights affect the handling characteristics of the car at different speeds. Four engineers of different weights will participate as the passengers in this experiment. The car has two front seats and two rear seats. In how many different ways can these four people be seated in the car?

    Solution: Because the order matters in this seating arrangement, you must use the fundamental counting principle to figure out the number of different permutations (seating arrangements).

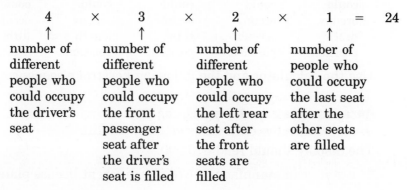

$$4 \quad \times \quad 3 \quad \times \quad 2 \quad \times \quad 1 \quad = \quad 24$$

| number of different people who could occupy the driver's seat | number of different people who could occupy the front passenger seat after the driver's seat is filled | number of different people who could occupy the left rear seat after the front seats are filled | number of people who could occupy the last seat after the other seats are filled |

    There are 24 different seating permutations.

Problems

1. Roosevelt Motors sold 500 automobiles during the month of February. The names of each of the 500 new car owners were placed in a box. One name will be selected at random, and the winner will be given one year of free car maintenance. Alice purchased a car at Roosevelt Motors during February.
    a.   What is the probability that her name will be selected?
    b.   What is the probability that her name will *not* be selected?

    c.   What are the odds of her winning one year of free car maintenance?

√ **2.** A car dealership is running a contest. In all, 10,000 entry blanks were mailed out, and 5,000 people returned their entry blanks. One of these will be selected at random, and the winner will receive a brand-new car. You returned your entry blank to the dealership.
    a. What is the probability that your entry blank will be selected?
    b. What is the probability that your entry blank will *not* be selected?
    c. What are the odds that your entry blank will be selected?

3. The Harrisons are considering buying either a Chevrolet or a Toyota. They are deciding among a two-door, a four-door, and a hatchback model.
    a. Draw a tree diagram to illustrate their possible choices.

    b. How many different combinations of car makes and door models are there?
    c. List all the outcomes that make up the sample space.

√ **4.** Mario is buying a new car. He must choose from the following interior styles: leather seats, cloth seats, and vinyl seats. The seats come in five different colors: black, white, tan, green, and maroon.
    a. Draw a tree diagram to illustrate his possible choices.

    b. How many different seat style and color combinations are in the sample space?
    c. List the different possibilities that make up the sample space.

5. A car manufacturer makes 3 different van models: Deluxe, Limited Edition, and Cargo. The vans can be ordered in 12 different colors. How many different combinations of models and colors are there?

√ **6.** One state issues license plates in which the first three characters are letters and the last two characters are numbers. How many different license plates of this type could be made?

7. An automobile manufacturer is experimenting with a new anti-drunk-driver lock. A five-digit number appears on the display for four seconds. The driver must then enter the five-digit code so that the locking device can be removed. How many different five-digit codes are possible?

✓ 8. A car dealership has six spots for displaying cars in the showroom. In how many different arrangements can a sports car, a van, a station wagon, a two-door car, a four-door car, and a truck be displayed?

9. A large car manufacturer offers 17 different paint colors on all its models. A customer can combine any two different colors to create a two-tone car. How many different two-tone cars can be made using the 17 colors?

10. A local custom-body shop restores old cars. The shop paints cars, adds pinstripes to cars, and replaces vinyl roofs. The body shop offers 200 paint colors, 29 roof colors, and 16 pinstripe colors. How many different color schemes can be created using these choices of colors for a car that is going to be painted, pinstriped, and have its vinyl roof replaced?

SECTION 4 • AUTOMOBILE INSURANCE

Most teenagers look forward to the convenience of driving their own cars. Owning an automobile is a tremendous responsibility. When used with care, an automobile can be a safe and pleasurable form of transportation. However, even responsible drivers run the risk of injuring themselves, other people, and damaging property. By law, all drivers are **liable** (responsible) to pay for damages they cause with their automobiles.

If you were a driver involved in an automobile accident, you could be responsible for paying these costs:

• medical expenses

• the repair of a damaged automobile

• the replacement of damaged property.

You could also be sued for being **negligent** (at fault) if you cause an accident. Because most drivers cannot afford the costs that result from an automobile accident, drivers purchase **automobile insurance.**

An **automobile insurance policy** is a contract between a driver and an insurance company. The driver agrees to pay an insurance premium and the company agrees to cover certain accident costs.

Any automobile insurance company is in business to make a profit. The company loses money if a high percentage of insured drivers get into accidents. Therefore, insurance companies do not like to insure people who are considered **high risks** (having a greater than average probability of getting into an accident). An insurance company can refuse to insure a driver who has a poor driving record (someone who has received many summonses for traffic violations or has been involved in accidents).

Insurance companies classify drivers according to their age, sex, marital status, driving record, and the territory they live in. Your insurance rate is based on the probability of a driver with your classification getting into an accident. For example, a 17-year-old unmarried male driver may pay more for insurance than a 36-year-old married female driver. A driver who has been given three speeding tickets may also pay more for insurance than a driver with no tickets.

In some states automobile insurance is mandatory, while in other states it is optional. There are several types of insurance coverage available to licensed drivers.

- **Personal Injury Protection (PIP).** This protection is sometimes referred to as **no-fault insurance.** Your PIP insurance will pay you and people in, on, around, or under your car for medical treatment that is necessary because of an auto accident. PIP insurance does not cover any damages to the car or property.

- **Bodily Injury Liability (BI).** If you are at fault in an automobile accident, you can be held responsible for paying the medical expenses of anyone injured in the accident. You may even be sued. BI liability insurance will cover your financial responsibility that results from your negligence. You can purchase as much BI liability coverage as you want; you are insured up to the coverage limit that you buy.

- **Property Damage Liability (PD).** This coverage pays for damage to other people's property caused by your driving negligence. It does *not* cover damage that you do to your own property. Usually, the property damaged is another car. However, you are financially responsible if you damage a telephone pole, a fire hydrant, a store front, or any other property. You can purchase as much PD liability coverage as you want; you are insured up to the coverage limit that you buy.

- **Uninsured and Underinsured Motorist Protection (UMP).** This coverage pays you for injuries to you or your passengers caused by a driver who has no insurance or who does not have enough insurance to cover your losses.

- **Comprehensive insurance.** This covers damages to *your* car only. It pays you for the repair or the replacement of parts of your car damaged by tree sprays and by fire, flood, winds, earthquake, vandalism, missiles, falling objects, riots, and other disasters. Comprehensive insurance also covers your car if it is stolen.

- **Collision insurance.** This pays you for the repair or replacement of your car if it is damaged in a collision with another vehicle or object or if it overturns.

- **Car-rental insurance.** Your company pays you for part of the cost of a rented car if your car is disabled because of a collision or a comprehensive covered repair.

- **Emergency road service insurance.** This coverage pays for towing or road service when your car is disabled. Only the road service fee is covered. Gas, oil, and parts are not covered.

Laws and insurance regulations vary from state to state. You should familiarize yourself with the insurance requirements of your state.

Skills and Strategies

Here you will learn how to work out problems concerning automobile insurance coverage and payments.

1. Charleen's total annual premium is $1,200. Assuming that she would choose one of the following common methods of payment, how much would her payments be under each plan?

Solution:

Plan	Number of Payments Per Year	Amount of Each Payment
Annually	1	$1,200
Semi-annually (every six months)	2	$\frac{600}{2)\,1,200}$ ◄— each payment
Quarterly (every three months)	4	$\frac{300}{4)\,1,200}$ ◄— each payment
Monthly	12	$\frac{100}{12)\,1,200}$ ◄— each payment

Charleen would pay $1,200 annually, $600 semiannually, $300 quarterly, or $100 monthly.

2. Ted Spooner's annual premium is $960. He does not pay his premium annually, semiannually, quarterly, or monthly. He pays his premium three times a year. The first payment is 40% of the annual premium, and the second and third payments are *each* 30% of the annual premium. What is the amount of each payment that Ted must make?

Solution: This payment method is sometimes called the 40% – 30% – 30% plan.

$$\begin{array}{ll} \$960 & \text{annual premium} \\ \underline{\times\ .40} & \text{percent paid (decimal equivalent)} \\ \$384.00 & \text{first payment} \end{array}$$

$$\begin{array}{ll} \$960 & \text{annual premium} \\ \underline{\times\ .30} & \text{percent paid (decimal equivalent)} \\ \$288.00 & \text{second and third payments} \end{array}$$

Ted's first payment is $384, his second payment is $288, and his third payment is $288. (Note that these three payments add up to $960.)

3. You can buy as much bodily injury (BI) liability insurance as you want. The amount that you purchase is called the **coverage limit**. Here are a few examples of bodily injury liability coverage limits.

   10/20   25/50   100/300   500/1,000

   Each of these numbers is in thousands. For example, 10 represents $10,000 and 500 represents $500,000.

   The first number in the BI liability coverage limit represents the maximum amount your insurance company will pay to any one person hurt as a result of your driving negligence. The second number represents the maximum amount your insurance company will pay in total to *all* people hurt because of your driving negligence. Look at this example:

   > Bob Forrester hurt one person in an auto accident caused by his driving negligence. Bob has 25/50 bodily injury liability insurance. The injured person was awarded $80,000 in a court case against Bob. How much of this amount will Bob's insurance company pay?

   Solution: Since Bob has 25/50 BI liability coverage, his insurance company will pay only $25,000 for one person injured in each accident.

4. Joan has 15/30 BI liability insurance. Four people were injured in an accident that a court determined was her fault. The four people were awarded $2,000 each. How much must Joan's insurance company pay?

   Solution: Since Joan has 15/30 BI liability coverage, her insurance company will pay up to $30,000. The total award is $8,000.

   Joan's insurance company will pay $8,000

5. Vincent has 100/300 BI liability insurance. Two people were injured in an auto accident caused by his driving negligence. A court awarded one person $150,000 and the other person $20,000. How much must Vincent's insurance company pay?

   Solution: Since Vincent has 100/300 BI liability coverage his company will pay only $100,000 of the $150,000 claim. The insurance company will pay the second person $20,000.

Vincent's insurance company must pay $120,000.

6. Hamed has $10,000 worth of property damage liability insurance. Yesterday he caused an accident that damaged a $750 fire hydrant and resulted in $11,000 worth of repairs to a sports car.
   a. What are the total damages?
   b. How much will Hamed's insurance company pay?
   c. How much of the damages must Hamed personally pay?

   Solutions:
   a. $11,000   damage to sports car
       <u>+ 750</u>   damage to fire hydrant
       $11,750   total property damage

   The total property damage was $11,750.

   b. Hamed's insurance company will pay $10,000 since that is the PD liability coverage limit bought.

   c. $11,750   total PD damages
       <u>− 10,000</u>   amount the insurance company will pay
       $ 1,750   amount Hamed must pay

   Hamed will personally have to pay $1,750.

7. Comprehensive insurance and collision insurance are sold on a **deductible** basis. If your car is damaged and you make a claim for repair under your comprehensive or collision insurance, your insurance will not pay for all the damages. You must pay part of the damages, and that part is called the deductible. The insurance company will pay the rest. Read through this sample problem.

   Barry backed his car into a telephone pole and did $700 worth of damage to his car. Barry has collision insurance with a $200 deductible. How much of the repair will be covered by his insurance company?

   Solution:

   $700   damages to car
   <u>− 200</u>   deductible (the amount Barry must pay)
   $500   amount the insurance company will pay

   The insurance company will pay $500 for repairs.

Problems

1. After Ronald Kivetsky bought a new car, he called his insurance agent for coverage costs. The following coverage and costs were considered best for him:

Coverage	Cost
personal injury protection	$ 98.00
bodily injury liability 25/50	$114.00
property damage liability ($10,000)	$ 94.50
uninsured motorist protection	$ 6.00
$500-deductible comprehensive	$215.00
$200-deductible collision	$298.25
emergency road service	$ 8.00

What is Ronald's total annual premium?

✓ 2. Amy Abrahams pays an annual auto insurance premium of $876.30. She makes her payments semiannually.
   a. How many payments does she make in one year?
   b. How much is each payment?

3. Ed Bowe pays $1,476 annually for auto insurance. He makes his payments quarterly.
   a. How many payments does he make in one year?
   b. How much is each payment?

4. Bruce Smith pays his auto insurance premium monthly. Each monthly payment is $77.19. What is Bruce's total annual premium?

✓ 5. Gloria Howard pays her $980 annual auto insurance premium under the 40% – 30% – 30% plan.
   a. What is the amount of her first payment?
   b. How much is her second payment?
   c. How much is her third payment?

6. Ruth Bowden has decided to drop her collison insurance because her car is getting old. Her total annual premium is $916, of which $170.60 covers collision insurance.
   a. What will her annual premium be after she drops the collision insurance?
   b. What will her quarterly payments be after she drops the collision insurance?

✓7. Gary has $10,000 worth of property damage liability insurance. He collides with two parked cars and causes $12,000 worth of damage.
   a. How much money will his insurance company pay for these damages?
   b. How much money must Gary pay?

8. Craig has a 100/300 bodily injury liability insurance policy. He injures three people in an auto accident, which a court determines is his fault. Each of the persons hurt is awarded $40,000. What is the total amount that Craig's insurance company will pay?

9. Leslie has comprehensive insurance with a $500 deductible on her van. On Halloween her van is vandalized, and the damages total $1,766. Leslie submits a claim to her insurance company.
   a. How much does Leslie have to pay for this repair?
   b. How much will the insurance company pay?

10. Felix Waltham has a $200-deductible collision insurance policy. In a snowstorm his car swerved off the road into a tree. As a result, his car needed $886 worth of repairs. He submits a claim to his insurance company.
   a. How much must Felix pay for this repair?
   b. How much will his insurance company pay?

✓11. Omar Garcia has $10,000 worth of PD liability insurance and a $400-deductible collision policy. He had a tire blowout while driving, and he destroyed a $1,400 fire hydrant. The accident caused $700 in damages to his own car.

    a.   Which insurance covers the damage to the fire hydrant?

    b.   How much will Omar's insurance company pay for the destroyed fire hydrant?

    c.   Which insurance covers the damage to Omar's car?

    d.   How much will Omar's insurance company pay for this damage?

12.   Carol currently pays $412 per year for auto insurance. The insurance company notified her that rates will be raised by 15% next year. What will Carol's annual premium be next year?

13.   Ruth and Elsie live next door to each other. They are the same age, they drive exactly the same kind of car, and they buy the same insurance coverage from the same company. Ruth has been charged with three accidents and has been given two speeding tickets, but Elsie has a perfect driving record. Who pays more for insurance? Why?

14.   Ed saves money each month for his insurance premium. His annual premium is $1,332. What is the average amount that Ed must save each month to pay this premium?

15.   The Schuster family just bought a second car. The insurance agent quoted them a price of $727 to insure the car, but since they insure two cars with the company, they receive a 10% multicar discount. What will the annual premium be after the discount?

SECTION 5 • AUTOMOBILE MAINTENANCE COSTS

Responsible drivers not only carry insurance and wear seat belts, but they also keep their cars in safe and reliable running condition. An automobile is made up of many parts, all of which can break down. Once the warranty on a car has expired, it is up to the owner to pay for all necessary repairs. (You may want to reread Chapter 1, Section 1 (pages 1–49), to refresh your memory about warranties.) Automobile part guarantees are usually **nontransferable**. This means that if you buy a new car and sell it before the warranty has expired, the parts covered under the warranty are not guaranteed for the new owner.

Keeping a safe and well-running car requires regular maintenance.

- changing the oil

- changing filters

- inspecting brakes and suspension

- checking fluid levels

- checking hoses and belts

- checking tire pressure

Occasionally, you may have to replace some parts. Here is a list of some of the parts that may need attention as a car ages.

- exhaust system   - transmission

- tires   - radiator

- brakes   - alternator

- battery   - carburetor

You may know how to do some auto maintenance yourself. If not, there are books you can study and courses you can take to help you learn. You can pay to have a trained mechanic repair your car rather than fix it yourself.

Any person who drives a car has the potential to get stuck in a disabled car at some time. For this reason, all drivers should learn about basic auto maintenance.

Skills and Strategies

Here you will learn how to compute costs of car repairs. Read each step carefully.

1. Maple Place Garage charges a labor fee of $38 per hour. John had these parts replaced on his car:

    exhaust pipe, $51
    muffler, $28
    tail pipe, $31
    muffler clamps, $8
    pipe hangers, $12

    The mechanic took $3\frac{1}{2}$ hours to complete the job. What is the total cost of John's repair, including a sales tax of 8%?

    Solution: Find the total cost for parts by adding the individual prices. The cost of the parts is $130.

    Then find labor cost by multiplying the hourly labor charge by the number of hours worked.

    $$\overset{19}{\cancel{38}} \times \frac{7}{\cancel{2}_{1}} = 133 \quad \text{labor charge}$$

    The labor charge is $133.

Then add the cost of the parts and the labor charge to get the subtotal.

$130   parts cost
+ 133   labor cost
$263   subtotal

Multiply the subtotal by the sales tax rate.

$263   subtotal
× .08   sales tax rate
$21.04   sales tax

The sales tax is $21.04

To find the total cost of John's car repair, including sales tax, add:

$263.00   parts and labor charges
+ 21.04   sales tax
$284.04   total cost of repair

The total cost of John's car repair is $284.04.

Try this computation with your calculator.

AC 51 M+ 28 M+ 31 M+ 8 M+ 12 M+

Computes and stores total price of parts

38 × 3.5 = M+ MRC × 8 % + MRC =

	Recalls	
Computes	total cost	Adds
and stores	and com-	total cost
labor	putes	to sales
charge	sales tax	tax

The display should read 284.04.

Problems

1. Bill's Garage spent $2\frac{1}{2}$ hours making electrical repairs to Tom's car. The labor charge was $30 per hour, and the mechanic used these parts:

   alternator, $89.00
   voltage regulator, $44.50
   fan belt, $11.75
   fuse, $1.00

   a. What is the total labor charge?
   b. What is the total cost of parts?
   c. What is the total cost of parts and labor?
   d. Including a sales of tax of 6%, how much did Tom pay to have his car fixed?

2. The Glen Oaks Fix-It Garage buys parts from a parts dealer and marks them up by 10% to sell to customers. If the garage buys a radiator for $178 and marks it up by 10%, what will be its selling price?

✓ 3. Beep's Auto Electric charges $48 per hour to find and fix electrical wiring problems in cars. How much would the shop charge for a job that takes $4\frac{1}{4}$ hours?

4. The Kwikie-Kwiet Muffler Shop regularly installs mufflers for $29. This week they are having a 20%-off special. What would it cost to have a muffler installed this week?

✓ 5. The Neverflat Tire Store had a 25%-off sale. Tony bought four tires that regularly sell for $80 each. How much did Tony pay for four tires, including a 5% sales tax?

6. A local department store guarantees its tires for 25,000 miles. When Pat bought her tires at this store, she had driven 29,476 miles. The mileage on her car is now up to 52,321 miles. Are Pat's tires protected by the guarantee? Explain your answer.

✓7. Roberto is estimating costs to restore his 1972 Camaro to brand-new condition. Chen's Restoration Clinic quotes him these prices:

bodywork, $3,000
upholstery, $600
carpeting, $100
engine rebuilding (parts only), $1,200

The engine will take 11 hours to rebuild. Chen's Clinic labor charges are $42 per hour. What is the total cost of the entire restoration, including parts and labor?

8. Chuckdan's Antique Auto Parts ships parts for old cars all over the world. A 15% shipping charge is added to all orders. What would the shipping charge be on a $700 order?

9. The price of antifreeze is $4.98 per gallon. A customer buying 2 gallons gets a $2.50 rebate check from the manufacturer. What is the total cost of 2 gallons after the rebate check is received?

✓10. A case of oil contains 12 one-quart cans. What is the price of one can if the case sells for $5.88?

SECTION 6 ● DRIVING DATA

The dashboard of an automobile is an information center for the driver. It supplies data on fuel, speed, time, and engine-operating conditions. The **odometer** indicates the distance the car has traveled since it left the factory. Two types of odometers are shown at the top of the next page.

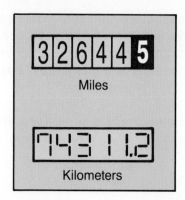

Some dashboards on new cars give odometer readings in both miles and kilometers.

The **speedometer** tells the driver the rate at which the car is traveling. The rate, or speed, is reported in miles per hour (mph) or kilometers per hour (kph).

Drivers are concerned not only with distance traveled and speed but also with the amount of gasoline used. Gasoline is sold by the gallon or by the liter. Over the past 20 years, the price of gasoline has changed dramatically.

Car buyers are usually interested in the number of miles a car can be driven on 1 gallon of gas. This number is called **miles per gallon (mpg)**. A car that "gets 28 mpg" can travel about 28 miles on 1 gallon of gas. Always look for the mpg estimate on the car's window sticker when shopping for a new car.

Although a dashboard can give you much information about the car's ability to *go*, it gives little or no information on the car's ability to *stop*. It takes time to stop a moving car safely. Even during the time your foot switches from the gas pedal to the brake pedal, the car continues to travel. The average, alert driver takes approximately three-quarters of a second — called the **reaction time**—to switch from the gas pedal to the brake pedal. During the reaction time, the car travels a greater distance than most people think. This distance is called the **reaction distance**. The distance a car travels while braking to a complete stop is called the **braking distance**.

Most people think they can "stop on a dime." Take a look at these facts:

- There are 5,280 feet in one mile.

- A car traveling 55 miles per hour covers 290,400 feet in one hour.

- A car traveling 55 miles per hour covers 4,840 feet in one minute.

- A car traveling 55 miles per hour covers over 80 feet in one second.

By thinking about these facts you can understand how speeding, tailgating, and driving while intoxicated can cost you your life.

Skills and Strategies

1. A car travels at an average rate of speed of 50 miles per hour for six hours. How far does the car travel?

    Solution: Use this formula.

    $$\text{distance} = \text{rate} \times \text{time traveled}$$
    $$D = R \times T$$

50	rate
× 6	number of hours traveled
300	distance traveled

    The car travels 300 miles.

2. You will be taking a 1,300-mile trip by car. If you plan to average 50 miles per hour, how many driving hours will the trip take?

    Solution: Use the formula $D = R \times T$ as a guide.

    $$D = R \times T$$
    $$1{,}300 = 50 \times \text{?}$$

    To find the time, you must divide:

    $$\text{average speed} \rightarrow 50\overline{)1{,}300} \quad \substack{\leftarrow \text{hours} \\ \leftarrow \text{miles}}$$

    The trip will take approximately 26 driving hours.

3. Denise bought a new car that averages 31 miles per gallon. The car has a 14-gallon gas tank. About how far can the car travel on one full tank of gas?

Solution: Use this formula.

distance = miles per gallon × number of gallons

$D = MPG \times G$

$$
\begin{array}{r}
31 \\
\times\ 14 \\
\hline
434
\end{array}
\quad
\begin{array}{l}
\text{miles per gallon} \\
\text{gallons} \\
\text{distance}
\end{array}
$$

Denise's car could travel about 434 miles on one full tank of gas.

4. Juliana wants to compute the number of miles she traveled on her cross-country trip. When she left on the trip, the odometer read 17,649.2 miles. When she returned home, the odometer read 26,171.4 miles. How many miles did she travel?

Solution: Juliana must subtract:

$$
\begin{array}{r}
26,171.4 \\
-\ \ 17,649.2 \\
\hline
8,522.2
\end{array}
\quad
\begin{array}{l}
\text{second odometer reading} \\
\text{first odometer reading} \\
\text{miles traveled}
\end{array}
$$

Juliana traveled 8,522.2 miles on her trip.

5. Joshua wants to check how many miles per gallon his car gets. He fills up the gas tank and records the odometer reading. He uses the car for the next few days and has the tank filled again. He records the 15.2 gallons that he purchases from the station attendant. Then he looks at his odometer and finds that he has traveled 357.2 miles since the last time he filled up the tank. How many miles per gallon did Joshua get from his car?

Solution: Since Joshua's car took 15.2 gallons the second time he filled up the tank, the car must have used up 15.2 gallons driving the 375.2 miles. Use the formula:

$$
\begin{array}{ccc}
D & = & MPG \times G \\
357.2 & = & ?\ \ \times\ 15.2
\end{array}
$$

To find the miles per gallon, you must divide. Use your calculator and the following keystroke sequence:

`AC` 357.2 `÷` 15.2 `=`

The display should read 23.5.

Joshua's car got 23.5 miles per gallon.

6. Nancy is planning to drive 1,200 miles. Her car gets 25 miles per gallon. Approximately how many gallons of gas should she expect to use to go 1,200 miles?

Solution: Use this formula.

$$D = MPG \times G$$
$$1,200 = 25 \times ?$$

Nancy must divide:

$$\text{mpg} \rightarrow 25\overline{)1,200} \leftarrow \text{miles}$$

48 ← number of gallons needed

Nancy can expect to use approximately 48 gallons of gas.

7. What is the approximate reaction distance for a car traveling 48 miles per hour?

Solution: The reaction distance is the approximate distance covered in the three-quarters of a second that an average driver takes to switch from the gas pedal to the brake pedal. There is an easy rule you can use to approximate the reaction distance if you know the car's speed.

In three-quarters of a second, a car travels *approximately* one foot for each mile per hour of speed.

48 miles per hour ← car's speed
approx. 48 feet ← reaction distance

A car traveling 48 miles per hour has a reaction distance of 48 feet.

8. What is the approximate braking distance for a car traveling 48 miles per hour?

Solution: You must use the **braking distance formula** to approximate the distance it takes to stop the car safely. The braking distance formula was developed by scientists. The formula assumes that the car's brakes are in good condition, that the road is in good condition, and that the driver is alert.

braking distance = $(.1 \times \text{car speed})^2 \times 5$

The formula involves three steps:

Step 1:   48   car speed
$$\begin{array}{r} 48 \\ \times\ .1 \\ \hline 4.8 \end{array}$$

Step 2: Use your answer from the first step, and multiply that answer by itself.

$$\begin{array}{r} 4.8 \\ \times\ 4.8 \\ \hline 23.04 \end{array}$$ answer from first step
answer from first step

Step 3: Use your answer from the second step and multiply by 5.

$$\begin{array}{r} 23.04 \\ \times\ 5 \\ \hline 115.2 \end{array}$$ answer from second step
braking distance

The approximate braking distance for a car traveling at 48 miles per hour is 115.2 feet which can be rounded to 115 feet. Different cars may take more or fewer feet to stop safely. Certainly, poor road conditions, poor brakes, or an unresponsive driver will make the braking distance longer.

9. Kim, Jean, and Linda have formed a **car pool**. This means they split the cost of driving to work. They use Kim's car every day. Last week the expenses for gas, tolls, and oil were $28.20. How much should each person pay?

Solution: The expenses are split three ways, so you must divide:

number of
people in   9.40 ←amount each person must pay
car pool → 3) 28.20 ←total expenses

Each person must pay $9.40.

Problems

1. Arthur travels for three hours on a freeway. His average speed is 55 miles per hour. How far does he travel?

√ **2.** Joan Larkin is planning a 775-mile trip to visit her daughter in Connecticut. She plans to average 50 miles per hour on the trip. At that speed, approximately how many driving hours will the trip take?

3. Caryl's car has a 17-gallon gas tank. The car gets an estimated 24 miles per gallon. Approximately how far can the car run on half a tank of gas?

4. Lori is planning a 2,100-mile trip to St. Louis to enter college. Her car averages 30 miles per gallon. About how many gallons will her car use on the trip?

√ **5.** Liu used his car for business last weekend. When he reports the exact number of miles he traveled, the company will pay him 22 cents for each mile. At the beginning of the weekend, the odometer in Liu's car read 74,902.6 miles. At the end of the weekend, it read 75,421.1 miles.
    a. How many miles did Liu drive during the weekend?

    b. How much money should his company pay him for the driving?

6. Lenny's car gets approximately 20 miles per gallon. He is planning a 750-mile trip.
    a. About how many gallons of gas should Lenny plan to buy?
    b. At an average price of $1.20 per gallon, how much should Lenny expect to spend for gas?

7. Mindy is driving 32 miles per hour as she nears an elementary school. A first-grade student runs into the street after a soccer ball, and Mindy reacts in about three-quarters of a second. What is her approximate reaction distance?

√ **8.** Edward is driving 52 miles per hour on a one-lane road. He must make a quick stop because there is a stalled car ahead.
    a. What is his approximate reaction distance?
    b. What is his approximate braking distance?
    c. About how many feet does the car travel from the time he switches pedals until the car has completely stopped?

9. Complete the chart.

Speed	Reaction Distance	Braking Distance
40 mph	a.	b.
30 mph	c.	d.
20 mph	e.	f.
15 mph	g.	h.
5 mph	i.	j.

10. Complete the chart.

Number of Gallons Purchased	Price Per Gallon	Total Cost of Gas Purchased	Number of People in Car Pool	Gas Cost per Person
10	$1.15	a.	2	b.
12	1.36	c.	3	d.
17	1.10	e.	2	f.
26	1.30	g.	4	h.

SECTION 7 • RENTING A CAR

As you can tell from the many advertisements on radio and television and in newspapers and magazines, the car-rental business is very big.

People rent cars for many reasons:

- they are on vacation.

- they need a car for business use.

- their own car is in need of repair.

- they don't own a car.

Different car-rental companies charge different rates, so it is best to shop around. All companies require the driver to have a valid driver's license. The companies also set a minimum age for renters, which is usually between 18 and 25 years of age. Most companies require the renter to have a major credit card. This requirement is necessary because the car that is rented is valuable and the company wants proof that the renter is financially responsible.

There are five main charges you should be aware of before you sign a car-rental contract:

- **Basic charge.** This is the rate you pay for each day or week you rent the car. You pay this rate regardless of how much you use the car.

● **Mileage charge.** Most companies charge the renter a few cents for each mile that the rented car is driven. Some companies offer an **unlimited free mileage** deal, which means there is no mileage charge.

● **Collision damage waiver (CDW).** Car-rental companies have deductible collision insurance on their cars. The deductible is usually very high (hundreds or thousands of dollars). If you as a renter cause collision damage to a rented car, *you* must pay the deductible. If you purchase the collision-damage waiver ($5 to $15 per day), the *company* will pay the deductible for any collision repairs.

● **Gas expenses.** The renter pays for the gasoline that is used. Many car-rental companies rent their cars with full tanks of gas and require renters to return them with full tanks of gas. If the car is not returned with a full tank, the company charges the renter the cost of filling up the tank.

● **Drop-off charge.** Some companies charge an extra fee if a renter returns a car to a location other than where the car was originally rented. Drop-off charges can be very high.

You should be aware of the various car-rental procedures before you rent a car.

Skills and Strategies

Here you will learn how to compute costs for renting a car. Examine each problem carefully.

1. Elliot's Rent-A-Car charges customers $22.50 per day to rent a compact car. The deal includes unlimited free mileage. The collison-damage waiver costs $11 per day. What is the total cost of renting this car for two days?

Solution:

$22.50   per-day basic charge
  × 2   number of days
$45.00   two-day charge

$11   collision-damage waiver per day
× 2   number of days
$22   two-day collision-damage waiver charge

$45   two-day charge
+ 22   two-day collision-damage waiver charge
$67   total cost

The total cost of renting the car for two days is $67.

2. Classic Rent-A-Car charges $38 per day to rent an intermediate-size car. The company also charges 12 cents per mile and $9 per day for the collison-damage waiver. What would Classic charge a customer to rent this car for a one-day, 300-mile trip, including the cost for the collision-damage waiver?

Solution: First compute the mileage charge.

300   miles driven
× .12   cost per mile
$36.00   mileage charge

$38   basic charge for one day
9   collision-damage waiver for one day
+ 36   mileage charge
$83   total cost

Classic would charge $83 to rent the car.

3. Bel-Air Car Rental put this ad in the newspaper:

Bel-Air Car Rental
SPECIAL
BRAND-NEW LUXURY CAR
$42 per day • 600 free miles
Mileage charge $.42 per mile over 600 miles. Collision-damage waiver $12 per day.

At the bottom of the ad, in small print, it said, "Mileage charge $.42 per mile over 600 miles. Collison-damage waiver $12 per day." What would Bel-Air charge to rent the luxury car for a three-day, 1,000-mile trip, including the cost for the collision-damage waiver?

Solution: First compute the basic charge.

$42 basic charge per day
× 3 number of days
$126 three-day charge

Next compute the collision-damage waiver.

$12 collision-damage waiver for one day
× 3 number of days
$36 collision-damage waiver for three days

Then compute the mileage charge.

1,000 miles traveled
− 600 number of free miles
400 miles that must be paid for

400 miles that must be paid for
× .42 mileage charge per mile
$168.00 total mileage charge

Then add the three charges.

$126 three-day charge
36 collision-damage waiver for three days
168 total mileage charge
$330 total rental cost

Bel-Air would charge $330 for the car rental.

Problems

✓**1.** Lyndon's Rent-A-Car charges $41 per day to rent a station wagon. There is also a $6-per-day charge for a collision-damage waiver and a 20-cent-per-mile mileage charge. What would Lyndon's charge a customer to rent a station wagon for a four-day, 600-mile trip, including the collision-damage waiver?

2. Buffy's Rent-A-Car is having a special offer — unlimited free mileage on all cars. The basic charge is $49 per day plus a $10 CDW charge per day. What would a three-day rental from Buffy's cost, including a 6% sales tax?

3. Planet Car Rental charges a $150 drop-off charge on all cars not returned to the original place of rental. The company also charges $273 per week, $7 per day for a CDW, and 14 cents per mile driven. How much would Planet charge to rent a car for a one-week, 1,700-mile trip if the car is not returned to the original place of rental and the customer purchases a CDW?

√4. Mutley's Car Rental charges $28.50 per day to rent a compact car. The company also charges $8 per day for a CDW and 14 cents per mile after 400 free miles. What would Mutley's charge a customer to rent a compact car for a five-day, 840-mile trip? (Include a CDW.)

5. Woody rented a car from Brookdale Rent-A-Car. When the car was checked out, the odometer read 17,489 miles. When Woody returned the car, the odometer read 19,003 miles. Brookdale charges renters 45 cents per mile with 500 free miles.
   a. How many miles did Woody drive the car?
   b. What would the mileage charge be for Woody's rental?

√6. Astro Rent-a-Car has a $3,000-deductible collision policy on every car. Seymour rented a car from Astro, but he did not purchase the CDW. After Seymour crashed into a tree, the damage estimate on his car amounted to $4,100.
   a. How much money must Seymour pay for the damage?
   b. How much money will the insurance company pay for the damage?
   c. How much money will the car-rental company pay for the damage?

7. Napoleon's Rent-A-Car charges $217 to rent a van for one week. The mileage charge is 11 cents per mile, and the CDW costs $11 per day. The company offers a 15% discount on the basic weekly charge to business travelers only.

a.   What is the basic weekly charge for business travelers who get the discount?

b.   What would be the total cost of a one-week, 200-mile trip with the business traveler's discount and the CDW?

✓ 8.   Read these two car-rental company ads from local newspapers.

Federal Rent-A-Car
$26 per day
19¢ per mile
$11-per-day collision-damage waiver
200 FREE miles
Do you dare to compare?

Sunshine Car Rental
"Cheapest Guys in Town!"
$31 per day
12¢ per mile
$11-per-day collision-damage waiver
300 FREE MILES

Janet is planning to rent a car for a three-day, 700-mile trip. She wants to compare Federal's price with Sunshine's price.

a.   What is the total cost of a rental from Federal, including a CDW?

b.   What is the total cost of a rental from Sunshine, including a CDW?

c.   Which company offers the better deal? By how much? Sunshine;

9.   Barbara has car-rental insurance. Her own car was in for a two-week repair, and she rented a car to use during that time. The total two-week cost of the rented car was $258.11. Barbara's insurance company paid her $13 per day toward the cost of the rented car.

a.   How much did Barbara's insurance company pay toward the two-week car rental?

b.   How much did Barbara have to pay?

c.   What was the average amount that Barbara had to pay per day? (Round your answer to the nearest cent.)

10.   Wesley rented a car for 17 days from Yonge's Rentals. The basic rate was $229 per week, including unlimited free mileage. Each extra day's rental cost $29. The collision-damage waiver cost $10 per day. What was the total cost of renting the car, including the collision-damage waiver?

SECTION 8 • USING A ROAD MAP

Knowing how to read a road map is a practical skill that you will use throughout your life. For example, when you are driving into an area you are not familiar with, you often must rely on a road map for directions. Many people who own cars consult road maps which they usually keep in the glove compartments of their cars. Most car-rental companies distribute free maps to people who rent cars from them. You will find that it is not difficult to learn how to read a road map.

Skills and Strategies

Road maps have four main features: letters and numbers along the edges; an index; a mileage table; and a legend or key.

Letters and numbers across the top, bottom, and sides of the map help you locate specific places.

1. Each location on the map can be found by using the coordinates of that location. The **coordinates** are the letter and number that specify a particular location. Look at the blank map on the next page. You can use the map coordinates to describe any area on a map. (Note that the arrows point to the F–9 area of this map.)

2. The **map index** lists alphabetically the names of places and gives the coordinates of each place on the map. Sometimes the map index gives the population of each place listed. See Figure 3.1 on page 157. On the map index, you can see that Ellenville can be found by looking near K–12 on the map. Ellenville's population is 4,405.

3. **Mileage tables** can be used to find distances between selected major cities and towns. (Not all maps give these tables.) Look at the mileage table in Figure 3.2 on page 158. In Figure 3.2 the distance between Denver and Philadelphia can be found by looking down the Denver column and across the Philadelphia row until the two intersect. The distance is 1,726 miles.

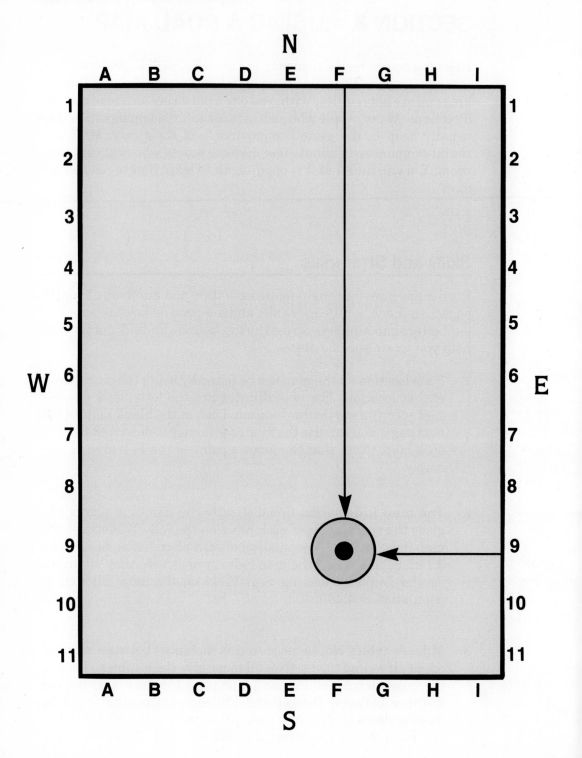

Cities & Towns	E. Meadow, 47300 .. M-3	Kill Buck, 600 .... J-3	Latham, 8000 .... H-13	Stanfordville, 400 .... J-13
Accord, 500 .... K-12	E. Moriches, 1800 ... M-7	Kinderhook, 1377 ... I-13	Orwell, 300 .... E-9	Stanley, 300 .... H-6
Acra, 400 .... I-13	E. Northport, 22200 ... L-4	King Fy, 400 .... H-7	Ossining,	Star L., 800 .... D-11
Adams, 1701 .... E-9	E. Norwich, 3650 .... M-4	Kings Pk., 4000 ..... L-5	20196 ...... M-13, K-2	Steamburg, 400 ..... J-2
Adams Cen., 800 ..... E-9	E. Palmyra, 125 ...... G-6	Kings Point, 5234 .... *E-7	Oswegatchie,	Stephens Mills,
Addison, 2028 .... J-6	E. Patchogue,	Kingston, 24481 ..... J-13	500 .... D-10	250 .... I-5
Adirondack, 150 ... E-13	8300 .... M-6	Kirkland, 100 .... G-10	Oswego, 19793 ...... F-7	Stephentown,
Afton, 982 .... I-10	E. Pembroke, 550 ... M-6	Kirkville, 300 .... G-9	Otego, 1089 .... I-10	300 .... H-14
Airmont, 1900 ... *A-3	Eastport, 1308 .... M-7	Kirkwood, 850 .... J-9	Otisco, 200 .... H-8	Sterling, 240 .... F-7
Akron, 2971 .... G-3	E. Randolph, 655 ... J-2	Knowlesville, 350 ... F-4	Otisville, 953 .... L-12	Stewart Manor,
Alabama, 250 .... G-4	E. Rochester, 7596 .. G-6	Knox, 400 .... H-13	Otto, 400 .... I-3	2373 .... *G-8
Albany, 101727 ..... H-13	E. Rockaway,	Lackawanna,	Ovid, 666 .... H-7	Stilesville, 100 .... J-10
Albertson, 11200 .... M-3	10917 .... *H-8	22701 .... H-2, C-4	Owasco, 400 .... H-8	Stillwater, 1572 ..... G-13
Alden, 2488 .... G-3	E. Setauket, 1440 ... L-5	Lacona, 582 .... E-8	Owego, 4364 .... J-8	Stittville, 500 .... F-10
Alder Creek, 300 .... F-10	E. Williamson, 500 .. G-6	La Fargeville, 500 .... D-9	Owls Head, 200 .... B-12	Stockbridge, 100 .... G-9
Alexander, 483 ...... G-4	E. Worcester, 400 .. H-11	Lafayette, 400 .... G-8	Oxbow, 200 .... C-9	Stockport, 350 ...... I-13
Alexandria Bay,	Eaton, 450 .... H-9	L. Carmel, 4796 ..... L-14	Oxford, 1765 .... I-9	Stockton, 300 .... I-1
1265 .... C-9	Eddyville, 300 .... J-13	L. Clear, 300 .... C-12	Oyster B., 7200 ..... M-4	Stone Ridge, 700 ... K-13
Alfred, 4967 .... I-5	Eden, 3000 .... H-3	Lake Delta, 2400 ... F-10	Painted Post, 2196 ... J-6	Stony Bk., 6600 ..... L-5
Alfred Sta., 200 1-5	Edmeston, 600 ..... H-10	Lake Erie Beach,	Palatine Br., 604 .... G-12	Stony Cr., 450 ...... F-13
Allaben, 300 ... J-12	Edwards, 561 .... C-10	3500 .... H-2	Palenville, 300 .... J-13	Stony Pt., 8270 ..... L-13
Allegany, 2078 .... J-3	Elba, 750 .... G-4	L. George, 1046 .... F-13	Palisades, 1000 .... *B-6	Stormville, 150 ..... K-13
Allentown, 400 ...... J-4	Elbridge, 1099 ...... G-8	L. Grove, 9692 ..... M-5	Palmyra, 3729 ...... G-6	Stottville, 1300 ..... I-13
Almond, 568 .... I-5	Eldred, 700 .... L-11	L. Hill, 450 .... J-12	Pamelia Four Cors.,	Stow, 250 .... J-1
Alpine, 200 .... I-7	Elizabethtown,	L. Huntington, 350 .. K-11	60 .... D-9	Stratford, 250 ...... G-11
Altamont, 1292 ... H-13	650 .... C-13	L. Katrine, 1092 ..... J-13	Panama, 511 .... J-1	Strykersville, 400 .... H-4
Alton, 450 .... G-7	Ellenburg, 300 ...... A-13	Lakemont, 160 ...... I-7	Panther L., 50 .... F-9	Stuyvesant, 450 .... I-13
Altona, 400 .... A-13	Ellenburg Cen.,	L. Placid, 2490 ..... C-13	Parish, 535 .... F-8	Stuyvesant Falls,
Amagansett, 1800 ... L-9	300 .... A-13	L. Pleasant, 300 ... F-12	Parishville, 550 ..... B-11	700 .... I-13
Amawalk, 800 ... L-13	Ellenburg Depot,	Lakeport, 300 .... G-9	Parma Cen., 180 .... F-5	Suffern,
Amenia, 1157 ...... K-14	350 .... A-13	L. Ronkonkoma,	Patchin, 250 .... H-3	10794 ...... M-13, K-1
Amherst,	Ellenville, 4405 ..... K-12	9600 .... M-5	Patchogue, 11291 ... M-6	Sugar Loaf, 300 ..... L-12
66100 ...... G-3, B-4	Ellicottville, 713 ..... I-3	L. Success, 2396 .... *F-8	Patterson, 950 ...... L-14	Sullivan, 140 .... G-9
Amityville, 9076 ...... N-4	Ellington, 500 .... I-2	L. View, 4600 .... H-2	Pattersonville, 400 .. G-13	Sullivanville, 200 .... J-7
Amsterdam,	Ellisburg, 307 .... E-8	Lakeville, 950 .... H-5	Paul Smiths, 600 .... C-12	Summitville, 500 .... K-12
21872 .... G-12	Elma, 2800 .... H-3	Lakewood, 3941 .... J-2	Pavilion, 550 .... H-4	Swain, 100 .... I-5
Andes, 372 .... J-11	Elmira, 35327 .... J-7	Lancaster, 13056 ... G-3	Pawling, 1996 ...... K-14	Swan L., 950 .... K-11
Andover, 1120 ...... J-5	Elmira Hts. 4279 .... J-7	Lanesville, 220 .... J-12	Pearl River,	Swormville,
Angelica, 982 .... I-4	Elmont, 30000 .... *G-8	Langford, 250 .... H-3	17146 .... M-13, L-2	350 .... G-3, B-5
Angola, 2292 .... H-2	Elmsford,	Lansing, 3039 .... I-8	Peconic, 800 .... L-8	Sylvan Bch., 1243 ... G-9
Angola On the Lake,	3361 .... M-13, L-3	Laona, 300 .... I-2	Peekskill, 18236 ..... L-13	Syosset, 10200 ..... M-4
1573 .... H-2	Elwood, 15400 ..... M-4	Laphams Mills,	Pekin, 250 ...... G-3, A-4	Syracuse, 170105 .... G-8
Annadale on	Endicott, 14457 ...... J-8	100 .... B-14	Pelham, 6848 ...... *D-7	Taberg, 500 .... F-9
Hudson, 100 ..... J-13	Endwell, 15999 ...... J-7	Larchmont,	Pelham Manor,	Taborton, 200 ...... H-14
Antwerp, 749 .... D-9	Erieville, 200 .... H-9	6308 .... M-13, L-3	6130 .... L-3, *D-7	Tallman, 900 .... *A-3
	Erin, 300 .... J-7	Lassellsville,	Pembroke, 100 ..... G-4	Tannersville,
		150 .... G-11	Penfield, 9600 .... G-6	685 .... I-10

Figure 3.1 Map Index for New York State

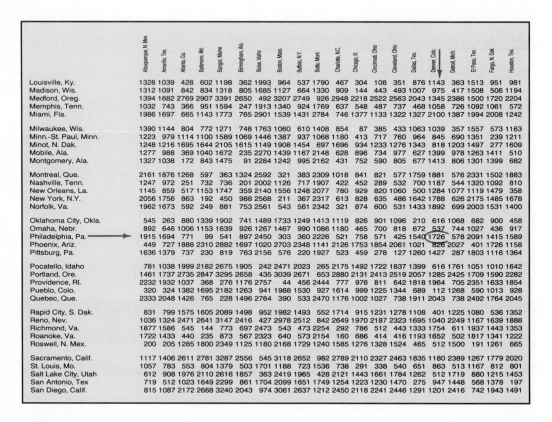

	Albuquerque, N. Mex.	Amarillo, Tex.	Atlanta, Ga.	Baltimore, Md.	Bangor, Maine	Birmingham, Ala.	Boise, Idaho	Boston, Mass.	Buffalo, N.Y.	Butte, Mont.	Charlotte, N.C.	Chicago, Ill.	Cincinnati, Ohio	Cleveland, Ohio	Dallas, Tex.	Denver, Colo.	Detroit, Mich.	El Paso, Tex.	Fargo, N. Dak.	Houston, Tex.
Louisville, Ky.	1328	1039	428	602	1198	362	1993	964	537	1790	467	304	108	351	876	1143	363	1513	951	981
Madison, Wis.	1312	1091	842	834	1318	805	1685	1127	664	1330	909	144	443	493	1007	975	417	1508	506	1194
Medford, Oreg.	1394	1682	2769	2907	3391	2650	492	3207	2749	926	2948	2218	2522	2563	2043	1345	2386	1500	1720	2204
Memphis, Tenn.	1032	743	366	951	1594	247	1913	1340	924	1769	637	548	487	737	468	1058	726	1092	1061	572
Miami, Fla.	1986	1697	665	1143	1773	765	2901	1539	1431	2784	746	1377	1133	1322	1327	2100	1387	1994	2008	1242
Milwaukee, Wis.	1390	1144	804	772	1271	748	1763	1060	610	1408	854	87	385	433	1063	1039	357	1557	573	1163
Minn.-St. Paul, Minn.	1223	979	1114	1100	1589	1069	1446	1387	937	1068	1180	413	717	760	964	845	690	1351	239	1211
Minot, N. Dak.	1248	1216	1695	1644	2105	1615	1149	1908	1454	697	1696	934	1233	1276	1343	818	1203	1497	277	1609
Mobile, Ala.	1277	988	369	1040	1672	235	2270	1439	1167	2148	628	896	734	977	627	1399	978	1263	1411	510
Montgomery, Ala.	1327	1038	172	843	1475	91	2284	1242	995	2162	431	752	590	805	677	1413	806	1301	1399	682
Montreal, Que.	2161	1876	1268	597	363	1324	2592	321	383	2309	1018	841	821	577	1759	1881	576	2331	1502	1883
Nashville, Tenn.	1247	972	251	732	736	201	2002	1126	717	1907	422	452	289	532	700	1187	544	1320	1092	810
New Orleans, La.	1145	859	517	1153	1747	359	2140	1556	1248	2077	780	929	820	1060	500	1284	1077	1119	1479	358
New York, N.Y.	2056	1756	863	192	450	988	2568	211	367	2317	613	828	635	486	1642	1788	626	2175	1485	1678
Norfolk, Va.	1962	1673	592	249	881	753	2561	543	561	2342	321	874	600	531	1433	1892	699	2003	1531	1400
Oklahoma City, Okla.	545	263	880	1339	1902	741	1489	1733	1249	1413	1119	826	901	1096	210	616	1068	682	900	458
Omaha, Nebr.	892	646	1006	1153	1639	926	1267	1467	990	1086	1180	465	700	818	672	537	744	1027	436	917
Philadelphia, Pa.	1915	1694	771	99	541	897	2450	303	360	2226	521	758	571	425	1540	1726	578	2091	1415	1589
Phoenix, Ariz.	449	727	1888	2310	2882	1697	1020	2703	2348	1141	2126	1753	1854	2061	1021	826	2027	401	1726	1158
Pittsburg, Pa.	1636	1379	737	230	819	763	2156	576	220	1927	523	459	278	127	1260	1427	287	1803	1116	1364
Pocatello, Idaho	781	1038	1999	2182	2675	1905	242	2471	2023	265	2175	1492	1722	1837	1399	616	1761	1051	1010	1642
Portland, Ore.	1461	1737	2735	2847	3295	2658	435	3039	2671	653	2880	2131	2413	2519	2057	1285	2425	1709	1590	2282
Providence, R.I.	2232	1932	1037	368	276	1176	2757	44	456	2444	777	976	811	642	1818	1964	705	2351	1633	1854
Pueblo, Colo.	320	324	1382	1695	2182	1263	941	1988	1530	927	1614	999	1225	1344	689	112	1268	590	1013	928
Quebec, Que.	2333	2048	1426	765	228	1496	2764	390	533	2470	1176	1002	1027	738	1911	2043	738	2492	1764	2045
Rapid City, S. Dak.	831	799	1575	1605	2089	1498	952	1982	1493	552	1714	915	1231	1278	1108	401	1225	1080	536	1352
Reno, Nev.	1036	1324	2471	2641	3147	2416	427	2978	2512	842	2649	1970	2187	2323	1695	1040	2249	1167	1639	1888
Richmond, Va.	1877	1586	545	144	773	697	2473	543	473	2254	292	786	512	443	1333	1754	611	1937	1443	1353
Roanoke, Va.	1722	1433	440	235	873	567	2323	640	573	2154	160	686	414	416	1193	1652	502	1817	1341	1222
Roswell, N. Mex.	200	205	1285	1800	2349	1125	1180	2168	1729	1240	1585	1276	1328	1524	465	512	1500	191	1261	665
Sacramento, Calif.	1117	1406	2611	2781	3287	2556	545	3118	2652	982	2789	2110	2327	2463	1835	1180	2389	1267	1779	2020
St. Louis, Mo.	1057	783	553	804	1379	503	1701	1188	723	1536	738	291	338	540	651	863	513	1167	812	801
Salt Lake City, Utah	612	908	1976	2110	2616	1857	363	2419	1965	428	2121	1443	1661	1784	1262	512	1719	880	1215	1453
San Antonio, Tex	719	512	1023	1649	2299	861	1704	2099	1651	1749	1254	1223	1230	1470	275	947	1448	568	1378	197
San Diego, Calif.	815	1087	2172	2668	3240	2043	974	3061	2637	1212	2450	2118	2241	2446	1291	1201	2416	742	1943	1491

Figure 3.2   Mileage Table One

Look at another type of mileage table from a New York State road map:

1. Albany
2. Amsterdam
3. Batavia
4. Binghamton
5. Boston, Mass.
6. Bridgeport, Conn.
7. Buffalo
8. Cleveland, Ohio
9. Dunkirk
10. Elmira
11. Geneva
12. Glens Falls
13. Hartford, Conn.
14. Hornell
15. Ithaca
16. Jamestown
17. Kingston
18. Lockport
19. Montreal, Que.
20. Newburgh
21. New York
22. Niagara Falls
23. Ogdensburg
24. Olean
25. Oneonta
26. Owsego
27. Peekskill
28. Philadelphia, Pa.
29. Pittsfield, Mass.
30. Plattsburgh
31. Poughkeepsie
32. Rochester
33. Schenectady
34. Scranton, Pa.
35. Syracuse
36. Toronto, Ont.
37. Troy
38. Utica
39. Watertown

Mileage table (each entry is *destination-number — miles*):

1: 2-33, 3-249, 4-140, 5-166, 6-127, 7-290, 8-441, 9-327, 10-197, 11-191, 12-54, 13-108, 14-259, 15-166, 16-354, 17-51, 18-286, 19-231, 20-85, 21-148, 22-302, 23-224, 24-304, 25-78, 26-171, 27-105, 28-236, 29-38, 30-169, 31-71, 32-225, 33-16, 34-172, 35-143, 36-386, 37-8, 38-91, 39-174

2: 3-218, 4-129, 5-202, 6-160, 7-259, 8-448, 9-296, 10-186, 11-160, 12-46, 13-144, 14-228, 15-153, 16-323, 17-84, 18-254, 19-219, 20-118, 21-271, 22-200, 23-283, 24-67, 25-140, 26-109, 27-138, 28-267, 29-71, 30-157, 31-104, 32-16, 33-16, 34-175, 35-112, 36-355, 37-31, 38-60, 39-143

3: 4-164, 5-426, 6-376, 7-43, 8-227, 9-80, 10-114, 11-70, 12-264, 13-368, 14-60, 15-114, 16-107, 17-300, 18-37, 19-352, 20-334, 21-397, 22-55, 23-225, 24-78, 25-220, 26-109, 27-354, 28-353, 29-287, 30-338, 31-320, 32-34, 33-234, 34-214, 35-111, 36-139, 37-249, 38-158, 39-168

4: 5-307, 6-198, 7-205, 8-365, 9-237, 10-57, 11-96, 12-169, 13-242, 14-121, 15-50, 16-219, 17-132, 18-201, 19-335, 20-131, 21-184, 22-217, 23-208, 24-164, 25-62, 26-112, 27-148, 28-187, 29-178, 30-279, 31-140, 32-140, 33-128, 34-61, 35-78, 36-301, 37-143, 38-93, 39-151

5: 6-159, 7-463, 8-648, 9-502, 10-364, 11-364, 12-166, 13-102, 14-427, 15-334, 16-529, 17-204, 18-469, 19-324, 20-200, 21-215, 22-273, 23-393, 24-475, 25-248, 26-349, 27-197, 28-317, 29-134, 30-306, 31-205, 32-398, 33-184, 34-299, 35-315, 36-565, 37-174, 38-262, 39-344

6: 7-417, 8-526, 9-454, 10-225, 11-294, 12-177, 13-59, 14-319, 15-248, 16-417, 17-104, 18-413, 19-354, 20-70, 21-59, 22-429, 23-351, 24-362, 25-193, 26-298, 27-50, …

7: 8-191, 9-44, 10-147, 11-111, 12-305, 13-405, 14-92, 15-155, 16-71, 17-341, 18-22, 19-394, 20-375, 21-438, 22-21, 23-267, 24-74, 25-261, 26-111, 27-395, 28-287, 29-328, 30-379, 31-361, 32-76, 33-275, 34-247, 35-152, 36-102, 37-290, 38-199, 39-210

8: 9-150, 10-308, 11-296, 12-498, 13-578, 14-247, 15-333, 16-146, 17-512, 18-213, 19-591, 20-479, 21-486, 22-211, 23-461, 24-197, 25-425, 26-440, 27-495, 28-437, 29-518, 30-601, 31-389, 32-263, 33-465, 34-380, 35-359, 36-299, 37-481, 38-386, 39-402

9: 10-180, 11-148, 12-342, 13-444, 14-112, 15-192, 16-29, 17-378, 18-65, 19-431, 20-412, 21-475, 22-65, 23-304, 24-72, 25-298, 26-188, 27-385, 28-368, 29-365, 30-416, 31-398, 32-113, 33-312, 34-274, 35-189, 36-146, 37-237, 38-236, 39-247

10: 11-59, 12-226, 13-299, 14-64, 15-33, 16-162, 17-189, 18-151, 19-347, 20-188, 21-241, 22-168, 23-220, 24-107, 25-119, 26-113, 27-205, 28-244, 29-235, 30-312, 31-197, 32-99, 33-185, 34-100, 35-90, 36-249, 37-200, 38-126, 39-163

11: 12-206, 13-306, 14-68, 15-46, 16-155, 17-242, 18-105, 19-305, 20-227, 21-280, 22-123, 23-178, 24-114, 25-134, 26-62, 27-244, 28-290, 29-229, 30-280, 31-262, 32-46, 33-176, 34-157, 35-53, 36-207, 37-191, 38-100, 39-121

12: 13-168, 14-274, 15-199, 16-369, 17-105, 18-301, 19-180, 20-139, 21-202, 22-317, 23-173, 24-320, 25-107, 26-186, 27-59, 28-293, 29-83, 30-118, 31-125, 32-240, 33-41, 34-215, 35-158, 36-401, 37-47, 38-106, 39-175

13: 14-362, 15-291, 16-464, 17-91, 18-427, 19-336, 20-98, 21-115, 22-415, 23-335, 24-410, 25-190, 26-291, 27-95, 28-217, 29-76, 30-271, 31-103, 32-340, 33-126, 34-197, 35-257, 36-507, 37-116, 38-204, 39-286

14: 15-83, 16-110, 17-253, 18-97, 19-373, 20-229, 21-20, 22-276, 23-246, 24-87, 25-171, 26-130, 27-269, 28-307, 29-297, 30-348, 31-434, 32-60, 33-254, 34-164, 35-181, 36-194, 37-159, 38-170, 39-189

15: 16-188, 17-182, 18-151, 19-314, 20-181, 21-234, 22-167, 23-187, 24-133, 25-88, 26-80, 27-198, 28-236, 29-204, 30-279, 31-190, 32-90, 33-154, 34-111, 35-57, 36-251, 37-169, 38-93, 39-130

16: 17-351, 18-93, 19-458, 20-350, 21-386, 22-92, 23-531, 24-55, 25-281, 26-215, 27-367, 28-338, 29-392, 30-443, 31-349, 32-140, 33-339, 34-256, 35-216, 36-173, 37-354, 38-163, 39-174

17: 18-337, 19-282, 20-34, 21-97, 22-353, 23-275, 24-296, 25-89, 26-22, 27-54, 28-184, 29-69, 30-207, 31-67, 32-113, 33-121, 34-194, 35-194, 36-437, 37-59, 38-142, 39-225

18: 19-381, 20-371, 21-434, 22-22, 23-254, 24-87, 25-257, 26-138, 27-391, 28-394, 29-324, 30-362, 31-357, 32-63, 33-270, 34-251, 35-148, 36-100, 37-285, 38-195, 39-197

19: 20-316, 21-379, 22-403, 23-127, 24-419, 25-284, 26-243, 27-336, 28-461, 29-264, 30-62, 31-302, 32-318, 33-218, 34-392, 35-257, 36-341, 37-224, 38-248, 39-184

20: 21-66, 22-387, 23-309, 24-295, 25-123, 26-256, 27-20, 28-155, 29-97, 30-254, 31-19, 32-310, 33-101, 34-107, 35-228, 36-471, 37-93, 38-176, 39-259

21: 22-450, 23-372, 24-331, 25-186, 26-319, 27-46, 28-110, 29-155, 30-317, 31-77, 32-373, 33-164, 34-121, 35-291, 36-534, 37-156, 38-239, 39-322

22: 23-276, 24-95, 25-273, 26-160, 27-407, 28-425, 29-340, 30-384, 31-373, 32-85, 33-287, 34-268, 35-164, 36-85, 37-302, 38-211, 39-219

23: 24-292, 25-202, 26-116, 27-329, 28-391, 29-257, 30-123, 31-295, 32-191, 33-216, 34-269, 35-130, 36-226, 37-217, 38-140, 39-57

24: 25-226, 26-176, 27-312, 28-355, 29-343, 30-394, 31-304, 32-103, 33-290, 34-201, 35-167, 36-176, 37-305, 38-214, 39-235

25: 26-142, 27-143, 28-246, 29-116, 30-222, 31-109, 32-196, 33-66, 34-108, 35-95, 36-357, 37-81, 38-62, 39-145

26: 27-276, 28-301, 29-209, 30-224, 31-242, 32-75, 33-156, 34-173, 35-34, 36-238, 37-171, 38-80, 39-59

27: 28-143, 29-109, 30-274, 31-31, 32-330, 33-121, 34-114, 35-248, 36-491, 37-113, 38-196, 39-279

28: 29-254, 30-396, 31-173, 32-350, 33-249, 34-128, 35-261, 36-517, 37-244, 38-313, 39-332

29: 30-202, 31-78, 32-263, 33-52, 34-190, 35-181, 36-424, 37-40, 38-129, 39-212

30: 31-240, 32-299, 33-156, 34-330, 35-238, 36-349, 37-162, 38-186, 39-165

31: 32-296, 33-87, 34-126, 35-214, 36-457, 37-79, 38-162, 39-245

32: 33-210, 34-201, 35-87, 36-163, 37-225, 38-134, 39-134

33: 34-174, 35-128, 36-371, 37-15, 38-76, 39-159

34: 35-139, 36-349, 37-180, 38-154, 39-212

35: 36-248, 37-143, 38-52, 39-73

36: 37-386, 38-295, 39-218

37: 38-91, 39-174

38: 39-83

Figure 3.3 Mileage Table Two

To find the mileage between two places on the table shown in Figure 3.3, use the numbers next to each place. Notice that the list is in alphabetical order. Use the column that corresponds to the place with the lower number. For example, Buffalo is number 7 and Toronto is number 36. Look under the column headed "7" in the mileage table. Look down to number 36. The number 102 means that the distance from Buffalo to Toronto is 102 miles.

4. All maps have a **map legend**, or **map key**, to explain what the symbols on the map mean.

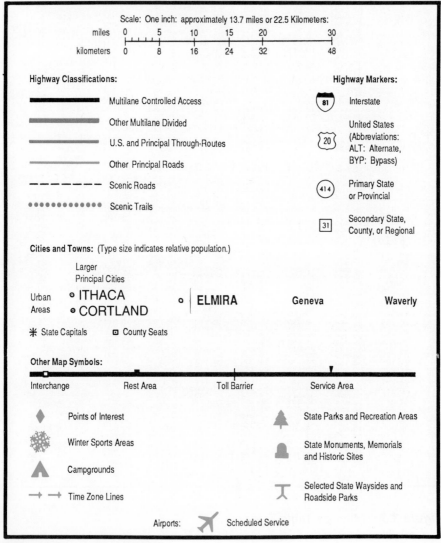

Figure 3.4 Map Legend

Read through the following examples. They will help sharpen your map-reading skills.

1. What is the population of Oswego, New York?

   Solution: Use Figure 3.1 on page 157. Look up Oswego alphabetically. Find this line:

   ```
   Orwell, 300 ........ E-9
   Ossining,
       20196 ...... M-13, K-2
   Oswegatchie,
       500 ........... D-10
   Oswego, 19793 ..... F-7
   Otego, 1089 ....... I-10
   Otisco, 200 ........ H-8
   Otisville, 953 ....... L-12
   Otto, 400 ........... I-3
   Ovid, 666 .......... H-7
   Owasco 400       H-8
   ```

   According to the map index, the population of Oswego is 19,793.

2. What coordinates given in Figure 3.1 could you use to find Oswego on the road map?

   Solution: Look up Oswego alphabetically in the map index. Find this line:

   ```
   Orwell, 300 ........ E-9
   Ossining,
       20196 ..... M-13, K-2
   Oswegatchie,
       500 ........... D-10
   Oswego, 19793 ..... F-7
   Otego, 1089 ....... I-10
   Otisco, 200 ........ H-8
   Otisville, 953 ....... L-12
   Otto, 400 ........... I-3
   Ovid, 666 .......... H-7
   Owasco 400       H-8
   ```

   You could look near F–7 to find Oswego.

3.   How far is Phoenix, Arizona, from Atlanta, Georgia?

Solution: Use Figure 3.2. Look at the row and column high-lighted below:

	Albuquerque, N	Amarillo, Tex.	Atlanta, Ga.	Baltimore, Md.
Louisville, Ky.	1328	1039	428	6(
Madison, Wis.	1312	1091	842	8:
Medford, Oreg.	1394	1582	2769	29(
Memphis, Tenn.	1032	743	366	9!
Miami, Fla.	1986	1697	665	11‹
Milwaukee, Wis.	1390	1144	804	7'
Minn.-St. Paul, Minn.	1223	979	1114	11(
Minot, N. Dak.	1248	1216	1695	16‹
Mobile, Ala.	1277	988	369	10‹
Montgomery, Ala.	1327	1038	172	8‹
Oklahoma City, Okla.	545	263	880	13:
Omaha, Nebr.	892	646	1006	11!
Philadelphia, Pa.	1915	1694	771	!
Phoenix, Ariz.	449	727	1888	23'
Pittsburg, Pa.	1636	1379	737	2:

The distance between Phoenix and Atlanta is 1,888 miles.

4.   How far is Rochester, New York, from Glens Falls, New York?

Solution: Use Figure 3.3. Glens Falls is represented by number 12, and Rochester is represented by number 32.

Find the column headed "12" in the mileage table. Look down to number 32.

	12	
15-192		18-151
16-29	13-168	19-314
17-378	14-274	20-181
18-65	15-199	21-234
19-431	16-369	22-167
20-412	17-105	23-187
21-475	18-301	24-133
22-65	19-180	25-88
23-304	20-139	26-80
24-72	21-202	27-198
25-298	22-317	28-236
26-188	23-173	29-204
27-385	24-320	30-279
28-368	25-107	31-190
29-365	26-186	32-90
30-416	27-159	33-154
31-398	28-293	34-111
32-113	29-83	35-57
33-312	30-118	36-251
34-274	31-125	37-169
35-189	32-240	38-93
36-146	33-41	39-130

The distance between Glens Falls and Rochester is 240 miles.

5. The mileage tables in this section give exact mileage between points. It is uncommon for a traveler to report exact distances. Usually, travelers round distances to the nearest 50 miles. They might use numbers such as these:

   50, 100, 150, 200, 250,...950, 1,000,...

   The approximation symbol (≈) can be used.

   Round 438 to the nearest 50 miles.

   Solution:

   Is 438 nearer 400 or 450? The number 425 is halfway between 400 and 450, so 438 should be rounded to 450 (nearest 50 miles). You can write 438 ≈ 450.

6. What is the approximate driving time for a 741-mile highway trip?

   Solution: Round 741 to the nearest 50 miles.

   741 ≈ 750

   For most long trips, 50 miles per hour can be used as a reasonable average speed.

   $$\begin{array}{r} 15 \leftarrow\text{number of hours} \\ \text{mph} \rightarrow 50\ \overline{)750} \leftarrow\text{approximate number of miles} \end{array}$$

   The 741-mile trip would take approximately 15 hours.

7. Using Figure 3.5, give driving directions for a trip from Watkins Glen, New York (C–8), to Corning, New York (A–10). The solution to this problem is at the top of page 165.

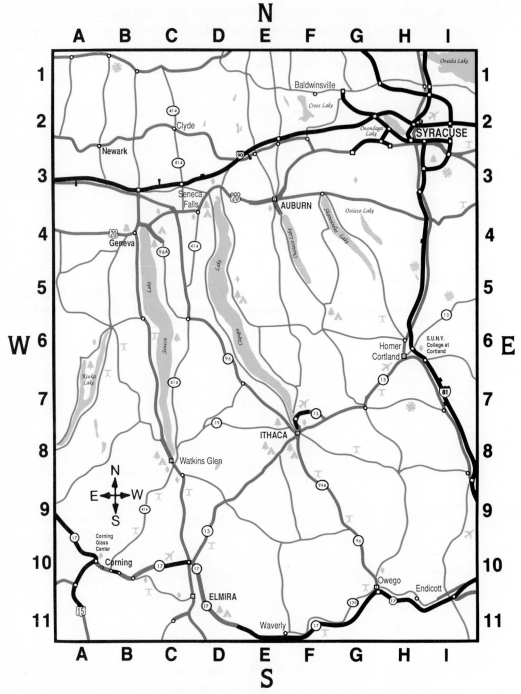

Figure 3.5 Map Section of New York State

Solution: Locate Corning and Watkins Glen on the map. Look for main roads that connect these two places. Look for the route numbers on each road. Be sure to include north, south, east, or west with each route number you report.

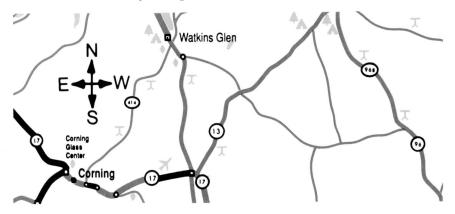

To drive from Watkins Glen to Corning, take Route 414 south.

Most maps are similar to Figure 3.5. By acquiring good map reading skills, you will be able to read any map.

Problems

1. Use Figure 3.1, page 157, to find the map coordinates for the following locations.

a.	Alfred	**d.**	Elmira
b.	Parishville	**e.**	Stockbridge
c.	Syosset	**f.**	Lake George

✓ 2. Find the distance between each of the following New York State locations. Use Figure 3.3, page 159.

    a. Troy and Utica
    b. Buffalo and Syracuse
    c. Plattsburgh and Newburgh
    d. Geneva and Peekskill
    e. Schenectady and Ithaca

3. Find the distance between each of the following United States cities. Use Figure 3.2, page 158.

    a. Pittsburgh, Pennsylvania, and Amarillo, Texas

    b. Miami, Florida, and Chicago, Illinois

    c. St. Louis, Missouri, and Boise, Idaho

    d. San Diego, California, and Baltimore, Maryland

    e. Omaha, Nebraska, and Detroit, Michigan

4. Round each of the following mileages to the nearest multiple of 50:

    a. 715   f. 624

    b. 699   g. 625

    c. 420   h. 1,071

    d. 940   i. 101

    e. 626   j. 88

✓ 5. John is planning a trip from Binghamton, New York, to Elmira, New York. Use Figure 3.3.

    a. How far apart are these two cities?

    b. Round this distance to the nearest 50 miles.

    c. At an average speed of 50 miles per hour, about how long would the trip take?

6. Paul is planning a trip from New York City to Buffalo, New York.

    a. How far apart are these two cities?

    b. Round this distance to the nearest 50 miles.

    c. At an average speed of 50 miles per hour, about how long would the trip take?

✓ 7. George is driving home from college in Newburgh, New York, to his home in Rochester, New York.

    a. According to Figure 3.3, how far must he drive?

    b. Round this distance to the nearest 50 miles.

    c. George's car gets 20 miles per gallon. Approximately how many gallons of gas will he need for the trip?

    d. George's car has an 11-gallon gas tank. Would he make it home on one tank of gas? Explain your answer.

e. If he pays $1.35 per gallon of gas, approximately how much will George spend on gas for this trip?

f. At an average speed of 50 miles per hour, approximately how long will the trip take?

8. Use the map in Figure 3.5, page 164, to give directions between each of the following locations.

   a. Ithaca (E–8) to Cortland (H–6)
   b. Owego (G–10) to Elmira (D–10)
   c. Watkins Glen (C–8) to Ithaca (E–8)

   d. Corning Glass Center (A–10) to SUNY College at Cortland (H–6)

9. Sonia examines the map legend on a map of the United States. She looks at the scale of miles and reads that 1 inch represents 18 miles. How many miles apart are two cities that are 4 inches from each other on the map?

10. Phil reads on his California road map that 1 inch represents 24 kilometers. Two famous beaches Phil wants to visit are $6\frac{1}{2}$ inches apart on the map. How many kilometers apart are these two beaches?

● KEY TERMS

To find the definition of any term introduced in the chapter, refer to the Glossary in the back of this book.

annually
automobile insurance
automobile insurance policy
basic charge
bodily injury liability (BI)
braking distance
braking distance formula
car pool
car-rental insurance
classified
classified ads

collision-damage waiver
collision insurance
comprehensive insurance
coordinates
coverage limit
data
deductible
drop-off charge
emergency road service insurance
equally likely

events
fundamental counting
  principle of probability
gas expenses
high risks
liable
map index
map key
map legend
mean
median
mileage charge
mileage tables
miles per gallon (mpg)
mode
monthly
negligent
no-fault insurance
nontransferable
odds
odometer

outcomes
permutation
personal injury protection
  (PIP)
premium
probability
property damage liability
  (PD)
quarterly
random
ratio
reaction distance
reaction time
sample space
semiannually
speedometer
statistics
tree diagram
uninsured and underinsured
  motorist protection (UMP)
unlimited free mileage

● REVIEW PROBLEMS

1. The *Garden City Tribune* charges $18 for a four-line classified
    ad. Each additional line costs $4.40. What would a six-line ad
    cost, including a sales tax of 4%?

2. Barbara wants to buy a 1972 Buick Skylark. Five 1972 Sky-
    larks are listed for sale in this week's *Newsdate* magazine.
    Barbara records the prices of the five cars:
    $1,200
    $ 900
    $ 200
    $3,400
    $ 750
    Find the median price, and explain why the median is more
    useful to Barbara than the mean.

3. A person filling out an automobile insurance application is going to be classified according to his or her answers to the following items:

   • Sex (male, female)

   • Age (under 25, 25 or older)

   • Marital status (single, married)

   • Number of accidents (fewer than 3, 3, more than 3)

   Draw a tree diagram and list the sample space of all possible categories into which an applicant can be placed. Refer to: Additional Responses

4. Peter accidentally backed his car into Stan's brand-new limousine. He did $495 worth of damage to Stan's car and $800 worth of damage to his own car. Peter has a $10,000 property damage liability policy and a $250-deductible collision policy. How much must Peter's insurance company pay, in total, for the damage to both cars?

5. For a class project, 50 students from Plainview High School visited local insurance agents and priced insurance for each of their cars. Of the total, 7 went to Howes Insurance, 20 went to Kohler Insurance, and the rest went to Derham Insurance. The school principal is going to select a student at random to conduct an assembly on auto insurance. What is the probability that the student chosen will have visited Derham Insurance?

6. Terry's Garage charges $44 per hour for labor. Winnie had these parts replaced on her car:

   radiator, $240
   water pump, $120
   hoses, $23
   fan belt, $8

   The mechanic worked $3\frac{3}{4}$ hours on the job. What is the total cost of Winnie's car repairs, including a 7% sales tax?

7. George is driving his car at 54 miles per hour on a dark two-lane highway. He puts on the brakes immediately when he

sees a deer on the road ahead of him. About how far will George's car travel from the moment he lifts his foot from the gas pedal to the time the car comes to a complete stop?

8. Diane and Bobby are planning a round-trip from Milwaukee, Wisconsin, to Boston, Massachusetts. Use Figure 3.2, page 158. Their car gets about 20 miles per gallon, and they estimate that gas will cost approximately $1.20 per gallon. What is the approximate total gas expense for the round trip?

9. Joan wants to rent a compact car for one day to travel from Albany, New York, to New York City. (Use Figure 3.3, page 159.) She will drop off the car at Kennedy Airport in New York City. The Troy Rental Company charges $36 per day plus 9 cents per mile driven. The company also adds on a $52 drop-off charge and an 8% sales tax. How much will the car rental cost Joan?

10. Four college students plan to drive 900 miles to go home for the Thanksgiving holiday weekend. If they split the driving time equally and travel at an average speed of 50 miles per hour, approximately how long will each of the four students spend driving the car?

CHAPTER 4

BE YOUR OWN TRAVEL AGENT

SECTION 1 ● ELAPSED TIME

How is traveling by car different from traveling by plane, train, or bus? When you drive, you can decide when you want to leave and control how much time you will spend traveling. When you travel by plane, train, or bus, you have to travel at the times arranged by the airline, the railroad, or the bus company. This information can be found in timetables or schedules from which you choose times that are convenient to you. It is important to read timetables and schedules carefully. A mistaken reading can cause a long delay, a missed ride, or even a trip cancellation.

You should know the following terms in order to plan a trip by plane, train, or bus.

Departure time is the time at which a plane, train, or bus leaves a location.
Arrival time is the time at which the plane, train, or bus gets to its destination.
Elapsed time is the amount of time the trip takes.

You can get the schedules you need to plan a trip from the airline, railroad, or bus company. Because these companies carry people to their destinations, they are often called **carriers**. You can also get timetables and schedules from a travel agent. Usually only departure and arrival times are shown, so it is up to you to compute elapsed times.

Nichole knew that her bus was scheduled to leave at six o'clock. She arrived at six at night, but there was no bus. What went wrong? Nichole forgot that most carriers operate 24 hours a day. She arrived at 6:00 PM for a bus that left at 6:00 AM. It is not enough to know that a bus leaves "at 6:00." You should always specify travel times as AM (before noon) or PM (after noon). Remember 12:00 can be confusing; be sure to check if noon or midnight is meant.

Skills and Strategies

Here you will learn how to compute elapsed time for any journey. In many cases, drawing an arrow diagram will help. An **arrow diagram** is a technique that can be used to show the amount of time that elapses between two given times.

1. A train departs at 6:43 AM and arrives at 11:00 AM. What is the elapsed time for the trip?

   Solution: Use an arrow diagram.

	17 minutes		4 hours	
6:43 AM	⟶	7 AM	⟶	11 AM
departure time		next whole hour		arrival time

   The elapsed time for the trip by train is 4 hours and 17 minutes.

2. A plane leaves at 10 AM and arrives at 3 PM. What is the elapsed time for the trip?

   Solution: Use an arrow diagram.

	2 hours		3 hours	
10 AM	⟶	noon	⟶	3 PM
departure time		Use noon to change from AM to PM		arrival time

2 hours	time traveled before noon
+ 3 hours	time traveled after noon
5 hours	elapsed time

The elapsed time for the trip by plane is 5 hours.

3. A train leaves at 9:43 AM and arrives at 3:15 PM. How long does the trip take?

Solution: Use an arrow diagram.

	17 minutes		2 hours		3 hours		15 minutes	
9:43 AM	⟶	10 AM	⟶	noon	⟶	3 PM	⟶	3:15 PM
departure time		next whole hour		use noon to change from AM to PM		arrival hour		arrival time

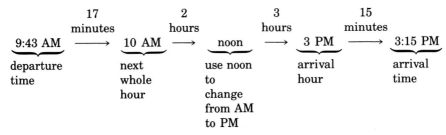

Add the hours and the minutes separately.

2 hours	17 minutes
+ 3 hours	+ 15 minutes
5 hours	32 minutes

The trip by train is 5 hours and 32 minutes.

4. A bus departs from its terminal at 9:43 AM and arrives at its destination at 7 AM the next day. What is the elapsed time for the bus trip?

Solution: Use an arrow diagram.

	17 minutes		2 hours		12 hours		7 hours	
9:43 AM	⟶	10 AM	⟶	noon	⟶	midnight	⟶	7 AM
departure time	next whole hour			There are 12 hours between noon and midnight.				arrival time

Add the hours.

2 hours	17 minutes	time traveled before noon
12 hours		time between noon and midnight
+ 7 hours		time traveled after midnight
21 hours	17 minutes	total time traveled

The elapsed time for the trip by bus is 21 hours and 17 minutes.

Problems

✓ **1.** Find the elapsed time for each trip.

Departure Time	Arrival Time	Elapsed Time
7:13 PM	9:28 PM	a.
4:37 AM	5:00 PM	b.
4:00 PM	11:57 PM	c.
3:50 AM	8:16 PM	d.
12:26 PM	midnight	e.
1:30 AM	1:35 PM	f.
1:30 AM	1:25 AM	g.

2. A bus departs from its terminal at 12:26 PM and reaches its destination at 9:00 PM. What is the elapsed time for the trip?

✓ **3.** A plane leaves at 1:18 AM and arrives at 3:04 AM. What is the elapsed time for the flight?

4. A train leaves Pennsylvania Station in New York City at 8:11 PM and arrives in Washington, DC, at 11:02 PM. What is the elapsed time for this train ride?

5. A flight from Miami to Boston was scheduled to leave at 8 AM, but is delayed 30 minutes. The flight takes 2 hours and 45 minutes. What time will it arrive in Boston?

6. A bus leaves Binghamton, New York, at 3:05 PM and arrives in Syracuse at 6:00 PM. What is the elapsed time for this bus trip?

✓ **7.** Eve is taking her son to a baseball doubleheader. The first game begins at 1:45 PM, and there is a one-hour show between the two games. Each game is about $2\frac{1}{2}$ hours long. At approximately what time will the second game be over?

8. Tom is planning a summer vacation in Seattle. The trip will take approximately 17 hours by automobile. He is leaving at 3:00 PM Friday, the last day of school. Approximately what day and time should Tom arrive in Seattle?

✓ **9.** The Zip Line bus leaves a local terminal for New Orleans at 10:00 AM. It arrives at 6:15 PM. What is the elapsed time for the bus trip?

10. Last week, Arlene visited Albuquerque. She arrived at 11:00 PM on Wednesday. Her bus left Albuquerque at 3:20 AM on the following Sunday. What was the length of Arlene's stay in Albuquerque?

SECTION 2 • TIME ZONES

Imagine that it is the year 1993. John lives in a small Arizona town near the California border. He decides to visit California. He leaves Arizona in 1993 and arrives in California in 1992. 1992? Yes! It sounds impossible, doesn't it? To find out how this can happen, you need to understand **time zones**. See Figure 4.1 at the top of page 176.

How do you know when it is noon? One way is to look for the sun. You know that it is noon when the sun is at its highest point in the sky. But when the sun is overhead in Texas, it is night on the other side of the earth. When it is noon in Texas, it is close to midnight in India. The earth takes 24 hours to rotate once. Therefore, the earth is divided into 24 time zones. There is a one-hour difference between each time zone. It is noon in each time zone when the sun is at its high point.

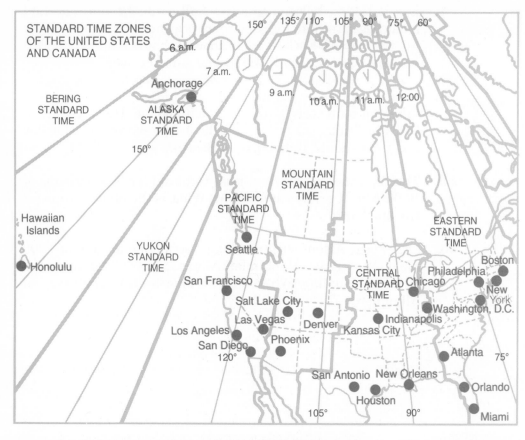

Figure 4.1 Time Zones of the United States and Canada

Look at the New York and Hawaii clocks in the photo above. They do not show the same time. Hawaii and New York are in two different time zones. (See Figure 4.1.)

The United States extends over seven time zones. The mainland United States is divided into four time zones—Pacific, mountain, central, and eastern. These time-zone names are listed on many plane, train, and bus schedules.

Pacific standard time (PST)
mountain standard time (MST)
central standard time (CST)
eastern standard time (EST)

When the clocks are set ahead in the spring for **daylight saving time**, the time-zone names change from standard to daylight.

Pacific daylight time (PDT)
mountain daylight time (MDT)
central daylight time (CDT)
eastern daylight time (EDT)

You should become familiar with these terms so that you can read and interpret schedules of different carriers.

This section began with John's "trip back in time." Have you figured out how John could leave in 1993 and arrive in 1992? Here is the way it's done.

It is January 1, 1993 at 12:15 AM MST. John is traveling on an Arizona highway towards California. It takes him five minutes to reach the border. He crosses into California and looks at the clock in a gas station. The clock reads 11:20 PM PST. John has gone back into 1992!

Skills and Strategies

Here you will learn how to apply what you know about time zones. Read each example carefully.

1. In what time zone is Denver, Colorado?

    Solution: Use the map on page 176.

    Denver is in the mountain time zone.

2. When it is 3:42 PM in Denver, Colorado, what time is it in San Francisco, California?

Solution: Use the map on page 176.

Denver can be found by looking under mountain time. San Francisco can be found by looking under Pacific time. Use the clocks above each time zone to help you.

When it is 3:42 PM in Denver, it is one hour earlier, or 2:42 PM, in San Francisco.

Problems

✓ **1.** Use the map, Figure 4.1, page 176 to help you identify the time zone of each city.
  a. San Antonio, TX
  b. Phoenix, AZ
  c. Seattle, WA
  d. Atlanta, GA
  e. Philadelphia, PA
  f. Orlando, FL
  g. San Diego, CA

✓ **2.** Complete the chart.

When it is:	It is:
a. 2:37 AM PST	EST
b. 6:12 AM MDT	PDT
c. 7:07 PM EDT	CDT
d. 1:10 PM CST	MST
e. 3:15 AM MST	CST
f. 9:23 PM PDT	EDT
g. noon EST	PST

3. The Super Bowl often begins at 6 PM EST. What time is it in Los Angeles, California, when the Super Bowl begins on the East Coast?

✓ 4. Night games in the World Series often start at 8:30 PM EDT. What time is it in Phoenix, Arizona, when a World Series night game begins on the East Coast?

5. A plane leaves Houston, Texas, at 7 PM for New York City. What is the time in New York City when the plane leaves Houston?

6. Rich flies from Miami, Florida, to New Orleans, Louisiana, and forgets to reset his watch. When his watch reads 3:30 PM, what time is it in New Orleans?

✓ 7. Jennifer takes a train from Washington, DC, to Kansas City, Missouri. She forgets to reset her watch. When her watch reads 4:30 AM, what time is it in Kansas City?

8. A plane leaves Boston, Massachusetts, at 7 PM EST and arrives in Seattle, Washington, at 8:20 PM PST. What is the elapsed time for this flight? Hint: First change departure time to PST.

9. A bus leaves Chicago, Illinois, at 1:00 PM CST and arrives in Indianapolis, Indiana, at 2:12 PM CST. What is the elapsed time for this trip?

10. When it is 11:20 PM on New Year's Eve (December 31) in Denver, Colorado, what date and time is it in New York City?

SECTION 3 • PURCHASING AIRLINE TICKETS

Have you ever purchased a ticket for a concert? If so, the seller probably told you that the ticket was nonrefundable. This means that if you decided not to attend the concert, you would not be able to get your money back. There are many restrictions on tickets for concerts, plays, and sporting events. For example, if your ticket is stolen or lost, there is no way to identify the actual owner. Anyone who finds the ticket could use it. There are also strict rules about how many people an auditorium can seat. Because of fire and safety regulations, an auditorium can sell only as many tickets as there are available seats.

Not all of these ticketing policies are true for airlines. Airline ticketing policies are more flexible. Air travel is expensive, and it is important for consumers to be familiar with airline rules and regulations.

Once you purchase a ticket for a certain flight, you receive a **confirmed reservation.** That reservation entitles you to several benefits. If you miss the flight for any reason, you are usually entitled to a refund. If you have purchased the ticket in advance and discover that you cannot make the flight, you can usually exchange the ticket for another or get a refund. You also are protected in case the ticket is stolen. Because your name is printed on the ticket and stored in the airline's computer, you can be easily identified as the actual owner of the ticket.

However, there are some regulations concerning air travel that can be inconvenient to a traveler. Consider Allen, for example. Allen was planning to fly to San Diego, California, on Flight 542, and he had a confirmed reservation. He arrived only a few minutes before the flight and found out that it was already full. The practice of selling more confirmed reservations than the number of seats on the plane is called **overbooking.** The airline arranged for Allen to take a different flight later that evening.

Why is overbooking allowed? The main reason is that airline tickets are refundable. Think about what that means to the airline. Suppose an airline sells exactly 100 confirmed reservations for a 100-seat airplane. If ten customers decide to refund their tickets at the last minute, the plane will have to fly with ten empty seats. Empty seats are not profitable to the airline. The government permits airlines to overbook flights as a way of protecting them against flying with empty seats. In this way, a plane can fly without empty seats, even if some customers cancel at the last minute.

The airlines use probability and statistics to predict the number of people who will not show up for a flight. For example, the airline may determine, by using previous records, that 20 people usually do not show up for a certain flight. This airline might decide to sell 320 reservations for a plane that has 300 seats. If 20 people do not show up, the plane is still full.

But what happened on Allen's flight? The airline used the estimations above. Unfortunately, 306 of the confirmed reservations were claimed. Six people could not get on the plane; they were denied boarding, or **bumped.** Bumped passengers are usually put on the next available flight. In some cases, bumped passengers are entitled to a payment for their inconvenience. This payment is called **denied boarding compensation.**

The government limits the number of confirmed reservations that an airline can overbook for a flight. Once all of the confirmed reservations are sold, a **waiting list** is established. The waiting list includes all customers who wish to purchase a ticket for the flight. They will not receive tickets unless a confirmed reservation is canceled. They will be notified by telephone if a ticket becomes available.

If a confirmed reservation is not available on the day of the flight, a traveler can go to the airport and wait near the boarding gate, hoping for a last-minute cancellation. This is called flying **standby.**

Skills and Strategies

Here you will learn how the rules and regulations of air travel work. You will see how problems concerning these policies can be easily solved. Read each example carefully.

1. Blair Air sells discount airline tickets on a 25-percent penalty basis. This means that if the ticket is returned for any reason, the purchaser will receive only 75 percent of the ticket price as a refund. If Sue must return a $650 Blair Air discount ticket, how much will she receive as a refund?

Solution:

$$\begin{array}{rl} \$650 & \text{ticket price} \\ \times\ .25 & \text{penalty rate expressed as a decimal} \\ \hline \$162.50 & \text{penalty} \end{array}$$

$$\begin{array}{rl} \$650.00 & \text{ticket price} \\ -\ 162.50 & \text{penalty} \\ \hline \$487.50 & \text{amount of refund} \end{array}$$

Sue would receive $487.50 as a refund.

2.   Sunshine Airlines has a daily flight to Florida that seats 287 people. Three hundred confirmed reservations were sold for yesterday's flight. Twenty confirmed-reservation holders did not show up for the flight. How many empty seats were there?

Solution:

300	confirmed reservations sold
− 20	cancellations
280	passengers

287	seats on the plane
− 280	passengers
7	empty seats

The plane flew with seven empty seats.

3.   Public Airways overbooks a 200-seat plane by 5 percent. How many confirmed reservations could be sold for this plane?

Solution:

200	seats on the plane
× .05	overbooking rate expressed as a decimal
10.00	overbooked seats

200	seats on the plane
+ 10	overbooked seats
210	confirmed reservations

Public Airways is permitted to sell 210 confirmed reservations for this plane.

Problems

1.   Jiffy Airlines sold Vinny a $140 ticket to California. The ticket was sold on a 25-percent penalty basis. Vinny had to cancel his flight because of a change in his work schedule. How much did he receive as a refund?

✓ 2.   Joanne bought a discount airline ticket to Hawaii for $420. There was a 20-percent penalty for returning the ticket. Joanne decides to return the ticket. How much will she receive as a refund?

3. Global Air Flight 76 to New Orleans has 175 seats. The airline sold 200 confirmed reservations, but 8 of these people didn't make the flight. How many people were bumped?

✓ 4. Seven people were bumped from Planet Airways Flight 17 to Miami. The airplane seats 190 people. How many people holding confirmed reservations showed up for the flight by departure time?

5. Skylark Air overbooked a 220-seat flight by 10 percent. How many confirmed reservations were sold for this flight?

6. Spoon Air overbooked a 180-seat flight by 5 percent. How many confirmed reservations were sold for this flight?

✓ 7. Family fares on Albatross Airways are set as follows:

    • Adults pay full fare

    • Children between 12 and 18 years of age pay 70 percent of full fare

    • Children under 12 pay 40 percent of full fare

    Mr. Ramirez is traveling with his 16-year-old daughter and 10-year-old son. What is his family's airfare cost on an Albatross Airways flight that has a full fare of $190?

8. Just Flyers Travel Agency is running a contest. The 250 people they booked on a flight to Arizona are eligible to win. One name will be selected at random. First prize is a trip to Hawaii. Seymour Fier, his wife, and their three children are aboard the Arizona flight. What is the probability that someone from the Fier family will win the contest?

✓ 9. Vincent is a member of the Northside Flyer Bonus Program. He will receive a free trip to anywhere in the United States after he shows that he has flown more than 20,000 miles. Vincent currently has 19,238 miles to his credit. He needs to make two business trips to Boston this week. Each round trip is 310 miles. How many miles will Vincent need to reach the 20,000-mile mark after he has completed his two Boston trips?

10. Super Air overbooked a 300-seat flight by 11 percent. On the day of the flight, 307 people showed up to board the plane. How many people had to be bumped?

SECTION 4 • READING PLANE, TRAIN, AND BUS SCHEDULES

Kurt was planning to take a bus to visit his grandparents. He received the bus schedules he needed from a travel agent. That's when his troubles started. He could barely tell which side was up! The schedule looked like a confusing jumble of numbers and letters. Luckily, his sister showed him how the information was organized. Then she explained the abbreviations. Kurt was able to read the schedule easily in no time.

Plane, train, and bus schedules can be very confusing the first time you see them. However, they are not difficult to read once you learn how. The first step is to look at the way the schedule is organized. How is each column labeled? What are the labels on the rows that go across? Next, look for a key on the schedule. The key will tell you what the abbreviations stand for. Remember to take your time, read the abbreviations carefully, and double-check your reading to make sure you have found the correct information. That way you'll be sure to catch the right ride.

Skills and Strategies

Here you will learn how to read a plane, train, or bus schedule. Read through the examples carefully. Look at the schedule in each section. Compare the ways that information is organized on each.

Airline Schedules

Look at the airline schedule in Figure 4.2 on page 185.

MEALS:

B Breakfast **L** Lunch **D** Dinner **S** Snack

Symbols shown alone indicate food service for both sections; symbols to left of slash (/) indicate food service in First Class section only; symbols to right of slash (/) indicate food service in Coach section.

FREQUENCY CODES: All Flights Daily Except as Noted

1—Monday 3—Wednesday 5—Friday 7—Sunday
2—Tuesday 4—Thursday 6—Saturday X—Except

MISCELLANEOUS SYMBOLS:

★ Early morning or late evening flights offering Off-Peak First Class/Off-Peak Coach fares at substantial savings over regular day fares and more discount seats than available on other flights

AIRPORT CODES

ATL—Atlanta   CVG—Cincinnati
BOS—Boston   DFW—Dallas/Ft. Worth
🎬—Movies in flight   ⛐—Helicopter Service Available

From DENVER, CO

Column headings for each schedule: **Lv | Ar | Flt No/Mls | Stops or Via | Rmks**

To AKRON/CANTON, OH

Lv	Ar	Flt No/Mls	Stops or Via	Rmks
1035a	430p	472/1559	CVG	S

To ALBANY, GA

Lv	Ar	Flt No/Mls	Stops or Via	Rmks
800a	335p	972/1738	ATL	B
1120a	735p	434/1739	ATL	
245p	915p	804/1740	ATL	S X6

To ALBANY, NY

Lv	Ar	Flt No/Mls	Stops or Via	Rmks
1035a	655p	472/1818	BOS	S X6

To AMARILLO, TX

Lv	Ar	Flt No/Mls	Stops or Via	Rmks
700a	110p	224/1017	DFW	B
1010a	420p	414/1087	DFW	L
445p	1059p	210/1051	DFW	D

To ANNISTON, AL

Lv	Ar	Flt No/Mls	Stops or Via	Rmks
800a	140p	972/1743	ATL	B
1120a	535p	434/1744	ATL	
245p	905p	804/1745	ATL	S X6

To ASHEVILLE, NC

Lv	Ar	Flt No/Mls	Stops or Via	Rmks
1120a	625p	434/1748	ATL	X6
245p	930p	804/1749	ATL	S 🎬

To ATHENS, GA

Lv	Ar	Flt No/Mls	Stops or Via	Rmks
245p	1000p	804/1753	ATL	S X6

To ATLANTA, GA

Lv	Ar	Flt No/Mls	Stops or Via	Rmks
800a	1230p	972	0	B
1120a	346p	434	0	
245p	717p	804	0	S 🎬
540p	1006p	332	0	
800p	150a	616/1274	DFW	★

To AUGUSTA, GA

Lv	Ar	Flt No/Mls	Stops or Via	Rmks
800a	210p	972/1441	ATL	B
1120a	545p	434/1448	ATL	
245p	920p	804/1442	ATL	S 🎬
540p	1150p	332/686	ATL	

To AUSTIN, TX

Lv	Ar	Flt No/Mls	Stops or Via	Rmks
700a	1255p	224/1220	DFW	B
1010a	240p	414/1103	DFW	L
445p	840p	210/1169	DFW	D
800p	1150p	616/1196	DFW	★

To BALTIMORE, MD ⛐

Lv	Ar	Flt No/Mls	Stops or Via	Rmks
800a	305p	972/930	ATL	B
1010a	500p	414/1100	DFW	
1120a	620p	434/1153	ATL	
245p	955p	804/1090	ATL	S 🎬
445p	1135p	210/1130	DFW	D X6

To BRYAN/ COLLEGE STATION, TX

Lv	Ar	Flt No/Mls	Stops or Via	Rmks
700a	1106a	224/1981	DFW	B X6
700a	100p	224/1942	DFW	B
1010a	225p	414/1933	DFW	L X6
135p	740p	530/1963	DFW	X6
445p	1125p	210/1978	DFW	D

To BURLINGTON, VT

Lv	Ar	Flt No/Mls	Stops or Via	Rmks
1035a	845p	472/1825	BOS	S X6

To CHARLESTON, SC

Lv	Ar	Flt No/Mls	Stops or Via	Rmks
800a	230p	972/1417	ATL	B
1120a	550p	434/1052	ATL	
245p	920p	804/408	ATL	S 🎬
540p	1155p	332/294	ATL	

To CHARLESTON, WV

Lv	Ar	Flt No/Mls	Stops or Via	Rmks
1035a	435p	472/1579	CVG	S

To CHARLOTTE, NC

Lv	Ar	Flt No/Mls	Stops or Via	Rmks
800a	410p	972/324	ATL	B
1120a	550p	434/1206	ATL	
245p	920p	804/422	ATL	S 🎬

To CHATTANOOGA, TN

Lv	Ar	Flt No/Mls	Stops or Via	Rmks
800a	250p	972/1221	ATL	B
1035a	440p	472/1617	CVG	S
1120a	627p	434/1287	ATL	X6
245p	900p	804/1242	ATL	S 🎬
540p	1130p	332/1284	ATL	

To CINCINNATI, OH

Lv	Ar	Flt No/Mls	Stops or Via	Rmks
1035a	245p	472	0	S
1120a	610p	434/704	ATL	
245p	945p	804/598	ATL	S 🎬
445p	1042p	210/586	DFW	D
540p	105a	332/986	ATL	

To CLEVELAND, OH

Lv	Ar	Flt No/Mls	Stops or Via	Rmks
800a	300p	972/319	ATL	B
1035a	410p	472/1432	CVG	S
1120a	640p	434/1216	ATL	
245p	950p	804/1202	ATL	S 🎬
540p	1230a	332/384	ATL	

To COLUMBIA, SC

Lv	Ar	Flt No/Mls	Stops or Via	Rmks
800a	215p	972/1208	ATL	B
1120a	550p	434/1404	ATL	
245p	920p	804/1050	ATL	S 🎬
540p	1232a	332/686	ATL	

To COLUMBUS, GA

Lv	Ar	Flt No/Mls	Stops or Via	Rmks
800a	220p	972/619	ATL	B X6
1120a	530p	434/1666	ATL	
245p	850p	804/1473	ATL	S 🎬
540p	1135p	332/1668	ATL	X6

To BOTMAN, AL

Lv	Ar	Flt No/Mls	Stops or Via	Rmks
800a	140p	972/1672	ATL	B
1120a	645p	434/1674	ATL	
245p	855p	804/1675	ATL	S X6

To EVANSVILLE, IN

Lv	Ar	Flt No/Mls	Stops or Via	Rmks
1035a	335p	472/1622	CVG	S

To FT. LAUDERDALE, FL
Ft. Lauderdale-Hollywood Int'l. Airport

Lv	Ar	Flt No/Mls	Stops or Via	Rmks
800a	305p	972/67	ATL	B
1010a	545p	414/802	DFW	
1120a	625p	434/98	ATL	
135p	825p	530/140	DFW	🎬
540p	144a	332/895	ATL	

To FT. MYERS, FL

Lv	Ar	Flt No/Mls	Stops or Via	Rmks
800a	300p	972/553	ATL	B
1120a	758p	434/643	ATL	
135p	525p	530/342	DFW	
245p	945p	804/545	ATL	S 🎬

To FT. WALTON BEACH, FL

Lv	Ar	Flt No/Mls	Stops or Via	Rmks
800a	335p	972/1678	ATL	B
1120a	505p	434/1679	ATL	
245p	850p	804/1680	ATL	S X6

To FT. WAYNE, IN

Lv	Ar	Flt No/Mls	Stops or Via	Rmks
800a	255p	972/468	ATL	B
1035a	405p	472/1574	CVG	S
245p	1103p	804/598	ATL	S 🎬

To FRANKFURT, GER

Lv	Ar	Flt No/Mls	Stops or Via	Rmks
1120a	745a	434/14	ATL	
1120a	745a	434/14	ATL	
1120a	845a	434/14	ATL	
135p	920a	530/22	DFW	
135p	920a	530/22	DFW	
135p	1020a	530/22	DFW	
245p	1125a	804/LH439	ATL	
245p	1225p	804/LH439	ATL	

To GADSDEN, AL

Lv	Ar	Flt No/Mls	Stops or Via	Rmks
800a	215p	972/1681	ATL	B X6
245p	815p	804/1724	ATL	S X6

To GREENSBORO/HIGH POINT/ WINSTON-SALEM, NC

Lv	Ar	Flt No/Mls	Stops or Via	Rmks
800a	225p	972/1236	ATL	B
1120a	545p	434/306	ATL	
245p	930p	804/604/ATL		S 🎬
540p	1159p	332/1140	ATL	X6

To GREENVILLE/ SPARTANBURG, SC

Lv	Ar	Flt No/Mls	Stops or Via	Rmks
800a	240p	972/1684	ATL	B

Figure 4.2 Airline Schedule,
Adapted from Delta Airlines System schedule

Examine the headings at the top of each column.

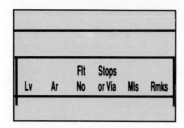

Lv — Leave (the departure time)

Ar — Arrive (the arrival time)

Flt No — Flight number

Stops or Via — Cities the plane stops in before arrival at the final destination

Mls — Meals served on the plane

Rmks — Remarks about the flight

The schedule key explains the symbols and abbreviations found in the table. The airline schedule (Figure 4.2) lists flights from Denver to many other cities. These cities are listed in alphabetical order.

1. What time does Flight 804 to Atlanta leave Denver?

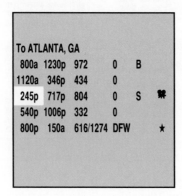

Solution:

Flight 804 leaves Denver at 2:45 PM MST.

2. Where does Flight 224/1220 from Denver to Austin stop?

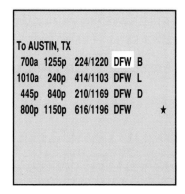

To AUSTIN, TX
700a 1255p 224/1220 DFW B
1010a 240p 414/1103 DFW L
445p 840p 210/1169 DFW D
800p 1150p 616/1196 DFW ★

Solution:

Flight 224/1220 stops in Dallas/Fort Worth. Notice that whenever two flight numbers are listed, there is a stopover.

Train Schedules

Look at the train schedule in Figure 4.3 on page 188. The headings at the top of each column in Figure 4.3 are highlighted below.

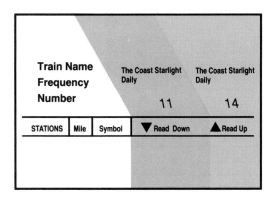

Train Name
Frequency
Number

The Coast Starlight
Daily

The Coast Starlight
Daily

11   14

| STATIONS | Mile | Symbol | ▼ Read Down | ▲ Read Up |

Train name — The name assigned to a particular train

Frequency — How often the train travels

Number — The number assigned to a particular train

Stations — Places the train stops

Mile — Mileage information

Symbol — Services that are offered

🚐　Via direct motor coach.
●　Tickets cannot be purchased at this location. You may purchase your tickets on the train (without penalty) or from any appointed travel agency.
♿　The station and/or platform area is accessible to handicapped and elderly passengers.

Seattle… Portland… Eugene… Sacramento… San Francisco… **Los Angeles**

Train Name							
Frequency					The Coast Starlight Daily　　R		The Coast Starlight Daily　　R
Number					11		14
STATIONS	Mile	Symbol	▼	Read Down		▲	Read Up
Connecting Motor Coach 87							
Vancouver, BC — *Downtown (PDT)*			Dp	7 00A		Ar	10 15P
(Burlington Northern) **Seattle, WA** — King St. Sta. (PDT) (Vancouver, BC🚐, Victoria, BC)	0	♿	Dp	11 05A		Ar	6 00P
Tacoma, WA	40			11 59A			4 50P
East Olympia, WA	75	● ♿		12 38P			4 03P
Centralia, WA	94	♿		1 00P			3 46P
Kelso-Longview, WA	135	● ♿		1 49P			3 00P
Vancouver, WA	174	♿	▼	2 32P			2 21P
Portland, OR (Bend🚐)	184	♿	Ar	3 05P		Dp	2 00P
(Southern Pacific) **Portland, OR** (Bend🚐)	184	♿	Dp	3 15P		Ar	1 50P
Salem, OR	237	♿		4 25P		▲	12 15P
Albany, OR (Corvallis)	264	♿		4 54P			11 45A
Eugene, OR	308	♿		5 36P			11 08A
Chemult, OR	429	● ♿		8 24P			8 13A
Klamath Falls, OR	503	♿		10 09P			6 56A
Dunsmuir, CA	608	♿		12 35A			3 58A
Redding, CA	665	● ♿		2 16A			2 12A
Chico, CA	739	● ♿		3 38A			12 50A
Marysville, CA (Yuba City)	783	●		4 21A			12 07A
Sacramento, CA	835	♿		6 00A			11 02P
Davis, CA	848	♿		6 22A			10 24P
Martinez, CA (Concord)	892	♿		7 07A			9 36P
Richmond, CA (BART Station)	912	♿	▼	7 36A			9 05P
Oakland, CA	921	♿	Ar	8 05A		Dp	8 52P
San Francisco, CA/Via 🚐 — Transbay Term. - Amtrack Sta. — Caltrain/SP Sta.	928	●	Ar Ar	8 35A 8 45A			8 15P 8 00P
— Caltrain/SP Sta. — Transbay Term. - Amtrack Sta.		●	Dp Dp	6 45A 7 50A			9 12P 9 02P
Oakland, CA	921	♿	Dp	8 25A		Ar	8 32P
San Jose, CA (Caltrain/SP)	965	♿		9 43A			6 57P
Salinas, CA (Monterey🚐)	1032	♿	▼	11 01A		▲	5 34P
San Luis Obispo, CA (Hearst Castle)	1166	♿	Ar Dp	2 10P 2 17P		Dp Ar	2 53P 2 46P
Santa Barbara, CA	1285	♿		4 35P		▲	12 05P
Oxnard, CA	1322	♿		5 19P			11 21A
Glendale, CA	1382	♿	▼	6 28P			10 13A
Los Angeles, CA (PDT)	1388	♿	Ar	7 10P		Dp	9 55A

Figure 4.3　Train Schedule
Adapted from Amtrak National Train Timetables

Read Down — Times the train stops at each station, when traveling from the first station listed to the last station listed

Read Up — Times the train stops at each station when traveling from the last station listed to the first station listed

Dp — Departure

Ar — Arrive

3. What time does Train 11 leave Vancouver, British Columbia?

					11		14
Vancouver, BC — *Downtown (PDT)*				Dp	7 00A	Ar	10 15P
(Burlington Northern) **Seattle, WA** — King St. Sta. (PDT) *(Vancouver, BC■, Victoria, BC)*	0		⌀	Dp	11 05A	Ar	6 00P
Tacoma, WA	40		⌀		11 59A		4 50P
East Olympia, WA	75	•	⌀	↓	12 38P	↑	4 03P

Solution:

Train 11 leaves Vancouver BC at 7:00 AM PST.

4. What time does Train 14 leave Oakland, California?

					11		14
Davis, CA	848		⌀		6 22A	↑	10 24P
Martinez, CA (Concord)	892		⌀		7 07A		9 36P
Richmond, CA (BART Station)	912	⌀	⌀	↓	7 36A		9 05P
Oakland, CA	921		⌀	Ar	8 05A	Dp	8 52P
San Francisco, CA/Via ■ — Transbay Term. - Amtrack Sta. — Caltrain/SP Sta.	928		•	Ar Ar	8 35A 8 45A		8 15P 8 00P
— Caltrain/SP Sta. — Transbay Term. - Amtrack Sta.			•	Dp Dp	6 45A 7 50A		9 12P 9 02P

Solution:

Train 14 leaves Oakland at 8:52 PM PST.

5. How many miles is the train ride from Seattle, Washington, to San Jose, California?

				11		14
Oakland, CA	921	⌀	Dp	8 25A	Ar	8 32P
San Jose, CA (Caltrain/SP)	965	⌀		9 43A		6 57P
Salinas, CA (Monterey 🚌)	1032	⌀		11 01A		5 34P
San Luis Obispo, CA (Hearst Castle)	1166	⌀	Ar / Dp	2 10P / 2 17P	Dp / Ar	2 53P / 2 46P
Santa Barbara, CA	1285	⌀		4 35P		12 05P
Oxnard, CA	1322	⌀		5 19P		11 21A
Glendale, CA	1382	⌀		6 28P		10 13A
Los Angeles, CA (PDT)	1388	⌀	Ar	7 10P	Dp	9 55A

Solution:

The train ride is 965 miles.

6. How many miles is the train ride from Chico, California, to Santa Barbara, California?

Solution:

$$
\begin{array}{rl}
1285 & \text{mileage from Santa Barbara to Seattle} \\
- \ 739 & \text{mileage from Chico to Seattle} \\
\hline
546 & \text{mileage from Chico to Santa Barbara}
\end{array}
$$

The train ride is 546 miles.

Bus Schedules

Look at the bus schedule in Figure 4.4 on page 191. Examine the headings at the top of each column. Bus schedules are similar to train schedules.

RENO—LOS ANGELES

READ DOWN				READ UP	
6007	6003	←SCHEDULE Nos. →		6002	6008
		554			

All bus routes are assigned numbers. The bus route from Reno, Nevada, to Los Angeles, California, is Number 554. Two buses travel from Reno to Los Angeles each day. One leaves Reno at 8:20

READ DOWN	6007	6003	SCHEDULE Nos. 554	6002	6008	READ UP
	8 20	10 40	Lv RENO, NEV. ....Ar	10 20	6 45	
	9 10	11 30	Carson City	9 30	5 55	
	9 35	11 55	Gardnerville-Minden	9 05	5 30	
	f	f	Holbrook Jct.	f	f	
	10 05	12 25	Ar Topaz Lodge, Nev. Lv	8 35	5 00	
	10 20	12 40	Lv Topaz Lodge, Nev ....Ar	8 20	5 00	
	f	f	Coleville, Cal.	f	f	
	f	f	Walker	f	f	
	f	f	Sonora Jct.	f	f	
	11 15	1 35	Bridgeport	7 25	4 05	
	11 50	2 10	Leevning	6 50	3 30	
	f	f	June Lake Jct.	f	f	
	f	f	Crestview	f	f	
	12 35	2 55	Mammoth Lakes	6 05	2 45	
	f	f	Rock Creek	f	f	
	1 35	3 55	Ar Bishop Lv	5 05	1 50	
	2 05	4 10	Lv Bishop ....Ar	4 30	1 30	
	2 23	4 28	Big Pine	4 10	1 10	
	2 55	5 00	Independence	3 37	12 37	
	3 13	5 18	Lone Pine	3 19	12 19	
	f	f	Olancha	f	f	
	f	f	Little Lake	f	f	
	4 50	6 55	Ridgecrest (LB)	1 45	10 45	
	f	f	N.W.C. Main Gate (LB)	f	f	
	6 00	8 05	Ar Mojave (LB) Lv	12 35	9 35	
	6 40	8 45	Mojave (LB) Ar	11 55	9 15	
	6 56	9 01	Rosamond	11 39	9 00	
			Mira Loma "Hospital"			
			Mira Loma "Facility"			
	7 10	9 15	Lancaster	11 25	8 45	
	7 25	9 30	Palmdale	11 05	8 25	
		10 05	Solemint Jct.			
			Magic Mountain x			
		f	Saugus			
		10 25	Newhall	10 10		
	8 25	10 45	San Fernando	9 50	7 20	
			Glendale (Burbank)			
	8 45	11 05	North Hollywood	9 30	7 00	
	9 00	11 20	Hollywood	9 10	6 45	
	9 20	11 40	Ar LOS ANGELES, CAL. Lv	8 45	6 20	

f symbolizes flag stop—the driver will only stop if asked by a passenger or flagged by a ticketholder. Not a scheduled stop.

Figure 4.4 Bus Schedule
Adapted from Greyhound Bus Schedules

AM. The other leaves at 10:40 AM. Two buses also travel from Los Angeles to Reno each day. The lightface type represents AM, and the boldface type represents PM. The arrows remind you to read up or read down in each column.

7. What times do the buses on Route 554 leave Los Angeles, California?

8 25	10 25	Newhall	10 10	
	10 45	San Fernando	9 50	7 20
		Glendale (Burbank)		
8 45	11 05	North Hollywood	9 30	7 00
9 00	11 20	Hollywood	9 10	6 45
9 20	11 40	Ar LOS ANGELES, CAL. Lv	8 45	6 20

Solution:

The buses on Route 554 leave (Lv) Los Angeles each day at 8:45 AM and 6:20 PM.

Problems

Use the plane, train, and bus schedules in Figures 4.2, 4.3, and 4.4 to help you answer each question.

✓ **1.** What time does Flight 472 from Denver to Cincinnati arrive at its destination?

2. How many nonstop flights from Denver to Amarillo are scheduled?

3. When does Flight 972/1221 from Denver to Chattanooga leave Denver?

4. Where does Flight 972/1208 stop on its way from Denver to Columbia, South Carolina?

✓ **5.** What meal is served on Flight 472/1622 from Denver to Evansville, Indiana?

6. How many flights are there from Denver to Baltimore?

7. A plane leaves New York City at 8:22 AM and arrives in Miami, Florida, at 10:59 AM. What is the elapsed time for this flight?

✓ **8.** Look up Flight 224/1220 from Denver to Austin, Texas.
   a. When does it leave Denver?
   b. What time zone is Denver in?
   c. When does it arrive in Austin?
   d. What time zone is Austin in?
   e. What is the elapsed time for this trip?

✓ **9.** What time does Train 14 leave Eugene, Oregon?

10. What time does Train 11 leave Sacramento, California?

11. How many miles is Davis, California, from Seattle, Washington?

12. What is the distance from Portland, Oregon, to San Francisco, California?

✓ 13. How many miles is Los Angeles from San Francisco?

14. What is the elapsed time of the trip from Los Angeles to Klamath Falls, Oregon, on Train 14?

✓ 15. What is the elapsed time of the trip from Oakland, California, to Santa Barbara, California, on Train 11?

16. What time does Bus 6007 leave Bishop?

17. What time does Bus 6002 leave Hollywood?

18. What is the elapsed time of the entire trip from Reno to Los Angeles on Bus 6007?

✓ 19. What is the elapsed time of the entire trip from Los Angeles to Reno on bus 6002?

20. Which bus schedule between Reno and Los Angeles takes less time, 6007 or 6002? By how much?

SECTION 5 • VACATION EXPENSES

How much does a vacation cost? That might sound like an easy question until you think of the many expenses linked to a vacation. In fact, you cannot know ahead of time exactly how much a vacation will cost. A wise traveler, however, should have a good idea of the vacation's cost from the beginning.

June was planning a vacation. She found the exact rates of the hotels she would use, the train fares, and the cost of her car rental. It is easy to find the *exact* costs of plane, train, or bus fares, hotels, and car rentals. Other expenses can be *estimated* in advance. June estimated how much she would spend on gasoline, tolls, meals, entertainment, and souvenirs. To be safe, she overestimated her expenses. That way she could be almost certain that she would take enough money.

Once you have decided how much money will be required, you need to know what form of payment you plan to use for each expense. Most travelers don't like to carry large amounts of cash with them on vacation. June decided to buy **traveler's checks** at a local bank. Unlike cash, traveler's checks can be replaced if they are lost or stolen. You can use traveler's checks as cash in most hotels, restaurants, and shops. Many travelers also bring along a credit card, which can be used instead of cash or traveler's checks in case of an unplanned expense or an emergency.

Another expense associated with a vacation is insurance. Most people have insurance that covers their homes, health, cars, and so forth. However, this insurance often does not cover emergencies or injuries while on vacation. Insurance companies sell insurance specifically to cover these costs. Three types of **travel insurance** are available.

- **Trip cancellation insurance** covers nonrefundable vacation payments if you cancel your trip because of illness or injury.

- **Baggage insurance** covers lost, stolen, or damaged baggage.

- **Travel accident insurance** covers certain medical expenses resulting from accidents that occur while on vacation.

Skills and Strategies

Here you will learn how to compute the costs for travel expenses. Read the problems carefully.

1. A family of five is planning a two-week vacation. The parents are trying to estimate total meal expenses. They expect that each meal will cost $5 per person. How much money should they set aside for meals?

   Solution:

5	number of family members
× 3	number of meals per day per person
15	total number of daily meals
15	total number of daily meals
× 14	number of days in two weeks
210	total number of meals for entire vacation

210   total number of meals for entire vacation
× $5   estimated cost per meal
$1,050   approximate meal expenses

This family should set aside approximately $1,050 for meal expenses.

2. Margaret wants to buy $100,000 of travel accident insurance for her three-week European vacation. What premium must she pay for this amount of insurance?

Solution: Use Table 4.1 on page 196.

There are 21 days in three weeks, so look down the Length of Coverage column and find the row labeled "21 Days." Look across this row to the $100,000 column to find Margaret's **premium**, the amount paid to purchase the insurance policy. The premiums are inexpensive because the probability of having an accident while on vacation is low. The premium for three weeks of $100,000 worth of travel accident insurance is $35.25.

3. Dorothy Fontak plans to insure $800 of baggage for her ten-day vacation. What premium must she pay?

Solution: Use Table 4.2 on page 197.

Look down the Length of Coverage column and find the 10 Days row. Look across this row to the $800 column to find Dorothy's premium. Dorothy will pay $19.75 to insure her baggage.

4. Amy is planning a $2,300 European vacation. She would like to purchase cancellation insurance in case she misses the trip because of illness or injury. How much will $2,300 of trip-cancellation insurance cost her? The solution to this problem appears at the top of page 198.

Travel Accident Insurance

Maximum Benefit →	$15,000	$25,000	$50,000	$100,000
Length of Coverage ↓	Premium	Premium	Premium	Premium
1 Day	$ .70	$ 1.15	$ 2.20	$ 4.30
3 Days	1.40	2.25	4.40	8.60
5 Days	2.05	3.40	6.60	12.90
8 Days	3.08	5.05	9.90	19.30
10 Days	3.75	6.15	12.10	23.50
15 Days	4.62	7.57	14.80	28.85
17 Days	4.95	8.10	15.95	30.95
21 Days	5.65	9.25	18.15	35.25
22 Days	5.77	9.43	18.52	35.92
24 Days	6.00	9.80	19.25	37.25
27 Days	6.35	10.35	20.35	39.25
31 Days	6.85	11.20	22.00	42.40
45 Days	8.55	13.95	27.45	53.25
60 Days	10.30	16.75	32.95	64.15
90 Days	13.00	21.25	41.75	81.65
120 Days	14.70	24.00	47.25	92.55
150 Days	16.45	26.80	52.75	103.45
180 Days	18.15	29.60	58.20	114.35

Table 4.1   Adapted from Mutual of Omaha Travel Insurance Brochure

Baggage Insurance

Length of Coverage	Amount of Insurance			
	$300.00 Premium	$500.00 Premium	$800.00 Premium	$1,000.00 Premium
1-3 Days	$ 4.25	$ 6.00	$ 8.50	$ 10.25
5 Days	5.75	8.50	12.00	14.25
8 Days	7.75	11.25	17.50	21.50
10 Days	8.25	12.75	19.75	24.00
15 Days	10.25	15.50	24.25	29.50
17 Days	11.00	16.75	26.50	31.25
21 Days	12.75	19.75	31.00	36.50
22 Days	13.25	21.00	32.50	40.25
24 Days	13.75	21.75	34.00	42.25
27 Days	14.25	22.50	36.00	44.75
31 Days	15.50	24.50	39.00	49.00
45 Days	18.75	30.75	49.00	61.00
60 Days	22.50	36.75	58.25	73.75
90 Days	27.75	46.00	73.00	91.25
120 Days	33.00	55.00	87.50	109.00
150 Days	38.25	64.00	102.00	126.50
180 Days	43.50	73.25	116.50	144.00

Table 4.2   Adapted from Mutual of Omaha Travel Insurance Brochure

Solution: Use Table 4.3.

Cancellation Insurance

Cost	Coverage
$5.80	$100

Table 4.3

$$\frac{23}{100) \ \$2,300} \leftarrow \text{number of \$100's in \$2,300} \\ \leftarrow \text{cost of vacation}$$

$$\begin{array}{ll} \$ \ \ 5.80 & \text{premium per \$100 of coverage} \\ \underline{\times \ 23} & \text{number of \$100's in \$2,300} \\ \$133.40 & \text{total premium} \end{array}$$

Amy must pay $133.40 for trip-cancellation insurance.

Problems

Find the answer to problems 6 through 10 by using Tables 4.1, 4.2, and 4.3 to help you.

1. Audrey and Vincent Ibelli have three children. The entire family is planning a two-week trip to Mount Rushmore. They plan to eat three meals a day and they estimate that an average meal will cost $6 per person. What is their estimated meal cost for the vacation?

2. Mr. Schuster and his daughter Jill are planning a ten-day trip to Canada. They expect to spend about $7 for each meal. What are their estimated meal expenses for the entire trip?

3. Yung Chou-chen is planning a 15-day trip to Israel. He wants to purchase $25,000 of travel accident insurance. What premium must he pay?

✓ **4.** Delia is planning a 60-day cross-country summer vacation. She has decided to purchase $15,000 of travel accident insurance. What premium must she pay?

5. Lloyd will be vacationing in Ireland from December 21 to January 10. He wants to purchase an $800 baggage insurance policy to cover his entire vacation. Compute the cost of his baggage insurance premium.

✓ **6.** Jackie did not purchase cancellation insurance for her vacation to Europe. The cruise tickets cost $2,400. Because of illness, she cancelled her trip. The cruise company refunded 60 percent of the ticket price. How much did Jackie get for her unused ticket?

7. The Ross family purchased a vacation package from Temptation Travel Agency for $4,500. They also bought cancellation insurance to cover the price of the package. Compute their cancellation insurance premium.

8. Jimmy Mack will be touring Europe for a total of eight weeks and four days. He wants to purchase $1,000 of baggage insurance to cover his entire trip. What is the cost of Jimmy's baggage insurance premium?

9. The McCartneys flew from Liverpool, England, to New York City. Mr. and Mrs. McCartney paid $510 each, their two teenage sons paid $470 each, and their baby daughter's ticket cost $150. What is the average price per person?

✓ **10.** Marina booked a $2,800 cruise through her travel agent. The money is refundable up to one month before the cruise. People who cancel within one month of the cruise receive only 65 percent of their fare as a refund. Marina is forced to cancel her trip 20 days before the cruise, and she has no travel insurance. How much should Marina receive as a refund on her $2,800 fare?

• KEY TERMS

To find the definition of any term introduced in the chapter, refer to the Glossary in the back of this book.

arrival time	elapsed time
arrow diagram	overbooking
baggage insurance	standby
bumped	time zones
carriers	travel accident insurance
confirmed reservation	traveler's checks
daylight saving time	travel insurance
denied boarding compensation	trip cancellation insurance
departure time	waiting list

• REVIEW PROBLEMS

1. Melanie is planning an automobile trip that will take approximately 19 hours. She is driving from New York City to Chicago. If she leaves at 6:30 AM, what time (CST) should she arrive in Chicago?

2. A $5\frac{1}{2}$ hour Miami-Seattle plane trip is being delayed 20 minutes because of weather conditions. The plane was scheduled to leave Miami at 4:40 PM EST. What time (PST) will the plane arrive in Seattle?

3. Five high school students plan to go to Fort Lauderdale, Florida, for spring break. Each will pay $210 for a round-trip ticket. The tickets can be returned, but there is a 20 percent penalty. If all five students must return their tickets, what would be the total penalty?

4. Nomad Airways overbooked Flight 601 to Honolulu by 15 percent. The plane can carry 200 passengers. How many confirmed reservations were sold for this flight?

5. The seven members of the Zorn family are planning a 12-day vacation. They estimate that each meal will cost $7.50 per person. What is a good estimate of their total meal expenses for the vacation?

6. A bus leaves Trenton, New Jersey, at 3:00 AM Wednesday and arrives in Denver, Colorado, at 6:30 PM Friday. What is the elapsed time for this trip?

7. Use the train schedule, Figure 4.3, page 188, to find the elapsed time of the trip from Los Angeles, California, to Vancouver, British Columbia.

8. Vicente is taking a train from Boise, Idaho, to Denver, Colorado. The train arrives at 10:45 AM in Denver. Vicente is planning to meet his sister at the train station and travel together by plane to Cleveland. Use the airline timetable, Figure 4.2, page 185, to find the number of the first flight they could take.

9. The Trinidades family is planning to visit the Wonder World Amusement Park. They will stay at a hotel in the park that charges $140 a night for one room, plus 6 percent sales tax. If the family stays in one room for 6 nights, how much will the Trinidades pay for hotel expenses?

10. Elizabeth wants to purchase travel insurance for a three-week vacation. She would like $50,000 of travel accident insurance, $1,000 of baggage insurance, and $2,400 of trip-cancellation insurance. How much will Elizabeth pay for all of this insurance? Use Tables 4.1, 4.2, and 4.3.

1. Go to a local new-car dealership. Pick out a car and make a list of the options you would order for it. Find out the price of the car, the price of each option, and the total cost. Compute the sales tax and make a complete list of any extra charges the dealer puts on new cars. Report your findings to the class. Write a thank-you letter to the car dealer.

2. Suppose that you are old enough to drive and have a license. Pick any new or used car you would like to own. Make a complete list of the options you would like the car to have. Visit a local insurance agent and find out the cost of insurance for the car you picked. Again, be sure to write a thank-you letter to the insurance agent after your visit.

3. Visit your local motor-vehicle department. Make a list of the forms needed to get license plates for a car in your state. If possible, get sample copies of each form. Show and explain each form to the class.

4. Make an appointment to interview a local travel agent. Before the interview make a list of questions you want to ask. Include the questions and answers from the interview in a report.

5. Talk to your teacher about having an insurance agent speak to your class. Have the class submit questions about automobile insurance. Copy their questions neatly on a sheet of paper and give it to the agent a day or two before the session.

6. Write an ad to sell a used car. Call several newspapers to find the price of running the ad for one week. Report your findings to the class. If there is only one newspaper in your area, find out how much it would cost to run the ad for three days, for one week, and for two weeks.

7. Pick out a new or used car that you own or would like to own. Choose one of the following repair jobs to be done on the car:

   - complete brake job

   - complete tune-up

   - complete exhaust-system replacement

   Go to a garage or repair shop and get a price estimate for the job. Be sure that the estimate includes parts and labor. Then go to a local auto-supply store and find out what each of the parts would cost. Compare the garage or repair shop's estimate of parts and labor to the cost of fixing the car yourself. Report your findings to the class.

8. Ask an insurance agent, your parents, or your friends who drive for the address of an automobile-insurance company. Write a business letter to the company requesting a brochure on their policies. Report your findings to the class.

9. Go to a local library and find the address of your state's chamber of commerce. Write to the chamber of commerce and request tourist information and a state road map. When you receive these items, read them and pick five places of interest in your state. Using the road map, write directions showing how to get to each of the five places from your home or school.

ESTIMATING DISTANCES ON A GLOBE

In Chapter 3, you learned about distance, speed, and how to use a scale of miles on a flat, two-dimensional map. In Chapter 4 you learned about airline travel and elapsed times.

Have you ever realized that an airplane must cover more distance than the ground distance between the two points it flies? Examine this picture:

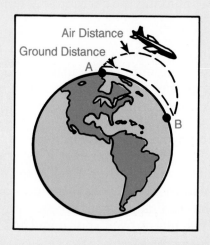

From the picture you can see that airplanes that fly higher altitudes must cover longer air distances. If two cities are 1,000 ground miles apart, and an airplane makes this trip in two hours, you may think that the plane traveled an average of 500 mph. However, the plane actually covered more than 1,000 miles in the two hours, so its average airspeed was more than 500 mph.

This manipulative activity will teach you about ground distances on earth.

Directions: You will need a globe, some string, and a ruler or yardstick. To find the distance between two cities, stretch the string across the globe between the two cities. Mark the length of string between the cities with your fingers. Then, measure the string against the ruler and use the scale of miles to find the distances between the two cities.

  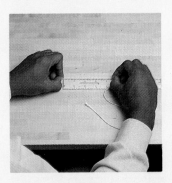

Complete the following chart: (Ask for help if you can't find the cities.)

Trip	Ground Distance
New York City-Los Angeles	
Honolulu-San Francisco	
Miami-London	
Moscow-Washington, DC	
Paris-St. Louis	
Rome-Peking	
Tel Aviv-Dublin	

Use the string to find the circumference of the earth at the equator _____.

TOPIC *2* COMPUTER APPLICATION

VACATION EXPENSES

It is very important to plan a vacation well in advance. You need to determine if the vacation that you have in mind can comfortably fit within your budget. This program will help you to approximate the total cost of taking your car when you go on vacation. However, you will need some information before running the program. On a sheet of paper, write down the following:

1. Find three different locations within the continental United States that appeal to you as choice vacation spots. If you don't have some special places in mind, you can look in the travel section of your local newspaper — usually in the Sunday edition.

2. Determine the approximate distance you will be driving (round trip) on each vacation. This information can be found by using a driving atlas or an encyclopedia. Each of the three locations is to be treated separately.

3. Decide how many days you have to spend on each vacation.

4. Also decide how many people will be traveling with you on each of the three vacation trips.

   Directions: To determine the cost of traveling to each of the three vacation spots you have chosen, you will fill out the blanks under Trip 1, Trip 2, and Trip 3. Follow the start-up procedures for your computer which are found in Appendix A. Select Topic 2 titled *Vacation Expenses* from the Main Menu. Follow the instructions on your computer screen to complete the following chart. Do not write in this book. Put your answers on a piece of paper.

Vacation Expenses

	Trip 1	Trip 2	Trip 3
Destination			
Round Trip Distance			
Length in Days			
Number of Riders			
Room Costs			
Food Expenses			
Gas/Oil Costs			
Total Cost			
Individual Cost			

TOPIC **3**
THE STOCK MARKET

Every successful attempt to manage money is based on careful planning and setting realistic goals. Such goals can be short-term, such as contact lenses, tickets to a baseball game, or a vacation with your best friend's family. Goals can also be long-term, such as a job-training program, your own video store, or your own car. Whatever your plans are, they probably require more money than you have now. That is why you may decide on an investment plan—to watch your savings grow. As you learn about investing and the stock market, you will see that different investments offer different rewards and risks. In order to choose your investments well, you should also become aware of the many ways financial information is reported and displayed.

CHAPTER 5

INVESTING IN STOCKS AND BONDS

SECTION 1 • TYPES OF BUSINESS ORGANIZATIONS

It's easy to take the things you use every day for granted. Yet every single item — from the pen you write with to the television you watch in the evening — had to be invented. Have you ever wondered who designed the first paper clip? How contact lenses are made? How computers work? What do you know about the people who invented staples, light bulbs, straws, telephones, toothbrushes, airplanes, and air conditioners? Have you ever heard of an idea and thought, "I can do that better," or "I wish I had thought of that"? You can. All inventions started out as a dream, or as a chance happening. From that point, it took some luck, imagination, and effort to transform the inventions into useful products and, finally, money-making businesses.

Brenda learned how to silk-screen designs onto fabric in an art class. She liked silk-screening so much that she printed T-shirts for everyone in her family. They were a hit. Her softball team liked her work so much that they asked Brenda to make team T-shirts. Soon lots of people — school clubs, stores, even a local rock band — were asking her to print shirts for them. As a result, Brenda decided to go into business. She took a few orders, bought supplies, and started silk-screening.

At this point, Brenda's business is known as a **sole proprietorship,** a business owned by just one person. Brenda may pay people wages to work for her, but she alone is responsible for paying all the bills. The money left over after she pays the expenses is called **profit.** The owner of a sole proprietorship is entitled to all the profits of the business. These profits need not be shared with anyone. However, the owner is also responsible, or **personally liable,** for any losses. If Brenda does not sell enough T-shirts to cover expenses, Brenda, as the owner, must still pay the bills. If a large sum of money is involved, she may be forced to sell her car or other personal possessions in order to make these payments.

Suppose the business does well. Brenda wants to expand and open a store. One of her first needs is more money — to lease the store, purchase equipment, hire employees, make more clothes, and so on. Another need is for someone to share the risk. A bigger operation can produce more profits, but it can also mean more losses.

Because of these needs, Brenda looks for a partner. After a short search, she finds Pablo, who has the money to invest in the business.

Pablo also is good at handling money. When they join together, they form a partnership. The feature that makes a business a **partnership** is that two or more people share ownership. They also share the profits and the responsibility for any losses of the business.

Pablo has some great ideas. Not only can he balance the books, but he also knows how to sell. As a result, the business becomes very successful. To keep growing, Brenda and Pablo now need a full-scale printing factory, delivery trucks, and some advertising. Money used to start or expand a business is called **capital.** Pablo estimates that they need $1 million to expand the business. At this point, Brenda and Pablo begin to worry. The possibility of having to repay $1 million is frightening. They go to a lawyer to get advice.

The lawyer suggests that they form a corporation. A **corporation** is a special form of business that is owned by one person or by a group of people, each of whom invests money in the business and owns shares in the business, called **shares of stock.** These shares are represented by **stock certificates,** which are documents that give evidence of ownership. The owners of the corporation, or **shareholders,** have limited liability. **Limited liability** means that each owner cannot lose more than he or she has invested in the business. For example, if Joan puts $500 into Brenda and Pablo's corporation, that is the most she could lose. Even if the company lost the entire $1 million, Joan's loss would be limited to $500.

Shareholders *own* the corporation, but they don't necessarily *run* the corporation. A corporation can have thousands, even millions, of shareholders. They elect a **board of directors** to run the corporation. Shareholders are kept informed of corporate dealings through shareholders' meetings and **annual reports.**

Skills and Strategies

Let's look at how businesses operate.

1. Steve, Marty, and Robbie formed a partnership and own the Brothers Three Video Store. Steve owns 20% of the business, Marty owns 50%, and Robbie owns 30%. Their profits for January were $9,000. How much money should each brother receive as his portion of the profits?

Solution:

$9,000 total profit
× .20 Steve's share, expressed as a decimal
$1,800.00 Steve's profit for January

$9,000 total profit
× .50 Marty's share, expressed as a decimal
$4,500.00 Marty's profit for January

$9,000 total profit
× .30 Robbie's share, expressed as a decimal
$2,700.00 Robbie's profit for January

Steve should receive $1,800, Marty should receive $4,500, and Robbie should receive $2,700.

2. Nelson invests $3,000 in a partnership that has four other partners. The total investment of all five partners is $12,000. What percent of the business does Nelson own?

Solution: Recall that all percents can be expressed as a fraction with the denominator 100. You can represent the unknown percent in this problem as the ratio:

$$\frac{P}{100}$$

Since Nelson invests $3,000 of the total $12,000, his share can be represented as the ratio:

$$\frac{3,000}{12,000}$$

Form an equation by making the two ratios equal.

$$\frac{P}{100} = \frac{3,000}{12,000}$$

An equation in which two ratios are equal is called a **proportion.**

Simplify the ratio $\frac{3,000}{12,000}$ to lowest terms.

$$\frac{3,000}{12,000} = \frac{3}{12} = \frac{1}{4}$$

Write $\frac{1}{4}$ as an equivalent decimal:

$$\begin{array}{r} .25 \\ 4\overline{)\,1.00} \end{array}$$

$$\frac{1}{4} = .25$$

Replace $\dfrac{3{,}000}{12{,}000}$ with .25 in the proportion $\dfrac{P}{100} = \dfrac{3{,}000}{12{,}000}$.

$$\frac{P}{100} = .25$$

This equation can be written as this division example:

$$\begin{array}{r} .25 \\ 100\overline{)\,P} \end{array}$$

You can find P as if you were checking a division example:

$$P = .25 \times 100$$
$$P = 25$$

Nelson owns 25% of the business.

The following sequence of calculator keystrokes can be used to find Nelson's share:

[AC] 3,000 [÷] 12,000 [%]

The display should read 25.

3. Cruz owns two-fifths of a florist shop that has one other partner. The florist shop is worth \$17,000. What is the value of Cruz's share of the business?

Solution: Find $\frac{2}{5}$ of \$17,000.

$$\frac{2}{5} \times \frac{17{,}000}{1} = 6{,}800$$

The value of Cruz's share of the business is \$6,800.

The following sequence of calculator keystrokes can be used to find the value of Cruz's share.

[AC] 2 [÷] 5 [×] 17,000 [=]

The display should read 6,800.

Problems

1. A partnership is owned equally by five partners. The total value of the business is $170,000. What is the value of each partner's share?

✓ 2. A baseball team's stock is owned by three people. Mark owns 95%, Margie owns 4%, and Gary owns 1%. If the team is worth $97,000,000, what is the value of Margie's shares?

3. A corporation originally issued 70,000 shares of stock. The 70,000 shares are owned by stockholders all over the country. Joe owns 1,400 shares of stock in this corporation. What percent of the corporation does he own?

✓ 4. A new corporation is going to distribute 60,000 shares of stock next week. These shares represent the entire ownership of the corporation. Jonathan plans to buy 1,200 shares in this corporation. What percent of the company would Jonathan own if he made this purchase?

5. Leslie owns three-eighths of an auto-parts store that is worth $48,000. What is the value of his share?

6. Elliot and Juan formed a partnership ten years ago. Elliot owns one-fourth of the partnership, and Juan owns the rest. The partnership is worth $19,000.
    a. What fraction of the partnership does Juan own? $\frac{3}{4}$
    b. What is the value of Elliot's share?
    c. What is the value of Juan's share?
    d. Elliot has decided to sell his share to two friends. How much should each friend pay Elliot, if the two friends want to be equal partners?

✓ 7. Kim and Jean are partners in a boutique that is worth $125,000. Kim owns 80% of the business, and Jean owns the rest. What is the value of Jean's share of the business?

8. Samuel and three of his friends are planning to buy a total of 70,000 shares in a brand new corporation. They will each buy the same number of shares. How many shares of stock in the corporation will each of them own?

✓ **9.** Roseann, Willie, Barbie, and Lou are purchasing a new restaurant worth $200,000. They will each own an equal share of the business. What percent of the business will each of them own?

10. Jan owns five-eighths of the Happy Haircutting Salon. Does Jan own more than half of this business? Explain your answer.

SECTION 2 • READING THE NEW YORK STOCK EXCHANGE TICKER

People buy stock with hopes of making money. Shares of stock can increase or decrease in value. Shareholders can sell their stock at any time to another individual. Stock, however, can be bought and sold only through licensed **stockbrokers.** Individuals cannot buy and sell shares on their own. When stock is bought or sold, a **trade** has been made.

A **stock exchange** is a place where brokers meet to trade stocks. There are ten stock exchanges in the United States:

> American Stock Exchange
> Boston Stock Exchange
> Chicago Board Options Exchange
> Cincinnati Stock Exchange
> Intermountain Stock Exchange
> Midwest Stock Exchange
> New York Stock Exchange
> Pacific Stock Exchange
> Philadelphia Stock Exchange
> Spokane Stock Exchange

Most trades can be handled through telephone calls to brokers. Not all brokers work at stock exchanges; most work in offices. When customers want to buy or sell stock, they call their brokers first. These brokers relay the customers' orders to brokers at a stock

exchange, where the actual trade takes place. For example, a broker with an order to buy 100 shares of General Motors stock meets with a broker who has an order to sell 100 shares of General Motors stock. Like participants in an auction, these brokers arrive at a price for the shares. Each **transaction** (trade) is recorded and displayed on a stock exchange **ticker,** which can be electronic or paper. A ticker display gives brokers instant information about recent transactions. The brokers use this information when buying from and selling to other brokers.

The paper tickers print trades on **ticker tape.** You may have seen the ticker on television or in newspapers.

The New York Stock Exchange (NYSE) is the largest in the United States. The NYSE ticker is displayed in thousands of brokerage offices throughout the country. Learning how to read the NYSE ticker tape is not difficult.

Skills and Strategies

Each company that is traded on the NYSE is given a symbol for the ticker. Here are some examples.

Coca-Cola, KO
Ford, F
General Motors, GM
International Business Machines, IBM
Quaker Oats, OAT
Toys "R" Us, TOY
Xerox, XRX

Examine the ticker tape in Figure 5.1.

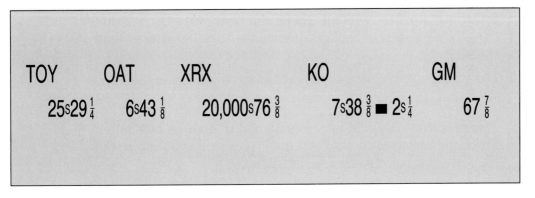

Figure 5.1 Ticker Tape

1. How many shares of Toys "R" Us stock were traded during the transaction shown on the ticker tape in Figure 5.1?

   Solution: Find the symbol TOY on the ticker tape. Look to the right and find 25s $29\frac{1}{4}$.

   If fewer than 10,000 shares are traded, the number to the left of the letter *s* indicates the number of groups of 100 shares traded.

100	number by which shares below 10,000 are grouped
× 25	number to the left of the *s*
2,500	number of Toys "R" Us shares indicated on ticker tape

   The ticker tape displays a trade of 2,500 shares of Toys "R" Us stock.

2.   How many shares of Xerox stock were traded during the transaction shown on the ticker tape in Figure 5.1?

Solution: Find the symbol XRX on the ticker tape. Look to the right and find 20,000s 76 $\frac{3}{8}$.

Sales of 10,000 or more shares are not displayed in groups of 100 shares. For such sales, the number to the left of the *s* indicates the exact number of shares traded.

The ticker tape displays a trade of 20,000 shares of Xerox stock.

3.   How many shares of General Motors stock were traded during the transaction shown on the ticker tape in Figure 5.1?

Solution: Find the symbol GM on the ticker tape. Notice that there is no *s* on the display; this means that 100 shares were traded.

The ticker tape displays a trade of 100 shares of General Motors stock.

4.   Stocks are usually sold at prices quoted in eighths of a dollar. Fractions are used to save space. For easier computation, the fractions can be converted to decimals.

Fraction	Decimal Equivalent	Monetary Amount
$\frac{1}{8}$	.125	$12\frac{1}{2}$ ¢
$\frac{1}{4}$	.25	25¢
$\frac{3}{8}$	.375	$37\frac{1}{2}$ ¢
$\frac{1}{2}$	.50	50¢
$\frac{5}{8}$	.625	$62\frac{1}{2}$ ¢
$\frac{3}{4}$	.75	75¢
$\frac{7}{8}$	.875	$87\frac{1}{2}$ ¢

At what price was one share of Quaker Oats stock traded as shown on the ticker tape in Figure 5.1?

Solution: Find the symbol OAT on the ticker tape. Look to the right and find 6s 43 $\frac{1}{8}$. The number to the right of the *s* gives the price of each share traded.

The ticker tape shows that one share of Quaker Oats stock was traded at the price of $43.125.

5. How many shares of Coca-Cola stock were traded during the transactions shown on the ticker tape in Figure 5.1?

   Solution: Find the symbol KO on the ticker tape. Look to the right and find 7s 38 $\frac{3}{8}$ ■ 2s $\frac{1}{4}$. This is interpreted as follows:

7s 38$\frac{3}{8}$	■	2s$\frac{1}{4}$
700 shares were traded at a price of $38.375 per share.		In another trade, 200 shares of Coca-Cola were traded at a price of $38.25 per share.

   The ticker tape shows that 900 shares of Coca-Cola were traded. Notice that the dollar amount ($38) was not repeated to save space.

6. What is the total value of the Quaker Oats trade indicated on the ticker tape in Figure 5.1?

   Solution:

   $$\begin{array}{rl} \$43.125 & \text{price of one share, expressed as a decimal} \\ \times\ 600 & \text{number of shares traded} \\ \hline \$25,875.00 & \text{total value of all shares} \end{array}$$

   The total value of the Quaker Oats trade is $25,875.

7. What is the total value of the Coca-Cola trades indicated on the ticker tape in Figure 5.1?

   Solution: Use the following calculator keystroke sequence.

   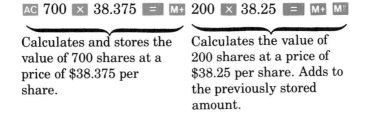

Calculates and stores the value of 700 shares at a price of $38.375 per share.	Calculates the value of 200 shares at a price of $38.25 per share. Adds to the previously stored amount.

The display should read 34,512.50

The total value of the Coca-Cola trades is $34,512.50.

Problems

Use the ticker tape in Figure 5.2 to answer Problems 1 through 10.

OAT   KO   XRX   IBM   GM

13s48 $\frac{1}{2}$ 17s39 $\frac{1}{8}$ ▪ 5s $\frac{1}{4}$ 74 $\frac{3}{4}$ 11,000s127   6s68 $\frac{5}{8}$

Figure 5.2   Ticker Tape

1. How many shares of Xerox Stock were traded?

✓ **2.** How many shares of General Motors stock were traded?

3. At what price per share were the shares of IBM stock traded?

✓ **4.** At what price per share were the shares of Quaker Oats stock traded?

5. What is the total value of the General Motors trade?

✓ **6.** What is the total value of the Xerox trade?

7. What is the total value of the IBM trade?

8. How many shares of Coca-Cola stock were traded?

9. At what prices were the Coca-Cola shares traded?

10. What is the total value of the Coca-Cola trade?

11. Represent the following trade on a ticker tape.
    900 shares of GM stock at $17.50 per share

✓ 12. Represent the following trade on a ticker tape.
    17,000 shares of IBM stock at $42.375 per share

13. Represent the following trade on a ticker tape.
    100 shares of GM stock at $73 per share

14. Represent the following trade on a ticker tape.
    9,200 shares of IBM stock at $137.25 per share

15. Harry sees the following display on a ticker tape:

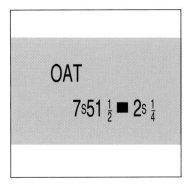

What is the total of this trade?

SECTION 3 • READING NEWSPAPER STOCK TABLES

There are millions of shareholders in the United States today. Many of these investors read the business section of the newspaper to help them make informed decisions. Every day the business section publishes trading information on thousands of corporations.

Skills and Strategies

Figure 5.3 is a sample of the New York Stock Exchange stock tables published after one trading day.

New York Stock Exchange Issues

52-Week High	52-Week Low	Stock	Div	Sales 100s	High	Low	Last	Chg.
12	10⅛	GGInc n	.25e	10	11½	11½	11½	+ ⅛
1⅝	¾	viGlbM	.12j	349	1¼	1	1⅛	...
5	2¼	viGlM pf	1.75j	36	2⅞	2⅝	2¾	...
10	8¼	GlbYld n	.41e	346	8¾	8⅝	8⅝	...
16	9⅛	GldNug		294	9½	9¼	9⅜	...
4	1⅛	GldN wt		153	1¼	1⅛	1⅛	− ⅛
46¾	29¾	GldWF	.20	77	36	35½	35¾	− ¼
47⅞	32⅛	Gdrich	1.56	27	44⅞	44⅝	44⅝	− ¼
50	29	Goodyr	1.60	6376	41¾	41¼	41¾	+ ⅛
22½	16⅜	GordnJ	.52	16	19⅜	19⅛	19¼	− ¼
21⅝	13¾	Gotchk n		12	20¼	20¼	20¼	+ ¼
32¾	14¾	Gould	.34j	460	17¾	17⅜	17⅝	− ⅛
60¾	45¼	Grace	2.80	537	50½	50	50⅛	− ⅛
32	19	Graco	.60	37	25⅝	25⅜	25⅜	...
46½	37¼	Graingr	.72	81	45½	45⅛	45½	+ ¼
24¾	13⅝	GtAFt s	.40	140	18⅝	18⅜	18½	+ ⅛
27¾	19¼	GtAtPc	.30	105	24¼	23⅞	24	− ⅛
27	15¼	GNIrn	2.72e	21	26⅝	26¼	26⅝	+ ⅜
68¾	39⅞	GtNNk	1.72	162	65½	65¼	65½	− ⅛
48¼	32	GtWFin	1.20	450	46⅝	46¼	46⅜	− ⅜
30⅞	19⅜	GMP	1.80	7	27	26⅞	26⅞	...
29¼	16⅜	GrenT s		433	25	24¾	24¾	− ⅛
38	27⅛	Greyh	1.32	293	32¼	31⅞	32	− ¼
57½	46	Greyh pf	4.75	z30	57½	57½	57½	+1
14	5¾	Grolier		217	10	9⅞	10	...
12¾	10	GrowGp	.30b	84	11⅝	11⅜	11½	+ ⅛
10¾	8¾	GthStk n		130	9	8¾	8⅞	− ⅛
10¾	4⅞	GrubEl	.08	502	5¼	5⅛	5⅛	...
33⅝	23	Grumn	1.00	119	26¼	26	26	− ⅛
28¾	26⅜	Grum pf	2.80	20	27⅝	27½	27⅝	+ ⅛
10¼	6⅜	Gruntal	.16	101	6⅞	6¾	6⅞	+ ⅛
29	21	Gulfrd s	.60	7	25¾	25⅝	.25⅝	...
72½	47⅝	GlfWst	.90	1600	64⅞	64½	64⅝	− ⅛
15⅜	10¼	GulfRs		126	11¼	11	11⅛	− ⅛
15	7	GlfStUt	.67i	1367	7⅝	7⅜	7½	− ⅛
53¼	27⅛	GlfSU pf	5.59e	25	28⅛	27⅞	28	...
32½	22½	GlfSU pr	3.85	11	25¼	25	25¼	+ ¼
34⅞	25	GlfSU pr	4.40	29	27⅛	26⅞	27	+ ⅛

52-Week High	52-Week Low	Stock	Div	Sales 100s	High	Low	Last	Chg.
20¼	12¾	Jostn s		299	18⅝	18⅛	18½	...
34¾	19⅝	JoyMfg	1.40	2565	34¾	34⅝	34⅝	...
19⅛	10¼	KDI	.30	15	13⅞	13¾	13¾	...
23⅞	17½	KLM	.69e	587	18⅝	18⅜	18⅜	− ¼
57⅜	33⅝	K mart	1.48	224	44⅜	43⅞	44	...
24¼	15⅝	KN En n	1.48	49	21	20⅝	20¾	− ¼
23¼	12½	KaisrAl	.15j	168	13⅝	13⅜	13⅝	+ ⅛
27⅜	13¼	KaisCe	.20	43	27⅜	27¼	27¼	...
25⅞	14½	KaiC pr	1.37	3	25½	25½	25½	...
13	6⅛	KanbE n	2.40	154	6⅞	6⅜	6¾	+ ¼
7½	2⅛	Kaneb	.14j	620	2¾	2½	2⅝	...
32¼	22⅛	KCtyPL	2.00	554	29⅝	29⅜	29⅜	...
43	32	KCPL pf	3.80	500	42½	42½	42½	...
52½	40	KCPL pf	4.50	210	51¾	51	51	−1½
26¼	19⅝	KCPL pf	2.20	1	25⅛	25⅛	25⅛	− ⅛
64⅞	46½	KCSou	1.08	74	48¾	48¼	48⅝	+ ⅜
16¾	11¼	KCSo pf	1.00	z50u	17	17	17	+ ½
23½	13½	KanGE	1.36	405	23⅜	23	23¼	+ ¼
65	39⅜	KanPLt	3.16	105	56¼	55⅝	55⅞	− ¼
29	22	KaPL pf	2.23	56	27¾	27½	27½	− ⅝
20½	12⅞	Katyln		21	14¾	14½	14¾	+ ¼
25⅞	10½	KaufB s	.33	65	18⅛	17¾	17¾	− ¼
139	83	Kauf pf	8.75	3	108	108	108	−1
58¾	32⅜	Kellog s	1.08	674	53⅛	52¾	53	− ⅛
26	15⅜	Kelwd s		67	23¾	23½	23¾	+ ⅜
26¾	20	Kenmt	1.00	90	24¼	24	24¼	...
24	14⅞	KPToy		68	18⅝	18⅜	18½	+ ⅛
48⅛	29⅞	KyUtil	2.52	86	41⅝	41⅜	41⅝	+ ¼
17½	11	KerrGl	.44	9	13⅜	13¼	13⅜	+ ⅛
34	23½	KerrMc	1.10	54	28⅞	28⅝	28⅝	− ⅛
30⅝	21	Keycp s	1.00	184	23½	23	23½	+ ½
9¾	3⅛	KeysCo		19	7⅛	7	7⅛	+ ⅛
19⅝	11⅜	Keylnt	.48b	21	14⅝	14⅝	14⅝	+ ⅛
38½	28⅜	Kidde	1.20	116	31⅞	31½	31½	− ⅛
88	70	Kid prB	4.00	x2	74⅛	74⅛	74⅛	− ⅜
92⅝	63⅜	KimbCl	2.48	77	82⅜	82⅛	82⅜	+ ⅛
19¼	9½	KngWd s		183	14	13⅝	14	+ ½
10	9¾	Klnwrt n		44	9⅞	9⅞	9⅞	...

Figure 5.3 New York Stock Exchange Sample

Examine the column headings shown at the top of page 223.

These column headings can be interpreted as follows:

52-Week High — The highest price at which a share of the corporation's stock was traded in the past year.

52-Week Low — The lowest price at which a share of the corporation's stock was traded in the past year

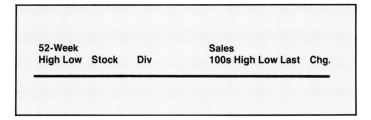

52-Week High Low	Stock	Div		Sales 100s High Low Last	Chg.

Stock — Abbreviation of the corporation's name

Div. — The annual dividend paid for one share of stock (Dividends will be discussed in Section 6.)

Sales 100's — The number of groups of 100 shares that were traded during the day's trading

High — The highest price at which a share of stock was traded during the day's trading

Low — The lowest price at which a share of stock was traded during the day's trading

Last — The price of a share at the last trade of the day; sometimes called the **close**

Chg. — The **net change**, or the difference between the previous trading day's closing price and the reported day's closing price

Look at the day's trading for the Goodyear Tire and Rubber Company.

52-Week High Low	Stock	Div	Sales 100s High Low Last	Chg.
50 29	Goodyr	1.60	6376 41¾ 41¼ 41¾	+ ⅛

Refer to Figure 5.3 as you follow through these questions and solutions.

1. What was the highest price paid for one share of Goodyear stock during the past year?

   Solution: Look in the column headed "52-Week High." The highest price paid for Goodyear stock during the past year was $50 per share.

2. How many shares of Goodyear stock were traded during the day's trading?

   Solution: Look in the column headed "Sales 100's."

   $$
   \begin{array}{ll}
   6{,}376 & \text{from "Sales 100's" column} \\
   \underline{\times\ 100} & \text{number by which shares are grouped} \\
   637{,}600 & \text{number of shares traded}
   \end{array}
   $$

   During the day's trading, 637,600 shares of Goodyear stock were traded.

3. Express as a decimal the lowest price paid for a share of Goodyear stock during the day's trading.

   Solution: Look in the column headed "52-Week Low."

   The lowest price paid for a share of Goodyear stock during the day's trading was $41\frac{1}{4}$ or $41.25 per share.

4. What was the net change?

   Solution: Look in the column headed "Chg."

   The net change was $+\frac{1}{8}$. This means that the last price for Goodyear *increased* $.125 over the previous day's last price. (A negative sign indicates a *decrease* in price.) Dots (....) in the Chg. column indicate a net change of zero.

5. At what price did Goodyear stock close on the previous day of trading?

   Solution: Look in the columns headed "Last" and "Chg."

   $$
   \begin{array}{ll}
   \text{Last} & 41\frac{3}{4} \\
   \text{Net Change} & +\frac{1}{8}
   \end{array}
   $$

Since net change is a positive number, the stock increased in value from the previous day. You must *subtract* to find the previous day's close:

$41\frac{3}{4}$ last price
$-\frac{1}{8}$ change

Use common denominators:

$41\frac{6}{8}$ last price
$-\frac{1}{8}$ change
$41\frac{5}{8}$ previous day's close

The previous day's close for Goodyear was $41\frac{5}{8}$, or $41.625.

Problems

Refer to Figure 5.3 to answer Problems 1 through 10. (These tables represent only one day's trading.)

1. Express the last price of Kmart stock as a decimal.

2. The B. F. Goodrich Corporation is listed as Gdrich in the stock tables. How many shares of Goodrich stock were traded?

✓ 3. Express as a decimal the lowest price of the year for Kaiser Aluminum (KaisrAl) stock.

4. Express as a decimal the net change for the Gulf and Western Corporation (GlfWst) stock.

5. How many shares of KLM stock were traded?

✓ 6. Express as a decimal the highest price of the year for Kellogg (Kellog) stock.

7. How many shares of the Grace Corporation stock were traded?

8. Did the last price of Grumman Aerospace Corporation (Grumn) stock increase or decrease when compared with the previous day's price? Explain your answer.

✓ **9.** Did the last price of Grolier stock increase or decrease when compared with that of the previous day? Explain your answer.

10. a. Express the net change for Kimberly-Clark (KimbCl) stock as a decimal.

    b. Did the last price of Kimberly-Clark stock increase or decrease when compared with the previous day's close?

    c. How many shares of Kimberly-Clark stock were traded?

    d. Express as a decimal the day's high for Kimberly-Clark stock.

    e. Express as a decimal the day's low for Kimberly-Clark stock.

✓ Complete the table.

Wednesday's Last Price	Wednesday's Net Change	Tuesday's Last Price
$31\frac{3}{4}$	$+\frac{1}{4}$	**a.**
$31\frac{3}{4}$	$-\frac{1}{4}$	**b.**
$17\frac{1}{8}$	$-\frac{5}{8}$	**c.**
$16\frac{5}{8}$	....	**d.**
$134\frac{1}{2}$	$-\frac{5}{8}$	**e.**
65	$+\frac{3}{8}$	**f.**

12. Is it possible for the high of the day to be the same as the low of the day? Explain.

13. Is it possible for the low of the day to be lower than the low of the year? Explain.

14. If the high price and the low price of the day are equal, must the net change be equal to zero? Explain.

15. If the last prices of two consecutive trading days are the same, must the net change (on the second day) be equal to zero? Explain. Yes; net change is the difference between two consecutive days' lasts.

SECTION 4 ● STOCK TRANSACTIONS

Most shareholders buy and sell stock in multiples of 100 shares. These groups of 100 shares are called **round lots.** A purchase of less than 100 shares is called an **odd lot.**

Suppose that you bought a round lot of 200 shares of Chrysler stock. Each day you follow the stock market tables, and you are pleased when the price of one share increases. Keep in mind, however, that you haven't made a profit until you actually *sell* the stock at a higher price than you paid for it. The price could go down; remember there is always a risk in buying or selling stock.

If the shares are sold at a higher price than you paid, you make money. The difference between the selling price of the shares and the purchase price of the shares is called **gross capital gain.**

If the shares are sold at a lower price than you paid, you lose money. In this case, there is a loss, or a **negative gross capital gain.**

Most high school students can only afford to purchase odd lots. As soon as you purchase stock — even if it's only one share — you begin your investment portfolio. A **portfolio** is a list of all the shares of stock you currently own. Every portfolio has the potential for a capital gain or loss.

Skills and Strategies

These sample problems will show you how to compute the purchase and sale of stock.

1. Last year Dr. Reyes purchased stock for $5,250. She sold the stock last week for $6,112. What was her gross capital gain?

   Solution:

$6,112	selling price
− 5,250	purchase price
$ 862	gross capital gain

   Dr. Reyes's gross capital gain was $862.

2. Last month Harry Johnson bought an odd lot for $700. Yesterday he sold the stock for $620 because he needed money for college books. What was his gross capital gain?

   Solution:

$700	purchase price
− 620	selling price
$ 80	difference between purchase price and selling price

   Since the selling price was lower than the purchase price, Harry Johnson sold at a loss.
   His gross capital gain was − $80.

3. Cathy Girolomo bought 300 shares of stock in an oil company at $51\frac{1}{4}$ per share. She sold them at $63\frac{1}{2}$ per share. What was her gross capital gain?

   Solution:

$51.25	purchase price of one share, expressed as a decimal
× 300	number of shares
$15,375.00	purchase price of 300 shares

$63.50	selling price of one share, expressed as a decimal
× 300	number of shares
$19,050.00	selling price of 300 shares

$19,050	selling price
− 15,375	purchase price
$ 3,675	gross capital gain

The following calculator keystroke sequence could be used to find Cathy Girolomo's gross capital gain:

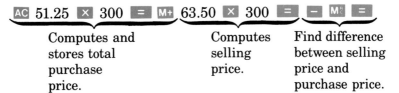

| Computes and stores total purchase price. | Computes selling price. | Find difference between selling price and purchase price. |

The display should read 3,675.

NOTE: If the capital gain is negative, the calculator will display the negative sign, indicating a loss.

Cathy Girolomo's capital gain was $3,675.

4. Debbie Lawson plans to buy seven shares of stock at $9.125 per share. How much should she pay for these shares?

Solution:

$ 9.125	price for one share
× 7	number of shares
$63.875	total

Debbie should pay $63.88 (rounded to the nearest cent) for the shares.

Problems

1. Two years ago Anita bought shares of stock for $7,300. Last week she sold the shares for $9,112. What was her gross capital gain?

✓ 2. Last summer Ralph bought a round lot of Meridien Corporation stock for $1,132. He sold the shares last week for $715. What was his gross capital gain?

3. Last month Lucy bought an odd lot of stock for $488.25. Yesterday she sold the stock for $412. What was her gross capital gain?

4. On Burt Weidermeier's last birthday, his wife, Anna Marie, bought him a round lot of Honeymoon Furs stock for $1,055.50. Last week he sold the shares for $2,000. What was his gross capital gain?

✓ **5.** Helen bought 17 shares of Shirley Pool Table Corporation stock at $10\frac{3}{8}$ per share. How much did she pay for the shares?

6. Don Faversham bought 210 shares in a typewriter company at $12\frac{3}{8}$ per share. How much did he pay for the shares?

✓ **7.** Last winter Joseph and Sally Walker bought 900 shares of stock at $7\frac{1}{2}$ per share. Yesterday they sold the shares at $11\frac{1}{8}$ each. What was their gross capital gain?

8. Last August Tom Condlin bought 700 shares of stock at $12\frac{1}{8}$ per share. Last week he sold them at $9\frac{1}{4}$ per share. What was his gross capital gain?

✓ **9.** Jane Lieberman bought 2,100 shares of Beepco stock at $19\frac{1}{2}$ per share. She sold the stock at $17\frac{7}{8}$ per share. What was her gross capital gain?

10. When her child was born, Juanita Waters set up a stock portfolio with the following purchases:
  37 shares in an automobile company at $75\frac{3}{8}$ per share
  200 shares in a steel company at $92\frac{3}{8}$ per share
  15 shares in an electronics company at 81 per share

Ten years later, Juanita sold the portfolio at these prices:
  automobile company shares at $69\frac{7}{8}$ per share
  steel company shares at 99 per share
  electronics company shares at $84\frac{1}{4}$ per share

  a. What was Juanita's gross capital gain on the automobile company shares?
  b. What was Juanita's gross capital gain on the steel company shares?
  c. What was Juanita's gross capital gain on the electronics company shares?
  d. How much money did Juanita gain from the sale of the portfolio?

SECTION 5 • STOCKBROKER COMMISSIONS

Stockbrokers perform services for their customers. Stockbrokers give investment advice, and they are licensed to buy and sell stocks. They are paid by investors for these services. Different brokers charge different fees.

Some people make their own investment decisions and do not rely on advice from stockbrokers. They still must buy and sell through brokers, but they may choose to use **discount brokers.** Discount brokers charge low fees to make stock transactions, but they don't give investment advice.

Most stockbrokers are paid a fee based on the value of the shares they buy or sell for a customer. This fee is often about 2% of the value of the shares traded, and it is called a **commission.** Brokers are not the only people paid by commission; many travel agents, car sales-people, and insurance agents are also paid by commission.

The commission you pay brokers reduces the profit you get when selling stock for more than you paid for it. Your **net proceeds** (income) is the amount of money you make after broker's fees are deducted. The net proceeds is the amount of profit you must report on your income taxes. Net proceeds can be negative if money was lost on the trade.

Skills and Strategies

Here you will learn how to determine fees paid to stockbrokers during the purchase or sale of stock.

1. Mary bought $3,000 worth of stock in an electric company. She has to pay her broker a 2% commission for the purchase of the stock. What is the broker's fee?

    Solution:

$3,000	total cost of the shares
× .02	broker's commission rate, expressed as a decimal
$60.00	broker's fee

    The broker's fee is $60.

2. Tony bought $2,300 worth of IBM stock. He has to pay a 2% commission to his broker. What is his total expense, including the broker's fee?

    Solution:

$2,300	total cost of the shares
× .02	broker's commission rate, expressed as a decimal
$46.00	broker's fee

$2,300	total cost of the shares
+ 46	broker's fee
$2,346	total expense

    Tony's total expense is $2,346.

3. Bill sold $2,750 worth of General Mills stock. The broker will take a 1% fee before sending Bill a check for the sale. How much should Bill receive?

    Solution:

$2,750	total selling price of the shares
× .01	broker's commission, expressed as a decimal
$27.50	broker's fee

$2,750.00	total selling price of the shares
− 27.50	broker's fee
$2,722.50	amount Bill should receive

    Bill should receive a check for $2,722.50.

4. At Luis' request, his broker purchased 70 shares of stock at $15\frac{1}{4}$ per share. Luis has to pay him a 2% broker's fee. What is Luis' total expense?

Solution:

$15.25	purchase price per share
× 70	number of shares
$1,067.50	total purchase price

$1,067.50	total purchase price
× .02	broker's commission rate, expressed as a decimal
$21.35	broker's fee

$1,067.50	total purchase price
+ 21.35	broker's fee
$1,088.85	total expense

Luis' total expense is $1,088.85.

The following calculator keystroke sequence could be used to find Luis' total expense.

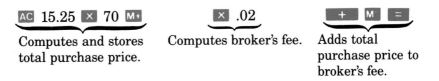

Computes and stores total purchase price.   Computes broker's fee.   Adds total purchase price to broker's fee.

The display should read 1,088.85.

5. Last year Trudy bought 60 shares of stock in a steel company at $39\frac{1}{4}$ per share. She had to pay a 2% fee to her broker. Yesterday she sold the 60 shares at $48\frac{1}{2}$ per share. She had to pay another 2% fee to her broker. What are her net proceeds?

Solution: Follow the steps in these stock purchase computations:

$39.25	purchase price of one share
× 60	number of shares
$2,355	total purchase price

$2,355	total purchase price
× .02	broker's commission rate, expressed as a decimal
$47.10	broker's fee

$2,355.00	total purchase price
+ 47.10	broker's fee
$2,402.10	total expense

These are the stock sale computations:

$48.50   selling price of one share
× 60   number of shares
$2,910.00   total selling price

$2,910   total selling price
× .02   broker's commission rate, expressed as a decimal
$58.20   broker's fee

$2,910.00   total selling price
− 58.20   broker's fee
$2,851.80   amount Trudy receives from sale of stock

$2,851.80   amount Trudy receives from sale of stock
− 2,402.10   Trudy's total expense
$ 449.70   net proceeds

Trudy's net proceeds are $449.70.

Problems

1. Lee purchased $7,200 worth of General Motors stock. She has to pay a 2% commission to her broker.
    a.   What is the amount of the broker's fee?
    b.   What is Lee's total expense?

✓ 2. Kwok purchased 200 shares of oil company stock at $17\frac{1}{8}$ per share. His broker charges a 1% commission.
    a.   What is the total purchase price for the 200 shares?
    b.   What is the broker's fee?
    c.   What is Kwok's total expense?

3. Kenneth purchased 90 shares of stock at $7\frac{1}{2}$ per share. His broker charges a 2% commission.
    a.   What is the total purchase price for the 90 shares?
    b.   How much money should the broker receive in commission?
    c.   What is Kenneth's total expense?

✓ 4. Eli sold 1,200 shares of stock at $6\frac{3}{4}$ per share. The broker will send Eli a check after deducting a 2% commission.
    a.   What is the total selling price for Eli's shares?

   b. How much money does Eli's broker receive for this sale?

   c. How much money should Eli receive from his broker?

5. Last year Elaine bought 200 shares of stock at $17\frac{1}{2}$ per share. Her broker charged her a 2% commission for the purchase. Last week Elaine sold the 200 shares at $24\frac{1}{2}$ per share. Her broker charged her a 1% commission for the sale.
   a. What was the purchase price for all 200 shares?
   b. How much money did the broker receive for the stock purchase?
   c. What was Elaine's total expense?
   d. What was the total selling price for Elaine's 200 shares?

   e. How much money did the broker receive for the stock sale?

   f. How much money did the broker send Elaine after deducting the commission?
   g. What were Elaine's net proceeds?
   h. What was Elaine's gross capital gain?

6. Two years ago Marta bought 100 shares of stock in an electronics company at 81 per share. She was charged a 2% broker's fee. To get some money to finish her college education, Marta had to sell her shares at $77\frac{3}{4}$ per share and pay a 2% broker's fee for this transaction.
   a. What was the total purchase price of the 100 shares?

   b. What was the broker's fee for the stock purchase?
   c. What was Marta's total expense?
   d. What was the total selling price of the 100 shares?
   e. What was the broker's fee for the sale of the stock?
   f. What were Marta's net proceeds?

✓ **7.** Last year Ravi bought 120 shares of stock in a musical instrument manufacturing company at $12\frac{1}{8}$ per share. Yesterday he sold all 120 shares at $18\frac{7}{8}$ per share. His broker charged him a 3% fee on *each* transaction. What are Ravi's net proceeds?

8. Last year Carole bought 600 shares in a clothing company at $3\frac{1}{2}$ per share. Last week she sold the 600 shares at $6\frac{1}{2}$ per share. What was her gross capital gain?

9. In Problem 8, Carole had to pay her broker a 2% fee on each transaction. What was her net proceeds?

✓ 10. Sylvan is a discount stockbroker. He charges a $\frac{1}{2}$% commission on all transactions.
   a. Express $\frac{1}{2}$ as a decimal.
   b. Express $\frac{1}{2}$% as an equivalent decimal.
   c. Is $\frac{1}{2}$% greater than or less than 1%?
   d. Does $\frac{1}{2}$% = 50%? Explain your answer.

SECTION 6 ● DIVIDEND INCOME

Sections 4 and 5 dealt with earnings from stock sales. Keep in mind that gross capital gain and net proceeds cannot be computed until the stock is actually sold. However, your stock portfolio *can* earn income before you sell the shares.

Shareholders in a corporation are entitled to part of the profits, since the shareholders own the corporation. Profit split among the shareholders is called a **dividend.** Money received from dividends is called **dividend income.** The board of directors of a corporation sets the **annual** (yearly) **dividend** for one share of stock, and this can be found under the column headed "Div." in a newspaper stock table. The board of directors can meet to change the dividend, but it is not changed often.

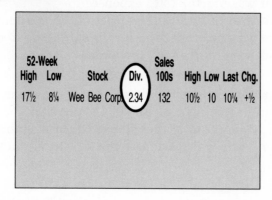

52-Week				Sales				
High	Low	Stock	Div.	100s	High	Low	Last	Chg.
17½	8¼	Wee Bee Corp	2.34	132	10½	10	10¼	+½

Your total dividend income depends on the number of shares you own. Some corporations do not pay a dividend because their profits are being used to improve the corporation. Some corporations do not pay a dividend because they have no profits; they are operating at a loss.

Dividend checks are mailed to shareholders **quarterly** (four times a year). They are usually sent at the beginning of each quarter — January 1, April 1, July 1, and October 1. Dividend checks can range in value from a few cents to thousands of dollars.

Skills and Strategies

Here you will learn how to compute dividend income.

1. Last year George received $728.80 in annual dividends from his shares in a software company. What amount did he receive on a quarterly dividend check?

   Solution: Divide the amount in annual dividends by the number of payments in one year.

   182.20 ← amount received on a quarterly dividend check
   4)728.80 ← total annual dividend

   There are four quarterly
   payments sent each year.

   The amount of George's quarterly dividend check was $182.20.

2. Ruth owns 300 shares of stock in the Toshico Corporation. Toshico pays an annual dividend of 74 cents per share. What annual dividend does Ruth receive for her 300 shares?

   Solution:

   300   number of shares
   × .74   annual dividend per share
   $222.00 total annual dividend for 300 shares

   Ruth receives an annual dividend of $222.

3. Sue owns 150 shares in the Chickesse Chicken Company, which pays an annual dividend of $1.14 per share. What is the amount of Sue's quarterly dividend check?

Solution: Use your calculator and the following keystroke sequence.

AC 150 × 1.14 =   ÷ 4 =

Computes the total   Computes the
annual dividend.   quarterly
                        dividend.

The display should read 42.75.

The amount of Sue's quarterly dividend check is $42.75.

Problems

✓ **1.**   Lenny receives $1,727 in annual dividends from his shares in the Base Steel Corporation. What amount does he receive on a quarterly basis?

2.   Wally is reviewing his yearly income before preparing his income tax form. Last year he received four dividend checks, each for $371.87. What was his total annual dividend?

3.   Francesca owns 200 shares in the Abramson Tool Company. Each share pays an annual dividend of $1.20.
  a.   What is Francesca's total annual dividend?
  b.   How much should she receive on a quarterly basis?

✓ **4.**   Darryl owns 750 shares of Brooklyn Beeper Company stock. The company pays an annual dividend of 16 cents per share. How much is Darryl's quarterly dividend check?

5.   Anita has 400 shares of El Camino stock, which pays an annual dividend of $1.62 per share. She received a quarterly dividend check for $118.23, and she thinks the company made an error on her check.
  a.   What is the total annual dividend for Anita's 400 shares?

  b.   What amount should she have received on her quarterly dividend check?
  c.   How much money does El Camino owe Anita?

✓ **6.** The amount of Barbara's car loan payment each month is $191.68. Barbara receives $2,268 per year in dividends from her Skylark Air stock.
   a. How much is Barbara's quarterly dividend check?
   b. What is Barbara's average dividend income per month?

   c. Does Barbara earn enough in dividends each month to pay her monthly car loan? Explain.

7. Harry and Ceil set up a stock portfolio for their grandchildren.
   Les owns 40 shares in the Somerville Company.
   Robbie owns 60 shares in the Sixties Corporation.
   Barbara owns 80 shares in the Type Company.
   Nancy owns 40 shares in the DiMonte Company.
   The annual dividend for one share of each stock is as follows:
   Somerville Company, $1.93
   Sixties Corporation, $.22
   Type Company, $1.30
   DiMonte Company, $2.10
   a. What is the annual dividend income for the 40 shares of Somerville stock?
   b. What is the quarterly dividend income for the 40 shares of Somerville stock?
   c. What is the annual dividend income for the 60 shares of Sixties Corporation stock?
   d. What is the quarterly dividend income for the 60 shares of Sixties Corporation stock?
   e. What is the annual dividend income for the 80 shares of Type Company stock?
   f. What is the quarterly dividend income of the 80 shares of Type Company stock?
   g. What is the annual dividend income for the 40 shares of DiMonte stock?
   h. What is the quarterly dividend income for the 40 shares of DiMonte stock?
   i. What is the combined annual dividend income for the grandchildren's stock portfolio?

8. Jessie owns 400 shares of Tellco Corporation stock. Each share pays an annual dividend of $1.70. How much should Jessie receive on a quarterly basis?

✓ **9.** Laura owns 60 shares of stock in the Slipstream Corporation. Each share pays an annual dividend of 80 cents. How much should Laura receive on a quarterly basis?

✓ **10.** Joel owns 200 shares in the Burden Tennis Equipment Corporation. He receives $840 in annual dividends.
   a. How much does Joel receive on a quarterly dividend check?
   b. How much is the annual dividend for one share of Burden Corporation stock?

SECTION 7 • CORPORATE BONDS

Are you familiar with United States government savings bonds? A **bond** is a loan agreement. When you purchase a city, town, or federal government bond, you are actually lending money. Governments borrow money to help pay for projects such as highways, transit systems, sewers, and other improvements. The government promises to pay back the money that it borrowed, plus **interest.** Interest is the extra money a borrower pays to a lender for the use of the lender's money.

People buy bonds because bonds pay interest. Investing in bonds is less risky than investing in stocks. The interest is predetermined and does not change.

Sometimes corporations need to borrow money to finance special projects. These corporations can borrow money from banks or sell bonds to the public. Corporate bonds are usually issued in $1,000 amounts. Each bond represents a $1,000 loan to a corporation. The amount of the loan (usually $1,000) is called the **face value** of the bond.

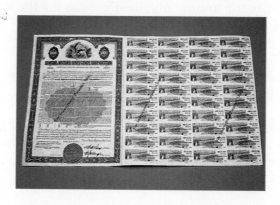

The face value must be paid to the owner of the bond on the date specified on the bond. This is the date of **maturity.** Interest payments are made twice a year, or **semiannually.** The bondholder must cut off a dated **coupon** (with the amount of interest shown) from the bond. This coupon can be cashed in at a bank.

Bondholders do not have to keep the bond until the maturity date; they can sell it at any time to another person. They use a broker to make the sale. The new bondholder receives all the interest from the coupons that remain. Bond quotations based on the previous trading day's sales can be found in the newspaper near the stock quotations.

Skills and Strategies

Here you will examine ways to determine interest on corporate bonds. Read each problem carefully.

1. Rick purchased a corporate bond that matures in 15 years. How many coupons are attached to the bond?

   Solution: Remember that interest on a corporate bond is paid semiannually.

15	number of years until maturity
× 2	coupons per year
30	total number of coupons attached

   Rick's bond has 30 coupons attached to it.

2. Louise bought a corporate bond that has 21 coupons attached to it. Each coupon is worth $47.25. How much interest would Louise receive if she held the bond until maturity?

   Solution:

$47.25	value of each coupon
× 21	number of coupons attached
$992.25	total interest received

   Louise would receive $992.25 in interest.

3. Although interest rates are most often expressed as percentages, you should change a percent to an equivalent decimal to multiply. For example, the Blackgold Oil Company pays 8.7%

interest on its corporate bonds. Suppose you had a $1,000 bond. How would you figure the interest for one year?

Solution:

$$\begin{array}{ll} \$1,000 & \text{face value of the bond} \\ \underline{\times\ .087} & \text{8.7\% expressed as a decimal} \\ \$87.00 & \text{interest for one year} \end{array}$$

You would earn $87 interest for one year.
You could also use the following calculator keystroke sequence.

$$\boxed{\text{AC}}\ \ 1{,}000\ \ \boxed{\times}\ \ 8.7\ \ \boxed{\%}$$

The display should read 87.

4. Write $8\frac{1}{4}\%$ as an equivalent decimal.

Solution: Recall that:

$$8\tfrac{1}{4}\% = 8.25\% = .0825$$

Change $\frac{1}{4}$ to an equivalent decimal.

Move the decimal point two places to the left.

The equivalent decimal of $8\frac{1}{4}\%$ is .0825.

5. Karen is planning to buy a $1,000 corporate bond that pays $7\frac{1}{2}\%$ annual interest. How much money would she receive in interest annually?

Solution: The interest rate is always based on the face value of the bond.

$$\begin{array}{ll} \$1,000 & \text{face value of the bond} \\ \underline{\times\ .075} & \text{decimal equivalent of } 7\tfrac{1}{2}\% \\ \$75.00 & \text{annual interest} \end{array}$$

Karen would receive $75 in interest annually.

6. Evan bought a $1,000 corporate bond that pays $69.40 in annual interest. How much is each semiannual coupon worth?

Solution:

$$34.70 \leftarrow \text{value of each coupon}$$
$$\text{two coupons per year} \rightarrow 2\overline{)69.40} \leftarrow \text{annual interest}$$

Each semiannual coupon is worth $34.70.

Problems

1. Enid bought a $1,000 corporate bond that matures in 17 years.
   a. How many coupons are attached to the bond?
   b. How much money must the corporation pay Enid when the bond matures after all interest coupons have been cashed in?

✓ 2. Steve purchased a $1,000 corporate bond that pays $6\frac{1}{4}\%$ interest per year.
   a. Express $6\frac{1}{4}\%$ as an equivalent decimal.
   b. How much interest should Steve receive annually from this investment?
   c. What is the value of a semiannual coupon for this bond?

3. Jean purchased a $1,000 bond from the Ward Corporation. The bond pays $11\frac{3}{4}\%$ annual interest. What is the value of a semiannual coupon for this bond?

4. Karen purchased a $1,000 Swarthout Corporation bond. The bond pays $9\frac{1}{2}\%$ annual interest, and there are 13 semiannual coupons attached to the bond.
   a. How much interest should Karen receive annually from this bond?
   b. What is the value of a semiannual coupon for this bond?
   c. How much interest will Karen collect if she keeps the bond until maturity?

✓ 5. Maureen is considering buying a $1,000 O'Dea Corporation bond. The bond pays 6.35% annual interest, and it matures in $9\frac{1}{2}$ years.
   a. Express 6.35% as an equivalent decimal.
   b. How much should Maureen receive in annual interest?

    c. What is the value of a semiannual coupon for this bond?

    d. How many coupons should be attached to the bond?
    e. How much interest will Maureen receive if she holds the bond until maturity?

✓ **6.** Complete the following chart for a corporate bond with a face value of $1,000.

Bond Interest	Equivalent Decimal	Annual Interest	Value of Each Semiannual Coupon
9%	a.	b.	c.
5%	d.	e.	f.
10%	g.	h.	i.
8.5%	j.	k.	l.
$11\frac{1}{4}$%	m.	n.	o.
5.4%	p.	q.	r.
9.8%	s.	t.	u.

7. Dr. Meredith purchased a $1,000 corporate bond that pays an annual interest rate of 6.38%. The bond will mature in 15 years.
    a. What is the annual interest on the bond?
    b. How many coupons should be attached to the bond?
    c. How much is each coupon worth?
    d. How much interest will Dr. Meredith receive if he holds the bond until maturity?

8. Henry Weintraub purchased a $1,000 corporate bond that pays interest at an annual rate of 8.55%. The bond matures in six years. How much interest will Henry receive if he holds the bond until maturity and withdraws the interest annually?

9. Bess purchased a $1,000 corporate bond from the Teitelbaum Corporation. The bond pays 9% interest per year, and it matures in $10\frac{1}{2}$ years. How much interest will Bess receive if she holds the bond until maturity and withdraws the interest annually?

10. Herman purchased a $5,000 corporate bond that matures in $12\frac{1}{2}$ years. It pays 7.5% interest per year. How many coupons should be attached to the bond?

● KEY TERMS

To find the definition of any term introduced in the chapter, refer to the Glossary in the back of this book.

annual dividend	net proceeds
annual reports	odd lot
board of directors	partnership
bond	personally liable
capital	portfolio
commission	profit
corporation	proportion
coupon	quarterly
discount brokers	round lots
dividend (div.)	sales 100
dividend income	semiannually
face value	shareholders
52-week high	shares of stock
52-week low	sole proprietorship
gross capital gain	stock
high	stockbroker
interest	stock certificates
last (close)	stock exchange
limited liability	ticker
low	ticker tape
maturity	trade
negative gross capital gain	transaction
net change (chg.)	

• REVIEW PROBLEMS

1. William, Barney, and Ethel plan to sell the partnership they own. William owns 70%, Barney owns 25%, and Ethel owns the remainder. If the partnership is sold for $675,000, how much money would Ethel receive as her share?

Use the ticker tape in Figure 5.4 to solve questions 2 and 3.

NEW   **ZRN**   **STN**

$7s41\frac{1}{2}$ $13s5\frac{1}{4}$ $31,000s14\frac{7}{8}$

Figure 5.4   Ticker Tape

2. What is the total value of the Zorn Corporation (ZRN) stock trade indicated on the ticker tape?

3. Catherine purchased the Stone Corporation (STN) shares indicated on the ticker tape. She has to pay her broker a 2% fee for the transaction. How much money does her broker receive?

4. On January 17 the Liverbird Corporation closed at $73\frac{7}{8}$ with a net change of $-2\frac{3}{4}$. At what price did Liverbird close on January 16?

5. Ted has been following the stock trading of the Ro-Bear Corporation. He has copied these numbers down from the Sales 100's column for the past five days:

    761
    3,512
    3,590
    4,411
    6,100

What is the average number of shares sold per day over the last five days?

6. Rachael bought 70 shares of Apple Airline stock at $68\frac{1}{8}$ per share. Five months later she sold all 70 shares at $75\frac{1}{4}$ per share. What was her gross capital gain?

7. Jesse bought $9,200 worth of stock in an automobile company. He had to pay his broker a 2% commission. Four months later he sold the stock for $10,800. Again, he paid his broker a 2% commission. What was Jesse's net proceeds?

8. Marianne bought 20 shares of stock in Porko Industries at $32\frac{1}{4}$ per share. Three years later she sold all 20 shares at $45\frac{5}{8}$ per share. Her discount broker makes 1% commission on all sales and purchases. How much did Marianne pay in broker's commissions?

9. Bank of New Merrick stock pays an annual dividend of $1.92 per share. How much would you receive in a Bank of New Merrick quarterly interest check if you owned 120 shares?

10. Alfred bought 11 corporate bonds. Each bond has a face value of $1,000 and pays 9.8% interest. If Alfred holds the bonds for eight years, what would be the total interest earned?

CHAPTER 6

USING GRAPHS TO DISPLAY BUSINESS INFORMATION

SECTION 1 ● BAR GRAPHS

Maria Kayanan is president of the Recycling Club at her school. She has been asked to prepare a report for the Town Council, which is considering an increase in funds for their town's recycling program. She realizes that the council members are busy and that a concise report presenting information in a well-organized, easily read format would work best. Maria decides to use graphs to convey the information quickly and efficiently.

To present data on the different kinds of materials that the club collects for recycling, she decides to use a **bar graph.** This kind of visual aid has vertical and horizontal border lines called **axes** (the plural of **axis**) and uses bars to show the individual data. Maria uses the **vertical axis** to show the number of pounds of recycling material that the club collected last year. The individual bars, which rest on the **horizontal axis,** can represent the different kinds of materials collected last year. She makes a rough draft of a bar graph that looks like the one which follows and is pleased with the results.

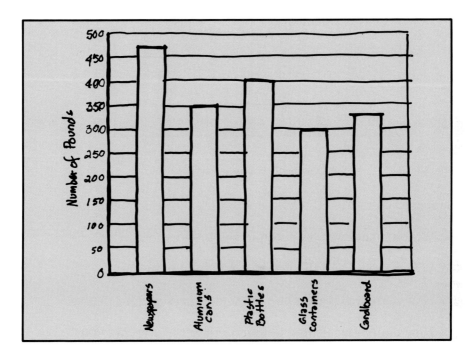

Skills and Strategies

In business, bar graphs are often used to present information to stockholders at meetings or in newspaper articles and annual reports. Before making investments, people in business rely on information which is often displayed in a bar graph.

Study the information in Table 6.1 at the top of page 250.

Chevrolet Passenger Car Production, U.S. Plants, 1983

Model	Number Produced
Full-sized Chevrolet	91,228
Corvette	28,174
Monte Carlo	124,926
Celebrity/Malibu	244,480
Camaro	193,118
Citation	86,878
Cavalier	308,461
Chevette	201,841

Table 6.1   Source: *World Almanac & Book of Facts, 1985,* Newspaper Enterprise Association, Inc.

Suppose you needed the answers to the following questions:

- Which model was produced in the greatest quantity?

- Which model had the lowest production figure?

- How many models had production figures under 115,000?

- How many models had production figures over 200,000?

- Which model had production figures between 150,000 and 200,000?

To answer these questions, you must carefully look up and down the list several times. Imagine how difficult it would be if the list was several pages long. Now look at the same information displayed on a bar graph in Figure 6.1 on page 251. Notice how much easier it is to use the bar graph to answer the questions.

- The Cavalier model was the leader in numbers produced.

- The Corvette model had the lowest production figure.

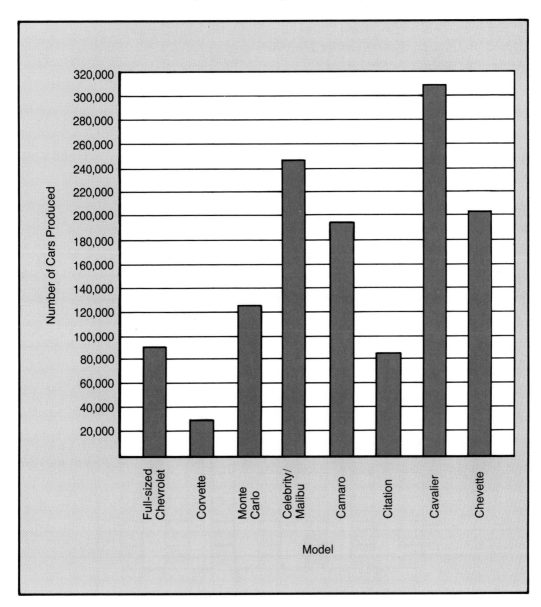

Figure 6.1 Chevrolet Passenger Car Production, U.S. Plants, 1983

- Three models — full-sized Chevrolet, Corvette, and Citation — had production figures under 115,000.

- Three models — Chevette, Cavalier, and Celebrity/Malibu — had production figures over 200,000.

- Only Camaro had between 150,000 and 200,000 cars produced.

As you can see, a bar graph presents information in an efficient, easy-to-read format.

The horizontal and vertical "borders" of a bar graph are called axes. Each axis must be clearly labeled. The graph should have a descriptive title so that the reader can determine what the two axes are comparing.

Examples 1–3 in this section refer to the bar graph shown in Figure 6.2.

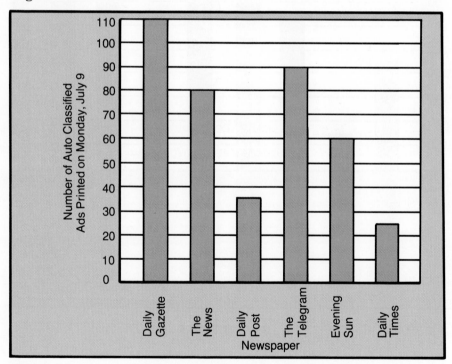

Figure 6.2 Number of Auto Classified Ads, Monday, July 9

1. How many automobile classified ads appeared in the *Daily Gazette?*

Solution: Find the bar labeled *Daily Gazette* on the horizontal axis. Find the number on the vertical axis that corresponds to the top of the bar.

The *Daily Gazette* published 110 automobile classified ads.

2. How many automobile classified ads appeared in the *Daily Post?*

    Solution: Notice that the top of the *Daily Post* bar corresponds to a number halfway between 30 and 40 on the vertical axis.

    The *Daily Post* published 35 automobile classified ads.

3. How many more automobile classified ads were published in *The Telegram* than in the *Evening Sun?*

    Solution:

90	number of ads in *The Telegram*
− 60	number of ads in the *Evening Sun*
30	difference

    The Telegram published 30 more ads.

4. Construct a bar graph using the following information:

    Number of Bumped Passengers on Four New Year's Day Airline Flights

Flight Number	Number of Bumped Passengers
Flight 18	5
Flight 353	3
Flight 1007	7
Flight 602	9

    Solution: Using a ruler and a sheet of graph paper, draw the horizontal axis. Under this axis show the flight numbers. Space them evenly under the axis with an equal amount of blank space in between. Draw the vertical axis at the left side, connecting with the horizontal axis. Where the lines meet, show a zero. Then list the number of bumped passengers, reading up from one to nine. Leave equal space between the numbers. (See Figure 6.3.)

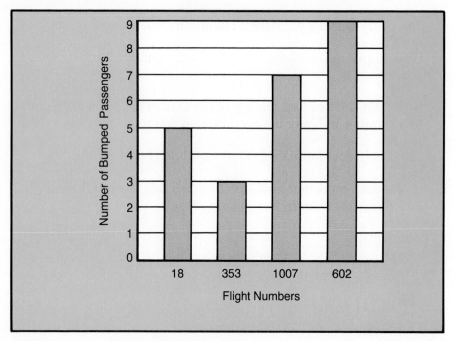

Figure 6.3   Number of Bumped Passengers on Four New Year's Day Airline Flights

Problems

Use Figure 6.4 at the top of page 255 to answer questions 1–6.

✓ **1.**   How many shares of KenCo stock were traded on Wednesday?

2.   How many shares of KenCo stock were traded on Friday?

✓ **3.**   How many more shares of KenCo stock were traded on Thursday than on Monday?

4.   How many fewer shares were traded on Friday than on Tuesday?

5.   On what two days were the same number of shares traded?

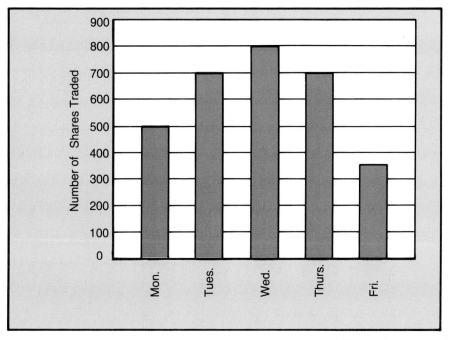

Figure 6.4 Number of KenCo Shares Traded During Week of August 10

✓ **6. a.** What was the total number of KenCo shares traded during the week?

b. What was the average number of shares traded per day during the week of August 10?

c. What was the median number of shares traded during the week of August 10?

d. What was the mode number of shares traded during the week of August 10?

Use Figure 6.5 at the top of page 256 to answer questions 7–13.

7. What county has the greatest number of stockbrokers?

8. What county has the least number of stockbrokers?

✓ **9.** What is the total number of brokers in the five neighboring counties?

10. How many counties have more than six brokers?

11. How many more brokers does York County have than Mexico County?

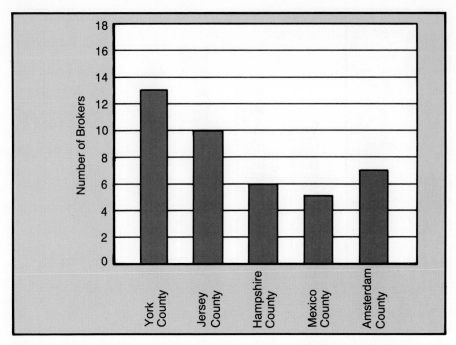

Figure 6.5 Number of Stockbrokers in Five Neighboring Counties

✓ **12.** How many fewer brokers does Amsterdam County have than Jersey County?

13. Arrange the counties in increasing order according to the number of brokers.

14. Construct a bar graph using the following information. (Be sure to label your graph.)

Factory Outlets in Russell County

Type of Outlet	Number of Outlets
Clothing	16
Dinnerware	2
Furniture	7
Leather	5
Shoes	3

15. Construct a bar graph using the following information. (Be sure to label your graph.)

Catalog Phone Orders on Six Holidays

Holiday	Number of Catalog Phone Orders
Mother's Day	2,000
Memorial Day	2,400
Father's Day	1,500
Independence Day	1,600
Labor Day	900
Veterans' Day	3,600

SECTION 2 • LINE GRAPHS

In preparing her report for the Town Council meeting, Maria decides that she should include a graph showing how much recycled material the club collected each month. She hopes that this information will impress the council members because the amount collected each month was greater than the amount collected the previous month. Since **line graphs** are often used to depict changes over a period of time, she decides to use a line graph.

Skills and Strategies

Line graphs are frequently found in newspapers and news-magazines. The reader gains information from a line graph quickly and easily. Businesses use line graphs to report sales figures, earnings, dividends, and other information in annual reports and other documents.

Examine the line graph in Figure 6.6.

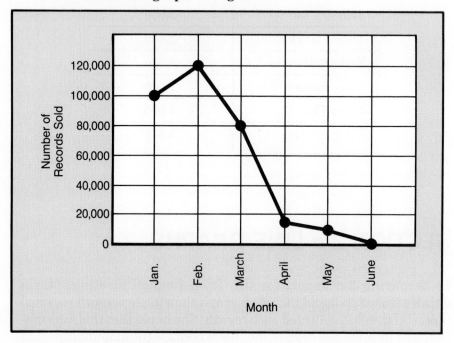

Figure 6.6 Semiannual Sales Report of the Penguin Record Company

Note that at a glance you can detect a downward trend in record sales. By using the axes, you can obtain more specific information. Line graphs are also useful in reporting weather statistics, sports statistics, and current-events data.

It is important to clearly label the horizontal and vertical axes of a line graph. In most line graphs, the horizontal axis represents different points in time. Questions 1–3 refer to the line graph in Figure 6.6.

1. How many Penguin records were sold in March?

   Solution: On the horizontal axis, find the line labeled *March*.

Follow that line up to the point representing March sales. This point is the intersection of the vertical line through March and the horizontal line through 80,000.

The Penguin Record Company sold 80,000 records in March.

2. How many records were sold by Penguin Records in May?

Solution: Note that the record sales for May are halfway between 0 and 20,000.

The Penguin Record Company sold *approximately* 10,000 records in May. Although the *exact* number of sales cannot be determined from the line graph, reasonable approximations can quickly be determined.

3. What is the only month that had a sales increase over the preceding month?

Solution: Look for a "peak" in the graph to see where sales increases occurred. February's sales showed an increase over January's sales.

February is the only month that had a sales increase over the preceding month.

4. Construct a line graph using the information given in the following table.

Stock Sales of the Watson Corp.
During a One-Week Period

Date	Shares of Stock Sold (in hundreds)
May 1	55
May 2	10
May 3	5
May 4	20
May 5	30

Solution: Use a ruler and a sheet of graph paper. Draw the horizontal and vertical axes. Be sure to leave enough room to label the axes.

Determine a numbering pattern for the vertical axis. In the solution shown in Figure 6.7, the space between two consecutive horizontal lines represents 500 shares of stock sold.

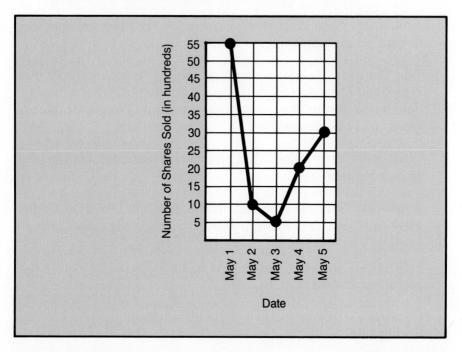

Figure 6.7   Stock Sales of the Watson Corp. over a One-Week Period

5.   It is possible to present two groups of data using the same set of axes. Look at the line graph in Figure 6.8 at the top of the next page. Two separate line graphs could have been used, but the single graph allows the reader to compare the two real-estate brokers easily. How many homes were sold by each broker in 1988?

Solution: The solid line represents Friendly's sales, and the broken line represents Pudgy's sales. Look for the year 1988 on the horizontal axis. Use the vertical axis to determine the number of houses sold by each real-estate broker.

In 1988 Friendly's sold 14 houses and Pudgy's sold 11 houses.

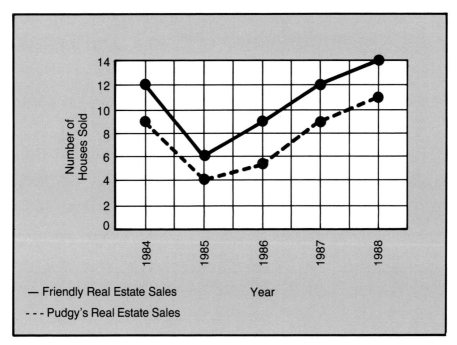

Figure 6.8 Housing Sales of Two Local Real Estate Brokers, 1984–1988

6. Examine the line graph in Figure 6.9 below.

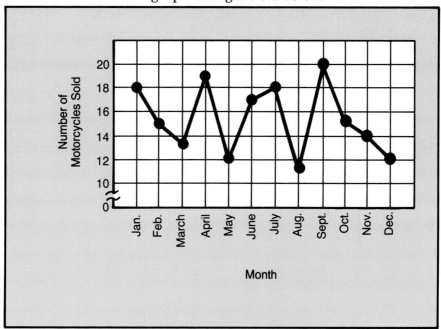

Figure 6.9 Woody's Cycle Shop: Last Year's Sales

How many motorcycle sales are represented by the space between consecutive horizontal lines?

Solution: Examine the horizontal lines labeled 10, 12, 14, 16, 18, and 20. Each line represents an increase of two motorcycles from the line below it. Note that because there were no months with fewer than 10 sales, it was unnecessary to have lines depicting 2, 4, 6, or 8 sales. To show that these lines were left out, there is a break in the vertical axis above the zero line. Keep this in mind when reading or interpreting line graphs.

Problems

Use the line graph in Figure 6.10 to answer Problems 1–6.

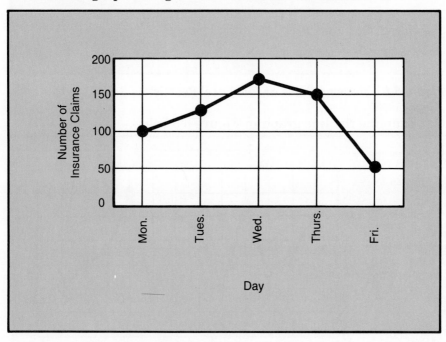

Figure 6.10 Insurance Claims Submitted to Derham Insurance Co. Last Week

✓ 1. How many claims were submitted to the Derham Insurance Company on Thursday?

2. How many claims were submitted to the Derham Insurance Company on Monday?

3. On which days did the Derham Insurance Company receive fewer than 150 claims?

4. Approximately how many claims were filed on Wednesday?

5. Did the total number of claims for the week exceed 550?

✓ **6.** How many fewer claims were filed on Friday than on Thursday?

Use the line graph in Figure 6.11 to answer Problems 7–13.

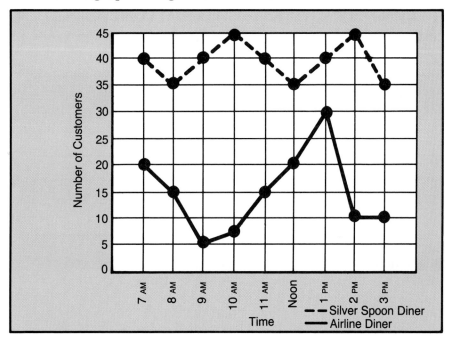

Figure 6.11 Number of Customers in Two Local Diners on May 30

7. How many customers were in the Silver Spoon Diner at 2 PM?

✓ **8.** How many customers were in the Airline Diner at 8 AM?

9. How many customers were in both diners at 9 AM?

✓ **10.** What is the average number of customers in both these diners at 1 PM?

11. Between which two hours did both diners show a decrease in the number of customers?

12. Which diner had more customers at 1 PM?

✓ 13. How many more customers were in the Silver Spoon Diner at 11 AM than were in the Airline Diner at 11 AM?

14. Construct a line graph using the following information.

Number of Blair High School Students Who Use Calculators

Year	Number of Students
1973	20
1976	60
1979	95
1982	95
1985	90
1988	164

15. Construct a line graph using the following information.

Number of Automobile Batteries Sold at Art's Auto Supplies

Month	Number of Batteries
October	7
November	6
December	7
January	13
February	30
March	18

SECTION 3 ● CIRCLE GRAPHS

After Maria made rough drafts of the bar graph and the line graph for her report, she wondered whether she should include another kind of visual aid. In math class she had learned that a **circle graph** is often constructed to present data given in percentages. Maria decided that her report should include a circle graph showing the percentage of the combined total of recycled material that each kind of collected material represented. She used her calculator to figure out each percentage, and she added the percentages to make sure that the sum was 100 percent. She then used a compass and a protractor to draw the circle graph. As you can see, Maria is determined to make her report look professional as well as be informative.

Skills and Strategies

When information can be presented as percentages, a circle graph is often drawn. The parts of a circle graph are expressed as percents, and the parts together equal 100 percent.

Circle graphs can be found in newspapers, magazines, annual reports, and many other publications. The simple format makes a circle graph easy to read and interpret.

Consider the following situation: Infotron Industries has sales offices throughout the country. In order to improve communications, the board of directors set up five regional offices. The percentage of Infotron employees working in each region is shown below:

Western Region, 30%
Eastern Region, 25%
Southern Region, 20%
Northern Region, 15%
Central Region, 10%

Each employee works in one of the company's five regions. Since 100 percent of Infotron employees work within the five regions, the sum of the percentages listed for those regions must be 100% (30% + 25% + 20% + 15% + 10% = 100%).

Figure 6.12 illustrates the distribution of Infotron employees by region.

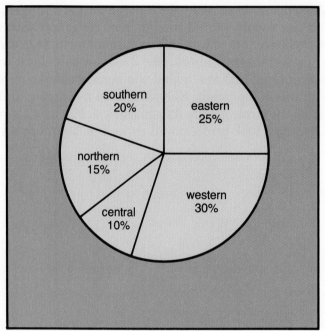

Figure 6.12   Distribution of Infotron Employees by Region

Note that the five radii in this circle divide 100% of the area of the circle into five regions, called **sectors.** The percentage of the total area of each sector corresponds to the percentage of Infotron employees working in the given region. Since 30% of the employees work in the Western Region, the sector labeled *Western* contains 30% of the area in the circle.

Read the following examples, which refer to Figure 6.12.

1.   Infotron employs 524,600 workers throughout the country. How many employees work in the Western Region?

   Solution:

524,600	total number of employees
× .30	Western region percentage expressed as decimal
157,380	30% of 524,600

There are 157,380 people employed by Infotron who work in the Western Region.

2. How many more employees work in the Eastern Region than in the Central Region?

Solution: The following keystroke sequence can be used to solve this problem.

AC 524,600 ☒ .10 M+ 524,600 ☒ .25 ⊟ M⁺ ⊟

| Calculates and stores 10% of 524,600 in memory. | Calculates and displays 25% of 524,600. | Subtracts number stored in memory from display. |

The display should read 78,690.
There are 78,690 more Infotron employees working in the Eastern Region than there are in the Central Region.

Problems

Jack was assigned a consumer math project to follow the stock market action of Shannon Industries for 60 days. He made the circle graph in Figure 6.13, shown at the top of page 268, to illustrate the daily net-change quotations for Shannon shares.

1. For how many days did Shannon stock show a positive net change?

✓ 2. For how many days did Shannon stock show a negative net change?

✓ 3. For how many days did Shannon stock show zero net change?

The circle graph in Figure 6.14 at the bottom of page 268 illustrates last year's annual income for E-Z Rest Inns, Inc. During the year of the report, the total income of the company was $1,940,000.

4. How much money did the company spend on new construction?

5. How much profit did the company make?

6. How much more money did the company spend on salaries than on advertising?

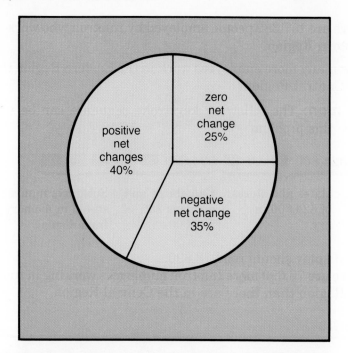

Figure 6.13 Net Changes for Shannon Corp. over 60 Days

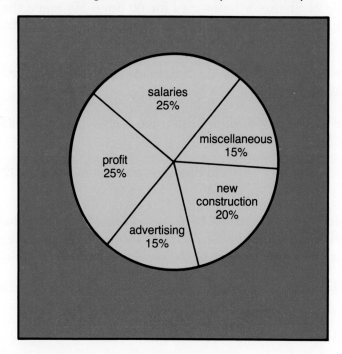

Figure 6.14 Annual Income for E-Z Rest Inns, Inc.

The circle graph in Figure 6.15 illustrates Allison's transportation stock portfolio, which consists of 1,200 shares of stock.

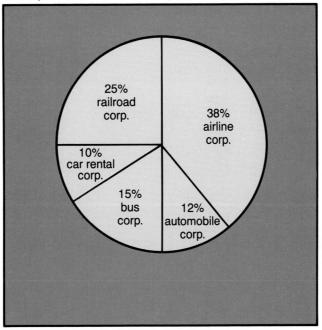

Figure 6.15 Transportation Stock Portfolio

7. How many shares of airline corporation stock does Allison have in her portfolio?

8. How many shares of automobile corporation stock are in her portfolio?

9. What percentage of the portfolio is made up of railroad, car rental, and bus corporation stocks combined?

10. How many more shares of railroad corporation stocks than car rental corporation stocks are in the portfolio?

SECTION 4 • PICTOGRAPHS

Maria also decided to make a **pictograph** for her report. Pictographs are found in magazines and newspapers. This kind of visual aid presents mathematical information in an attractive form.

Skills and Strategies

Examine the pictograph shown in Figure 6.16.

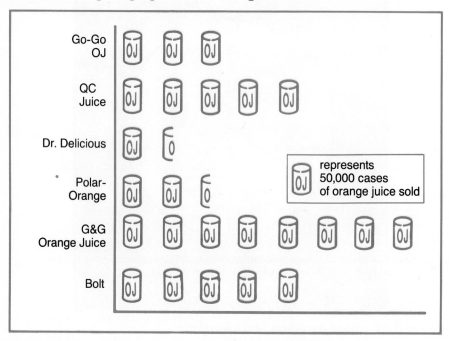

Figure 6.16 July Sales for Six Orange Juice Manufacturers

This pictograph reports sales figures for the orange juice industry. The picture that is repeated instantly identifies the subject matter of the pictograph. You can immediately see that Figure 6.16 deals with orange juice. Look through some magazines at home or in the library to see how many pictographs you can find.

These examples refer to Figure 6.16.

1. How many cases of Go-Go OJ were sold in July?

   Solution: Each symbol represents 50,000 cases of juice. The Go-Go OJ sales are represented by 3 symbols.

50,000	number of cases represented by each symbol
× 3	number of symbols pictured
150,000	total Go-Go OJ sales

   In July, 150,000 cases of Go-Go OJ were sold.

2. How many cases of Polar-Orange were sold in July?

Solution: Since each symbol represents 50,000 cases of juice, half of a symbol represents 25,000 cases of juice. The Polar-Orange sales are represented by $2\frac{1}{2}$ symbols.

100,000	number of cases represented by 2 symbols
+ 25,000	number of cases represented by half of a symbol
125,000	total number of Polar-Orange cases sold

OR

Recall your fraction skills from Chapter 1.

$$2\frac{1}{2} \times 50,000 = 125,000$$

Number of symbols representing Polar-Orange sales.   Each symbol represents 50,000 cases sold.

3. What percentage of the total juice sales for all six companies are QC Juice sales?

Solution:

$$\frac{5}{25}$$ number of cans representing QC Juice sales
    total number of cans

The following calculator keystroke sequence can be used to convert the fraction to a percent.

AC 5 ÷ 25 %

The display should read 20.

QC Juice sales represent 20% of the total sales of the six corporations.

Problems

Use the pictograph in Figure 6.17 at the top of page 272 to answer questions 1–5.

1. How many flights were canceled on Monday?

2. How many more flights were canceled on Wednesday than on Friday?

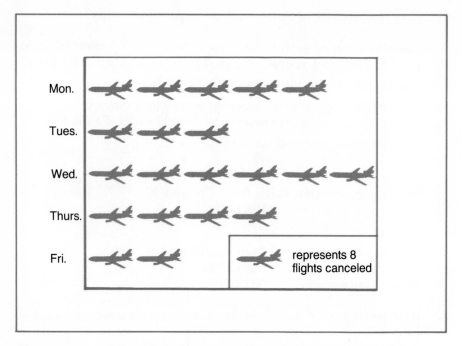

Figure 6.17 Airline Flights Canceled During a Snowy January

3. How many flights were canceled in all?

✓ **4.** What is the average number of flights canceled per day?

✓ **5.** What percentage of all canceled flights were canceled on Thursday?

Use the pictograph in Figure 6.18 at the top of page 273 to answer questions 6–10.

6. How many Forrester guitars were sold last year?

✓ **7.** How many Lawson guitars were sold last year?

✓ **8.** What was the total number of guitars sold by the five leading manufacturers last year?

9. What was the average number of guitars sold by all manufacturers?

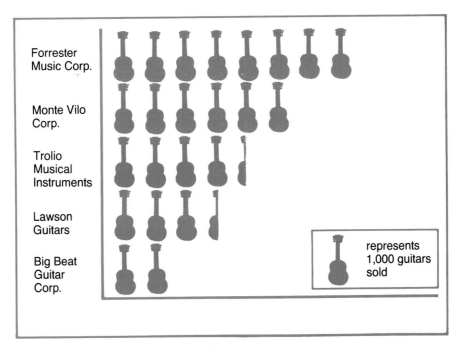

Figure 6.18 Guitar Sales of Five Leading Manufacturers for Last Year

10. Construct a pictograph by using the following information.

Number of Television Sets Sold
During One Week

Selling Days	Sets Sold
Monday	10
Tuesday	8
Wednesday	2
Thursday	4
Friday	8
Saturday	4
Sunday	7

Let each ⊡ represent two television sets sold.

SECTION 5 ● GRAPHING STOCK TRENDS

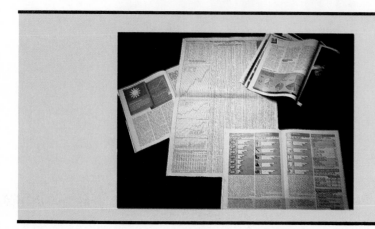

Different types of magazines and newspapers rely on bar graphs, line graphs, circle graphs, and pictographs to help illustrate important articles. The financial pages of the newspaper often feature a different type of graph that is designed to give you a great deal of information.

Skills and Strategies

Figure 6.19 on page 275 shows this week's trades of Dowling Corporation stock.

The vertical axis is broken into two parts. This axis gives you several pieces of information, including the day's high, the day's low, the close (last) price, and the day's sales in hundreds of shares. As an investor, you can easily see trends in stock trading by keeping a graph such as the one in Figure 6.19.

Look for similar graphs in business newspapers and magazines. The graphing skills from the previous sections will help you interpret graphs from the financial pages of different publications.

Use Figure 6.19 for questions 1–4 which appear on page 276.

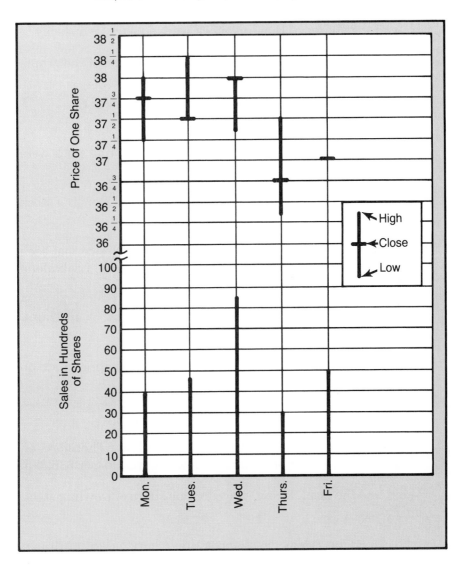

Figure 6.19 Stock Prices of Dowling Corporation During a One-Week Period

1. How many shares of Dowling stock were sold on Wednesday?

   Solution: Use the bar graph on the lower portion of the graph.

100	the axis shows sales in 100s
× 85	number of groups of 100 shares sold Wednesday
8,500	number of shares sold Wednesday

   On Wednesday, 8,500 shares of Dowling Corporation stock were sold.

2. What was the highest price paid for one share of Dowling stock on Thursday?

   Solution: Use the upper portion of the graph. Notice that each drawing displays a high, a low, and a closing price. Look along the Thursday line.

   The highest price paid for one share of Dowling stock on Thursday was $37\frac{1}{2}$, or $37.50.

3. What was the lowest price for one share of Dowling stock on Thursday?

   Solution: Look along the Thursday line.

   The lowest price is midway between $36\frac{1}{4}$ and $36\frac{1}{2}$. Therefore, on Thursday the low for one share of Dowling was $36\frac{3}{8}$, or $36.375.

4. What was the last (closing) price for one share of Dowling stock on Friday?

   Solution: The Friday graph has a single horizontal line drawn at the $37 mark. Therefore, on Friday the high, the low, and the close for Dowling were all the same.

   On Friday the last price for one share of Dowling stock was $37.

Problems

Use Figure 6.20 at the top of page 277 to answer questions 1–10.

1. How many shares of Omnipop stock were sold on April 3?

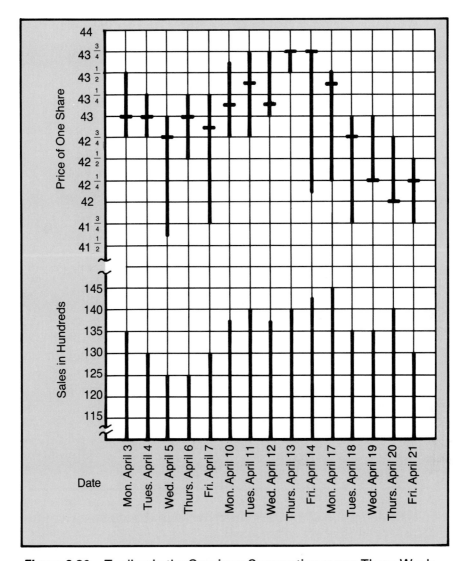

Figure 6.20   Trading in the Omnipop Corporation over a Three-Week
Period in April

2. Approximately how many shares of Omnipop stock were
    sold on April 12?

✓ 3. What was the total number of shares sold during the week of
    April 3?

4.   What was the average number of shares sold per day during the week of April 17?

✓ 5.   What was the day's high for Omnipop on April 11?

6.   What was the day's low for Omnipop on April 5?

✓ 7.   **a.**   What was the day's close for Omnipop on April 13?
   b.   What was the day's close for Omnipop on April 14?
   c.   What was the net change for Omnipop on April 14?

8.   **a.**   What was the day's last for Omnipop on April 4?
   b.   What was the day's last for Omnipop on April 5?
   c.   What was the net change for Omnipop on April 5?

✓ 9.   **a.**   On which days did the day's low equal the day's last?

   b.   On which days did the day's high equal the day's last?

10.   **a.**   What was the highest price for one share of Omnipop for the three-week period?
   b.   What was the lowest price for one share of Omnipop for the three-week period?

● KEY TERMS

To find the definition of any term introduced in the chapter, refer to the Glossary in the back of this book.

axes	line graphs
axis	pictograph
bar graph	sectors
circle graph	vertical axis
horizontal axis	

● REVIEW PROBLEMS

Use the bar graph in Figure 6.21 at the top of the next page to answer questions 1 and 2.

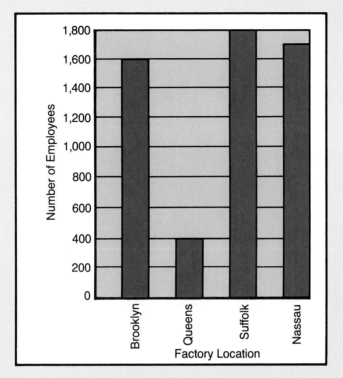

Figure 6.21   SUDOCON Employees

1. What is the average number of workers that SUDOCON employed at the four factory locations?

2. What is the median number of employees at the four SUDOCON factories?

Use the line graph in Figure 6.22 at the top of page 280 to answer questions 3 and 4.

3. How many more computers were sold in June than in January?

4. What percentage of all computers sold were sold in June?

Use the circle graph in Figure 6.23 at the bottom of page 280 to answer questions 5 and 6.

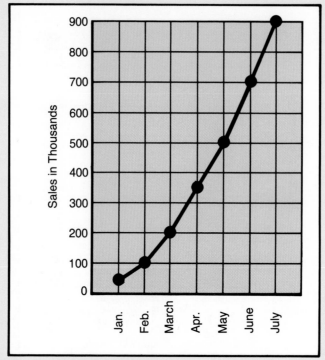

Figure 6.22 Computer Sales of Datakey Computers

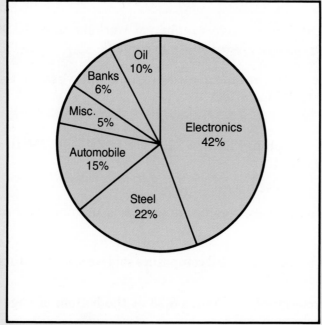

Figure 6.23 Stock Investments

Figure 6.23 illustrates the stock portfolio of the Kane Investment Corporation. Kane invested a total of $980,100.

5. How much money was invested in electronics stocks?

6. How much more money was invested in steel stocks than in automobile stocks?

Questions 7 and 8 refer to the Figure 6.24.

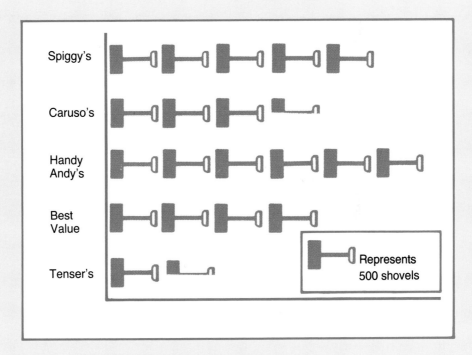

Figure 6.24   Snow Shovel Sales at Five Hardware Stores Last Winter

7. What was the total number of snow shovels sold by the five hardware stores?

8. What percentage of the total sales of snow shovels were Best Value's sales?

9. Construct a bar graph using the following information.

Local Stock Brokers and Their Clients

Stockbroker	Number of Clients
Harry Tenser	390
Steven Rozales	200
Pat Reynolds	140
Janet Saevitz	220
Susan Mitchell	330

10. Construct a line graph using the following information.

Sales of Synthesizers at Sound Foundations Music Outlets

Year	Number of Synthesizers Sold
January	25
February	61
March	180
April	473
May	810
June	1,003
July	1,130

TOPIC *3* ENHANCE/ADVANCE

1. Look at a newspaper containing the New York Stock Exchange quotations. Find a corporation that you are interested in following. Set up a chart to record the high, low, and closing prices of your stock for the next four weeks. Look in the paper daily to record the *prices*. When you have completed the chart, graph the results as shown in Chapter 6, Section 5. Report your findings to the class.

2. Look at a newspaper containing the New York Stock Exchange quotations. Find a corporation that you are interested in following. Set up a chart to record the daily sales in hundreds of this stock for the next four weeks. Look in the paper daily to record the *sales*. When you have completed the chart, graph the results as shown in Chapter 6, Section 5. Report your findings to the class.

3. Combine projects 1 and 2 on one chart. Graph the results on one set of axes, as shown in Chapter 6, Section 5. Report your findings to the class.

4. Pick a corporation you are interested in. Find the corporation's address on one of its products, or go to a library to find it. Write a letter requesting a copy of the corporation's annual report. Also request any information about various products and services.

5. Write a letter to the New York Stock Exchange requesting a list of the publications that the Exchange offers. The address is:

   New York Stock Exchange
   Publications Department
   11 Wall Street
   New York, NY 10003

   Share your materials with your classmates.

6. Write a letter to the New York Stock Exchange requesting a piece of ticker tape and a list of New York Stock Exchange corporate names and the symbols that are used on the ticker tape. Share your materials with your classmates.

7. Find out the address of a local stockbroker. (Use the phone book or go to a library.) Compile a list of questions you would

like to ask him or her. Call the broker and request an appointment for a short meeting. Interview the broker and report your findings to the class.

8. Find out the address of a local stockbroker. (Use the phone book or go to a library.) Talk to your teacher about setting up a class session featuring the stockbroker as guest speaker. Invite the broker to visit your class. Collect stock market questions that your classmates would like answered. During the session, you should conduct the question-answer period and present each question to the broker. Remember to write a thank-you letter to the broker after the session. Have the letter signed by the entire class.

9. Discuss stocks and savings with your parents, relatives, or guardians. Decide with them if you can purchase a reasonable amount of stock. If so, visit a broker with one of them and make a stock purchase. (Good luck!) Report this adventure to the class.

10. Discuss savings bonds with your parents, relatives, or guardians. Visit a bank, talk to a bank employee, and compare the interest rate on U.S. Government Savings Bonds with the interest rate that is being paid on a savings account.

TOPIC *3* MANIPULATIVE ACTIVITY

GRAPHING STOCK PRICES ON A GEOBOARD

Pick a stock that you would like to follow for the next few weeks. Each day you are going to look up the high, low, closing price, and sales in hundreds, and place this information on a special item you are going to make. It's called a geoboard.

Directions: You will need electrical tape, a $2'' \times 4''$ wooden stud, a hammer, box of nails, paint, a few very large rubber bands, and a few regular size rubber bands. Review Section 5: Graphing Stock Trends, from Chapter 6.

1. Cut the wooden stud to a six-foot length. You may want to paint it a light color at this point.

2. Wrap a piece of electrical tape around the stud, three feet from the top of the stud (the middle of the six-foot piece).

3. Draw a line across the piece, $2''$ from the top.

4. Continue drawing lines every $2''$ until you reach the bottom of the stud.

5. Hammer in rows of three evenly spaced nails on each $2''$ line from the top until you hit the piece of tape in the middle.

6. Hammer in one centered nail on each $2''$ line from the tape until the bottom of the stud.

7. Label the top rows as you labeled the vertical axes in Section 5. Find the current price of your stock, and label every other $2''$ line in $\frac{1}{4}, \frac{1}{2}, \frac{3}{4}$, and dollar amounts. Remember to skip a line between each line you label.

8. Label the bottom rows with numbers representative of the sales in hundreds action of your stock. Label the last row zero.

9. Label the axes by using signs made on paper and stapled to the wood.

You will use the rubber bands on a daily basis to display the action of your stock to the class. See the diagram and the photograph on pages 286 and 287.

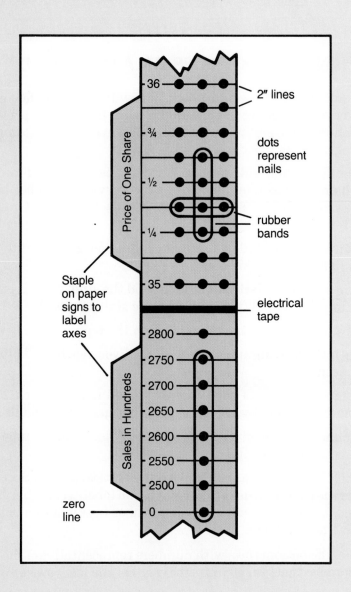

The top rubber bands show that the high was $35\frac{5}{8}$, the low was $35\frac{1}{4}$, and the close was $35\frac{3}{8}$. The bottom rubber band shows the sales in hundreds was 2750, which means 275,000 shares were sold.

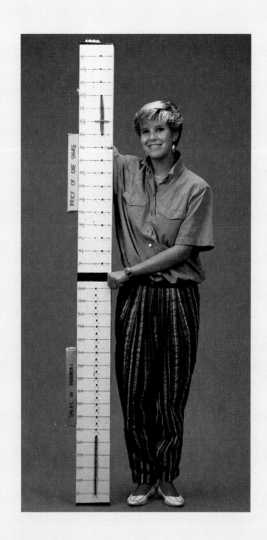

TOPIC 3 COMPUTER APPLICATION

BAR GRAPHS

At the end of a trading day, each stock can be identified as belonging to one of the following three categories:

Up   The stock closed at a higher price per share than it did on the previous trading day.

Down   The stock closed at a lower price per share than it did on the previous trading day.

Unchanged   The stock closed at the same price per share as it did on the previous trading day.

Knowing the number of stocks in each of the three categories gives you a good idea of market trends, or how the stock market is doing. The UP, DOWN, and UNCHANGED information for a trading day can be found in the business section of most newspapers.

Directions: In this computer application, you are to keep track of these three categories for one full week (Monday through Friday trading days). Keep in mind that each day's trading information will appear in the following day's newspaper.

If necessary, follow the start-up procedures for your computer which are found in Appendix A. Select Topic 3 titled *Bar Graphs* from the Main Menu. Follow the instructions on your computer screen to complete the following questions. Do not write in this book. Put your answers on a piece of paper.

Questions 1 through 5 refer to the *chart* on your screen only.

1. Which day had the most stocks closing DOWN?

2. Which day had the greatest difference between the number of stocks closing DOWN and the number of stocks closing UP?

3. On what day of the week did the largest daily number of stocks closing UNCHANGED occur?

4. What two days of the week had the most similar UP, DOWN, and UNCHANGED numbers?

5. On what day of the week did the least number of stocks close UP?

Questions 6 through 10 refer to the *bar graph* only.

6. Which day had the least stocks closing DOWN?

7. Which day had the greatest difference between the number of stocks closing UNCHANGED and the number of stocks closing UP?

8. On what day of the week did the largest daily number of stocks closing UP occur?

9. What two days of the week had the least similar UP, DOWN, and UNCHANGED numbers?

10. On what day of the week did the most number of stocks close UNCHANGED?

Now that you have ended the computer program, answer the following question. Was it easier to answer stock questions when the information was presented in chart form or bar graph form? Explain your answer.

TOPIC *4*

CONSUMER CREDIT

Sales clerks often ask whether you are paying with cash or a credit card. You've been learning all about paying with cash. But what about credit? Credit is a promise to pay in the future for what you buy or borrow today. Credit buying has advantages and disadvantages. Credit lets you enjoy purchases while you are paying for them. But if you use credit too often or without thinking, you may find that you have more bills to pay than cash to pay them with. If this happens to you often, then credit is not for you. But if you plan before you shop, credit can be a way to pay for an expensive purchase. Even if you now pay only with cash, you need to know how credit works in order to take advantage of installment plans, loans, and credit cards.

CHAPTER 7

BUY NOW/PAY LATER

SECTION 1 • BEGINNING A CREDIT HISTORY

Martin has a chance to participate in a cross-country bicycle tour. He would love to see the country, but he has a problem: his bicycle is too heavy. It's a three-speed bike he's had for ten years. The bike is great for riding to and from school, but it will make traveling 80 miles a day very difficult. He has saved some money, but not enough to pay for a new ten-speed touring bicycle. Is there any way he could get the bicycle in time to take advantage of this once-in-a-lifetime opportunity? Martin needs to find a way that he can buy now and pay later.

There are two ways that goods and services can be purchased. The first is buy now, pay now. You pay for the item when you purchase it. The second way to purchase goods and services is buy now, pay later. With this method, you pay for the item after you already have it. Using a buy-now, pay-later plan is called using **credit**. Martin can buy his bicycle if he can establish credit.

There are many goods and services that are commonly bought using credit. For example, every time you use electricity, you are using credit. You use the electricity before paying for it. If you have newspapers delivered to your house and pay at the end of the week, you are buying the newspapers on credit. People who use charge cards and those who take out loans are using credit. Try to think of some more examples of credit.

Any type of credit is based on honesty. The organization that is giving credit believes that the consumer intends to repay the debt. Organizations or people that give or extend credit are called **creditors.** People who use credit are called **debtors.** Debtors are responsible for paying back all the money they owe their creditors.

Martin decides to buy his bicycle on credit. However, he needs to look carefully at the advantages and disadvantages of using credit.

Advantages

- You don't have to wait until you can pay in full to purchase goods and services. Without credit, you would have to save for weeks, months, or even years to make certain purchases.

- You can shop without having to carry large sums of money. This is both convenient and safe.

- You can take advantage of sales even if you don't have cash available.

- You receive a written record of your purchases. This is helpful for income tax and warranty purposes.

- You can order merchandise over the telephone.

- You are better able to handle financial emergencies.

- You receive advance notice of sales from stores in which you've established credit.

Disadvantages

- There is usually an extra cost (called the **interest** or the **finance charge**) when using credit.

- You may spend more than you planned because you aren't limited to the cash you have on hand.

- If you do not make payments on time, merchandise you bought on credit can be **repossessed** (taken back by the creditor due to lack of payment).

An overwhelming majority of Americans use credit; possibly they feel that the advantages outweigh the disadvantages. However, not everybody can get credit. Creditors must determine the credit worthiness of anyone who applies for credit. If you apply for credit, creditors will use the following financial indicators to evaluate your application:

1. **Assets.** Assets are everything you own. They include items such as your home, personal possessions, and bank accounts. Creditors determine the value of these items.

2. **Earning Power.** Earning power is your ability to earn money now and in the future. Creditors are obviously interested in your income. They are also concerned about your expenses such as rent, insurance, and money you owe to other creditors.

3. **Credit Rating.** A credit rating is your credit "report card." The credit rating gives creditors information on how you've met past financial obligations. These reports are kept on file at **credit**

reporting agencies. These agencies compile financial records of all users of credit. These records are made available to creditors to help them evaluate applicants.

These three indicators help creditors judge your ability to repay debts.

Martin wants to use credit to buy his bicycle, but he has few assets, so he is going to try to use his earning power and credit rating to get credit. If you think you might want to use credit, it is a good idea to begin to establish a good credit rating right now. While in high school, you can do several things that will help improve your credit rating.

- Open a savings account.

- Get a job.

- Open a checking account.

- Pay all bills on time.

In the future, when you have a full-time job, you can improve your credit rating in several ways.

- Take out a loan and make all required payments.

- Use a credit card responsibly.

- Pay your rent and utility bills on time.

Remember, using credit is a privilege and a responsibility. If credit was not available, most people would not be able to purchase cars, homes, and other costly items.

Skills and Strategies

Managing your money wisely is very important. You may want to save ahead in order to pay cash for your purchases. Or you may want to take your purchases and pay them off at a certain rate each week or month. Here are some examples of each method.

1. Jessica wants to buy a $400 stereo system for her car. She is saving $25 a week toward this purchase. In how many weeks will she have enough money to get the car stereo?

Solution: Divide:

$$\begin{array}{r} 16 \leftarrow\text{number of weeks} \\ \text{weekly savings} \rightarrow 25\overline{)400} \leftarrow\text{cost of stereo system} \end{array}$$

Jessica will need 16 weeks to save $400. Notice that for the 16 weeks, she will be without a car stereo. If she purchased the stereo with credit, she could get it immediately.

2. Ronnie purchased a used drum set from his friend Earl. He agreed to pay $440 for the set, but he is paying for it at the rate of $80 a week. How many weeks will it take Ronnie to pay for the set?

Solution: Divide:

$$\begin{array}{r} 5.50 \leftarrow\text{number of weeks} \\ \text{weekly payment} \rightarrow 80\overline{)440.00} \leftarrow\text{cost of drum set} \end{array}$$

The quotient 5.50 shows that Ronnie will pay for the set after 5.5, or $5\frac{1}{2}$, weeks. (Actually, 6 weeks rounded up.)

3. Leslie needs money to have his pickup truck painted. His take-home pay is $1,700 a month, but he must spend $900 on rent, about $175 on car expenses, about $200 on food and miscellaneous expenses, and around $150 on utilities. Approximately how much money can Leslie save toward the paint job each month?

Solution: Find the approximate sum of Leslie's monthly expenses.

$$\begin{array}{rl} \$\ 900 & \text{rent} \\ 175 & \text{car expenses (approximate)} \\ 200 & \text{food and miscellaneous (approximate)} \\ +\ 150 & \text{utilities (approximate)} \\ \hline \$1,425 & \text{approximate monthly expenses} \end{array}$$

$$\begin{array}{rl} \$1,700 & \text{monthly take-home pay} \\ -\ 1,425 & \text{approximate monthly expenses} \\ \hline \$\ 275 & \text{approximate monthly savings} \end{array}$$

Leslie can save approximately $275 per month toward the paint job.

Problems

Round up your answers to the nearest full week.

√ **1.**   Courtney is planning to go to Alaska during her summer vacation. The round-trip plane fare is $600. She can save $40 per week for the plane tickets. In how many weeks will she have enough money for the tickets?

2.   Darren used credit to purchase a $500 set of tires for his van. He is going to pay $60 each week toward the cost of the tires. In how many weeks will he finish making payments?

3.   Ed saw a guitar on sale for $800. He decided to buy it on credit. He also bought a case at a cost of $200, and he paid 4% sales tax on his purchases. He pays $40 each month on the guitar and case.
   a.   What was the total cost of the guitar and case, including tax?
   b.   How many months will it take Ed to repay this amount?

√ **4.**   Alicia agreed to pay $700 for the used computer she bought recently. She gets paid every two weeks, and she pays $35 from each paycheck toward the cost of the computer.
   a.   How many paychecks will she need to receive to repay the $700?
   b.   How many weeks will she work to pay for the computer?

5.   Aiden, Christopher, and Gregg are sharing the cost of an exercise bicycle. The bicycle costs $630 plus 6% sales tax. How much should each person contribute?

6.   Stephanie is saving money to go on the junior class trip to Canada. The trip will cost $550. She can manage to save $45 each week. How many weeks will she need to save enough money for the trip?

✓ **7.** Ryan had his car painted at a cost of $750 plus 6% sales tax. He is paying $60 each week for the paint job. How many weeks will it take Ryan to repay the cost?

8. Helene and Paul are sharing the cost of exercise equipment for their home. The equipment cost $1,720 plus 8% sales tax. How much should each person pay?

✓ **9.** Jennifer's summer camp charges $480 per summer. She can save $20 per week. The full payment is due in three months.
   a. How many weeks will it take Jennifer to save the money?

   b. Will she be able to save the money within three months?

10. Jethro bought a saxophone on credit. The total cost of buying the saxophone on credit is $1,400. He pays $30 each week toward the cost of the instrument. Will he have repaid his debt within a year?

SECTION 2 • INSTALLMENT PURCHASES

Martin was able to buy his new bicycle on credit. He found a bicycle that would be perfect for his trip. The store agreed to accept Martin's payment on credit. He paid some money right away. He also signed an agreement stating he would pay a certain amount of money each month until he had paid for the bike. There was an added charge for the privilege of paying by credit, but Martin was happy. Credit made his cross-country trip possible.

Some stores offer creditworthy customers the convenience of credit through an **installment plan**. The customer pays for merchandise over a scheduled period of time. The customer must pay *part* of the selling price at the time of purchase. This part is called the **down payment.** The scheduled payments are usually made on a monthly basis and are called **installments.**

Installment buyers are charged a fee for the privilege of using this "easy-payment" plan. This fee is called **interest** or **finance charge.** It is added to the cost of the merchandise. The consumer must decide if the convenience of installment buying outweighs the extra cost. Installment buyers sign an agreement that specifices the down payment, interest, monthly payments, and payment schedule. Remember, before you sign any agreement, be sure you understand all the terms used in the agreement.

Skills and Strategies

Here you will learn how to compute charges associated with installment buying.

1. Ricardo is interested in purchasing a refrigerator for $750 on the installment plan from Stan's Appliance Store. The store requires a 10% down payment. How much is the down payment?

    Solution: Multiply the price by the down payment rate.

$750	cost of the refrigerator
× .10	down payment rate, expressed as an equivalent decimal
$75.00	down payment

    Ricardo must put down $75 to purchase the refrigerator.

2. Heather purchased a $400 color television on the installment plan. She signed an installment agreement requiring her to pay $100 down and 12 monthly installments of $30 each.
    a.   What was the total cost of the color television, with interest?

    Solution: Find the total amount of the monthly payments.

$ 30	each monthly payment
× 12	number of installments
$360	total amount of the monthly payments

    Add the down payment.

$360	total amount of the monthly payments
+ 100	down payment
$460	cost of the television, with interest

    The total cost of Heather's television, with interest, was $460.
    b.   How much interest did Heather pay?

Solution:

$460   cost of the television, with interest
− 400   cash price of the television
$ 60   interest

Heather paid $60 interest. It cost her $60 to use the installment plan.

3. Ellie bought a $700 pair of skis on the installment plan. She had to make a down payment of $100 and pay 12 monthly installments of $61 each. How much interest will she be paying?

Solution: Use the following calculator keystroke sequence:

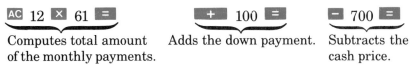

Computes total amount   Adds the down payment.   Subtracts the
of the monthly payments.   cash price.

The interest amounts to $132.

Problems

1. Monique wants to purchase a $4,700 central air conditioning system for her house. She can't afford to pay cash, so she is using the installment plan, which requires a 15% down payment. How much is the down payment?

✓ 2. Craig wants to purchase a small boat from Cousin's Boating House. The boat costs $1,420. Craig signs an installment agreement requiring a 20% down payment. How much is the down payment?

3. Jean bought a $1,980 snowplow on the installment plan. The installment agreement included a 10% down payment and 18 monthly installments of $116 each.
   a. How much is the down payment?
   b. What is the total amount of the monthly payments?
   c. How much will Jean pay for the snowplow on the installment plan?
   d. What is the finance charge?

✓ 4. Linda bought a $1,500 washer and dryer from Royal Ranch Laundry Supplies. She signed an installment agreement requiring a 12% down payment and monthly payments of $118 for one year.

   a. How much is the down payment?

   b. How many monthly payments must Linda make?

   c. What is the total amount of the monthly payments?

   d. How much will Linda pay for the washer and dryer on the installment plan?

   e. How much interest will she pay?

  5. Robert bought a $2,300 bobsled on the installment plan. He made a $450 down payment, and he has to make monthly payments of $93.50 for the next two years. How much interest will he pay?

✓ **6.** Ari purchased a $420 microwave oven on the installment plan. He made a 20% down payment and agreed to pay $19 per month for the next two years. How much interest will he pay?

  7. Alice bought a $620 exercise bicycle on the installment plan. She made a $100 down payment, and she agreed to pay $61.51 per month for the next year. How much interest will she pay?

  8. Bernie bought a refrigerator at a special sale. The refrigerator sold for $986 cash, but Bernie bought it on the installment plan. No down payment was required. Bernie has to pay $59 per month for the next two years. What is the finance charge for Bernie's installment purchase?

✓ **9.** Lillian purchased a $670 guitar from the Smash Music Store ten months ago. She paid 10% down and has been making monthly payments of $60. Her installment agreement is for one year.

   a. How many payments does she have left?

   b. How much money does she still owe Smash?

   c. What is the total amount of interest Lillian will pay on her installment purchase?

 10. Peterson's Appliance Store requires a down payment of one-third on all installment purchases. Norton's Home Appliance Center requires a down payment of 30% on all installment purchases. Which down payment rate is lower?

SECTION 3 • LENDING INSTITUTIONS

Suppose that you were going to buy a new car. Would you buy the first car you looked at? Probably not. You would most likely want to go to several dealers to compare prices. The same model could vary greatly in price from dealer to dealer.

Once you found the car you wanted at the best price, you might need to borrow money to pay for the car. A common way to borrow money is to take out a **loan.** The money you borrow must be paid back, plus an additional amount called interest. Interest is the fee you pay for using the money. Organizations that make loans are called **lending institutions.** The most common types of lending institutions are banks, credit unions, consumer finance companies, pawnbrokers, and life insurance companies.

Now suppose you have decided to take out a loan to pay for your new car. Just as you shopped around for the best price on the car, you should also shop around for the best loan possible. The interest charged on the money you want to borrow could vary greatly from lender to lender. You should go to several lending institutions and compare their offers.

When interest is expressed as a percent, it is called the **interest rate**, or the **annual percentage rate (APR).** There are laws set by the federal government that control all loans, but each lending institution has its own policies.

1. **Banks.** Most consumers apply for their loans at banks. There are different types of banks. Businesses deal mostly with **commercial banks**, while consumers bank at **savings banks**, or **savings and loan associations.** Banks offer good interest

rates, but they require loan applicants to have a good credit rating.

2. **Credit Unions.** A credit union is an organization that provides financial services for its members only. The members of the credit union have something in common, such as the place they work, where they live, or the school they attend. Members deposit money in a credit union account. This money is made available to members who apply for loans from the credit union. The interest rate is often lower than the interest rate of a bank, but you must be a member to borrow money.

3. **Consumer Finance Companies.** Consumer finance companies take more risks than banks or credit unions do. They will give loans to consumers whose credit ratings might not be acceptable at some other lending institutions. Finance companies charge higher interest rates than banks because they are willing to take more risks.

4. **Pawnbrokers.** Some people go to pawnshops to borrow money from pawnbrokers. The pawnbroker requires a borrower to leave personal property until the borrower pays back the loan, with interest. The personal property is called **collateral.** If the loan is not repaid on time, the pawnbroker notifies the borrower that the loan payment is due. The collateral could then be sold by the pawnbroker, who keeps part of the money made from the sale. The pawnbroker keeps an amount equal to the value of the loan plus interest. Any extra money from the sale is returned to the borrower. Pawnbrokers specialize in **single-payment loans** — the borrower pays back the entire loan, plus interest, at one time. Borrowers don't usually make monthly payments.

5. **Life Insurance Companies.** Life insurance companies make loans to their policyholders only. The amount of money that can be borrowed is limited. This limit is based on the amount of life insurance purchased and the length of time over which premiums have been paid. Life insurance companies can offer reasonable interest rates because there is little risk involved. If loans made by life insurance companies are not repaid, the amount owed can be deducted from the total value of the borrower's life insurance policy.

Regardless of where you shop for your loan, the **Equal Credit Opportunity Act** requires the creditor to treat you fairly. It is illegal to discriminate against applicants on the basis of race, sex, religion, marital status, age, nationality, or because a person may be receiving public assistance. Complaints against creditors can be filed with the federal government. You can find a listing of approprite federal agencies and their addresses in the library.

If your loan application is turned down, you are protected by the **Fair Credit Reporting Act.** The lending institution must give you the reason, in writing. If the loan has been denied because of a poor credit rating, the lending institution must give you the name of the credit reporting agency that supplied your credit history. You are entitled to see a copy of your credit rating free of charge if you have been denied credit. You can get a copy of your credit history for a fee if you haven't been denied credit.

When shopping for a loan, your main concern should be to compare the annual percentage rates (APRs) of the lending institutions you visit. Before you shop, decide how much you want to borrow and the length of time you need to repay the loan. Once you've determined these facts, keep in mind that the loan with the lowest APR will have the lowest interest for identical loans.

Skills and Strategies

In these examples, you will learn how to compare loan rates. Read each problem carefully.

1. Tina plans to take out a three-year, $5,000 loan. She compares the APRs of two local banks. North Savings Bank offers her a 13% APR, and Valley Bank offers her a 12.7% APR. Which bank charges less interest for the loan Tina wants?

   Solution: Tina must determine which APR is lower. Examine the numerical parts of the two APRs.

   Since 12.7 is less than 13, 12.7% APR is lower than 13% APR. Valley Bank offers Tina the lower APR.

2. Luke has decided to take out a two-year loan for $12,000. He checks out the APRs at two local banks. Shannon National Bank offers an APR of 11.65%, and Glen Shore Bank offers an APR of 11.7%. Which bank charges less interest?

Solution: Write the APRs as decimals.

Shannon National Bank, .1165
Glen Shore Bank,   .117

It is easier to compare two decimals if they have the same number of decimal places.

Recall that you can annex a zero to the right of .117 without changing its value. That is, .117 and .1170 are equivalent decimals.

Since Shannon National Bank's APR is equal to a four-place decimal and Glen Shore Bank's APR is equal to a three-place decimal, write Glen Shore's APR as a four-place decimal.

Shannon National Bank, .1165
Glen Shore Bank,   .1170

Now both decimals can be read as ten-thousandths. You can now see that $\frac{1,165}{10,000}$ is smaller than $\frac{1,170}{10,000}$.

Shannon National Bank charges a lower interest rate than Glen Shore Bank.

3. Luke (from Problem 2) decided to visit two more banks. He was given an APR of 11.645% from Liverpool Savings Bank and an APR of 11.75% from Royal Savings Bank. List the four APRs Luke was offered in **ascending** order (from lowest to highest).

Solution: Change all percents to equivalent decimals.

Shannon National Bank, .1165
Glen Shore Bank, .117
Liverpool Savings Bank, .11645
Royal Savings Bank, .1175

Use zeros to make five-place decimals.

Shannon National Bank, .11650
Glen Shore Bank, .11700
Liverpool Savings Bank, .11645
Royal Savings Bank, .11750

These decimals all represent fractions with the denominator 100,000. Without writing all these fractions, use their numerators to list the banks in ascending order, according to their APRs.

Liverpool Savings Bank,   11.645%
Shannon National Bank, 11.65%
Glen Shore Bank,   11.7%
Royal Savings Bank,   11.75%

4. Riverhead Bank offers a 14.7% APR on a $12,000, three-year loan. The Bank of Commack offers a $14\frac{3}{4}\%$ APR on the same loan. Which bank has the lower APR?

Solution: Express the fractional part of the APR as a decimal.

$14\frac{3}{4}\%$ = 14.75%
14.7% = 14.7%

Write each percent as an equivalent decimal without the percent sign.

14.75% = .1475
14.7% = .147

Write both decimals with the same number of decimal places. Then compare.

.1475
.1470

It is not always necessary to write the decimals as equivalent fractions. It is easy to see that .1470 is less than .1475.

Riverhead Bank has the lower APR.

5. Arrange the following lending institutions in **descending** order (from highest to lowest) according to their APRs for a $10,000, two-year loan:

East Meadow Savings, $13\frac{1}{2}\%$
Uniondale Credit Union, 13%
Westbury Trust, $13\frac{3}{8}\%$
The First Bank of Carle Place, 13.45%
Bellmore Consumer Finance Company, $23\frac{1}{4}\%$

Solution: Express all APRs as equivalent decimals of the same length.

$13\frac{1}{2}\%$	=	13.5%	=	.135	=	.13500
13%	=	13.0%	=	.130	=	.13000
$13\frac{3}{8}\%$	=	13.375%	=	.13375	=	.13375
13.45%	=	13.45%	=	.1345	=	.13450
$23\frac{1}{4}\%$	=	23.25%	=	.2325	=	.23250

Use the five-place decimal equivalents to arrange the banks in descending order according to their APRs.

Bellmore Consumer Finance Company, $23\frac{1}{4}$%
East Meadow Savings, $13\frac{1}{2}$%
The First Bank of Carle Place, 13.45%
Westbury Trust, $13\frac{3}{8}$%
Uniondale Credit Union, 13%

Problems

✓ **1.** Bruce wants to take out a two-year, $4,000 loan. He compares the APRs at three local banks. Smith Savings offers him a 14.25% rate, Omni Trust offers him a 14% rate, and Metro Savings offers him a 14.5% rate. Which of the three banks offers Bruce the lowest APR?

2. Jane comparison-shopped for her new-car loan and found two banks offering APRs of 12.1% and $12\frac{1}{4}$%. Her credit union offers her an APR of 10.5%.
  a. Which of the two APRs offered by the banks is lower?

  b. Does the credit union offer a better APR than the banks?

3. Augie has a poor credit rating. After being turned down for a loan by several banks, Augie visits two consumer finance companies. Home Finance Corporation offers him a 21.7% loan, and the Cash-on-Hand Finance Corporation offers him a $21\frac{3}{4}$% loan. Which finance company offers Augie the lower APR?

✓ **4.** Marilou belongs to two credit unions. She joined the Federal Plumbers Credit Union because she works as a plumber, and she joined the Queens College Student Credit Union because she is a college student. She is quoted two APRs for her three-year, $11,000 loan:
Federal Plumbers Credit Union, 10.4%
Queens College Student Credit Union, $10\frac{1}{2}$%

a. Convert the Federal Plumbers Credit Union APR to an equivalent decimal.
b. Convert the Queens College Student Credit Union APR to an equivalent decimal.
c. Which credit union offers the lower APR?

✓ **5.** Arrange the following lending institutions in ascending order, from lowest interest rate to highest interest rate, according to their APRs on a $13,000, three-year loan.

Larson County Trust, $15\frac{3}{4}\%$
Miller Credit Union, $15\frac{1}{8}\%$
The First Bank of Hanover, 15.33%
Glenlawn National Bank, $15\frac{3}{8}\%$

✓ **6.** Arrange the following lending institutions in descending order, from highest interest rate to lowest interest rate, according to their APRs on a $20,000, two-year loan.

The Robert National Bank, 16.2%
First Bank of Linden County, $16\frac{1}{4}\%$
Lauraton Teachers Credit Union, $16\frac{1}{8}\%$
Richardsville Trust, 16.32%
Emten Consumer Finance Company, $16\frac{5}{8}\%$

7. The policy of the Broadway Pawnshop is to lend up to 65% of the value of a borrower's collateral. John wants to use a $3,000 ring and a $1,200 necklace as collateral for a loan. What is the maximum amount that he could borrow from Broadway?

8. Brian wants to take out a $5,000 loan to buy a used car. He has been turned down by a bank because of his poor credit rating. The local pawnshop will lend him up to 75% of the value of his collateral. Brian wants to use $8,500 worth of jewelry as collateral. Will the pawnbroker lend him enough money so that he can buy the car? Explain your answer.

✓ **9.** Cooky's Pawnshop will lend up to 72% of the value of a borrower's collateral. Jeff plans to pawn his $3,000 violin because he needs $2,000 to get his car fixed. Will Cooky's lend Jeff enough money to get his car fixed? Explain your answer.

10. Ray made this list of seven APRs offered by local banks:
    $12\frac{3}{8}\%$, 12.2%, 16%, $12\frac{1}{2}\%$, 12%, 12.35%, 11%
    What is the median of the APRs offered by these banks?

SECTION 4 ● BORROWING MONEY

Whenever you borrow money, you must sign an agreement that states the conditions of the loan. This agreement is called a **promissory note,** and your signature confirms your promise to make payments on time. Read the entire promissory note carefully before you sign. Seek outside help if you don't understand any part of the note.

The **Truth-in-Lending Act** requires lenders to let consumers know the exact terms of the lending agreement. Borrowers can sue lending institutions that don't supply the required information.

The following information must be included on every promissory note:

● the amount borrowed, called the **principal**

● the APR

● the amount of each monthly payment

● the number of payments that must be made

● the finance charge

● due dates for each payment

● extra charges for late payments

Not all loan agreements are the same, so each promissory note describes the features of that particular loan. You should become familiar with the following terms:

Cosigner. This person agrees to pay back the loan if the borrower is unable to make the payments.

Life Insurance. A creditor often requires a borrower to take out life insurance to cover the loan in case the borrower dies before the loan is paid. This payment is included in the monthly payment and the finance charge.

Prepayment Privilege. This feature allows the borrower to make payments before the due date to reduce the amount of interest.

Prepayment Penalty. This agreement requires borrowers to pay a fee if they wish to pay back an entire loan before the due date.

Balloon Payment. The last monthly payment on some loans is much higher than the previous payments. These high payments are **balloon payments.**

Keep in mind that lending institutions are businesses, and the interest you pay on loans is part of their profit. Lending institutions make profit by charging interest, and promissory notes protect them as well as you.

Skills and Strategies

A table of monthly payments for several selected loans is given in Figure 7.1 on page 310. Refer to it when reading the examples on page 311 and 312.

10% APR — Monthly Payment

Principal	1 Year	2 Years	3 Years	4 Years	5 Years
2000	175.84	92.29	64.54	50.73	42.50
3000	263.75	138.44	96.81	76.09	63.75
4000	351.67	184.58	129.07	101.46	84.99
5000	439.58	230.73	161.34	126.82	106.24
6000	527.50	276.87	193.61	152.18	127.49
7000	615.42	323.02	225.88	177.54	148.73
8000	703.33	369.16	258.14	202.91	169.98
9000	791.25	415.31	290.41	228.27	191.23
10000	879.16	461.45	322.68	253.63	212.48
15000	1318.74	692.18	484.01	380.44	318.71

11% APR — Monthly Payment

Principal	1 Year	2 Years	3 Years	4 Years	5 Years
2000	176.77	93.22	65.48	51.70	43.49
3000	265.15	139.83	98.22	77.54	65.23
4000	353.53	186.44	130.96	103.39	86.97
5000	441.91	233.04	163.70	129.23	108.72
6000	530.29	279.65	196.44	155.08	130.46
7000	618.68	326.26	229.18	180.92	152.20
8000	707.06	372.87	261.91	206.77	173.94
9000	795.44	419.48	294.65	232.61	195.69
10000	883.82	466.08	327.39	258.46	217.43
15000	1325.73	699.12	491.09	387.69	326.14

12% APR — Monthly Payment

Principal	1 Year	2 Years	3 Years	4 Years	5 Years
2000	177.70	94.15	66.43	52.67	44.49
3000	266.55	141.23	99.65	79.01	66.74
4000	355.40	188.30	132.86	105.34	88.98
5000	444.25	235.37	166.08	131.67	111.23
6000	533.10	282.45	199.29	158.01	133.47
7000	621.95	329.52	232.51	184.34	155.72
8000	710.80	376.59	265.72	210.68	177.96
9000	799.64	423.67	298.93	237.01	200.21
10000	888.49	470.74	332.15	263.34	222.45
15000	1332.74	706.11	498.22	395.01	333.67

13% APR — Monthly Payment

Principal	1 Year	2 Years	3 Years	4 Years	5 Years
2000	178.64	95.09	67.39	53.66	45.51
3000	267.96	142.63	101.09	80.49	68.26
4000	357.27	190.17	134.78	107.31	91.02
5000	446.59	237.71	168.47	134.14	113.77
6000	535.91	285.26	202.17	160.97	136.52
7000	625.23	332.80	235.86	187.80	159.28
8000	714.54	380.34	269.56	214.62	182.03
9000	803.86	427.88	303.25	241.45	204.78
10000	893.18	475.42	336.94	268.28	227.54
15000	1339.76	713.13	505.41	402.42	341.30

14% APR — Monthly Payment

Principal	1 Year	2 Years	3 Years	4 Years	5 Years
2000	179.58	96.03	68.36	54.66	46.54
3000	269.37	144.04	102.54	81.98	69.81
4000	359.15	192.06	136.72	109.31	93.08
5000	448.94	240.07	170.89	136.64	116.35
6000	538.73	288.08	205.07	163.96	139.61
7000	628.51	336.10	239.25	191.29	162.88
8000	718.30	384.11	273.43	218.62	186.15
9000	808.09	432.12	307.60	245.94	209.42
10000	897.88	480.13	341.78	273.27	232.69
15000	1346.81	720.20	512.67	409.90	349.03

15% APR — Monthly Payment

Principal	1 Year	2 Years	3 Years	4 Years	5 Years
2000	180.52	96.98	69.34	55.67	47.58
3000	270.78	145.46	104.00	83.50	71.37
4000	361.04	193.95	138.67	111.33	95.16
5000	451.30	242.44	173.33	139.16	118.95
6000	541.55	290.92	208.00	166.99	142.74
7000	631.81	339.41	242.66	194.82	166.53
8000	722.07	387.90	277.33	222.65	190.32
9000	812.33	436.38	311.99	250.48	214.11
10000	902.59	484.87	346.66	278.31	237.90
15000	1353.88	727.30	519.98	417.47	356.85

16% APR — Monthly Payment

Principal	1 Year	2 Years	3 Years	4 Years	5 Years
2000	181.47	97.93	70.32	56.69	48.64
3000	272.20	146.89	105.48	85.03	72.96
4000	362.93	195.86	140.63	113.37	97.28
5000	453.66	244.82	175.79	141.71	121.60
6000	544.39	293.78	210.95	170.05	145.91
7000	635.12	342.75	246.10	198.39	170.23
8000	725.85	391.71	281.26	226.73	194.55
9000	816.58	440.67	316.42	255.07	218.87
10000	907.31	489.64	351.58	283.41	243.19
15000	1360.97	734.45	527.36	425.11	364.78

18% APR — Monthly Payment

Principal	1 Year	2 Years	3 Years	4 Years	5 Years
2000	183.36	99.85	72.31	58.75	50.79
3000	275.04	149.78	108.46	88.13	76.19
4000	366.72	199.70	144.61	117.50	101.58
5000	458.40	249.63	180.77	146.88	126.97
6000	550.08	299.55	216.92	176.25	152.37
7000	641.76	349.47	253.07	205.63	177.76
8000	733.44	399.40	289.22	235.00	203.15
9000	825.12	449.32	325.38	264.38	228.55
10000	916.80	499.25	361.53	293.75	253.94
15000	1375.20	748.87	542.29	440.63	380.91

20% APR — Monthly Payment

Principal	1 Year	2 Years	3 Years	4 Years	5 Years
2000	185.27	101.80	74.33	60.87	52.99
3000	277.91	152.69	111.50	91.30	79.49
4000	370.54	203.59	148.66	121.73	105.98
5000	463.18	254.48	185.82	152.16	132.47
6000	555.81	305.38	222.99	182.59	158.97
7000	648.45	356.28	260.15	213.02	185.46
8000	741.08	407.17	297.31	243.45	211.96
9000	833.72	458.07	334.48	273.88	238.45
10000	926.35	508.96	371.64	304.31	264.94
15000	1389.52	763.44	557.46	456.46	397.41

22% APR — Monthly Payment

Principal	1 Year	2 Years	3 Years	4 Years	5 Years
2000	187.19	103.76	76.39	63.02	55.24
3000	280.79	155.64	114.58	94.52	82.86
4000	374.38	207.52	152.77	126.03	110.48
5000	467.98	259.40	190.96	157.54	138.10
6000	561.57	311.27	229.15	189.04	165.72
7000	655.17	363.15	267.34	220.55	193.34
8000	748.76	415.03	305.53	252.05	220.96
9000	842.35	466.91	343.72	283.56	248.58
10000	935.95	518.79	381.91	315.07	276.19
15000	1403.92	778.18	572.86	472.60	414.29

Figure 7.1 Monthly Payment Tables

1. What is the monthly payment for a $4,000, two-year loan with an APR of 11%?

   Solution: The box labeled "11% APR" from Figure 7.1 is shown below. Look down the column headed "Principal" and find $4,000. Look across the $4,000 row for its intersection with the column headed "2 years."

11% APR					Monthly Payment
Principal	**1 Year**	**2 Years**	**3 Years**	**4 Years**	**5 Years**
2000	176.77	93.22	65.48	51.70	43.49
3000	265.15	139.83	98.22	77.54	65.23
4000	353.53	(186.44)	130.96	103.39	86.97
5000	441.91	233.04	163.70	129.23	108.72
6000	530.29	279.65	196.44	155.08	130.46
7000	618.68	326.26	229.18	180.92	152.20
8000	707.06	372.87	261.91	206.77	173.94
9000	795.44	419.48	294.65	232.61	195.69
10000	883.82	466.08	327.39	258.46	217.43
15000	1325.73	699.12	491.09	387.69	326.14

   The monthly payment is $186.44.

2. What is the total amount of the monthly payments for a $4,000, two-year loan with an APR of 11%?

   Solution: First find the total number of monthly payments.

12	number of months in one year
× 2	length of loan, in years
24	total number of monthly payments

   The monthly payment (found in Problem 1) is $186.44.

$186.44	amount of each monthly payment
× 24	total number of monthly payments
$4,474.56	total amount paid in the two years

   The total amount of the monthly payments is $4,474.56.

3.   What is the finance charge for a $4,000, two-year loan with an 11% APR?

   Solution: First find the total amount of the monthly payments (from Problem 2).

$4,474.56	total amount of the monthly payments
− 4,000.00	principal (amount borrowed)
$ 474.56	finance charge

   The finance charge is $474.56. This is the cost of borrowing the $4,000.

4.   Elsie wants to check the accuracy of the finance charge before signing a promissory note for a $9,000, three-year loan with a 15% APR.

   Solution: Elsie can use Figure 7.1 to check that the monthly payment entered on the promissory note is correct. She can use the following calculator keystroke sequence to verify that the finance charge is correct.

   AC 311.99 × 36 = − 9,000 =

   | Computes the total | Subtracts the |
   | amount to be paid. | principal. |

   The display should read 2,231.64.

   Elsie should pay $2,231.64 in finance charges. She should compare this amount to the entry on her promissory note.

Problems

Use Figure 7.1, page 310, to help you find the answers to Problems 1–5 and 8–10.

✓ 1.   Barry needs to borrow $7,000 from a local bank. He compares the monthly payments for a 12% loan for three different periods of time.
   a.   What is the monthly payment for a one-year loan?
   b.   What is the monthly payment for a five-year loan?
   c.   What is the monthly payment for a three-year loan?

2. Rachel took out a $10,000, three-year loan with an APR of 14%.
  a. What is the monthly payment?
  b. What is the total amount of the monthly payments?

  c. What is the finance charge?

✓ **3.** Melissa wants to check the accuracy of the finance charge on her promissory note. She took out a $6,000, four-year loan at an APR of 13%.
  a. What is the monthly payment?
  b. What is the total amount of the monthly payments?

  c. What is the finance charge?

4. Juliana is taking out an $8,000, five-year loan with an APR of 16%. What is the finance charge for this loan?

✓ **5.** Solomon is taking out a $15,000, two-year loan with an APR of 11%. What is the finance charge for this loan?

6. How many more monthly payments are made for a five-year loan than for a two-year loan?

7. How many monthly payments must be made for a $2\frac{1}{2}$-year loan?

✓ **8.** Alex wants to borrow $10,000 for the next two years. Merit Savings Bank offers a 12% APR, and Stewart Trust offers a 13% APR.
  a. Which bank charges less interest?
  b. What is the finance charge at Merit Savings Bank?

  c. What is the finance charge at Stewart Trust?
  d. How much could Alex save over the two-year period by borrowing from the lending institution with the lower rate?

9. Olivia is a teacher. She is considering becoming a member of the Regional Teachers Credit Union so that she can save money on a loan. The credit union will lend her $8,000 for two years at 11% APR. The same loan at her savings bank has an APR of 13%. How much would Olivia save in finance charges if she joined the credit union and took out her loan there?

✓**10.** Rob wants to purchase a $2,000 drum set. The music store offers him a two-year installment agreement requiring $500 down and monthly payments of $90.

   a. What is the interest on this installment agreement?

   b. Instead of using the store's installment plan, Rob can borrow the $2,000 (at an 18% APR for two years) from a local consumer finance company. What would be the monthly payment for this loan?

   c. How much interest would Rob pay if he borrowed the money from the finance company?

   d. Should Rob use the store's installment plan or borrow the money from the finance company? Explain your answer.

● KEY TERMS

To find the definition of any term introduced in the chapter, refer to the Glossary in the back of this book.

annual percentage rate (APR)	finance charge
ascending	installments
assets	installment plan
balloon payment	interest
banks	interest rate
collateral	lending institutions
commercial bank	life insurance
consumer finance company	life insurance companies
cosigner	loan
credit	pawnbrokers
creditors	prepayment penalty
credit rating	prepayment privilege
credit reporting agencies	principal
credit union	promissory note
debtors	repossessed
descending	savings and loan associations
down payment	savings banks
earning power	single-payment loans
Equal Credit Opportunity Act	Truth-in-Lending Act
Fair Credit Reporting Act	

• REVIEW PROBLEMS

1. Pat is saving money to buy a $1,800 pool table. She earns $109 per week at her part-time job. After expenses, she can save approximately $50 toward the pool table. How many weeks must she save to make this purchase, which includes 5% sales tax?

2. Gary is planning to buy a new television monitor on the installment plan. If he made a down payment of $150 and monthly payments of $48.25 for the next $2\frac{1}{2}$ years, what would be Gary's total cost for the monitor, including finance charges?

3. Eva bought a $2,000 jukebox on the installment plan. She paid $300 down and will make monthly payments of $62.50 for the next three years. How much interest will Eva pay for the convenience of using the installment plan?

4. Paul is shopping for a loan. He looks through the newspaper advertisements for lending institutions and finds this information relating to the kind of loan he wants:

   Blair Finance Company, 21.5%
   Wigmont Savings and Loan, $15\frac{1}{4}$%
   Fairmont Federal Savings, 15.35%

   Paul is a member of a credit union that will charge him a 14.1% APR. List the four lending institutions in order, according to their APRs, from lowest to highest.

5. Crazy Charlie, a pawnbroker, will lend up to 75% of the value of the collateral left by the borrower. If you pawned a $1,200 gold watch, what is the maximum amount Crazy Charlie would lend you?

6. How many more monthly payments would you have to make for a six-year loan than for a $3\frac{1}{2}$-year loan?

Use Figure 7.1 to help you answer Problems 7–9.

7. What is the total amount of the monthly payments on a three-year, $10,000 loan with an APR of 20%?

8. What is the finance charge on a four-year, $6,000 loan with an APR of 11%?

9. Martha needs to borrow $2,000 for home improvements. Bolton Savings Bank will lend her the money for two years at 14% APR. The Bank of Long Haven will lend her the money for three years at 14% APR.
   a. How much lower is the monthly payment for the three-year loan than for the two-year loan? $27.67
   b. How much higher is the finance charge for the three-year loan?

10. Bill's credit union will lend him $6,000 at an APR of $12\frac{3}{4}$% for one year. His monthly payments would be $535.20. Bill's savings bank will lend him $6,000 at an APR of $12\frac{3}{4}$% for three years. His monthly payments on the bank loan would be $201.44. How much would Bill save by taking out the loan for the shorter period of time?

CHAPTER 8

CREDIT CARDS

SECTION 1 • READING A MONTHLY STATEMENT

You have probably seen stickers in store windows that show credit cards. Those stickers tell you that the stores will accept payment by credit card. What kinds of stores accept payment by credit card? Think of as many examples as you can. Most department stores, gas stations, and restaurants accept credit cards. You can use credit cards in many stores that sell clothing, appliances, and other goods. Many businesses and services also honor credit cards. They can even be used when you shop by mail or by catalog. With so many possibilities, it is not surprising that so many Americans use credit cards. There are two types of credit card accounts:

- **Regular 30-day accounts** allow the cardholder to charge purchases in places that accept the credit card. The monthly bills for all purchases must be paid in full. Cardholders can have their credit cards taken away if they do not pay their bills in full.

- **Revolving charge accounts** also allow the cardholder to charge purchases in places that accept the card. The monthly bills for these purchases do *not* have to be paid in full. However, there is a charge (called the finance charge) each month the bill is not paid in full.

Using a credit card is both a convenience and a responsibility. You must be able to use the card wisely and carefully. It is important to understand the rules for using the card.

The Truth-in Lending Act protects you if your credit card is lost or stolen. If this happens, you should notify the creditor immediately. You are somewhat responsible for charges made by unauthorized users of cards you lose. Charges that occur *after* you notify the creditor are subject to interpretation by the laws in existence at that time.

In this chapter, you will learn how to check the accuracy of a **monthly statement**, or bill, for a credit card. The **Fair Credit Billing Act** protects you if there are any errors on your monthly statement. The act states that you must notify a creditor *in writing* within 60 days if you discover an error on your bill. You do not have to pay the amount that is disputed, or any finance charges based on that amount, until the problem is cleared up. You are still responsible for any other debts listed on the monthly statement.

If you find yourself unable to meet payments required by a creditor, notify that creditor immediately. The **Fair Debt Collection Practices Act** prohibits the creditor from threatening you or using any unfair means to collect the amount owed. Topic Four Enhance/ Advance Activity 1 will help you learn more about government credit legislation.

Skills and Strategies

How does shopping with a credit card work? Let's examine Jane Sharp's last purchase at Beadle's Department Store.

On January 5, Jane made these purchases at Beadle's:

jeans, $32.50
2 blouses, $29.99 each
sweater, $40.00

Jane used her Flash Card revolving credit card to charge the purchases. The cashier listed the items on the credit card invoice. A **credit card invoice** is a receipt used only for customers paying with credit cards. Examine Jane's credit card invoice for her purchases shown in Figure 8.1 at the top of page 319.

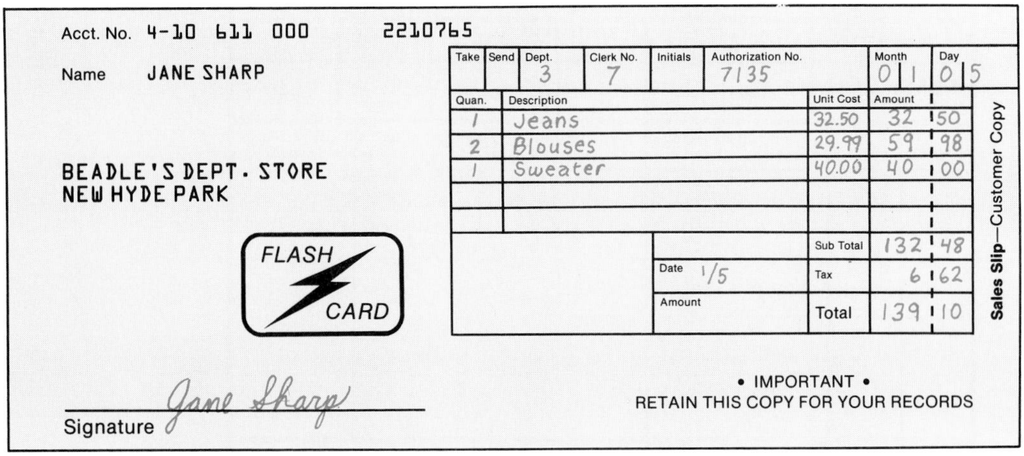
Acct. No. 4-10 611 000 2210765

Name JANE SHARP

Take	Send	Dept.	Clerk No.	Initials	Authorization No.	Month	Day
		3	7		7135	01	05

Quan.	Description	Unit Cost	Amount
1	Jeans	32.50	32 50
2	Blouses	29.99	59 98
1	Sweater	40.00	40 00
		Sub Total	132 48
	Date 1/5	Tax	6 62
	Amount	Total	139 10

BEADLE'S DEPT. STORE
NEW HYDE PARK

FLASH CARD

Sales Slip—Customer Copy

Signature Jane Sharp

• IMPORTANT •
RETAIN THIS COPY FOR YOUR RECORDS

Figure 8.1 Credit Card Invoice

Before Jane signed the invoice, she checked all the arithmetic on it. After she signed it, she received one copy of the invoice. Beadle's Department Store kept one copy and sent Flash Card one copy.

Jane saved her copy of the invoice until her monthly Flash Card statement, or bill, arrived. The monthly bill is a listing of all Flash Card purchases made since the last bill. Examine Jane's most recent Flash Card bill at the top of page 320.

Look at the terms below. These terms are commonly found on most credit card statements. You should be familiar with each of the terms and its meaning. Locate each term (A–V) on the statement in Figure 8.2 on page 320.

A. **Account Type.** This space contains the name of the credit card used to make the transactions listed on the bill. This is Jane's Flash Card bill. (She may get other bills for her other credit cards.)

B. **Account Number.** Each credit card account has a unique number. Jane's account number is 4-10611000.

C. **Credit Line.** This is the maximum amount you can owe at any specific time. Jane is not allowed to owe more than $2,000 at any time. This is her credit limit.

D. **Available Credit.** This is the difference between the maximum amount you can owe and the amount you actually owe. Jane's available credit is $1,636.52.

ACCOUNT TYPE	ACCOUNT NUMBER	CREDIT LINE	AVAILABLE CREDIT	BILLING DATE	PAYMENT DUE DATE
FLASH CARD	4-10611000	2,000	1,636.52	1/23	2/6

DATE POSTED	TRANS	REFERENCE NUMBER	TRANSACTION DESCRIPTION	DEBITS/ CREDITS(−)
1/11	1/2	6391235365	POWDERMAKER SHOP	75.00
1/12	1/3	2463107382	JEFFERSON RESTAURANT	31.85
1/15	1/5	8192653731	BEADLE'S DEPT. STORE	139.10
1/20	1/10	5251356999	RATHAUS BOOKS	38.50
1/21	1/21	20819408910	PAYMENT	−75.00

SUMMARY	PREVIOUS BALANCE	PURCHASES	PAYMENTS	FINANCE CHARGE	LATE CHARGE	NEW BALANCE	MINIMUM PAYMENT
	150.50	284.45	75.00	3.53	0	363.48	20.00

JANE SHARP HOLLY, PA	NUMBER OF DAYS IN BILLING CYCLE	ANNUAL PERCENTAGE RATE	AVERAGE DAILY BALANCE	MONTHLY PERIODIC RATE
FLASH CARD	30	18%	235.10	1.5%

Figure 8.2 Credit Card Statement

E. Billing Date. This is the date the bill was written. Jane's bill covers purchases made through January 23.

F. Payment Due Date. On this date the monthly payment must be received by the creditor. Flash Card wants Jane's payment by February 6.

G. Date Posted. These dates indicate when the creditor received its copy of the credit card invoices or payments. Notice that the invoice for Jane's purchases at Beadle's was posted on January 15.

H. Date of Transaction. These dates show when purchases were made or payments were received. Notice that Jane made her purchases at Beadle's on January 5.

I. **Reference Number.** These are numbers used by credit card companies to identify particular transactions.

J. **Transaction Description.** This section of the statement lists where purchases were made and what payments were made. Notice that during this billing period, Jane made purchases at four places and paid $75 to reduce her debt.

K. **Debits/credits (−).** A debit is the amount charged to your account; a credit is a payment made to reduce your debt. Credits are identified by a minus (−) sign.

L. **Previous Balance.** This amount is any money you owed before the current billing period. Notice that Jane owed $150.50.

M. **Purchases.** This amount is the sum of all purchases (debits) on the current bill. Notice that Jane made purchases totaling $284.45.

N. **Payments.** The total amount of money received by the creditor from the debtor.

O. **Finance Charge.** This is the cost of using the credit card for the current billing period. Notice Jane must pay $3.53 in finance charges.

P. **Late Charge.** This amount is the penalty charged for late payments.

Q. **New Balance.** This is the amount you currently owe. Notice that Jane owes $363.48.

R. **Minimum Payment.** This amount is the lowest payment the credit card company will accept for the current billing period.

S. **Number of Days in Billing Cycle.** This is the amount of time, in days, covered by the current bill. Jane's bill covers 30 days of transactions, up to January 23, the billing date.

T. **Annual Percentage Rate.** This is the yearly interest rate. Jane's Flash Card has an APR of 18%.

U. **Average Daily Balance.** This is the average amount Jane owed during the billing cycle.

V. **Monthly Periodic Rate.** This rate is used to compute finance charges. Jane's monthly periodic rate is 1.5%. The monthly periodic rate can be found by dividing the APR by 12.

In the next examples, you will learn how to read and verify credit card statements. Read each problem carefully.

1. Joan wants to verify the total of the purchases on her credit card statement. Her statement lists the following purchases:

Hobby Craft, $117.50
Spooner China Shop, $64.90
Manzee Shop, $231.45

What is the sum of these purchases?

Solution: Add to find the total.

$117.50   Hobby Craft purchase
   64.90   Spooner China Shop purchase
+ 231.45   Manzee Shop purchase
$413.85   total

The sum is $413.85. Joan should check that the purchases on her statement match this amount.

2. Pascual has a credit line of $2,000 on his Flash Card. His new balance is $643.12. How much available credit does Pascual have?

Solution: Pascual can owe up to $2,000 at any specific time. He now owes $643.12. Subtract to find his available credit.

$2,000.00   credit line
− 643.12   new balance
$1,356.88   available credit

Pascual has $1,356.88 available credit.

3. Sheldon's Flash Card has a 23.4% annual percentage rate. What is the monthly periodic rate?

Solution: There are 12 months in a year, and Sheldon must divide the annual rate by 12. The following calculator keystroke sequence can be used:

AC 23.4 ÷ 12 =

The display should read 1.95.

Sheldon's monthly periodic rate is 1.95%.

4. Myrna is examining the summary section of her Flash Card statement. Here is her statement:

	PREVIOUS BALANCE	PURCHASES	PAYMENTS	FINANCE CHARGE	LATE CHARGE	NEW BALANCE	MINIMUM PAYMENT
SUMMARY	1748.00	800.00	100.00	9.15	1.00	2758.15	25.00

Myrna has checked all the entries on her bill and agrees with everything except the new balance. Use the summary section to determine whether the new balance shown is correct.

Solution: Add the amounts in the four boxes that show money that Myrna must pay to Flash Card.

$1,748.00	previous balance
800.00	purchases
9.15	finance charge
+ 1.00	late charge
$2,558.15	total to be paid to Flash Card

Subtract the $100 payment Myrna has already made.

$2,558.15	total to be paid to Flash Card
− 100.00	payment
$2,458.15	new balance

Myrna's new balance should be $2,458.15. The new balance of $2,758.15 shown on her statement is incorrect. Under the Fair Credit Billing Act, Myrna must notify her creditor in writing within 60 days.

Problems

Use Figure 8.3 at the top of page 324 to help you answer Problems 1–5.

ACCOUNT TYPE	ACCOUNT NUMBER	CREDIT LINE	AVAILABLE CREDIT	BILLING DATE	PAYMENT DUE DATE
FLASH CARD	4-10700000	3,000	1,661.51	5/30	6/8

DATE POSTED	TRANS	REFERENCE NUMBER	TRANSACTION DESCRIPTION	DEBITS/ CREDITS(−)
5/9	5/4	3291684271	FANELLI FURS	975.00
5/12	5/7	594683219	BROOKLYN PETS	32.50
5/15	5/12	7677095385	MAPLE GARAGE	178.21
5/18	5/18	8765713281	PAYMENT	−150.00
5/21	5/19	321447162	CARUSO'S RESTAURANT	41.53

SUMMARY	PREVIOUS BALANCE	PURCHASES	PAYMENTS	FINANCE CHARGE	LATE CHARGE	NEW BALANCE	MINIMUM PAYMENT
	420.50	1,227.24	150.00	18.96	0	1,338.49	30.00

	NUMBER OF DAYS IN BILLING CYCLE	ANNUAL PERCENTAGE RATE	AVERAGE DAILY BALANCE	MONTHLY PERIODIC RATE
FLASH CARD	30	19.8%	1,149.28	1.65%

Figure 8.3 Flash Card Statement

1. How many purchases were made during the billing period shown?

2. What is the sum of all purchases made during the billing period shown?

3. a. When is the payment for this statement due?
   b. What is the minimum amount that can be paid?

4. How many days are in the billing cycle?

5. What is the previous balance?

6. Rollie has a Flash Card, and his credit line is $4,000. His new balance on his current statement is $1,251. What is Rollie's available credit?

✓ **7.** Rebecca has a credit line of $6,500 on her Flash Card. Her current statement shows a new balance of $2,111.65. What is Rebecca's available credit?

✓ **8.** The APR on Leslie's Flash Card is currently 21.6%. What is the monthly periodic rate for Leslie's account?

9. Examine this summary section of a Flash Card monthly statement.

	PREVIOUS BALANCE	PURCHASES	PAYMENTS	FINANCE CHARGE	LATE CHARGE	NEW BALANCE	MINIMUM PAYMENT
SUMMARY	359.02	103.65	80.00	5.34	0	548.01	18.00

Use the first five entries to determine whether the new balance is correct. If the new balance is incorrect, write the correct amount.

✓ **10.** Check the new balance entry on the monthly statement below by using the first five entries.

	PREVIOUS BALANCE	PURCHASES	PAYMENTS	FINANCE CHARGE	LATE CHARGE	NEW BALANCE	MINIMUM PAYMENT
SUMMARY	424.41	103.38	104.41	7.77	3.00	434.15	54.00

If the new balance is incorrect, write the correct amount.

SECTION 2 • CREDIT CARD FINANCE CHARGES

Consumers who use credit have many different spending habits. Some do most of their monthly shopping in a few days; other use their credit cards almost daily. Some people use their credit cards for all or most of their shopping; others use them only for major items. Some credit card users pay their bills in full; others pay only part of their bills each month.

Debtors who do not pay their bills in full are charged a finance charge for the convenience of extra payment time. The finance charge is computed on any statement in which the consumer has a previous balance. You should be able to determine whether the finance charge has been computed correctly. The finance charge is based on the average amount the debtor owed each day of the billing cycle. This average is called the **average daily balance**. Many consumers do not know how to compute the average daily balance. It's not difficult, so take out your calculator.

Skills and Strategies

Here you will learn how to compute an average daily balance. With this information, you will also be able to verify the correctness of a statement's finance charge and new balance. Figure 8.4 on page 327 shows Kim Montlack's last Flash Card statement.

1. Compute Kim's average daily balance and determine whether the entry on her statement is correct.

    Solution: Carefully follow Steps 1–9.

    Step 1. On a blank sheet of paper, draw a grid that has seven boxes across and five boxes down. Draw an arc in each corner, as shown in Figure 8.5 on page 328.

Account Type			Account Number	Credit Line	Available Credit	Billing Date	Payment Due Date
FLASH CARD			0-7365555	3,000	2,196.61	11/13	12/05

Date Posted	Trans	Reference Number	Transaction Description	Debits/ Credits (−)
10/25	10/11	73628195738	HILLDALE TRAVEL INC.	67.00
10/29	10/11	73629157233	FLYRITE LUGGAGE CO	55.00
11/05	11/05	7361914384	PAYMENT-THANK YOU	−160.00

Summary	Previous Balance	Purchases	Payments and Other Credits	Finance Charge	Late Charges	New Balance	
	829.30	122.0	160.00	12.09	0	803.39	Your Minimum Payment ▼

Your Minimum Payment 59.00

KIM MONTLACK
5771 BENITO STREET
MEADOW, MA

FLASH CARD

NUMBER OF DAYS IN BILLING CYCLE	*ANNUAL PERCENTAGE RATE	AVERAGE DAILY BALANCE	MONTHLY PERIODIC RATE
31	16.98%	854.46	1.415%

RETAIN THIS PORTION   *NOTICE: SEE REVERSE SIDE FOR IMPORTANT INFORMATION

Figure 8.4   Kim Montlack's Flash Card Statement

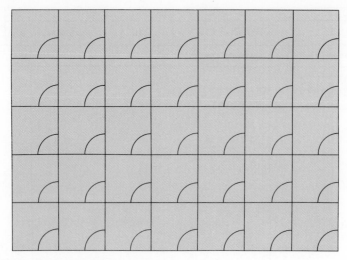

Figure 8.5 Blank 35-Day Calendar

Step 2. Find out the number of days in the billing cycle on Kim's statement. There are 31 days in the billing cycle.

Step 3. The blank calendar can represent a billing cycle of up to 35 days. Since Kim's billing cycle is 31 days, shade in the last four days on the calendar; these will not be used. (See Figure 8.6.)

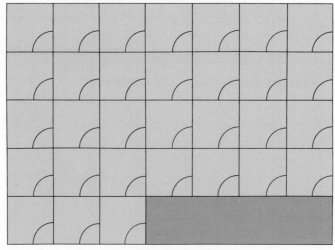

Figure 8.6 Billing Cycle Calendar (31 days)

Step 4. Enter the billing date in the corner section of the last day on the calendar. You can leave out the month. Then, number the days by counting down until the calendar is completely filled in, as in Figure 8.7.

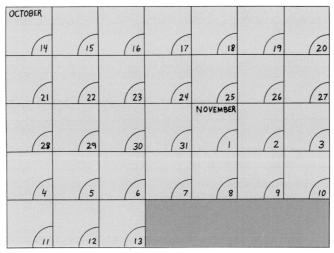

Figure 8.7 Calendar Dates

Notice that the billing cycle ended in November. The billing cycle includes some days from October, which has 31 days. If you need help with the number of days in any month, see Figure 1.1 in Chapter 1.

Step 5. Look at the posting dates of each of the charges (debits). Put a plus (+) sign on the calendar dates that have debits posted. Next look at the posting date of the payment that was made. Put a minus (−) sign on that calendar date. See Figure 8.8 at the top of page 330.

Step 6. The first day of the billing cycle is October 14. The previous balance ($829.30) is the amount Kim owed on October 14. Enter the previous balance on October 14. Notice that Kim made no purchases or payment until October 25, so on *each* day from October 14 to October 24, the daily balance is $829.30. Enter this number on each of these dates. See Figure 8.9. at the bottom of page 330.

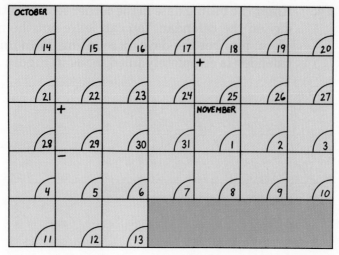

Figure 8.8   Posting Dates

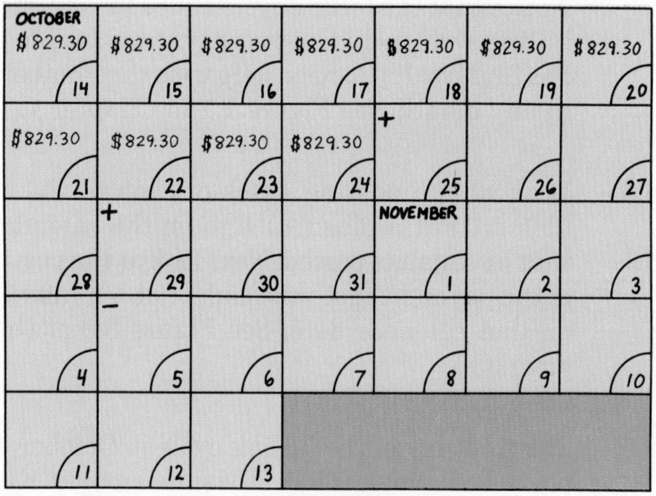

Figure 8.9   Calendar of Daily Balances

Step 7. Notice that a $67 purchase was made on October 25. The amount Kim owes on October 25 is increased by $67. The amount owed from October 25 to October 28 now is $896.30. (Examine Figure 8.10.)

OCTOBER $ 829.30	$ 829.30	$829.30	$829.30	$829.30	$ 829.30	$829.30
14	15	16	17	18	19	20
$829.30	$829.30	$829.30	$829.30	+ $896.30	$896.30	$896.30
21	22	23	24	25	26	27
$896.30	+			NOVEMBER		
28	29	30	31	1	2	3
–						
4	5	6	7	8	9	10
11	12	13				

Figure 8.10 Calendar of Daily Balances

Step 8. A $55 purchase was made on October 29, and a payment of $160 was made on November 5. The purchase must be added to the daily balance of October 28, and the payment must be subtracted from the daily balance of November 4. Complete the calendar as shown in Figure 8.11.

OCTOBER $ 829.30	$ 829.30	$829.30	$829.30	$829.30	$829.30	$829.30
14	15	16	17	18	19	20
$829.30	$829.30	$829.30	$829.30	+ $896.30	$896.30	$896.30
21	22	23	24	25	26	27
$896.30	+ $951.30	$951.30	$951.30	NOVEMBER $951.30	$951.30	$951.30
28	29	30	31	1	2	3
$951.30	– $791.30	$791.30	$791.30	$791.30	$791.30	$791.30
4	5	6	7	8	9	10
$791.30	$791.30	$791.30				
11	12	13				

Figure 8.11 Complete Calendar of Daily Balances

Step 9. To find the average daily balance, add up all the daily balances and divide by the number of days in the billing cycle, which is 31 here. The following keystroke sequence makes the addition easy. Follow the sequence and make sure you understand it. Notice that multiplication will be used to shorten the sequence.

Keystrokes	
AC	← Clears the memory.
829.30 × 11 = M+	← Calculates and stores the sum of the first 11 days.
896.30 × 4 = M+	← Calculates the sum of the next 4 days and adds this sum to the memory.
951.30 × 7 = M+	← Calculates the sum of the next 7 days and adds this sum to the memory.
791.30 × 9 = M+	← Calculates the sum of the next 9 days and adds this sum to the memory.
MR ÷ 31 =	← Recalls the sum of all 31 days from the memory and divides to find the average daily balance.

The display should read 854.46129.
Kim's average daily balance (rounded to the nearest cent) for this Flash Card bill should be $854.46. Compare this to the average daily balance on her statement, and notice that this entry is correct.

2. Compute Kim's finance charge to determine whether the finance charge entry on her statement is correct (see Figure 8.4).

Solution: If the previous Flash Card bill was paid *in full*, the previous balance for this billing cycle is $0, and the finance charge for this billing cycle is $0. If the previous balance is *not* $0, compute the finance charge as follows:

Multiply the average daily balance by the monthly periodic rate, expressed as a decimal. Use the following calculator keystroke sequence:

AC 854.46 × 0.01415 =

average	monthly periodic
daily	rate, expressed as
balance	a decimal

The display should read 12.090609.

Kim's finance charge (rounded to the nearest cent) for this Flash Card bill should be $12.09. Compare this to the finance charge on her bill, and notice that this entry is correct. Also, note that you can find the new balance by adding the finance charge ($12.09) to the daily balance ($791.30) that is listed on the last day of the billing cycle (November 13). (See the completed calendar.)

Problems

✓ **1.** Ralph just received his June Flash Card bill. He did not pay his May bill in full, so his June bill shows a previous balance and a finance charge. The average daily balance is $470, and the monthly periodic rate is 1.5%. What should Ralph's finance charge be?

2. Lauren did not pay her January Flash Card bill in full, so her February bill has a finance charge added on. The average daily balance is $510.44, and the monthly periodic rate is 2.5%. What should Lauren's finance charge be on her February statement?

✓ **3.** Jennifer did not pay her Flash Card bill in full in March, so there is a finance charge on her April bill. The average daily balance is $1,250, and the APR is 24%.
   a. What is the monthly periodic rate?
   b. What is the finance charge on the April statement?

4. Tanya did not pay her Flash Card bill in full in September. Her October bill shows a finance charge, and she wants to see whether or not it is correct. The average daily balance is $970.50, and the APR is 28.2%. Find the finance charge for her October statement.

✓ **5.** Lyndon paid his April Flash Card bill in full. His May bill shows an average daily balance of $270.31 and a monthly periodic rate of 1.95%. What is the finance charge on Lyndon's May statement?

Use Mark Gilley's Flash Card statement (Figure 8.12) to answer Problems 6–10. There is an error in his bill — the average daily balance, finance charge, available credit, and new balance spaces are not filled in.

ACCOUNT TYPE	ACCOUNT NUMBER	CREDIT LINE	AVAILABLE CREDIT	BILLING DATE	PAYMENT DUE DATE
FLASH CARD	7-6231-491	6,000		6/26	7/10

DATE POSTED	TRANS	REFERENCE NUMBER	TRANSACTION DESCRIPTION	DEBITS/ CREDITS(−)
5/31	5/30	63214987261	LINDA'S ART SHOP	251.00
6/12	6/5	62115497621	ARTISIGN'S INC	72.50
6/18	6/18	73216532116	PAYMENT THANK YOU	−200.00
6/20	6/17	73162225142	SYLVART CORP.	18.50

SUMMARY	PREVIOUS BALANCE	PURCHASES	PAYMENTS	FINANCE CHARGE	LATE CHARGE	NEW BALANCE	MINIMUM PAYMENT
	800.00	342.00	200.00		0		25.00

MARK GILLEY HOUSTON, TX	NUMBER OF DAYS IN BILLING CYCLE	ANNUAL PERCENTAGE RATE	AVERAGE DAILY BALANCE	MONTHLY PERIODIC RATE
FLASH CARD	31	18%		1.5%

Figure 8.12 Flash Card Bill

6. What is Mark's average daily balance?

7. What is Mark's finance charge?

8. What is Mark's new balance?

9. What is Mark's available credit?

10. If the $200 payment had been posted on 6/13, would Mark's finance charge for this billing cycle have been higher or lower? Explain your answer.

Use Ed Lubbock's Flash Card bill (Figure 8.13) to answer Problems 11–15. The entries for average daily balance, finance charge, new balance, and available credit are missing.

ACCOUNT TYPE	ACCOUNT NUMBER	CREDIT LINE	AVAILABLE CREDIT	BILLING DATE	PAYMENT DUE DATE
FLASH CARD	7-6234712	1,000		12/10	12/21

DATE POSTED	TRANS	REFERENCE NUMBER	TRANSACTION DESCRIPTION	DEBITS/ CREDITS(−)
11/24	11/21	632174293	RUSTY'S RIB PALACE	48.00
12/1	12/1	321446253	PAYMENT	−100.00
12/6	12/2	333261114	PETRELA SAILBOATS	30.00

SUMMARY	PREVIOUS BALANCE	PURCHASES	PAYMENTS	FINANCE CHARGE	LATE CHARGE	NEW BALANCE	MINIMUM PAYMENT
	421.50	78.00	100.00				30.00

	NUMBER OF DAYS IN BILLING CYCLE	ANNUAL PERCENTAGE RATE	AVERAGE DAILY BALANCE	MONTHLY PERIODIC RATE
ED LUBBOCK FLORAL PARK, NY	30	19.8%		1.65%

Figure 8.13   Flash Card Bill

11. What is Ed's average daily balance?

12. What is Ed's finance charge?

13. What is Ed's new balance?

14. What is Ed's available credit?

15. If the $30 charge to Petrela Sailboats had been posted on 12/9, would the finance charge for the billing cycle be higher or lower? Explain your answer.

● KEY TERMS

To find the definition of any term introduced in the chapter, refer to the Glossary in the back of this book.

account number	finance charge
account type	late charge
annual percentage rate	minimum payment
available credit	monthly periodic rate
average daily balance	monthly statement
billing date	new balance
credit	number of days in billing cycle
credit card invoice	payment due date
credit line	previous balance
date of transaction	purchases
date posted	reference number
debit	regular, 30-day account
Fair Credit Billing Act	revolving charge accounts
Fair Debt Collection Practices Act	transaction description

● REVIEW PROBLEMS

Questions 1–10 refer to Figure 8.14 on page 337, Linda George's Flash Card bill. Notice that several entries are missing.

1. How many days are in the billing cycle?

2. Does this bill include purchases made on April 1?

3. What is the total of all the purchases shown on this statement?

4. On what date did Linda purchase items from Safran's Music Store?

ACCOUNT TYPE	ACCOUNT NUMBER	CREDIT LINE	AVAILABLE CREDIT	BILLING DATE	PAYMENT DUE DATE
FLASH CARD	3-472916-1	2,500		5/12	5/23

DATE POSTED	TRANS	REFERENCE NUMBER	TRANSACTION DESCRIPTION	DEBITS/ CREDITS(−)
4/26	4/21	362149231	LARRY'S SPORTS	65.50
5/2	4/28	214769421	SAFRAN'S MUSIC	765.00
5/7	4/30	326471893	CAROLLO'S GUITARS	91.75
5/11	5/11	876241591	PAYMENT THANK YOU	−250.00

SUMMARY	PREVIOUS BALANCE	PURCHASES	PAYMENTS	FINANCE CHARGE	LATE CHARGE	NEW BALANCE	MINIMUM PAYMENT
	291.81						28.00

	NUMBER OF DAYS IN BILLING CYCLE	ANNUAL PERCENTAGE RATE	AVERAGE DAILY BALANCE	MONTHLY PERIODIC RATE
LINDA GEORGE NEW ORLEANS, LA	30	18%		1.5%

FLASH CARD

Figure 8.14 Flash Card Bill

5. What is the last date covered by this billing cycle (the billing date)?

6. What is the average daily balance?

7. What is the monthly periodic rate?

8. What is the finance charge?

9. What is the new balance?

10. What is the available credit?

1. Go to a library and find the address of the Federal Trade Commission in Washington, D.C. Also find the address of your local or state Office of Consumer Affairs. Write a business letter to each office requesting pamphlets explaining government laws on consumer credit. Share this information with your classmates.

2. Go to a local bank and ask the loan department if the bank offers *passbook loans*. Find out what a passbook loan is and what you must do to take out a passbook loan. Ask how the passbook loan rates compare to other loans at that lending institution. Write a short summary and report your findings to the class.

3. Visit two lending institutions in your area. Find out the APR, monthly payment, and finance charge for a $15,000, three-year loan at the two different lending institutions. Make a wall chart displaying all the data.

4. Call a lending institution in your area. Find out the APR, monthly payment, and finance charge for a car loan based on the car you priced in Topic 2 Enhance/Advance Activity 1. (Be sure to bring all the paperwork you have from the car-pricing project.) Prepare a wall chart about your car and all costs for the car itself, for insurance, and for the loan.

5. Find out from a lending institution the APR, monthly payment, and finance charge for a $20,000 loan over a one-year, two-year, three-year and four-year period. Prepare a wall chart that displays your findings.

6. Go to a library and find the names and addresses of five credit unions located in your state. Write a business letter to one of the credit unions. Ask about the requirements for becoming a member of the credit union. Share this information with the class.

7. Talk to your teacher about having a local banker come to your school to speak about borrowing money. Visit a local bank and invite a bank representative. Have your classmates prepare

questions for the banker in advance. Submit these questions to the banker before or during the session. Be sure to write a thank-you letter to the banker.

8. Ask to interview your parent or friends about how they use their credit cards. Find out how often they use their cards, how many cards they have, and why they use credit cards. Show them how to compute the average daily balance and verify the finance charge on one of their credit card statements.

9. Visit some of the stores in your area. Make a list of 25 local stores. Indicate what credit cards, if any, are accepted by each store. Submit a report of your findings to your teacher.

TOPIC *4* MANIPULATIVE ACTIVITY

CHARGE CARDS

Many consumers charge holiday purchases during November and December. Then they receive large bills and finance charges in January. It is possible to lower your finance charges by making purchases and payments at certain times in your billing cycle.

In this activity, you will manipulate cards that you design, and learn how credit card purchases and payments affect the average daily balance. After creating the cards, you can challenge your classmates to test their knowledge about averages and credit cards.

Directions: You will need 50 index cards (size $3\frac{1}{2}'' \times 5''$ or larger) masking tape, and 3 permanent markers (black, red, green). You will be making 3 decks of cards.

1. Review Chapter 8, Section 2.

2. Using the black marker, write each of the dates from November 20 through December 19 on 30 index cards (one date per card). Shuffle this deck of "date" cards.

3. Using the red marker, write "purchase" on each of 15 index cards. Then fill in a different amount of each purchase (your choice) on each card. Shuffle this deck of "purchase" cards.

4. Using the blue marker, write "payment" on each of 5 index cards. Then, fill in a different amount of payment (your choice) on each card. Shuffle this deck of "payment" cards.

Now you are ready to use this manipulative. Have another student pick 10 date cards, 7 purchase cards, and 3 payment cards at random. Put a piece of masking tape on each card so they can be taped to the chalkboard.

Make 2 columns on the chalkboard. Label them "date" and "transaction." Then have the student put the date cards in order, vertically down the date column. Next to each date card, the student must place a purchase or payment card so that the average daily balance for the November 20 to December 19 billing period is as low as possible. Have your teacher check your work and see if you and your classmates can discover a general rule for lowering the average daily balance.

Reshuffle the decks and have other students try!

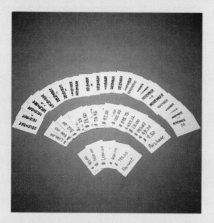
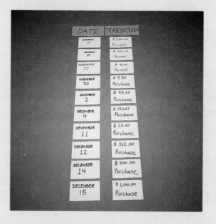

TOPIC 4 COMPUTER APPLICATION

LOAN PAYMENTS

Review the information on loans that you covered in Topic 4.

Directions: Now that you have reviewed that material, follow the start-up procedures for your computer which are found in Appendix A. Select Topic 4 titled *Loan Payments* from the Main Menu. Follow the instructions on your computer screen to answer these three situations. Do not write in this book. Put your answers on a piece of paper.

1. What effect does a shorter borrowing period have on the monthly payment and total interest paid over the life of a loan if the principal and the APR are the same in both situations?

Principal	APR	Length of Loan (years)	Number of Payments	Monthly Payments (dollars)	Total Interest (dollars)
$10,000	11%	5 years			
$10,000	11%	4 years			

2. What effect does a slightly lower APR have on the monthly payment and total interest paid over the life of a loan if the principal and the length of the loan are the same in both situations?

Principal	APR	Length of Loan (years)	Number of Payments	Monthly Payments (dollars)	Total Interest (dollars)
$10,000	10.5%	4 years			
$10,000	10%	4 years			

3. In the two situations that follow, the loan amount and the APR are the same. However, in the second instance the money is borrowed for a period twice as long as the first. What effect does this have on the monthly payments and total interest paid over the life of the loan?

Principal	APR	Length of Loan (years)	Number of Payments	Monthly Payments (dollars)	Total Interest (dollars)
$10,000	9%	4 years			
$10,000	9%	8 years			

How do people obtain the money they spend? You may already be familiar with a weekly allowance. But there are also other ways you may not have thought about: earnings from a job, gift of cash, and interest from savings in a bank. However, there are some expenses involved in all of these. Banks often charge fees for their services, and we pay taxes on earnings and gifts. You will need to learn about the different ways of earning money and the expenses involved.

CHAPTER **9**

GETTING A JOB

SECTION 1 ● LOOKING FOR EMPLOYMENT

How do you go about looking for a job? Begin by asking yourself, "What do I already know how to do? What do I enjoy doing? Am I good with cars? Do I have a green thumb? Am I handy with a calculator?" Next, turn your skills into a job by thinking about who would pay for your services. You can then start by looking for a help-wanted sign in a business such as a fast-food restaurant, a department store, or a gas station. The managers of these businesses will probably ask you to fill out a job application that includes a description of your skills and interests.

You can also look for job listings in the classified advertisements section of the newspaper. These help-wanted ads are similar to the classified ads for used cars that you learned about in Chapter 3. For example, examine this ad:

LEGAL SECY
Position open to qualified applicant with 10 yrs exp,
dictation 75 wpm, refs, great benefits. Salary 21K.
Apply to P.O. Box 459990

EXEC SECY to $390/wk
REAL ESTATE
Prestigious firm seeks exec secy with 5 years' exp,
75 wpm, refs req, pd vac, E.O.E. Call Ron (312) 555-
1300 for appt.

GENERAL SECY
Pay comm with exp. 5 yrs exp, dictation 55 wpm.
E.O.E. Call (312) 556-1561 for appt.

You will find it helpful to learn the special "shorthand" that is used in help-wanted classified ads. Study these abbreviations:

agcy — employment agency

appt — appointment

asst — assistant

avail — available

bi/ling — bilingual (able to speak and read more than one language)

comm — commission

dept — department

exec — executive

E.O.E. — equal opportunity employer

eves — evenings

exp — experience

exp nec — experience
necessary

fee pd — employment
agency fee paid
by employer

hr — hour

immed — immediate

K — $1,000 (for example,
15K = $15,000 per
year salary)

mo — month

pd vac — paid vacation

PT — part-time

refs — references

req — required

secy — secretary

to $400 — maximum
weekly salary
offered is $400

wpm — words per minute
(for dictation and/
or typing)

yr — year

If you apply for a job through a classified ad, you will have to send your résumé to the employer. A **résumé** is a short account of your career or qualifications. You will learn more about résumés in Topic 5 Enhance/Advance Activity 1. If the employer is impressed with your résumé, you will be invited to an interview and you might be hired!

You can also look for a job through an employment agency. An **employment agency** is a business that has lists of job openings. If you are placed in a job by an employment agency, you may have to pay a fee to the agency. When the employer is willing to pay this fee, the job is listed as **fee paid.** After you have been hired, your employer will ask you to fill out a **Form W-4: Employee's Withholding Allowance Certificate.** This form will be used by you and your employer for tax purposes.

As you can see, there are many ways of looking for employment. Good luck in your job hunting!

Skills and Strategies

Here you will compute a salary, an employment-agency fee, and the cost of printing a résumé.

1. John found a job listed in the classified ads that pays a yearly salary of $21K. What is the weekly salary based on this amount?

Solution: John must interpret what $21K means.

$1,000   K stands for $1,000
  × 21   number of thousands in $21K
$21,000   yearly salary

John can first *estimate* his weekly salary by rounding and dividing:

$$\frac{\$400}{50)\$20,000} \leftarrow \text{approximate weekly salary}$$
$$\leftarrow \text{John's salary rounded to the nearest } \$10,000.$$

↑
52 weeks rounded
to nearest 10 weeks

To find the exact weekly salary, John must divide the yearly salary by 52, the number of weeks in a year, and round to the nearest cent:

$$\frac{\$403.846}{52)\$21,000.000}$$

The following calculator keystroke sequence could be used to find the weekly salary:

AC 21,000 ÷ 52 =

The display, to three decimal places, should read 403.846.

The weekly salary based on $21,000 is $403.85, rounded to the nearest cent.

2. Dylan took a job through an employment agency. The job pays $195 per week. Dylan must pay a fee equal to 20% of his first four weeks' pay to the employment agency. How much money must Dylan pay the agency?

Solution:

$195   Dylan's weekly pay
  × 4   number of weeks used to compute fee
$780   Dylan's first four weeks' pay

$780   first four weeks' pay
× .20   20% expressed as a decimal
$156.00   fee

The following calculator keystroke sequence could be used to find the fee:

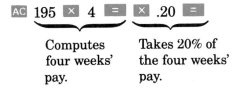

Computes	Takes 20% of
four weeks'	the four weeks'
pay.	pay.

The display should read 156.

3. Cara brought her typed résumé to a printer to have 300 copies made. The printer charged $10 for the first 100 copies and $8.50 for each additional set of 100 copies. How much did Cara pay for these copies, before sales tax?

   Solution: The first 100 copies cost $10. The remaining 200 copies represent two additional sets of 100 copies

$ 8.50	price per additional 100 copies
× 2	sets of additional 100 copies
$17.00	price of additional 200 copies

$10.00	price of first 100 copies
+ 17.00	price of 200 additional copies
$27.00	total cost

   Cara paid $27.00 to have 300 copies of her résumé printed.

Problems

1. Danny just answered a help-wanted ad. The ad states that the job pays $18K annually. What would Danny's monthly salary be if he gets this job?

✓2. Becky is looking for a new job as an account executive. She responds to a help-wanted ad for a position that pays $24K. What would Becky's weekly salary be if she gets this job? (Round your answer to the nearest cent.)

3. Eva got a job through an employment agency that charges a fee equal to 50% of the first five weeks' pay. The job pays $315

per week. How much money does Eva have to pay the employment agency?

4.   Melanie got a new job through the McDowell Employment Agency. The job pays $25,200 per year, and the agency fee is equal to one month's pay. How much must Melanie pay the agency?

✓ **5.**   The Bellerose Employment Agency just placed Howard Jacobson in a job as a pharmacist. The job pays $22.1K. The agency fee is equal to 40% of the first three weeks' pay.
   a.   What is Howard's weekly salary?
   b.   What will Howard earn during the first three weeks?

   c.   How much must Howard pay the employment agency?

6.   Bruce is applying for a job as a talent scout in Hollywood. He finds classified ads from seven different talent agencies that are looking for scouts. Since he lives in Nebraska, he rushes seven copies of his résumé through an overnight delivery service that charges $14.95 for each. What is the total cost of the rush delivery on these seven résumés?

✓ **7.**   Pat earns $370 per week at her new job. She must pay 20% of her first four paychecks to an employment agency. What is the total fee that she owes the employment agency?

✓ **8.**   Roger wants to have 400 copies of his résumé printed. His local printer charges $21.50 for the first 200 copies and $10 for every 100 additional copies. How much will the 400 copies cost, including a sales tax of 6%?

9.   Nina is looking for a job as a teacher. She will consider any job in the 123 schools within commuting distance of her home. She needs 123 copies of her résumé to send to these schools. Her local printer charges $12 per 100 copies, and sells them only in sets of 100.
   a.   How many copies must Nina purchase if she is to have enough résumés?
   b.   How much will the copies cost her, including a 5% sales tax?
   c.   How many copies will Nina have if she mails out 123 copies and accidentally rips four other copies?

✓ **10.** Carole spent $60 to have her résumé typeset by a printer. The printer charges $9.50 per 100 copies ordered. Carole orders 300 copies. What is the total cost of the copies and the typesetting, including a sales tax of 8%?

SECTION 2 • PAY PERIODS

Almost everybody looks forward to payday. Most high-school students are paid on a weekly basis, which means they receive 52 paychecks per year. Their paydays usually fall on the same day each week. Not all jobs, however, have a pay period of one week.

Some employees receive a paycheck every two weeks; they receive 26 paychecks per year. These people are paid **biweekly.** Their paydays fall on the same day of the week. Businesses that distribute paychecks to their employees biweekly save time and paperwork compared with businesses that pay their employees weekly.

Some businesses pay their employees twice a month, or **semimonthly.** Since there are 12 months in a year, these employees receive 24 paychecks per year. The paychecks are distributed on the same dates of each month. For example, an employer may choose to pay employees on the 1st and the 15th of each month. Note that biweekly and semimonthly payment schedules are slightly different.

Although it is not common, some businesses pay their employees **monthly.** These employees receive 12 paychecks per year. They are usually paid on the same date (for example, the first day) of each month.

When you take a job, be sure to ask about the pay periods so that you can look forward to payday too!

Skills and Strategies

Here you will learn to figure the dates and amounts of paychecks.

1. Pablo received his first paycheck on March 3. He is paid weekly. What are the dates of his next four paydays?

Solution: There are 7 days in a week.

March 3	date of first paycheck
+ 7	
March 10	payday
+ 7	
March 17	payday
+ 7	
March 24	payday
+ 7	
March 31	payday

Pablo will receive paychecks on March 10, March 17, March 24, and March 31.

2. Connie receives her paychecks biweekly. She received a paycheck on May 20. What is the date of her next paycheck?

Solution: There are 14 days in a biweekly pay period. Note that you can't just add 14 to May 20 to get the next pay date — there is no May 34th. Because there are 31 days in May, part of the pay period is in May and part is in June.

31	number of days in May
− 20	pay date
11	number of pay-period days in May

14	number of days in a biweekly pay period
− 11	number of pay-period days in May
3	June pay date

The date of Connie's next paycheck is June 3.
(*Note:* You can use the calendar in Chapter 1, on page 4, if you need help with this type of problem.)

3. Alice is paid biweekly. Her annual salary is $27,000. How much should her biweekly salary be?

Solution: There are 26 biweekly paychecks per year. Alice uses her calculator and the following keystroke sequence:

AC 27,000 ÷ 26 =

The display, to three decimal places, should read 1038.461.

Alice's biweekly salary (rounded to the nearest cent) should be $1,038.46.

Problems

✓ **1.** Arthur received his most recent paycheck on June 12. He is paid biweekly. When will he receive his next paycheck?

2. Joan is a teacher. She is paid biweekly. Her most recent payday was September 21. When will she receive her next paycheck?

3. Caryl is paid semimonthly. How many checks does she receive in a half-year?

✓ **4.** Lori works for a public-relations firm and receives a weekly paycheck. Her last payday was June 1. What are the dates of her next five paychecks?

5. Jamie is paid biweekly. His annual salary is $42,500. How much is his biweekly salary?

6. Mindy's semimonthly salary is $1,371.50. What is her annual salary?

7. Ceil gets paid biweekly. Her biweekly salary is $1,763.28. What is Ceil's annual salary?

8. Harry's weekly salary is $478.25. What is his annual salary?

✓ **9.** Ruth is paying back a two-year car loan of $8,000 with a 14% APR. Her annual salary is $37,400, and she is paid monthly.
   a. What is Ruth's monthly salary?
   b. Look at Figure 7.1, page 310. What is Ruth's monthly loan payment?
   c. How much of each monthly paycheck is left after Ruth deducts her loan payment?

10. Last year Jacob's annual salary was $38,350. This year he received a raise and now earns $46,462 annually. He is paid biweekly.
   a. What was Jacob's biweekly salary last year?
   b. What is Jacob's biweekly salary this year?
   c. On a biweekly basis, how much more does Jacob earn as a result of his raise?

SECTION 3 • HOURLY PAY

Most part-time jobs that students hold pay them a set amount for each hour they work. This amount is called the **hourly rate.** Many people in full-time careers also get paid at an hourly rate.

Certain jobs, whether full- or part-time, require the employee to work a specific number of hours per week. These are the employee's **regular hours.** Employees may work more hours than their regular hours; these are called **overtime hours.** The **overtime hourly rate** is usually greater than the hourly rate for the regular hours.

All employers must follow federal and state laws. Some of these laws involve pay rates. For example, there are federal laws involving the **minimum wage.** The minimum wage is the lowest hourly rate that can be paid to an employee in the United States. In Topic 5 Enhance/Advance Activity 2 you will learn more about labor laws in the United States and in your state.

It is important to have a clear understanding of your rights and responsibilities as an employee. This way you can be sure that you are being treated fairly by your employer.

Skills and Strategies

Here you learn to compute regular and overtime wages.

1. Maureen works at a local Chicken King restaurant. She is paid $4.90 per hour, and she regularly works 20 hours per week. What is her regular weekly pay?

    Solution:

    $$\begin{array}{ll} \$4.90 & \text{hourly rate} \\ \underline{\times\ 20} & \text{number of hours} \\ \$98.00 & \text{weekly pay} \end{array}$$

    Maureen's regular weekly pay is $98. This amount is sometimes referred to as **regular gross pay.**

2. If Maureen works overtime at her job, she is paid at $1\frac{1}{2}$ times her regular hourly rate. What is Maureen's hourly overtime rate?

    Solution: This overtime rate, sometimes referred to as *time and a half,* must be computed.

$2.45 ← half of the hourly rate

2)$4.90 ← regular hourly rate

$2.45 half of the hourly rate

+ 4.90 regular hourly rate

$7.35 overtime rate

The following calculator keystroke sequence could be used to find Maureen's hourly overtime rate.

| Stores the regular hourly rate in memory. | Finds the half-hour rate. | Adds the half-hour rate to the regular hourly rate. |

The display should read 7.35.
You could also use the keystroke sequence

AC 4.90 × 1.5 =

Multiplies hourly rate by $1\frac{1}{2}$.

Maureen's hourly overtime rate is $7.35.

3. Alex regularly earns $5.10 per hour. He receives $1\frac{1}{2}$ times his hourly rate for each hour of overtime he works. Last week he worked seven hours of overtime. What was his total overtime pay?

Solution: Alex must compute his hourly overtime rate.

$2.55 ← half of the hourly rate

2)$5.10 ← regular hourly rate

$2.55 half of the hourly rate

+ 5.10 regular hourly rate

$7.65 hourly overtime rate

$7.65 hourly overtime rate

× 7 number of overtime hours

$53.55 total overtime pay

Alex received $53.55 in total overtime pay last week.

4. Erin regularly works 40 hours per week, and she receives $7 per hour. Erin receives *double time* (twice her hourly rate) for each hour of overtime she works. Erin worked 46 hours last week. What was her total pay?

Solution: Erin must compute her regular pay and overtime pay and then add them together.

$$
\begin{array}{rl}
\$\ \ 7.00 & \text{regular hourly rate} \\
\underline{\times\ 40} & \text{regular hours} \\
\$280.00 & \text{regular gross pay}
\end{array}
$$

$$
\begin{array}{rl}
\$\ 14.00 & \text{overtime rate (twice the regular hourly rate)} \\
\underline{\times\ 6} & \text{number of overtime hours} \\
\$\ 84.00 & \text{total overtime pay}
\end{array}
$$

$$
\begin{array}{rl}
\$280.00 & \text{regular gross pay} \\
\underline{+\ 84.00} & \text{total overtime pay} \\
\$364.00 & \text{total pay for the week}
\end{array}
$$

Erin's total pay for the week was $364. This amount is also referred to as **gross pay.**

The following calculator keystroke sequence could also be used to compute Erin's total gross pay.

AC 7 × 40 = M+ 7 × 2 = × 6 = M+ M

Computes and stores regular gross pay.

Computes hourly overtime rate; then computes total overtime pay and adds it to regular gross pay.

The display should read 364.

Erin's total gross pay was $364.00.

Problems

1. Hector works in a gas station and earns $4.60 per hour. Last week he worked 20 hours. What was his gross pay?

✓ 2. Eddie works at Beep-N-Kleen car wash. He earns $4.80 per hour. Last week he worked $18\frac{1}{2}$ hours. What was his gross pay?

✓ 3. Lynn regularly earns $7 per hour. She receives time-and-a-half pay for each hour of overtime she works. Last week she worked six hours overtime.
   a. What is her hourly overtime rate?
   b. What is her total overtime pay?

4. Jill earns $5 per hour while working at Woody's Pet Supplies. She regularly works 40 hours per week. She receives time-and-a-half pay for each hour of overtime she works. Last week she worked 47 hours.
   a. What is her hourly overtime rate?
   b. How many overtime hours did Jill work last week?
   c. What is her total overtime pay?
   d. What is her gross pay for the week?

5. Nancy regularly works 20 hours at Pook's Dry Cleaners from Monday through Friday. She earns $4.70 per hour and receives double-time pay for working on a Sunday. Next week she will work her regular 20 hours as well as an additional eight hours on Sunday. What will her gross pay be for next week?

✓ 6. Tom earns $7 per hour at the Fairmont Golf Club. He regularly works 40 hours per week. He is paid a time-and-a-half rate for each overtime hour he works. Last week he worked 42 hours. What was his gross pay for the week?

7. Pedro regularly works 35 hours per week at Butelli's Deli. He earns $6.10 an hour and receives time-and-a-half pay for each hour of overtime he works. Last week he worked 41 hours and received a paycheck for $215.20.
   a. Find Pedro's overtime hourly rate.
   b. Find Pedro's total overtime pay.
   c. Find Pedro's regular gross pay.
   d. Find Pedro's total gross pay for the week.
   e. Pedro's paycheck was incorrect. How much money does his boss owe him?

✓**8.** Kerry earns $6 per hour at the Glen Oaks Bakery. He regularly works 40 hours per week, and he receives double-time pay for each hour of overtime he works. His time card for last week is shown in Figure 9.1. Use this time card to answer questions a-e at the top of page 357.

NAME   KERRY OSOMO

EMPLOYEE'S NO.   60390

CLOCK NO.   1

SOCIAL SECURITY NUMBER   405-84-3763

PERIOD _____

GLEN OAKS BAKERY

SIGNATURE ____*Kerry Osomo*____

AUTHORIZED _____

ALL DEVIATIONS FROM REGULAR TIME OFF FOR LUNCH AND BREAKS **MUST BE INDICATED** ON THE TIME CARD.

DAY	IN	OUT	IN	OUT	FOR PAYROLL USE ONLY	TOTAL
M	7 00 AM	5 00 PM				
T	7 00 AM	5 30 PM				
W	6 58 AM	6 30 PM				
TH	6 55 AM	4 55 PM				
F	9 00 AM	5 05 PM				

		HOURS	
SPECIAL		REGULAR	
S & A OR STD		SICK	
VARIABLE		OVERTIME	

Figure 9.1   Kerry Osomo's Time Card

   a. How many hours did Kerry work last week?
   b. What was Kerry's regular gross pay?
   c. How many overtime hours did Kerry work last week?
   d. What is Kerry's hourly overtime rate?
   e. What was Kerry's gross pay for last week?

✓ **9.** Find the time-and-a-half rate based on each of the following regular hourly rates. (Round each answer to the nearest cent.)
   a. $7.50   **b.** $6.20   **c.** $4.90
   d. $7.75   **e.** $6.55   **f.** $4.95

10. Jimmy and Cheryl work in different local supermarkets. Jimmy regularly earns $5.90 per hour, and he is paid time and a half for each hour of overtime he works. Cheryl regularly earns $4.10 per hour and gets double-time pay for each overtime hour. Who receives more for one hour of overtime pay? How much more?

SECTION 4 • COMMISSIONS AND ROYALTIES

Some employees are not paid by the number of hours they work. Their pay is based on the amount of sales they make. For example:

- Stockbrokers earn money based on the number of shares they trade.

- Travel agents earn money based on the value of the trips they book.

- Authors earn money based on how many copies of their books are sold.

- Rock musicians earn money based on record, tape, and disc sales.

- Vacuum-cleaner salespeople earn money based on the number of vacuum cleaners they sell.

These people are paid a **commission,** or a **royalty.** The commission or royalty rate is usually expressed as a percent. People who get paid commissions or royalties earn more money as more sales are made. Even if they work many hours, they can earn very little money if very few sales are made.

Some employees get a commission in addition to their regular salary. Can you think of any advantages and disadvantages of getting paid only by commission?

Skills and Strategies

Here you will learn how commissions and royalties are computed.

1. Ken sells new cars at a local dealership. He receives 8% in commission on every car he sells. How much commission would he make for selling a $23,000 sports car?

    Solution:

    $$
    \begin{array}{ll}
    \$23,000 & \text{selling price} \\
    \underline{\times\ .08} & \text{commission rate expressed as a decimal} \\
    \$1,840.00 & \text{commission}
    \end{array}
    $$

    Ken would receive a commission of $1,840.

2. Andrew Dell wrote a textbook for high-school students. He receives a 10% royalty based on the total sales of the book. The book sells for $7.95, and 17,000 copies were sold last year. How much did Andrew Dell receive in royalty payments for last year?

Solution: First, determine the total sales from the 17,000 books.

17,000	number of books sold
× 7.95	price per book
$135,150.00	total sales

$135,150	total sales
× .10	royalty rate expressed as a decimal
$13,515.00	total royalties

Andrew Dell received $13,515 in royalty payments for last year.

3. Dorothy sells cosmetics part-time from door to door. She is paid a monthly commission. She receives 11% of her first $900 in sales and 17% of the balance of her sales. Last month she sold $1,250 worth of cosmetics. How much commission did she earn last month?

Solution: Find the commission on the first $900 worth of sales.

$900	first $900 of total sales
× .11	commission rate expressed as a decimal
$99.00	commission based on first $900

$1,250	total sales
− 900	first $900 of total sales
$350	balance of sales

$350	balance of sales
× .17	commission rate expressed as a decimal
$59.50	commission on balance of sales

$99.00	commission based on first $900
+ 59.50	commission based on the $350 balance
$158.50	total commission for last month

Dorothy earned $158.50 in commission last month.

You could also have used the calculator keystroke sequence at the top of page 360.

AC `900` X `.11` = M+ `1250` − `900` = X `.17` = + M‖ =

Calculates and stores the commission based on the first $900 of sales.	Finds the balance over $900.	Computes commission on the balance.	Adds the two commissions together.

The display should read 158.50.

Problems

1. Rock musician Johnny Gale is paid 15% on his album and cassette sales. Last year he sold one million albums and 550,000 cassettes. The albums were sold to record stores for $4 each, and the cassettes were sold for $3.70 each.
    a. What was the total amount of album sales?
    b. What was the total amount of cassette sales?
    c. What was the combined total of album and cassette sales?

    d. How much did Johnny Gale receive in royalties last year?

2. Joan sells American-made trucks. She receives 9% on her sales. Last month she had two truck sales, one for $21,790 and one for $25,650. How much did she earn in commission?

✓ 3. Melissa is a travel agent. She receives a 7% commission based on the value of the trips she books. Today she spent four hours arranging a $3,300 cruise for a newlywed couple. How much commission did she earn?

4. Jerry works at Lucchessi's Computer Outlet. He receives a weekly salary of $200 plus 3% commission based on his sales. Last week he sold $29,700 worth of computer equipment. How much money did Jerry earn last week?

✓ 5. Sylvan sells magazine subscriptions from door to door. He receives 12% of the first $1,000 and 15% on the balance over $1,000. Last month he sold $7,500 worth of magazine subscriptions. What was his commission for last month?

6. Professional baseball player Rusty Raspberry earns $715,000 a year playing baseball. Last year a biography that he had written sold 300,000 copies at a price of $12 each. Raspberry received 10% in royalties on the book sales. What was his total salary last year from the book and his baseball career?

✓ 7. Claire Powers is a real-estate agent. She earns 6.5% commission on each sale she makes. Last month she sold a house for $250,000 and another for $310,000. What did Claire earn in commissions for the month?

8. Stephanie has a job selling magazine subscriptions by phone. She makes a base salary of $4.80 per hour plus a 5% commission on all sales. Last week Stephanie worked 35 hours and sold $230 worth of magazine subscriptions. What was her gross pay for the week?

9. Hillside Travel pays its employees $5 per hour plus 8% commission on all trips booked. Last week Vincent worked 20 hours and booked trips amounting to $2,100. What was his gross pay for last week?

✓ 10. Sandy is a stockbroker. She receives a commission based on the value of the trades she makes. Her last three weekly paychecks were $964.30, $711.10, and $612.10. What was Sandy's mean salary for the last three weeks?

SECTION 5 • PIECEWORK PAY

Some people are paid according to the *amount* of work that they do rather than the length of time that it takes them to do the job. These employees are called **pieceworkers.** Pieceworkers are paid a certain amount of money, called the **piecework rate,** for each item or piece that they complete. Although **piecework** is not as common as it used to be, there are still jobs in which workers are paid according to this method. Some farm workers are paid by the number of baskets of fruit or vegetables they pick. Some factory workers are paid by the number of items they produce.

Piecework pay is sometimes used in combination with an hourly wage. The employee gets paid by the hour and receives a certain amount of money for each piece of work completed. The greater the number of pieces completed, the more money the employee makes. This benefits both the employer and the worker.

Skills and Strategies

Here you will learn how piecework wages are computed.

1. Florence works in a factory that manufactures automobile parts. She is paid at a piecework rate of 75 cents per unit (piece) produced. Yesterday she produced 110 units. How much did she earn?

   Solution: Remember that 75¢ = $.75

110	number of units
× .75	piecework rate
$82.50	piecework pay

   Florence earned $82.50 yesterday.

2. Darren picks strawberries and gets paid at a piecework rate of 45 cents per basket for the first 200 baskets picked. He receives a bonus of 20 cents (in addition to the 45 cents) per basket for every basket over 200 that he picks. Last week he picked 270 baskets. How much did he earn?

   Solution: Recall that 45¢ = $.45 and 20¢ = $.20.

200	first 200 baskets picked
× .45	piecework rate
$90.00	piecework pay for 200 baskets

270	number of baskets picked
− 200	first 200 baskets picked
70	number of baskets picked over 200

70	number of baskets picked over 200
× .65	piecework rate (45¢ + 20¢)
$45.50	piecework pay for the additional 70 baskets

$90.00	piecework pay for first 200 baskets
+ 45.50	piecework pay for 70 additional baskets
$135.50	total piecework pay

Darren earned $135.50 for picking strawberries last week.

Darren could also use the following calculator keystroke sequence:

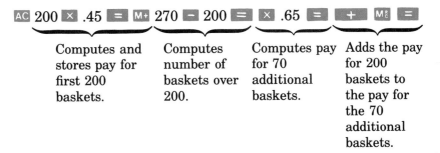

Computes and stores pay for first 200 baskets.	Computes number of baskets over 200.	Computes pay for 70 additional baskets.	Adds the pay for 200 baskets to the pay for the 70 additional baskets.

The display should read 135.5.

Problems

1. Sylvan picks berries at Seymour's Berry Farm. He receives 28 cents for each basket picked. Last week he picked 731 baskets. How much did he earn?

✓ 2. Barbara works in a local factory. She receives 92 cents for each of the first 100 units she produces and $1.01 for each unit over 100. Yesterday she produced 120 units. How much did she earn?

3. Bill works in Wagner's Winch Factory. He receives 25 cents for each unit he produces. Last week he produced 2,000 units. He received a check for $474, and he is certain the check is incorrect.
   a. What is Bill's correct total piecework pay?
   b. How much money does his boss owe him?

✓ 4. Audrey works in a factory. She receives a salary of $4 per hour and piecework pay of 12 cents per unit produced. Last week she worked 38 hours and produced 755 units.
   a. What was her piecework pay?
   b. What was her total pay for the week?

5. Anton picks corn at a local farm. He is paid 80 cents per bushel for the first 50 bushels, 90 cents per bushel for the next 50 bushels, and $1.00 per bushel for all bushels picked over 100. How much does Anton make if he picks 120 bushels?

✓ 6. Beatrice works in an exclusive dress factory. She is paid $78 for each dress she sews. Last month she sewed 30 dresses. What was her total pay for the month?

7. Barbara types papers for local college students. She charges $2.50 per page. How much would she receive for typing 22 pages?

✓ 8. Neil stuffs envelopes part-time for a local coupon company for 3 cents an envelope. Last week he stuffed 3,211 envelopes. What was his total pay for the week?

9. Last week Eric received a total piecework paycheck of $252.48. He receives 12 cents per unit produced. How many units did Eric produce last week?

✓ 10. Nancy receives 10 cents per unit produced at the Wiggy Factory. Her production record for last week was affected by a machinery breakdown on Tuesday. Here are her production results:

Monday, 375 units
Tuesday, 22 units
Wednesday, 410 units
Thursday, 390 units
Friday, 390 units

a. What is the mean number of units produced per day?
b. What is the median number of units produced?
c. Which statistic, the mean or the median, would best describe Nancy's daily production last week? Explain your answer.
d. What is the mode number of units produced?

SECTION 6 • INSURANCE AVAILABLE TO EMPLOYEES

In many states employees are covered by certain types of insurance plans. These plans differ from state to state and from job to job. Here are some of the more common types of plans:

Workers' compensation is an insurance plan through which eligible employees who are injured on the job receive cash payments and medical coverage.

Unemployment insurance supplies income to persons who have lost their jobs through no fault of their own. People who receive unemployment insurance must be ready and willing to accept a new job.

Disability insurance pays benefits to persons who are out of work because of an illness or injury that is not job-related.

Medical insurance plans are not offered to all employees. Medical insurance covers medical emergencies, hospital and doctor bills, and other expenses. Some plans cover the employee's spouse (husband or wife) and children.

Dental insurance plans cover dental work. Some plans cover the employee's spouse and children.

Retirement insurance provides income for employees after they stop working. There are certain age requirements that an employee must meet before collecting benefits. Retirement-insurance benefits are sometimes called **pensions.**

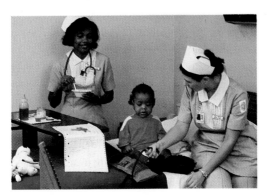

Topic 5 Enhance/Advance Activity 2 will help you find out specific information about these insurance plans.

Some insurance premiums are paid by the employee, and some are paid by the employer. Sometimes both the employer and the employee contribute money toward the premium. With all insurance plans, the policyholders have the potential to collect more in benefits than they pay in premiums.

When you get a job, it is important to ask your employer about the insurance plans that would be available to you.

Skills and Strategies

Here you will see how to compute an insurance premium and an annual pension.

1. Janet pays $8.50 per week in medical insurance premiums. What is her annual medical insurance premium?

   Solution:

   $$\begin{array}{ll} \$\ 8.50 & \text{weekly premium} \\ \underline{\times\ 52} & \text{number of weeks in one year} \\ \$442.00 & \text{annual premium} \end{array}$$

   Janet's annual medical insurance premium is $442.

2. Harriet is retiring from her job as a teacher. Her annual pension is computed by taking 60% of her average salary for the last three years she worked. Harriet's last three annual salaries were $40,000, $42,120, and $45,746. Compute Harriet's annual pension.

   Solution: First, find the average of her last three annual salaries:

   $$\left.\begin{array}{r} \$40,000 \\ 42,120 \\ +\ 45,746 \end{array}\right\} \text{last three annual salaries}$$

   $$\$127,866 \quad \text{total pay for last three years}$$

   $$\begin{array}{l} \quad\ \underline{\$42,622} \leftarrow \text{average of last three annual salaries} \\ 3\overline{)\$127,866} \leftarrow \text{total pay for last three years} \end{array}$$

$42,622   average of last three annual salaries
× .60   60% expressed as a decimal
$25,573.20   Harriet's annual pension

Harriet will receive $25,573.20 as her annual pension.

You could have used the following calculator keystroke sequence:

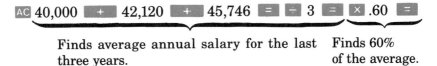

Finds average annual salary for the last three years.   Finds 60% of the average.

The display should read 25,573.2.

Problems

1. Doug collected $75 per week in unemployment insurance for the last 26 weeks. How much unemployment insurance did he receive?

√2. Marty has a dental insurance plan through his job at Dan's Supermarket. He pays $13.12 per month in premiums. What is his total dental insurance premium for the year?

3. Mindy's medical insurance plan costs $370 per year. She pays 10% of this premium, and her employer contributes 90% of the premium.
   a. How much does Mindy pay per year?
   b. How much does her employer pay?

√4. Denise broke her leg in a skiing accident, and she is unable to work for the next four weeks. She regularly earns $373.40 per week. Her disability insurance will pay her 45% of her regular weekly salary for each week she can't work.
   a. What will Denise's weekly disability payment be? $168.03
   b. How much disability insurance will Denise be paid for the four weeks?

5. Paul injured himself while working at his job as an electrician. He receives from his workers' compensation insurance 30% of

his weekly salary for each week he can't work. Paul's regular annual salary is $25,220, and he will miss two weeks of work as a result of the injury.
a. What is Paul's weekly salary?
b. What will Paul receive in weekly workers' compensation benefits?
c. How much workers' compensation will Paul receive for the two weeks he missed?

6. Ronald's annual pension is equal to 58% of the average of his last four years of earnings. Ronald's last four annual salaries are $54,780, $63,120, $62,000, and $67,920.
a. What is Ronald's mean salary for the last four years?

b. What is Ronald's median salary for the last four years?

c. What is the amount of Ronald's annual pension?

7. Debbie's employer pays 75% of each employee's medical insurance premiums. What percentage of the medical insurance premium must Debbie pay?

8. Jill receives an annual pension of $18,120. The pension checks are mailed out monthly. What is the amount of Jill's monthly pension check?

9. Ben's dental insurance plan pays for 80% of his dental expenses. Last month Ben had $1,412 worth of dental work done.
a. How much will Ben's insurance company pay toward this dental expense?
b. How much will Ben have to pay?

10. Anita contributes 3% of her weekly salary toward her pension. Her annual salary is $24,284. How much money does Anita contribute toward her pension each week?

● KEY TERMS

To find the definition of any term introduced in the chapter, refer to the Glossary in the back of this book.

biweekly	overtime hourly rate
commission	overtime hours
dental insurance	pensions
disability insurance	piecework
employee's withholding allowance certificate	piecework rate
	pieceworkers
employment agency	regular gross pay
fee paid	regular hours
Form W-4	royalty
gross pay	résumé
hourly rate	retirement insurance
medical insurance	semimonthly
minimum wage	unemployment insurance
monthly	workers' compensation

● REVIEW PROBLEMS

1. Nancy is looking for a job as a teacher. She finds two classified ads describing jobs that interest her. The Briar School is offering $24K annually, and the Berkely School is offering $22.8K. What is the difference between the monthly salaries of these two jobs?

2. Sylvia took a job with the Fairchild Balloon Company. She must pay a fee equal to her first three weeks' pay to the employment agency that arranged the job interview. Her annual salary is $18,200. How much does Sylvia have to pay the employment agency?

3. Ken regularly works 40 hours per week, and he receives $5.50 an hour. If Ken works overtime, he receives time-and-a-half pay. Last week Ken worked 43 hours. What was his gross pay?

4. Sue earns $4.90 per hour. Last week she worked $36\frac{1}{2}$ hours. How much did she earn?

5. Enrique sells brushes from door to door. He receives 9% commission based on his sales. Last month he sold $7,000 worth of brushes. How much in commission did Enrique earn last month?

6. Marie sews high-quality women's dresses. She is paid at a piecework rate of $67.50 per dress. Last week she made seven dresses. How much piecework pay did Marie earn last week?

7. Craig is a plumber. He places a classified ad stating that he will pay a helper $670 semimonthly. What annual salary is Craig offering?

8. An employer pays five employees $27,690 each a year. Their paychecks are made out biweekly. What is the amount of each biweekly paycheck?

9. Ted has three insurance plans through his job. From each weekly paycheck, Ted pays $3.17 in medical insurance, $1.19 in dental insurance, and $.98 in disability insurance. How much does Ted pay for all of this insurance per year?

10. Miguel earns $7 per hour, and he regularly works 40 hours per week. Last week he was injured in a car accident, and he is going to miss five weeks of work. His disability insurance will pay him 60% of his salary each week. How much will Miguel receive in disability insurance for the five weeks he does not work?

CHAPTER 10

INCOME TAXES

SECTION 1 ● SOCIAL SECURITY

In Chapter 9 you learned about several insurance plans available through employers. What if your employer does not offer one of these plans? An insurance program is also available jointly through your employer and the United States government. This insurance, called **social security**, covers 90% of all American jobs.

President Franklin D. Roosevelt started social security in 1935. It was established in the **Federal Insurance Contributions Act (FICA).** Social security offers limited protection for eligible workers and their families. Social security provides some income and medical benefits for people after they retire. It is somewhat like a pension. However, many retired people receive income from both social security and their pensions.

Under some conditions, social security pays benefits to family members of disabled workers. Social security can also act as a life insurance policy. If an eligible worker dies, benefits are paid to the surviving family members.

When you work at a job covered by social security, you must pay **social security tax**, or FICA tax, to cover this insurance. The costs of your social security are split evenly between you and your employer. The amount of social security tax that you pay depends upon the **social security percentage** and the **maximum taxable income** for that year. A percentage of each worker's salary is taken out of each paycheck, up to a set maximum amount. Any annual income above that amount is not subject to social security tax.

The employer must also contribute an equal amount toward the employee's social security account. The money that you and your employer contribute to social security is used to pay the *current* social security benefits to *someone else*. When *you* become eligible for social security, the people working at that time will be paying for your benefits. Your social security benefits will be based on the lifetime contributions in your account. Topic 5 Enhance/Advance Activity 4 will assist you in obtaining your own record of social security payments.

Records of all contributions are kept on file in social security offices around the country. Each person who contributes is given an identification number called a **social security number**. All records are listed under the person's social security number. Your social security number is unique — nobody else will ever be issued the same number. You will keep the same number throughout your life. You can write to your local social security office to obtain a social security number. The office will send you a **Form SS-5: Application for Social Security Number**. Eligible people who fill out the form will be issued a social security number.

Skills and Strategies

Here you will learn how social security payments have increased in recent years. You will also learn how to compute problems relating to social security tax.

1. The first year that Jack worked, he earned $19,200. The social security percentage for that year was 7.15%. The maximum taxable income was $43,800. What was the amount of Jack's social security tax that year?

   Solution: First look at Jack's income. Because his income was less than the maximum taxable income ($19,200 is less than $43,800), Jack paid social security tax on his entire income. Change 7.15% to an equivalent decimal.

   7.15% = .0715

Multiply the total income by the tax rate to find the tax amount.

$19,200.00 total income
$\times$ .0715 tax rate
$1,372.80 tax amount

Jack paid $1,372.80 in social security tax.

Because most social security tax computations are lengthy, it is advisable to use a calculator. You can use the following calculator keystroke sequence:

AC 19,200 × 7.15 %

The display should read 1,372.80.

Jack contributed $1,372.80 toward his social security account that year.

2. In 1987 the social security percentage was 7.15% on a maximum taxable income of $43,800. Mr. Harrison earned $76,000 in 1987. How much did he pay in FICA tax?

Solution: Mr. Harrison paid FICA tax only on the first $43,800 he earned. You can use the following calculator keystroke sequence:

AC 43,800 × 0.0715 =

The display should read 3,131.70.

Mr. Harrison paid $3,131.70 in FICA tax in 1987. This was the maximum amount that could be paid by employees that year. Mr. Harrison's employer also contributed $3,131.70 toward Mr. Harrison's social security account.

Problems

✓ 1. Convert each of the following percents to equivalent decimals.
   a. 5.85%   **b.** 6.05%   **c.** 6.13%   **d.** 6.65%
   e. 6.7%   **f.** 7.05%   **g.** 7.15%

2. Jerry is writing to his representative in Congress to inquire about FICA tax increases. He feels that FICA taxes increase

too much each year. Jerry compiles the information found in Table 10.1

FICA Taxes, 1977–1987

Year	Social Security Percentage	Maximum Taxable Income
1977	5.85%	$16,500
1978	6.05%	$17,700
1979	6.13%	$22,900
1980	6.13%	$25,900
1981	6.65%	$29,700
1982	6.7%	$32,400
1983	6.7%	$32,400
1984	6.7%	$37,800
1985	7.05%	$39,600
1986	7.15%	$42,000
1987	7.15%	$43,800

Table 10.1

a. What was the maximum FICA tax an employee could have contributed in 1977?

b. What was the maximum FICA tax an employee could have paid in 1987?

c. How much did the maximum FICA tax increase from 1977 to 1987?

3. Construct a line graph showing the social security maximum taxable income for each year from 1977 to 1987. Use information from Table 10.1.

4. What was the maximum FICA tax an employee could have contributed in 1980? (Use Table 10.1.)

✓ 5. Louis entered dental school in 1986. He was not employed in 1986, 1987, or 1988 because he needed time to study. In 1985

Louis earned $28,400. How much did he contribute in FICA tax in 1985? (Use Table 10.1.)

6. Mrs. Starr retired in 1987. She earned $41,670 during her last year of work. She now receives $966.20 in monthly social security benefits.
   a. What is her current annual social security benefit?

   b. What is the difference between her current annual social security benefit and her 1987 salary?

✓ 7. Mr. Epstein earned $24,000 during his last year of work. He is now retired and receives $876 a month in social security benefits.
   a. What was Mr. Epstein's average monthly salary during his last year of work?
   b. What is the difference between his monthly salary during his last year of work and his present monthly social security benefit?

8. In 1986 Mr. Wolfe received a monthly salary of $4,200.
   a. How much money did Mr. Wolfe receive over the first ten months of 1986?
   b. What was the maximum taxable income for FICA contributions in 1986? (Use Table 10.1.)
   c. How much did Mr. Wolfe contribute to social security during the first ten months of 1986?
   d. How much money did Mr. Wolfe contribute to social security during the last two months of 1986? Explain your answer.

✓ 9. In 1982 Mrs. Blair had two jobs. As an accountant during the day, she earned $23,111; as a waitress at night, she earned $10,000. Did Mrs. Blair earn more than the social security maximum taxable income in 1982? (Use Table 10.1.) Explain your answer.

10. In 1981 Mrs. Brala had two jobs. She earned $20,000 from her day job and $11,000 from her night job. Both employers took FICA taxes out of her paycheck.
   a. How much FICA tax did Mrs. Brala pay based on the salary of her day job? (Use Table 10.1.)

   b. How much FICA tax did Mrs. Brala pay based on the salary of her night job? (Use Table 10.1.)

   c. How much FICA tax did Mrs. Brala pay in 1981?

   d. What is the maximum amount of FICA tax that an employee should have paid in 1981?

   e. Mrs. Brala paid too much FICA tax in 1981, and the government had to send her the amount she overpaid. How much extra FICA tax did Mrs. Brala pay in 1981?

SECTION 2 ● READING TAX TABLES

How much money does it take to run your city? Think of the many costs for repairs and maintenance alone. Now imagine the amount of money it takes to run your city, state, and federal governments combined! Think of just a few services they provide:

- police forces

- fire departments

- political officers

- the space program

- legal professionals

- road building and maintenance

- teachers and educational resources

- health research

- military defense and national security

- public assistance programs

Where does the money for all these services come from? Taxpayers! People who earn income in the United States must pay taxes based on the amount of **taxable income** they earn. These taxes are called **income taxes**. Each taxpayer has a specific tax liability each year. Your **tax liability** is the amount of money you must pay to the government. It is the price you pay to benefit from government services. Your state, city, and federal governments collect income taxes. Although people don't *like* to pay taxes, they do so willingly because they realize taxes are necessary.

Federal taxes are collected by the **Internal Revenue Service (IRS).** Topic 5 Enhance/Advance Activity 5 will help you learn about the history of taxation in the United States.

You have already learned how to compute sales tax. Remember, sales tax is based on the price of something that is *sold*. Income tax is based on the income you *earn*. Your income tax liability changes as your income changes. You can find your tax liability by using a **tax table** or **tax schedule**.

You report your taxable income on a form that is mailed to the government. This form is called a **tax return**. You will learn how to fill out tax returns in Sections 4 and 5 of this chapter. When you mail a return to the government, you have **filed** your income taxes. Income taxes are based on your taxable income for the previous calendar year and on your filing status. Your **filing status** is a description of your marital and family status on the last day of the tax year. Study these terms:

Single — unmarried taxpayers

Married Filing Jointly — married people who fill out one tax return together

Married Filing Separately — married people who file one return for the husband and one return for the wife

Head of Household — a special filing status for certain unmarried taxpayers who support people in addition to themselves

Figure 10.1 on page 378 is a sample table of tax liabilities. These tables may change, but the skills involved in reading the sample table will help you read *any* tax table. Examine Figure 10.1.

If taxable income is—		And you are—				If taxable income is—		And you are—				If taxable income is—		And you are—			
At least	But less than	Single	Married filing jointly *	Married filing separately	Head of a household	At least	But less than	Single	Married filing jointly *	Married filing separately	Head of a household	At least	But less than	Single	Married filing jointly *	Married filing separately	Head of a household
		Your tax is—						Your tax is—						Your tax is—			
14,000						**17,000**						**20,000**					
14,000	14,050	1,727	1,360	2,057	1,655	17,000	17,050	2,352	1,840	2,834	2,212	20,000	20,050	3,054	2,375	3,726	2,827
14,050	14,100	1,737	1,368	2,070	1,664	17,050	17,100	2,364	1,848	2,848	2,222	20,050	20,100	3,067	2,384	3,742	2,839
14,100	14,150	1,747	1,376	2,082	1,673	17,100	17,150	2,375	1,856	2,862	2,232	20,100	20,150	3,080	2,393	3,759	2,851
14,150	14,200	1,757	1,384	2,095	1,682	17,150	17,200	2,387	1,864	2,876	2,242	20,150	20,200	3,093	2,402	3,775	2,863
14,200	14,250	1,767	1,392	2,107	1,691	17,200	17,250	2,398	1,872	2,890	2,252	20,200	20,250	3,106	2,411	3,792	2,875
14,250	14,300	1,777	1,400	2,120	1,700	17,250	17,300	2,410	1,880	2,904	2,262	20,250	20,300	3,119	2,420	3,808	2,887
14,300	14,350	1,787	1,408	2,132	1,709	17,300	17,350	2,421	1,889	2,918	2,272	20,300	20,350	3,132	2,429	3,825	2,899
14,350	14,400	1,797	1,416	2,145	1,718	17,350	17,400	2,433	1,898	2,932	2,282	20,350	20,400	3,145	2,438	3,841	2,911
14,400	14,450	1,807	1,424	2,157	1,727	17,400	17,450	2,444	1,907	2,946	2,292	20,400	20,450	3,158	2,447	3,858	2,923
14,450	14,500	1,817	1,432	2,170	1,736	17,450	17,500	2,456	1,916	2,960	2,302	20,450	20,500	3,171	2,456	3,874	2,935
14,500	14,550	1,827	1,440	2,182	1,745	17,500	17,550	2,467	1,925	2,974	2,312	20,500	20,550	3,184	2,465	3,891	2,947
14,550	14,600	1,837	1,448	2,195	1,754	17,550	17,600	2,479	1,934	2,988	2,322	20,550	20,600	3,197	2,474	3,907	2,959
14,600	14,650	1,847	1,456	2,207	1,763	17,600	17,650	2,490	1,943	3,002	2,332	20,600	20,650	3,210	2,483	3,924	2,971
14,650	14,700	1,857	1,464	2,220	1,772	17,650	17,700	2,502	1,952	3,016	2,342	20,650	20,700	3,223	2,492	3,940	2,983
14,700	14,750	1,867	1,472	2,232	1,781	17,700	17,750	2,513	1,961	3,030	2,352	20,700	20,750	3,236	2,501	3,957	2,995
14,750	14,800	1,877	1,480	2,245	1,790	17,750	17,800	2,525	1,970	3,044	2,362	20,750	20,800	3,249	2,510	3,973	3,007
14,800	14,850	1,887	1,488	2,257	1,799	17,800	17,850	2,536	1,979	3,058	2,372	20,800	20,850	3,262	2,519	3,990	3,019
14,850	14,900	1,897	1,496	2,270	1,808	17,850	17,900	2,548	1,988	3,072	2,382	20,850	20,900	3,275	2,528	4,006	3,031
14,900	14,950	1,907	1,504	2,282	1,817	17,900	17,950	2,559	1,997	3,086	2,392	20,900	20,950	3,288	2,537	4,023	3,043
14,950	15,000	1,917	1,512	2,295	1,826	17,950	18,000	2,571	2,006	3,100	2,402	20,950	21,000	3,301	2,546	4,039	3,055
15,000						**18,000**						**21,000**					
15,000	15,050	1,927	1,520	2,307	1,835	18,000	18,050	2,582	2,015	3,114	2,412	21,000	21,050	3,314	2,555	4,056	3,067
15,050	15,100	1,937	1,528	2,320	1,844	18,050	18,100	2,594	2,024	3,128	2,422	21,050	21,100	3,327	2,564	4,072	3,079
15,100	15,150	1,947	1,536	2,332	1,853	18,100	18,150	2,605	2,033	3,142	2,432	21,100	21,150	3,340	2,573	4,089	3,091
15,150	15,200	1,957	1,544	2,345	1,862	18,150	18,200	2,617	2,042	3,156	2,442	21,150	21,200	3,353	2,582	4,105	3,103
15,200	15,250	1,967	1,552	2,357	1,871	18,200	18,250	2,628	2,051	3,170	2,452	21,200	21,250	3,366	2,591	4,122	3,115
15,250	15,300	1,977	1,560	2,370	1,880	18,250	18,300	2,640	2,060	3,184	2,462	21,250	21,300	3,379	2,600	4,138	3,127
15,300	15,350	1,987	1,568	2,382	1,889	18,300	18,350	2,651	2,069	3,198	2,472	21,300	21,350	3,392	2,609	4,155	3,139
15,350	15,400	1,997	1,576	2,395	1,898	18,350	18,400	2,663	2,078	3,212	2,482	21,350	21,400	3,405	2,618	4,171	3,151
15,400	15,450	2,007	1,584	2,407	1,907	18,400	18,450	2,674	2,087	3,226	2,492	21,400	21,450	3,418	2,627	4,188	3,163
15,450	15,500	2,017	1,592	2,420	1,916	18,450	18,500	2,686	2,096	3,240	2,502	21,450	21,500	3,431	2,636	4,204	3,175
15,500	15,550	2,027	1,600	2,432	1,925	18,500	18,550	2,697	2,105	3,254	2,512	21,500	21,550	3,444	2,645	4,221	3,187
15,550	15,600	2,037	1,608	2,445	1,934	18,550	18,600	2,709	2,114	3,268	2,522	21,550	21,600	3,457	2,654	4,237	3,199
15,600	15,650	2,047	1,616	2,457	1,943	18,600	18,650	2,720	2,123	3,282	2,532	21,600	21,650	3,470	2,663	4,254	3,211
15,650	15,700	2,057	1,624	2,470	1,952	18,650	18,700	2,732	2,132	3,296	2,542	21,650	21,700	3,483	2,672	4,270	3,223
15,700	15,750	2,067	1,632	2,482	1,961	18,700	18,750	2,743	2,141	3,310	2,552	21,700	21,750	3,496	2,681	4,287	3,235
15,750	15,800	2,077	1,640	2,495	1,970	18,750	18,800	2,755	2,150	3,324	2,562	21,750	21,800	3,509	2,690	4,303	3,247
15,800	15,850	2,087	1,648	2,507	1,979	18,800	18,850	2,766	2,159	3,338	2,572	21,800	21,850	3,522	2,700	4,320	3,259
15,850	15,900	2,097	1,656	2,520	1,988	18,850	18,900	2,778	2,168	3,352	2,582	21,850	21,900	3,535	2,711	4,336	3,271
15,900	15,950	2,107	1,664	2,532	1,997	18,900	18,950	2,789	2,177	3,366	2,592	21,900	21,950	3,548	2,722	4,353	3,283
15,950	16,000	2,117	1,672	2,545	2,006	18,950	19,000	2,801	2,186	3,380	2,602	21,950	22,000	3,561	2,733	4,369	3,295
16,000						**19,000**						**22,000**					
16,000	16,050	2,127	1,680	2,557	2,015	19,000	19,050	2,812	2,195	3,396	2,612	22,000	22,050	3,574	2,744	4,386	3,307
16,050	16,100	2,137	1,688	2,570	2,024	19,050	19,100	2,824	2,204	3,412	2,622	22,050	22,100	3,587	2,755	4,402	3,319
16,100	16,150	2,147	1,696	2,582	2,033	19,100	19,150	2,835	2,213	3,429	2,632	22,100	22,150	3,600	2,766	4,419	3,331
16,150	16,200	2,157	1,704	2,596	2,042	19,150	19,200	2,847	2,222	3,445	2,642	22,150	22,200	3,613	2,777	4,435	3,343
16,200	16,250	2,168	1,712	2,610	2,052	19,200	19,250	2,858	2,231	3,462	2,652	22,200	22,250	3,626	2,788	4,452	3,355
16,250	16,300	2,180	1,720	2,624	2,062	19,250	19,300	2,870	2,240	3,478	2,662	22,250	22,300	3,639	2,799	4,468	3,367
16,300	16,350	2,191	1,728	2,638	2,072	19,300	19,350	2,881	2,249	3,495	2,672	22,300	22,350	3,652	2,810	4,485	3,379
16,350	16,400	2,203	1,736	2,652	2,082	19,350	19,400	2,893	2,258	3,511	2,682	22,350	22,400	3,665	2,821	4,501	3,391
16,400	16,450	2,214	1,744	2,666	2,092	19,400	19,450	2,904	2,267	3,528	2,692	22,400	22,450	3,678	2,832	4,518	3,403
16,450	16,500	2,226	1,752	2,680	2,102	19,450	19,500	2,916	2,276	3,544	2,702	22,450	22,500	3,691	2,843	4,534	3,415
16,500	16,550	2,237	1,760	2,694	2,112	19,500	19,550	2,927	2,285	3,561	2,712	22,500	22,550	3,704	2,854	4,551	3,427
16,550	16,600	2,249	1,768	2,708	2,122	19,550	19,600	2,939	2,294	3,577	2,722	22,550	22,600	3,717	2,865	4,567	3,439
16,600	16,650	2,260	1,776	2,722	2,132	19,600	19,650	2,950	2,303	3,594	2,732	22,600	22,650	3,730	2,876	4,584	3,451
16,650	16,700	2,272	1,784	2,736	2,142	19,650	19,700	2,963	2,312	3,610	2,743	22,650	22,700	3,743	2,887	4,600	3,463
16,700	16,750	2,283	1,792	2,750	2,152	19,700	19,750	2,976	2,321	3,627	2,755	22,700	22,750	3,756	2,898	4,617	3,475
16,750	16,800	2,295	1,800	2,764	2,162	19,750	19,800	2,989	2,330	3,643	2,767	22,750	22,800	3,769	2,909	4,633	3,487
16,800	16,850	2,306	1,808	2,778	2,172	19,800	19,850	3,002	2,339	3,660	2,779	22,800	22,850	3,782	2,920	4,650	3,499
16,850	16,900	2,318	1,816	2,792	2,182	19,850	19,900	3,015	2,348	3,676	2,791	22,850	22,900	3,795	2,931	4,666	3,511
16,900	16,950	2,329	1,824	2,806	2,192	19,900	19,950	3,028	2,357	3,693	2,803	22,900	22,950	3,808	2,942	4,683	3,523
16,950	17,000	2,341	1,832	2,820	2,202	19,950	20,000	3,041	2,366	3,709	2,815	22,950	23,000	3,821	2,953	4,699	3,535

Figure 10.1 Sample Tax Table

Skills and Strategies

Here you will learn how to read a tax table.

1. Vernon Graham is single. He wants to find his tax liability on his $20,172 taxable income. What is Mr. Graham's tax liability?

   Solution: Examine the section marked "20,000" in Figure 10.2.

If taxable income is—		And you are—			
At least	But less than	Single	Married filing jointly *	Married filing sepa- rately	Head of a house- hold
			Your tax is—		
20,000					
20,000	20,050	3,054	2,375	3,726	2,827
20,050	20,100	3,067	2,384	3,742	2,839
20,100	20,150	3,080	2,393	3,759	2,851
20,150	20,200	3,093	2,402	3,775	2,863
20,200	20,250	3,106	2,411	3,792	2,875
20,250	20,300	3,119	2,420	3,808	2,887
20,300	20,350	3,132	2,429	3,825	2,899
20,350	20,400	3,145	2,438	3,841	2,911

Figure 10.2 Using a Tax Table

Mr. Graham's taxable income of $20,172 is between $20,150 and $20,200, so use the line labeled:
   "At least 20,150 but less than 20,200."

Look across this line until it intersects with the column marked "Single."
Mr. Graham's tax liability is $3,093.

2. Mr. Willoughby is single. His taxable income is $52,156. Use Schedule X to compute his tax liability.

   Solution: The tax table in Figure 10.1 does not give tax liabilities for all incomes. Use Tax Schedule X as shown in Figure 10.3 on page 380. Look down the first two columns on the left side of Schedule X. Mr. Willoughby's income of $52,156 is
   "over 44,780 but not over 59,670"
   so use the line circled in Figure 10.4 at the top of page 381.

SCHEDULE X—Single Taxpayers

If taxable income is: Over—	but not over—	The tax is:	of the amount over—
$0	$2,480	—0—	
2,480	3,670	········ 11%	$2,480
3,670	4,750	$130.90 + 12%	3,670
4,750	7,010	260.50 + 14%	4,750
7,010	9,170	576.90 + 15%	7,010
9,170	11,650	900.90 + 16%	9,170
11,650	13,920	1,297.70 + 18%	11,650
13,920	16,190	1,706.30 + 20%	13,920
16,190	19,640	2,160.30 + 23%	16,190
19,640	25,360	2,953.80 + 26%	19,640
25,360	31,080	4,441.00 + 30%	25,360
31,080	36,800	6,157.00 + 34%	31,080
36,800	44,780	8,101.80 + 38%	36,800
44,780	59,670	11,134.20 + 42%	44,780
59,670	88,270	17,388.00 + 48%	59,670
88,270	········	31,116.00 + 50%	88,270

SCHEDULE Z—Heads of Household

If taxable income is: Over—	but not over—	The tax is:	of the amount over—
$0	$2,480	—0—	
2,480	4,750	········ 11%	$2,480
4,750	7,010	$249.70 + 12%	4,750
7,010	9,390	520.90 + 14%	7,010
9,390	12,730	854.10 + 17%	9,390
12,730	16,190	1,421.90 + 18%	12,730
16,190	19,640	2,044.70 + 20%	16,190
19,640	25,360	2,734.70 + 24%	19,640
25,360	31,080	4,107.50 + 28%	25,360
31,080	36,800	5,709.10 + 32%	31,080
36,800	48,240	7,539.50 + 35%	36,800
48,240	65,390	11,543.50 + 42%	48,240
65,390	88,270	18,746.50 + 45%	65,390
88,270	116,870	29,042.50 + 48%	88,270
116,870	········	42,770.50 + 50%	116,870

SCHEDULE Y—Married Taxpayers and Qualifying Widows and Widowers

Married Filing Joint Returns and Qualifying Widows and Widowers

If taxable income is: Over—	but not over—	The tax is:	of the amount over—
$0	$3,670	—0—	
3,670	5,940	········ 11%	$3,670
5,940	8,200	$249.70 + 12%	5,940
8,200	12,840	520.90 + 14%	8,200
12,840	17,270	1,170.50 + 16%	12,840
17,270	21,800	1,879.30 + 18%	17,270
21,800	26,550	2,694.70 + 22%	21,800
26,550	32,270	3,739.70 + 25%	26,550
32,270	37,980	5,169.70 + 28%	32,270
37,980	49,420	6,768.50 + 33%	37,980
49,420	64,750	10,543.70 + 38%	49,420
64,750	92,370	16,369.10 + 42%	64,750
92,370	118,050	27,969.50 + 45%	92,370
118,050	175,250	39,525.50 + 49%	118,050
175,250	········	67,553.50 + 50%	175,250

Married Filing Separate Returns

If taxable income is: Over—	but not over—	The tax is:	of the amount over—
$0	$1,835	—0—	
1,835	2,970	········ 11%	$1,835
2,970	4,100	$124.85 + 12%	2,970
4,100	6,420	260.45 + 14%	4,100
6,420	8,635	585.25 + 16%	6,420
8,635	10,900	939.65 + 18%	8,635
10,900	13,275	1,347.35 + 22%	10,900
13,275	16,135	1,869.85 + 25%	13,275
16,135	18,990	2,584.85 + 28%	16,135
18,990	24,710	3,384.25 + 33%	18,990
24,710	32,375	5,271.85 + 38%	24,710
32,375	46,185	8,184.55 + 42%	32,375
46,185	59,025	13,984.75 + 45%	46,185
59,025	87,625	19,762.75 + 49%	59,025
87,625	········	33,776.75 + 50%	87,625

Figure 10.3   Tax Computation Schedules

SCHEDULE X—Single Taxpayers			
If taxable income is:		The tax is:	of the amount over—
Over—	but not over—		
$0	$2,480	—0—	
2,480	3,670	········ 11%	$2,480
3,670	4,750	$130.90 + 12%	3,670
4,750	7,010	260.50 + 14%	4,750
7,010	9,170	576.90 + 15%	7,010
9,170	11,650	900.90 + 16%	9,170
11,650	13,920	1,297.70 + 18%	11,650
13,920	16,190	1,706.30 + 20%	13,920
16,190	19,640	2,160.30 + 23%	16,190
19,640	25,360	2,953.80 + 26%	19,640
25,360	31,080	4,441.00 + 30%	25,360
31,080	36,800	6,157.00 + 34%	31,080
36,800	44,780	8,101.80 + 38%	36,800
44,780	59,670	11,134.20 + 42%	44,780
59,670	88,270	17,388.00 + 48%	59,670
88,270	········	31,116.00 + 50%	88,270

Figure 10.4 Using a Tax Computation Schedule

Mr. Willoughby's tax is $11,134.20 plus 42% of the amount of taxable income over $44,780. Compute his tax liability as follows:

$52,156   taxable income
$\underline{- 44,780}$ from right-hand column of Schedule X
$ 7,376   amount of taxable income over $44,780

$ 7,376.00   amount of taxable income over $44,780
$\underline{\times .42}$ 42%, expressed as a decimal
$ 3,097.92   tax liability on amount over $44,780

$ 3,097.92   tax liability on amount over $44,780
$\underline{+ 11,134.20}$ tax liability on $44,780
$14,232.12   total tax liability

Mr. Willoughby's tax liability is $14,232.12. The following calculator keystroke sequence could also be used.

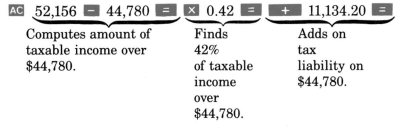

AC 52,156 ⊟ 44,780 ▤	⊠ 0.42 ▤	⊞ 11,134.20 ▤
Computes amount of taxable income over $44,780.	Finds 42% of taxable income over $44,780.	Adds on tax liability on $44,780.

The display should read 14,232.12.

Remember, these tables change each year. Familiarize yourself with this year's tax tables.

Problems

✓**1.** Use Figure 10.1 to find the tax liability on each of the following taxable incomes.
   a. $14,731   (single)
   b. $21,406   (married filing jointly)
   c. $17,773.50   (married filing separately)
   d. $16,244.21   (head of household)
   e. $19,732   (single)
   f. $19,749   (married filing jointly)
   g. $19,749.49   (married filing jointly)
   h. $19,750.95   (married filing jointly)
   i. $19,799   (single)
   j. $19,800   (single)
   k. $19,801   (single)

✓**2.** Use Figure 10.3 to compute the tax liability on each of the following taxable incomes.
   a. $43,240   (single)
   b. $64,128   (married filing jointly)
   c. $37,492   (head of household)
   d. $86,912   (single)
   e. $112,644   (married filing separately)
   f. $369,811   (single)
   g. $411,321   (married filing jointly)

3. Find the tax liability for a single person with a taxable income of $67,920. (Use Figure 10.3.)

4. Find the tax liability for a single person with a taxable income of $21,287. (Use Figure 10.1.)

✓**5.** On December 31, Rich Fiore was using Schedule X to compute his tax liability, as the year's end was approaching. He had earned $92,111 in taxable income during the year. On December 31, just before the New Year, Mr. Fiore's boss gave him an additional $10,000 bonus. What is Mr. Fiore's tax liability for the $10,000 bonus?

SECTION 3 • NET PAY

You have learned that employees have many expenses. They can include:

- federal income tax
- state income tax
- city income tax
- social security tax

- disability insurance
- pension plan
- dental insurance
- medical insurance

These expenses can add up to thousands of dollars each year. What do you think would happen if employees had to pay these all at once each year? This one-time charge would be extremely high, and many employees might have already spent their earnings in other ways. You can see that it is not practical to have employees pay for these costs in a single yearly payment.

Instead, these payments are distributed throughout the year. Each time an employee receives a paycheck, a certain amount is **deducted** (subtracted) from the employee's gross, or total pay. This deduction is based on information that employees submit on **Form W-4** when they are hired (see Chapter 9, page 345). These deductions pay for the identified employee expenses. By the end of the year, the employee has paid most of the expenses for that year.

The employer **withholds** these payments and sends the total accumulated to the appropriate government agency. Federal income tax is sometimes called federal **withholding tax** because employers withhold these taxes and send them to the federal government. State and city withholding taxes are handled in the same way. Social security payments are also withheld from each paycheck and sent to the government.

Not all withheld payments are sent to the government. For example, insurance payments that are withheld are sent to the insurance companies. In addition, if an employee is a member of a credit union (see Chapter 7), a deduction can be taken directly from each check.

All these deductions reduce the amount of each paycheck that the employee receives. The amount of money that the employee "takes home" is called **net pay** or **take-home pay**.

Employers and employees must keep accurate records of paycheck deductions. Most employers issue a paycheck stub with each check. The paycheck stub lists all the payments deducted. Be sure to save all your paycheck stubs, and check that the entries are correct each time you receive your pay.

At the end of each year, an employer must compile a list of each employee's deductions. Some of these annual deductions must be reported to the city, state, and federal governments. Employers put this information on a **Wage and Tax Statement**, which is also called **Form W-2**. By January 31, employees should receive W-2 forms for each job they had during the previous year. Six copies are made of every W-2 form. Three of the copies are for the employer's use, and three are for the employee. Employees use their W-2 forms when they file their income tax returns.

Skills and Strategies

Here you will learn how to make calculations based on reading paycheck stubs and W-2 forms. Figure 10.5 is the paycheck stub from Barbara Brady's last paycheck.

NAME		SOCIAL SECURITY NUMBER		PAY PERIOD	
BARBARA BRADY		000-00-0000		FEBRUARY 7 {WEEKLY}	
EARNINGS					
REGULAR HOURLY RATE	HOURS	REGULAR HOURS	OVERTIME HOURS	OVERTIME HOURLY RATE	GROSS PAY
$6.50	41	40	1	$9.75	$269.75
DEDUCTIONS:					
FICA TAX WITHHELD	FEDERAL WITHHOLDING TAX	STATE WITHHOLDING TAX	CITY WITHHOLDING TAX	RETIREMENT INSURANCE	
$19.29	$47.51	$12.62	$4.90	$9.10	
DISABILITY INSURANCE		MEDICAL INSURANCE	DENTAL INSURANCE	NET PAY	
$1.71		$2.11	$1.01	$171.50	

Figure 10.5 Paycheck Stub

1. Barbara Brady wants to verify that her net pay has been computed correctly. She has already verified that her gross pay is correct. Check to see that Barbara's net pay is correct.

Solution: Find the sum of all paycheck deductions.

$19.29 FICA tax withheld
47.51 federal withholding tax
12.62 state withholding tax
4.90 city withholding tax
9.10 retirement insurance
1.71 disability insurance
2.11 medical insurance
+ 1.01 dental insurance
$98.25 total paycheck deductions

Then subtract the deductions from the gross pay.

$269.75 gross pay
− 98.25 total paycheck deductions
$171.50 net pay
Barbara's paycheck stub shows the correct net pay, $171.50.

You could use the following calculator keystroke sequence:

Finds the sum of the paycheck deductions and stores the sum in memory.

Subtracts the paycheck deductions from gross pay.

The display should read 171.5.

2. Here is Barbara Brady's Wage and Tax Statement (Form W-2) for last year, shown at the top of page 386. How much did Barbara earn last year?

1 Control number 22222		OMB No. 1545-0008		
2 Employer's name, address, and ZIP code SQUIRE INDUSTRIES 100 NORTHEAST ST. FOREST HILLS, NY		3 Employer's identification number 123456		4 Employer's state I.D. number 789
		5 Statutory Deceased Legal 942 Subtotal Void employee rep. emp. ☐ ☐ ☐ ☐		
		6 Allocated tips		7 Advance EIC payment
8 Employee's social security number 000-00-0000	9 Federal income tax withheld $2,400.00	10 Wages, tips, other compensation $14,140.00		11 Social security tax withheld $1,011.01
12 Employee's name, address, and ZIP code BARBARA BRADY 63 BACK ROAD JACKSON HEIGHTS, NY 11358		13 Social security wages $14,140.00		14 Social security tips
		16		16a Fringe benefits incl. in Box 10
		17 State income tax $624.50	18 State wages, tips, etc. $14,140.00	19 Name of state NY
		20 Local income tax $259.00	21 Local wages, tips, etc. $14,140.00	22 Name of locality NYC

Form **W-2 Wage and Tax Statement**

Copy B To be filed with employee's FEDERAL tax return   Department of the Treasury
This information is being furnished to the Internal Revenue Service.   Internal Revenue Service

Figure 10.6   Form W-2: Wage and Tax Statement

Solution: Look at Box 10 on Barbara's W-2 form.

Barbara earned $14,140 last year.

3. How much FICA tax was withheld from Barbara's earnings last year?

Solution: Look at Box 11 on Barbara's W-2 form.

Remember, FICA tax is social security tax.

Barbara paid $1,011.01 in FICA tax last year.

Problems

Use Joseph Capidulupo's paycheck stub as shown in Figure 10.7 at the top of page 387 to answer Problems 1–10.

NAME	SOCIAL SECURITY NUMBER	PAY PERIOD
JOSEPH CAPIDULUPO	000-00-0000	MARCH 3 [WEEKLY]

EARNINGS					
REGULAR HOURLY RATE	HOURS	REGULAR HOURS	OVERTIME HOURS	OVERTIME HOURLY RATE	GROSS PAY
$8.10	45	40	5	$12.15	$384.75

DEDUCTIONS:				
FICA TAX WITHHELD	FEDERAL WITHHOLDING TAX	STATE WITHHOLDING TAX	CITY WITHHOLDING TAX	RETIREMENT INSURANCE
$27.51	$61.12	$21.03	$6.01	$4.12

DISABILITY INSURANCE		MEDICAL INSURANCE	DENTAL INSURANCE	NET PAY
$1.31		$7.01	$2.11	

Figure 10.7 Joseph Capidulupo's Paycheck Stub

1. How many overtime hours did Joseph work during this pay period?

2. What is Joseph's overtime hourly rate?

3. What was Joseph's total overtime pay during this pay period?

4. What was Joseph's gross pay for this pay period?

5. What is the sum of all of Joseph's paycheck deductions?

6. Joseph was so excited to get his paycheck, that he accidentally ripped part of the paycheck stub when he opened the paycheck envelope. He can't read the net-pay box. What was Joseph's net pay for this pay period?

✓ 7. What will be the dates of Joseph's next three paychecks?

8. How many paychecks does Joseph receive in one year?

✓ 9. Joseph pays $7.01 in medical insurance from each paycheck. What is his annual premium?

10. **a.** What is Joseph's regular hourly rate?
    b. What is Joseph's overtime hourly rate?
    c. Does Joseph receive time and a half, double time, or triple time for each hour of overtime?

Use Leslie Gerber's Wage and Tax Statement as shown in Figure 10.8 to answer Problems 11–15.

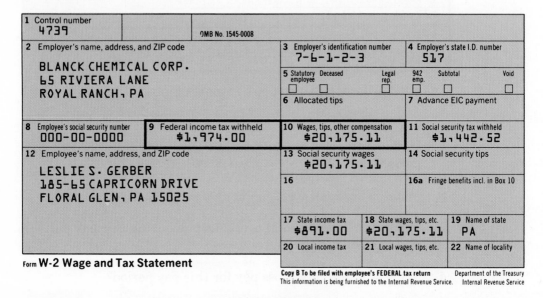

Figure 10.8   Leslie Gerber's Wage and Tax Statement

11. What was Leslie's annual salary last year?

12. How much FICA tax was withheld from Leslie's income?

✓13. Leslie is paid semimonthly. How many paychecks does she receive each year?

14. What is the number of the box that shows the address of Leslie's employer?

15. Leslie received a 12% raise this year. How much will she earn this year?

SECTION 4 • FILING TAX RETURNS

What is the difference between your annual income and your taxable income? The amount of money you earn in a year is your annual income. However, not all the money you earn is taxed. Certain tax laws allow part of your income to be nontaxable income. Your tax liability is based on your taxable income, not your annual income.

In Section 2 of this chapter, you learned how to find your tax liability based on your taxable income. It is common for a person's tax liability to be several thousand dollars. In Section 3, you learned that most people pay their tax liability over a period of a year. The employer withholds federal, state, and local taxes from each paycheck. At the end of the year, each employee's annual income and the amounts withheld for taxes are reported on Form W-2.

Once you get your W-2 form from your employer, you need to find out what your tax liability is for that year, based on your earnings. You should then compare your tax liability to the amount that your employer withheld during the year. If your tax liability is exactly equal to the amount withheld, your taxes are paid for the year. However, this is a very unlikely event. It is difficult for your employer to estimate exactly your tax liability in advance.

If your employer withholds more than your tax liability, you are entitled to a **refund**. If your employer withholds less than your tax liability, you owe the government the difference. In any case, you must furnish all this information to the government on a tax return. If you owe money to the government, you must include a check with the return. If the government owes you money, you will receive it after your return has been processed.

There are three basic Internal Revenue Service tax returns. **Form 1040EZ** and **Form 1040A** are short forms, and **Form 1040** is a long form. Tax forms may change from year to year. In this section, you will learn the skills that are essential for filling out any of these tax forms. Instruction booklets are also available from the Internal Revenue Service. Topic 5 Enhance/Advance Activity 7 will help you learn about *this* year's tax forms. It is not difficult to master the skills used in filling out federal and state tax forms. (See Figure 10.9 at the top of page 390.)

Skills and Strategies

On any tax form, you must fill out the name, address, social security number, filing status, and information about the family members

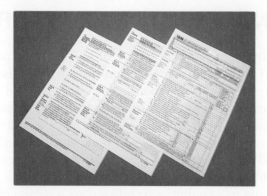

Figure 10.9 Internal Revenue Service Tax Returns

that you support financially. Each person you support is called a **dependent** or an **exemption**. Part of your nontaxable income is based on the number of exemptions you claim. Look for this information in the sample tax form shown in Figure 10.10

Form **1040**	Department of the Treasury—Internal Revenue Service **U.S. Individual Income Tax Return**			
For the year January 1-December 31,	or other tax year beginning	ending	, 19	OMB No. 1545-0074

Use IRS label. Other-wise, please print or type.	Your first name and initial (if joint return, also give spouse's name and initial)		Last name	**Your social security number**
	Present home address (number and street or rural route). (If you have a P.O. Box, see page 4 of Instructions.)			**Spouse's social security number**
	City, town or post office, state, and ZIP code		If this address is different from the one shown on your return, check here ▶	

| **Presidential Election Campaign** ▶ | Do you want $1 to go to this fund? . . . . | Yes | No | **Note:** Checking "Yes" will not change your tax or reduce your refund. |
| | If joint return, does your spouse want $1 to go to this fund?. . | Yes | No | |

Filing Status Check only one box.	1	Single	For Privacy Act and Paperwork Reduction Act Notice, see Instructions.
	2	Married filing joint return (even if only one had income)	
	3	Married filing separate return. Enter spouse's social security no. above and full name here.	
	4	Head of household (with qualifying person). (See page 5 of Instructions.) If the qualifying person is your unmarried child but not your dependent, enter child's name here.	
	5	Qualifying widow(er) with dependent child (year spouse died ▶ 19). (See page 6 of Instructions.)	

Exemptions Always check the box labeled	6a	Yourself	65 or over	Blind	} Enter number of boxes checked on 6a and b ▶
	b	Spouse	65 or over	Blind	
	c	First names of your dependent children who lived with you			} Enter number of children listed on 6c ▶

Figure 10.10 Sample Tax Form

Before you fill out any tax form, you must organize all your financial records and list important information on a **tax worksheet**. Keep together all forms that report income. Most of your income will probably be reported on Form W-2. However, bank interest, stock dividends, royalties, and prizes also must be listed as income on your tax return. Usually, a report of this income is sent to you on **Form 1099**. Figure 10.11 shows a sample Form 1099.

☐ CORRECTED (if checked)

PAYER'S name, street address, city, state, and ZIP code	Payer's RTN (optional)	OMB No. 1545-0112	**Interest Income**
FLORAL NATIONAL BANK 72-10 JILL STREET NEW PARK, DE		Statement for Recipients of	

PAYER'S Federal identification number	RECIPIENT'S identification number 000-00-0000	1 Earnings from savings and loan associations, credit unions, bank deposits, bearer certificates of deposit, etc. $ **$73.12**	**Copy B** **For Recipient**
RECIPIENT'S name (first, middle, last) BILL PACA		2 Early withdrawal penalty $	3 U.S. Savings Bonds, etc. $	This is important tax information and is being furnished to the Internal Revenue Service. If you are required to file a return, a negligence penalty or other sanction will be imposed on you if this income is taxable and the IRS determines that it has not been reported.
Street address 17 FLOYD STREET		4 Federal income tax withheld $	
City, state, and ZIP code NEW PARK, DE 19711		5 Foreign tax paid (if eligible for foreign tax credit)	6 Foreign country or U.S. possession
Account number (optional) 76321441		$	

Form **1099-INT**   Department of the Treasury - Internal Revenue Service

Figure 10.11 Sample Form 1099

This Form 1099 shows that Bill Paca received $73.12 in interest from his savings account at the Floral National Bank. This amount is included on his tax worksheet as income. Before preparing your return, list the income you received in each of the following categories:

1. wages

2. tips

3. interest

4. dividends

5. royalties

6. alimony

7. capital gain

8. pension

9. rent

10. business income

11. farm income

12. unemployment insurance benefits

13. social security benefits

14. prizes

Look for these categories on the income section of the sample tax form shown in Figure 10.12 on page 392.

Income	7	Wages, salaries, tips, etc. *(attach Form(s) W-2)*	**7**	
	8	Interest income *(also attach Schedule B if over $400)*	**8**	
Please attach Copy B of your Forms W-2, W-2G, and W-2P here.	9a	Dividends *(also attach Schedule B if over $400)* _____ , **9b** Exclusion _____		
	c	Subtract line 9b from line 9a and enter the result	**9c**	
	10	Taxable refunds of state and local income taxes, if any, from the worksheet on page 9 of Instructions.	**10**	
If you do not have a W-2, see page 4 of Instructions.	11	Alimony received	**11**	
	12	Business income or (loss) *(attach Schedule C)*	**12**	
	13	Capital gain or (loss) *(attach Schedule D)*	**13**	
	14	40% of capital gain distributions not reported on line 13 (see page 9 of Instructions)	**14**	
	15	Other gains or (losses) *(attach Form 4797)*	**15**	
	16	Fully taxable pensions, IRA distributions, and annuities not reported on line 17 (see page 9). .	**16**	
	17a	Other pensions and annuities, including rollovers. Total received ⌐17a⌐		
	b	Taxable amount, if any, from the worksheet on page 10 of Instructions	**17b**	
	18	Rents, royalties, partnerships, estates, trusts, etc. *(attach Schedule E)*	**18**	
	19	Farm income or (loss) *(attach Schedule F)*	**19**	
	20a	Unemployment compensation (insurance). Total received . . ⌐20a⌐		
Please attach check or money order here.	b	Taxable amount, if any, from the worksheet on page 10 of Instructions	**20b**	
	21a	Social security benefits (see page 10). . . . . ⌐21a⌐		
	b	Taxable amount, if any, from worksheet on page 11. { Tax-exempt interest _____ }	**21b**	
	22	Other income (list type and amount—see page 11 of Instructions) _____		
			22	
	23	Add the amounts shown in the far right column for lines 7 through 22. This is your **total income** . ▶	**23**	

Figure 10.12   Sample Tax Form

Line 23 of the sample tax form is used to report your total income for the year. Remember, part of this income is nontaxable, so this is not the amount that is used to determine your tax liability.

The nontaxable part of your income is a **deduction** from your total income. After all deductions have been subtracted, you are left with your taxable income. This amount will determine your tax liability. You should compare your tax liability with the amount withheld by your employer, to see whether or not you will receive a refund.

Sign and date your return. Staple a copy of Form W-2 to the tax return, and mail it to your Internal Revenue Service regional office. Always save a copy of your return for future use. The copy will help you fill out your state tax form. Here are some examples of this process.

1. William Base's employer withheld $2,138 in federal income tax. After completing his tax return, William has determined that his tax libility is $1,374. Will William get a refund, or does he owe the government money?

    Solution: First determine whether or not William's tax liability is greater than or less than the amount withheld.

    $1,374 < $2,138
        ↑
    "is less than"

He will receive a refund since his tax liability is less than the amount withheld. Subtract to find the amount of his refund.

$2,138   amount withheld by employer
− 1,374   tax liability
$ 764   tax refund

William will receive an income tax refund of $764.

2. Roberto Ross is filling out a tax worksheet to determine his income. He compiles the following list:
wages, $21,764.00
tips, $400.00
interest, $147.61
dividends, $27.95
state lottery prize, $1,000.00

What is his total income?

Solution: Add to find the total income. You can add using paper and pencil or the following calculator keystroke sequence:

AC 21,764 **+** 400 **+** 147.61 **+** 27.95 **+** 1,000 **=**

The display should read 23,339.56.

Roberto's total income is $23,339.56.

Problems

✓**1.** Ralph is a teacher who works as a musician on weekends. Here is part of his tax worksheet:

wages from teaching job,
wages from music job,
interest,
dividends,
royalties,

What is Ralph's total income?

2. Don is filling out his income tax return. His tax liability for last year is $973. His employer withheld $712 in federal taxes.
  a. Does Don get a refund, or does he owe the government money?
  b. What is the difference between Don's tax liability and the amount withheld by his employer?

✓ **3.** Sue's employer withheld $1,619 in federal taxes last year. Her tax liability is $1,708.
   a. Does Sue get a refund, or does she owe the government money?
   b. What is the difference between Sue's tax liability and the amount withheld by her employer?

4. Pat is single with a taxable income for last year of $21,355. Her employer withheld $2,100 in federal taxes.
   a. Use the tax table (Figure 10.1, page 378) to determine Pat's tax liability
   b. Does Pat get a tax refund?
   c. Find the difference between Pat's tax liability and the amount withheld by her employer.

5. Phil is married and is filing a joint tax return with his wife Lynn. They received $19,801.42 in taxable income last year. Their employers withheld $800 in federal taxes.
   a. Use the tax table (Figure 10.1, page 378) to determine their tax liability.
   b. Do they get a tax refund?
   c. Find the difference between their tax liability and the amount withheld by their employers.

✓ **6.** Alita is a single taxpayer. Her taxable income last year was $71,342. Her employer withheld $22,000 in federal taxes.
   a. Use Schedule X (Figure 10.3, page 380) to compute Alita's tax liability.
   b. Does Alita get a tax refund?
   c. What is the difference between Alita's tax liability and the amount withheld by her employer?

7. Janet is paying off a car loan. The monthly payment is $211.28. She is hoping to receive an income tax refund that is large enough to make one monthly loan payment. Her tax liability is $1,722, and her employer withheld $2,071 in federal taxes.
   a. How much of a refund will Janet receive?
   b. Will Janet be able to make one monthly payment on her car loan with the refund? Explain your answer.

✓ **8.** John wants to take out a car loan. He wants to use his income tax refund as the first month's payment. He borrowed $5,000 for two years at an APR of 14%

 a. Use Figure 7.1 on page 310 in Chapter 7 to find the amount of John's monthly payment.

 b. John's tax liability for last year is $1,300. His employer withheld $1,764 in federal taxes. How much of an income tax refund will John receive?

 c. Will John's refund pay for his first month's car payment? Explain.

 d. Will John's refund pay for *two* months' car payments? Explain.

In Problems 9 and 10, use the current short tax forms (Form 1040A and Form 1040EZ) and an instruction booklet.

 9. Laurie Tenser is single. She works in a fur store. Her Form W-2 is shown in Figure 10.13.

1 Control number **7701**		OMB No. 1545-0008	3 Employer's identification number	4 Employer's state I.D. number **105**
2 Employer's name, address, and ZIP code MEAD TERRACE FURS 662 ARTHUR AVE. BALDWIN, NH			5 Statutory employee □ Deceased □ Legal rep. □ 942 emp. □ Subtotal □ Void □	
			6 Allocated tips	7 Advance EIC payment
8 Employee's social security number 000-00-0000	9 Federal income tax withheld $1,131.00		10 Wages, tips, other compensation $21,265.50	11 Social security tax withheld
12 Employee's name, address, and ZIP code LAURIE TENSER 15 LOUIS ROAD CARYLVILLE, NH 03224			13 Social security wages	14 Social security tips
			16	16a Fringe benefits incl. in Box 10
			17 State income tax $900.00	18 State wages, tips, etc. $21,265.50	19 Name of state NH
			20 Local income tax	21 Local wages, tips, etc.	22 Name of locality

Form **W-2 Wage and Tax Statement**

Copy B To be filed with employee's FEDERAL tax return   Department of the Treasury
This information is being furnished to the Internal Revenue Service.   Internal Revenue Service

Figure 10.13 Laurie Tenser's W-2 Form

Laurie received $173 in interest from her bank account. Fill out a Form 1040EZ for Laurie.

10. Donald and Eve Colby are married with one child, Andrea. Donald is a teacher, and Eve is a salesperson. Their W-2 forms are shown in Figures 10.14 and 10.15.

1 Control number 8173	22222	OMB No. 1545-0008		
2 Employer's name, address, and ZIP code NORTHSIDE SCHOOLS 112 FRANKLIN AVE. COLUMBUS, OH		3 Employer's identification number		4 Employer's state I.D. number 472
		5 Statutory employee ☐ Deceased ☐	Legal rep. ☐	942 emp. ☐ Subtotal ☐ Void ☐
		6 Allocated tips		7 Advance EIC payment
8 Employee's social security number 000-00-0000	9 Federal income tax withheld $2,178.00	10 Wages, tips, other compensation $24,611.00		11 Social security tax withheld
12 Employee's name, address, and ZIP code DONALD COLBY 621 FOUNDATION DRIVE SOUNDVILLE, OH 45226		13 Social security wages		14 Social security tips
		16		16a Fringe benefits incl. in Box 10
		17 State income tax $1,211.00	18 State wages, tips, etc. $24,611.00	19 Name of state OH
		20 Local income tax	21 Local wages, tips, etc.	22 Name of locality

Form **W-2 Wage and Tax Statement**

Copy B To be filed with employee's FEDERAL tax return   Department of the Treasury
This information is being furnished to the Internal Revenue Service.   Internal Revenue Service

Figure 10.14   Donald Colby's W-2 Form

1 Control number 9987	22222	OMB No. 1545-0008		
2 Employer's name, address, and ZIP code WESTERN SALES INC. 382 MADISON LANE SOUNDVILLE, OH		3 Employer's identification number		4 Employer's state I.D. number 247
		5 Statutory employee ☐ Deceased ☐	Legal rep. ☐	942 emp. ☐ Subtotal ☐ Void ☐
		6 Allocated tips		7 Advance EIC payment
8 Employee's social security number 000-00-0000	9 Federal income tax withheld $1,331.00	10 Wages, tips, other compensation $18,222.00		11 Social security tax withheld
12 Employee's name, address, and ZIP code EVE COLBY 621 FOUNDATION DRIVE SOUNDVILLE, OH 45226		13 Social security wages		14 Social security tips
		16		16a Fringe benefits incl. in Box 10
		17 State income tax $1,100.00	18 State wages, tips, etc. $18,222.00	19 Name of state OH
		20 Local income tax	21 Local wages, tips, etc.	22 Name of locality

Form **W-2 Wage and Tax Statement**

Copy B To be filed with employee's FEDERAL tax return   Department of the Treasury
This information is being furnished to the Internal Revenue Service.   Internal Revenue Service

Figure 10.15   Eve Colby's W-2 Form

Eve and Donald also received $341.78 interest on bank deposits and $211 in stock dividends. Fill out a joint Form 1040A for Eve and Donald.

SECTION 5 • ITEMIZED DEDUCTIONS

Hundreds of laws concerning income taxes have been passed over the years. Many of these laws were designed to lessen the tax burden on employees. One common way to reduce this burden is to keep part of an employee's annual income nontaxable. In Section 4, you learned that part of an employee's income is nontaxable based on the number of exemptions the employee claims. There are many other ways that a taxpayer can claim nontaxable income.

Nontaxable income lowers the amount of taxable income, which in turn lowers a person's tax liability. Your local, state, and federal governments allow you to deduct certain expenses as nontaxable income. These expenses are called **itemized deductions**. They are listed on a form called **Schedule A**. You can file a Schedule A form only if you are filing a Form 1040. You cannot claim itemized deductions if you use Form 1040A or Form 1040EZ.

The information you need to fill out Schedule A is included in the Form 1040 instruction booklet. Before preparing Schedule A, you should set up a tax worksheet. You will use the worksheet to help you determine what expenses you can list as deductions. The following is a partial listing of the items you should consider before filling out Schedule A.

Medical Payments — doctors, dentists, hospitals, medical insurance premiums, prescriptions, eyeglasses, hearing aids, dentures, cosmetic surgery

Taxes — state income tax, local income tax, property tax

Interest — mortgage interest and more

Contributions — cash and noncash donations to qualified charities

Casualty and Theft Losses — some financial setbacks due to sudden unfortunate events

Miscellaneous — business-related expenses, work uniforms purchased or laundered, educational expenses, gambling losses

Such deductions are subject to certain limitations and restrictions. Topic 5 Enhance/Advance Activity 5 will help you learn what expenses qualify as tax deductions.

You can see that it is beneficial to know about deductions. The more you know, the more you save on your taxes. Even if you hire an accountant to prepare your taxes, you must fill out a tax worksheet for your accountant. You should learn what you need to tell your accountant about your finances. Activities in Topic 5 Enhance/Advance will help you keep up to date on the current allowable itemized deductions.

Skills and Strategies

Here you will learn how to determine what expenses are allowable tax deductions.

1. Maria had $2,100 in medical expenses last year. Her medical insurance covered 80% of these expenses. How much can she report on Schedule A under medical expenses?

    Solution: On Schedule A, Maria can enter only the medical expenses that were not covered by insurance.

$2,100	medical expenses
× .80	80%, expressed as a decimal
$1,680.00	amount paid by insurance company

$2,100	medical expenses
− 1,680.00	amount paid by insurance company
$ 420.00	medical expenses not covered by insurance

    Maria can enter $420 in medical expenses that were not covered by her insurance company. Part of this may be tax deductible.

2. Jake attended religious services every week throughout the past tax year. He donated $2 each week. What were his cash contributions to this religious institution for that year?

Solution: Multiply to find the total amount.

$ 2.00 weekly contribution
× 52 number of weeks in one year
$104.00 total contribution

Jake can deduct $104 on his tax return as a charity contribution. He can add this to other charitable contributions he may have made during the year.

3. Lauren is a licensed nurse. She attended college last year to receive more training in nursing skills. Here are her educational expenses for the courses she took:
   tuition, $3,212.50
   books, $73.74
   lab fees, $100.00

What are her total educational expenses for the year?

Solution: Use a calculator to add:

AC 3,212.50 + 73.74 + 100 =

The display should read 3,386.24.

Lauren spent $3,386.24 on educational expenses.

4. Mike is a licensed plumber. He took night courses in ceramics and photography last year. He spent $674 in tuition and supplies for the ceramics course and $715 in tuition and supplies for the photography course. How much of these educational expenses can he deduct on Schedule A?

   Solution: Mike cannot deduct *any* of these educational expenses because they are not sufficiently related to the improvement of his plumbing skills.

5. Gloria is single. Her total income before deductions was $20,505. She was able to reduce her total income $5,381 by filling out Schedule A. How much did she save in tax liability by using Schedule A?

   Solution: Use Figure 10.1 on page 378 to determine tax liability before and after deductions. The tax liability for a single person earning $20,505 is $3,184.

$20,505   income before deductions
− 5,381   Schedule A allowable deductions
$15,124   taxable income after Schedule A deductions

The tax liability on $15,124 for a single person is $1,947.
Then subtract the amount of tax liability after deductions from
the amount before deductions.

$3,184   tax liability on $20,505
− 1,947   tax liability on $15,124
$1,237   tax saving

Gloria saved $1,237 by using Schedule A.

Problems

1. Jeanne is covered by medical insurance. Her insurance policy
    paid 80% of her medical expenses, which were $2,321. How
    much of the expenses were not covered and can be entered on
    Schedule A?

2. Louis had $1,200 worth of dental expenses during the tax year.
    His dental policy covered 60% of this amount. The premiums
    for the dental insurance amounted to $176. What is the total
    amount Louis had to pay in dental insurance and dental
    expenses?

✓ 3. Charleen is single. Her taxable income was $19,816 before she
    completed Schedule A. Charleen was able to claim $3,014 in
    deductions from her income. What is Charleen's tax liability?
    (Use Figure 10.1, page 378.)

4. Robin contributed $5 per month to her brother's Boy Scout
    troop. What were her annual contributions to the troop?

✓ 5. Andy took courses to improve his teaching skills as an auto-
    shop teacher. He had the following expenses:
       tuition, $3,200
       books, $120
       course supplies, $50

What were Andy's total deductions for educational expenses?

6. Dominic had an annual income of $17,489.32 last year. His deductions totaled $2,845.82. What was Dominic's taxable income for last year?

✓ **7.** Jessica is filing her taxes under the status of head of household. She had a total annual income of $19,385 last year. Her total deductions were $5,240.80.

    a. What was Jessica's taxable income for last year?

    b. Use Figure 10.1 on page 378 to compute Jessica's tax liability for last year.

    c. Jessica's employer withheld $6,940.82 in federal tax last year. Will Jessica owe the government money?

    d. What is the difference between Jessica's tax liability and the amount that was withheld by her employer?

8. Mr. and Mrs. Delta are jointly filing their tax return. Together they had an annual income of $62,340 last year. Their total deductions were $16,848.50.

    a. What was Mr. and Mrs. Delta's taxable income last year?

    b. Use Figure 10.4 on page 381 to find the Delta's tax liability for last year.

    c. The combined total of the Deltas' federal withholding taxes was $18,947.30. Should they receive a refund?

    d. What is the difference between the Deltas' tax liability and the amount that was withheld by their employers?

✓ **9.** Complete the chart at the top of page 402. Use Figure 10.1 on page 378.

Annual Income of Single Taxpayer	Deductions	Taxable Income	Tax Liability
$21,955	$100	a.	b.
$21,955	200	c.	d.
$21,955	300	e.	f.
$21,955	400	g.	h.
$21,955	500	i.	j.
$21,955	600	k.	l.
$21,955	700	m.	n.

10. Use the information in the chart in Problem 9 to draw a bar graph depicting the effect that deductions have on an annual income of $21,955. Label the vertical axis "Tax Liability (Single)" and the horizontal axis "Deduction."

✓ 11. Complete the following chart. Use Figure 10.3 on page 380.

Annual Income of Single Taxpayer	Deductions	Taxable Income	Tax Liability
$53,210	$ 2,000	a.	b.
$53,210	6,000	c.	d.
$53,210	10,000	e.	f.
$53,210	14,000	g.	h.
$53,210	18,000	i.	j.
$53,210	22,000	k.	l.

12. Use the information in the chart in Problem 11 to draw a line graph depicting the effect that deductions have on an annual income of $53,210. Label the vertical axis "Tax Liability (Single)" and the horizontal axis "Deduction."

In Problems 13, 14, and 15, you will need a Form 1040, a Schedule A, and a Form 1040 instruction booklet.

13. Margaret and Brian O'Sullivan are married. They have three children: Carole, Maureen, and Debbie. Margaret is a photographer for a television studio, and Brian is a sportscaster. Their W-2 forms are shown in Figures 10.16 and 10.17.

1 Control number 7401	22222	OMB No. 1545-0008		
2 Employer's name, address, and ZIP code		3 Employer's identification number	4 Employer's state I.D. number 234	
FRIENDLY'S STUDIOS 37 HEMPSTEAD ST. BOSTON, MA		5 Statutory employee Deceased Legal rep. 942 emp. Subtotal Void		
		6 Allocated tips	7 Advance EIC payment	
8 Employee's social security number 000-00-0000	9 Federal income tax withheld $1,500.00	10 Wages, tips, other compensation $19,100.00	11 Social security tax withheld	
12 Employee's name, address, and ZIP code		13 Social security wages	14 Social security tips	
MARGARET O'SULLIVAN 682 ARLINGTON DRIVE SEATOWN, MA 01256		16	16a Fringe benefits incl. in Box 10	
		17 State income tax $700.00	18 State wages, tips, etc. $19,100.00	19 Name of state MA
		20 Local income tax $400.00	21 Local wages, tips, etc. $19,100.00	22 Name of locality

Form **W-2 Wage and Tax Statement**

Copy B To be filed with employee's FEDERAL tax return   Department of the Treasury
This information is being furnished to the Internal Revenue Service.   Internal Revenue Service

Figure 10.16   Margaret O'Sullivan's W-2 Form

1 Control number 441	22222	OMB No. 1545-0008		
2 Employer's name, address, and ZIP code		3 Employer's identification number	4 Employer's state I.D. number 405	
WROB-TV 121 SAEVITZ ST. BOSTON, MA		5 Statutory employee Deceased Legal rep. 942 emp. Subtotal Void		
		6 Allocated tips	7 Advance EIC payment	
8 Employee's social security number 000-00-0000	9 Federal income tax withheld $1,274.00	10 Wages, tips, other compensation $18,000.00	11 Social security tax withheld	
12 Employee's name, address, and ZIP code		13 Social security wages	14 Social security tips	
BRIAN O'SULLIVAN 682 ARLINGTON DRIVE SEATOWN, MA 01256		16	16a Fringe benefits incl. in Box 10	
		17 State income tax $616.00	18 State wages, tips, etc. $18,000.00	19 Name of state MA
		20 Local income tax $319.00	21 Local wages, tips, etc. $18,000.00	22 Name of locality

Form **W-2 Wage and Tax Statement**

Copy B To be filed with employee's FEDERAL tax return   Department of the Treasury
This information is being furnished to the Internal Revenue Service.   Internal Revenue Service

Figure 10.17   Brian O'Sullivan's W-2 Form

Margaret and Brian received the following income in addition to their salaries:

Interest: $275 from Boston Bank
$300 from Globe Savings
Dividends: $212
Prizes: $1,000 from the lottery

Here is a list of their itemized deductions:

Medical Expenses: prescriptions, $100
doctors, $300
dentists, $1,300
insurance, $700
Taxes: real estate tax, $3,000
Interest Paid: home mortgage loan, $4,600
Contributions: cash, $300
used clothing, $50

Use the above information to file a joint Form 1040 and Schedule A for the O'Sullivan family.

14. Bruce and Carole Kontchegulian are married. They have two children: Robert and Linda. Bruce is a musician, and Carole is a teacher. Their W-2 forms are shown in Figures 10.18 and 10.19 on page 405.

Bruce and Carole received the following income in addition to their salaries:

Interest: $342 from Beeper Bank
$49 from Nomad Savings
Dividends: $150
Prizes: $250 on a TV quiz show

Here is a list of their itemized deductions:

Medical Expenses: prescriptions, $200
doctors, $700
dentists, $1,000
hospitals, $420
insurance, $200
Taxes: real estate tax, $3,000
Interest Paid: home mortgage loan, $4,600
Contributions: cash, $750
used piano donated, $400

Use the above information to file a joint Form 1040 and Schedule A for the Kontchegulian family.

1 Control number 5491	22222	OMB No. 1545-0008			

2 Employer's name, address, and ZIP code

OMNI TALENT AGENCY
44 JERICHO ST.
HILLDALE, OH

3 Employer's identification number

4 Employer's state I.D. number 976

5 Statutory employee   Deceased   Legal rep.   942 emp.   Subtotal   Void ☐ ☐ ☐ ☐ ☐ ☐

6 Allocated tips

7 Advance EIC payment

8 Employee's social security number 000-00-0000

9 Federal income tax withheld $3,700.00

10 Wages, tips, other compensation $26,111.00

11 Social security tax withheld

12 Employee's name, address, and ZIP code

BRUCE KONTCHEGULIAN
12 MADISON ST.
CINCINNATI, OH 45227

13 Social security wages

14 Social security tips

16

16a Fringe benefits incl. in Box 10

17 State income tax $1,519.00

18 State wages, tips, etc. $26,111.00

19 Name of state OH

20 Local income tax

21 Local wages, tips, etc.

22 Name of locality

Form **W-2 Wage and Tax Statement**

Copy B To be filed with employee's FEDERAL tax return
This information is being furnished to the Internal Revenue Service.

Department of the Treasury
Internal Revenue Service

Figure 10.18 Bruce Kontchegulian's W-2 Form

1 Control number 6231	22222	OMB No. 1545-0008			

2 Employer's name, address, and ZIP code

LAKEWOOD HIGH SCHOOL
375 GLEN AVE.
LAKEWOOD, OH

3 Employer's identification number

4 Employer's state I.D. number 975

5 Statutory employee   Deceased   Legal rep.   942 emp.   Subtotal   Void ☐ ☐ ☐ ☐ ☐ ☐

6 Allocated tips

7 Advance EIC payment

8 Employee's social security number 000-00-0000

9 Federal income tax withheld $2,771.00

10 Wages, tips, other compensation $23,651.00

11 Social security tax withheld

12 Employee's name, address, and ZIP code

CAROLE KONTCHEGULIAN
12 MADISON ST.
CINCINNATI, OH 45227

13 Social security wages

14 Social security tips

16

16a Fringe benefits incl. in Box 10

17 State income tax $1,311.00

18 State wages, tips, etc. $23,651.00

19 Name of state OH

20 Local income tax

21 Local wages, tips, etc.

22 Name of locality

Form **W-2 Wage and Tax Statement**

Copy B To be filed with employee's FEDERAL tax return
This information is being furnished to the Internal Revenue Service.

Department of the Treasury
Internal Revenue Service

Figure 10.19 Carole Kontchegulian's W-2 Form

15. Nancy and Tom DiMonte are married and have three children: Jamie, Caryl, and Lori. Nancy is a teacher, and Tom is a computer programmer. Their W-2 forms are shown in Figures 10.20 and 10.21.

1 Control number			
2555	22222	OMB No. 1545-0008	

2 Employer's name, address, and ZIP code	3 Employer's identification number	4 Employer's state I.D. number
BUREN HIGH SCHOOL 232 HILLSIDE AVE. PHOENIX, AZ		977

5 Statutory employee	Deceased	Legal rep.	942 emp.	Subtotal	Void
☐	☐	☐	☐	☐	☐

6 Allocated tips	7 Advance EIC payment

8 Employee's social security number	9 Federal income tax withheld	10 Wages, tips, other compensation	11 Social security tax withheld
000-00-0000	$2,300.00	$24,176.00	

12 Employee's name, address, and ZIP code	13 Social security wages	14 Social security tips
NANCY DIMONTE 156 CONNECTICUT AVE. PHOENIX, AZ 85251	16	16a Fringe benefits incl. in Box 10

17 State income tax	18 State wages, tips, etc.	19 Name of state
$1,137.00	$24,176.00	AZ

20 Local income tax	21 Local wages, tips, etc.	22 Name of locality
$671.00	$24,176.00	

Form **W-2 Wage and Tax Statement**

Copy B To be filed with employee's FEDERAL tax return   Department of the Treasury
This information is being furnished to the Internal Revenue Service.   Internal Revenue Service

Figure 10.20   Nancy DiMonte's W-2 Form

1 Control number			
3477	22222	OMB No. 1545-0008	

2 Employer's name, address, and ZIP code	3 Employer's identification number	4 Employer's state I.D. number
PENNGRUMON CORP. 3716 ZEPHYR BLVD. PHOENIX, AZ		246

5 Statutory employee	Deceased	Legal rep.	942 emp.	Subtotal	Void
☐	☐	☐	☐	☐	☐

6 Allocated tips	7 Advance EIC payment

8 Employee's social security number	9 Federal income tax withheld	10 Wages, tips, other compensation	11 Social security tax withheld
000-00-0000	$3,100.00	$42,119.00	

12 Employee's name, address, and ZIP code	13 Social security wages	14 Social security tips
TOM DIMONTE 156 CONNECTICUT AVE. PHOENIX, AZ 85251	16	16a Fringe benefits incl. in Box 10

17 State income tax	18 State wages, tips, etc.	19 Name of state
$2,100.00	$42,119.00	AZ

20 Local income tax	21 Local wages, tips, etc.	22 Name of locality
$976.00	$42,119.00	

Form **W-2 Wage and Tax Statement**

Copy B To be filed with employee's FEDERAL tax return   Department of the Treasury
This information is being furnished to the Internal Revenue Service.   Internal Revenue Service

Figure 10.21   Tom DiMonte's W-2 Form

Nancy and Tom received the following income in addition to their salaries:
Interest: $301 from Dalton Savings Bank
$211 from Brooklyn Bank
Dividends: $35 from Coca-Cola
$173 from Xerox
Prizes: $100 from the state lottery
$600 in a supermarket contest

Here is a list of their itemized deductions:
Medical Expenses: prescriptions, $59
doctors, $490
dentists, $1,700
insurance, $812
Taxes: real estate tax, $2,140
Interest Paid: home mortgage loan, $3,400
Contributions: cash, $700
used violin, $50
used clothing, $150

Use the above information to file a joint Form 1040 and Schedule A for the DiMonte family.

● KEY TERMS

To find the definition of any term introduced in the chapter, refer to the Glossary in the back of this book.

deducted
deduction
dependent
exemption
Federal Insurance
    Contributions Act (FICA)
filed
filing status
Form SS-5: Application for
    Social Security Number
Form 1040

Form 1040A
Form 1040EZ
Form 1099
Form W-4
Form W-2
income taxes
Internal Revenue Service
    (IRS)
itemized deduction
maximum taxable income
net pay

refund
Schedule A
social security
social security number
social security percentage
social security tax
take-home pay
taxable income

tax liability
tax return
tax schedule
tax table
tax worksheet
Wage and Tax Statement
withholds
withholding tax

• REVIEW PROBLEMS

1. Harold's gross pay for last week was $449.58. Deductions for insurance, social security, and withholding taxes added up to $114.18. What was Harold's net pay?

2. Fred is paid biweekly. On each paycheck, $24 is deducted for medical insurance. What is Fred's total medical insurance premium for the year?

3. Use Figure 10.1 on page 378 to find the tax liability for a single person who has $19,211 in taxable income.

4. Use Figure 10.3 on page 380 to find the tax liability for a married couple (filing a joint return) who have $75,900 in taxable income.

5. Elsie is paid weekly. She can deduct her hospital and dental insurance premiums on Schedule A. From each paycheck $2.10 is deducted for dental insurance and $3 is deducted for hospital insurance. What does Elsie pay yearly for these medical insurance policies?

6. Eric is single. He earned $40,000 last year. After working on his tax return, Eric finds that $19,123 of his income is nontaxable. Use Figure 10.1 on page 378 to find Eric's tax liability.

7. List the names (letters and/or numbers) of five Internal Revenue Service forms you learned about in Topic 5.

8. Alfredo is single. His taxable income was $21,171 before he used Schedule A. After filling out Schedule A, Alfredo was able to claim $7,061 in deductions from his income. What is Alfredo's tax liability? (Use Figure 10.1, page 378.)

9. Juanita is married. She and her husband file separate returns. Juanita reduced her taxable income of $21,611 by compiling $6,298 in deductions. How much did she *save* on her tax liability by using Schedule A? (Use Figure 10.1 on page 378.)

10. Emily is divorced and files as a head of household. Her taxable income is $51,000. Brett is single, and her taxable income is also $51,000. How much higher is Brett's tax liability than Emily's? (Use Figure 10.3 on page 380.)

TOPIC *5* ENHANCE/ADVANCE

1. Prepare your first job résumé by going to the library and finding a book that explains how to set it up. You may also ask your English teacher or business teacher for help. Include your background, work experience, and references. Have it typed. You may want to make up schools, jobs, and references if you can't provide that information at this time in your life. Make sure the form, spelling, and typing are correct. Hand the résumé in to your teacher for display in the classroom.

2. Go to a library and find the address of the Department of Labor in your state. As a class, write a business letter requesting information on insurance and labor laws that apply to your state.

3. Cut out one page from the help-wanted section of a newspaper. Circle 25 abbreviated terms that are used in the ads. Prepare a wall chart with these expressions and their meanings. Display the chart in your classroom.

4. Go to a library and find the address of your local social security office. Choose one of the following assignments:
   a. Write a business letter requesting information about benefits paid under social security. Also request information on applying for a social security number. Report your findings to the class.
   b. Write a business letter to the office requesting Form SS-5: Application for Social Security Number. Ask your teacher to display this form in the classroom. If you do not already have a social security number, apply for one.
   c. Write a letter to the office requesting a form that can be used to apply for a copy of your social security account. Discuss this form with your parent or guardian. Fill out the form, and mail it in. Save the information that you receive.
   d. Write a business letter requesting information about this year's FICA tax. Be sure to find out what percentage is used to compute this year's FICA tax and to find out the maximum annual income that is subject to FICA tax. Prepare a wall chart of your findings, and hand it in to your teacher.

5. Go to a library and find the address of your regional Internal Revenue Service office. Write a business letter requesting a copy of the IRS booklet *Publication 17: Your Federal Income Tax*. Present this booklet to your classmates.

6. With clearance from your teacher, invite an accountant to speak to your class. Before the accountant's visit, have class members write questions they would like answered. Read these questions to the accountant during the session. Be sure to write a thank-you letter after the session.

7. Go to a post office and get several copies of current federal income tax forms. Also, pick up a copy of the instruction booklet used to fill out tax forms. Share these materials with your classmates.

8. Write an original story about a family that needs to have their tax returns prepared. You can model your story after the stories presented in the problems in Sections 4 and 5. Use your imagination. Present enough information so that a tax return can be completed for the family. Hand the story in to your teacher. Talk to your teacher about having the class complete tax returns for this year, based on your story.

TOPIC *5* MANIPULATIVE ACTIVITY

THE TAX BITE

In Topic 5, you learned how to compute tax liabilities for given taxable incomes. You learned how employers withheld taxes from employee paychecks to help employees meet their tax liabilities. Did you ever wonder what size chunk of your income your tax liability is? This activity will help you visualize how much of your income is paid in taxes. This amount is often called the "tax bite."

Directions: You will need a large piece of white poster board, several sheets of colored construction paper, a compass, protractor, ruler, glue, a magic marker, and a current Federal income tax instruction booklet. You will construct a circle graph, or pie chart. Slices of the pie will be used to represent the portion of income that is paid in taxes.

1. Copy and complete the following chart for a single taxpayer. Use the current tax instruction booklet and your calculator.

Pie Chart Number	Taxable Income TI	Tax Liability TL	Tax Liability Expressed as a Percent of Taxable Income (Tax Bite Percent) TI ÷ TL % (Round to the nearest %)
1	$ 15,000		
2	$ 30,000		
3	$ 60,000		
4	$100,000		

2. Use the compass to draw four large circles, one on each of four sheets of construction paper.

3. Cut out the four circles.

4. The central angle of a complete circle contains 360 degrees. For the first pie chart, use the tax bite percent to find how many degrees will be used to draw the sector that represents the tax bite. Round your answer to the nearest degree.

5. Use the protractor and the ruler to construct the tax bite sector for the first pie chart. Ask your teacher if you need help using the protractor.

6. Cut out the tax bite sector from the first pie chart. Glue the original circle and the tax bite sector onto the poster board. Label the pie chart.

7. Repeat steps 4, 5, and 6 with pie charts 2, 3, and 4.

8. Present your findings to the class in a chart similar to the one shown:

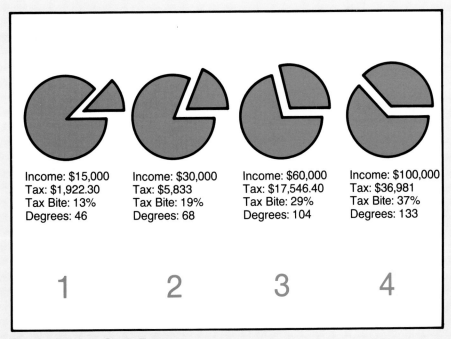

Income: $15,000
Tax: $1,922.30
Tax Bite: 13%
Degrees: 46

Income: $30,000
Tax: $5,833
Tax Bite: 19%
Degrees: 68

Income: $60,000
Tax: $17,546.40
Tax Bite: 29%
Degrees: 104

Income: $100,000
Tax: $36,981
Tax Bite: 37%
Degrees: 133

1   2   3   4

The Tax Bite for a Single Taxpayer

PAYCHECKS

In this computer application, you will run the PAYCHECKS program to examine the annual pay schedules for three different employees. The data needed about each employee follows with a list of questions to be answered for each.

Review the information you have covered about pay periods and taxes before you run the computer program. You will need to know the *current* social security percentage withholding, and the maximum taxable income level for social security.

Directions: If necessary, follow the start-up procedures for your computer which are found in Appendix A. Select Topic 5 titled *Paychecks* from the Main Menu. Follow the instructions on your computer screen and use the data generated by the computer to answer the questions under 1, 2, and 3. Do not write in this book. Put your answers on a piece of paper.

1.

Employee	Gross Annual Income	Pay Period	First Pay Date
Jane Michaels	$25,000	Weekly	January 7

    a. What is this employee's gross pay per check?

    b. By what date has Jane Michaels earned approximately 50% of her annual salary?

    c. What is the gross pay that Jane has earned as of the eleventh paycheck?

    d. How much Social Security Tax (FICA) does Jane pay per paycheck?

    e. What is the total amount of Social Security Tax that Jane must pay this year?

    f. What is Jane's net pay for the year?

2.

Employee	Gross Annual Income	Pay Period	First Pay Date
Toshiro Domo	$40,000	Bi-weekly	January 14

   a. What is this employee's gross pay per check?
   b. By what date has Toshiro Domo earned approximately 50% of her annual salary?
   c. What is the gross pay that Toshiro has earned as of the eleventh paycheck?
   d. How much Social Security Tax (FICA) does Toshiro pay per paycheck?
   e. What is the total amount of Social Security Tax that Toshiro must pay this year?
   f. What is Toshiro's net pay for the year?

3.

Employee	Gross Annual Income	Pay Period	First Pay Date
Maria Juarez	$40,000	Monthly	January 31

   a. What is this employee's gross pay per check?
   b. By what date has Maria Juarez earned approximately 50% of her annual salary?
   c. What is the gross pay that Jane has earned as of the eleventh paycheck?
   d. How much Social Security Tax (FICA) does Maria pay per paycheck?
   e. What is the total amount of Social Security Tax that Maria must pay this year?
   f. What is Maria's net pay for the year?

Have you thought about where you will be living in a few years? There are many possibilities. The end of your schooling means that you will begin to become independent. When this happens, you may find that you are spending a large part of your income on housing and household expenses. With so much money involved, you will want to spend carefully. You will have large bills that are the same every month, such as rent. You will also have expenses that change every month, such as food. How do people plan for expenses that vary? You will learn skills for managing household finances, budgeting, and bank transactions in the final chapters of *Dollars and Sense*.

CHAPTER *11*

WHERE TO LIVE

SECTION 1 ● FINDING A PLACE TO LIVE

Have you ever imagined what it would be like to have "a place of your own"? Most teenagers look forward to the day when they can afford to support themselves. Moving away from your family home is costly and a great responsibility. Topic 6 contains important information and presents practical skills that will help you make intelligent choices about independent living.

Once you have decided to find a place of your own, you will need the classified ads section of a newspaper. You have already learned how to read classified ads listing automobiles for sale and employment opportunities. Now let's examine the following ad from the real-estate classified section.

Note that it's difficult to understand parts of this advertisement. Since classified ads have a language all their own, you should become familiar with the following abbreviations.

appls — appliances (could include washer, dryer, refrigerator, and so on)

apt — apartment

balc — balcony

bdrm — bedroom

blks — blocks

bsmt — basement

bth — bathroom

cent air — central air-conditioning

contemp — contemporary (modern)

din rm — dining room

EIK — eat-in kitchen

fin — finished

frplce — fireplace   **liv rm** — living room

gar — garage   **mint** — excellent condition

gd — good   **nr all** — near all (close to

hi — high   schools, shops,

immac — immaculate   public

transportation, and

kit — kitchen   so on)

lge — large   **pvt** — private

lo — low   **rnch** — ranch

An informed consumer will compare several places before making a decision on where to live. The following factors might affect your choice:

- price

- room size

- location

- nearness to your job

- nearness to stores

- nearness to schools

- availability of public transportation

You can easily see that finding a place to live is a rather complicated task. *Caveat emptor!* (Let the consumer beware!)

Skills and Strategies

Here you will learn how to price a home and place a classified ad to sell the home.

1. The Santiago family plans to sell their house. Before taking out a classified ad, they must set a price for the house. During the past year, five similar houses on their block were sold. Here are the selling prices of the five houses:
   $215,000
   $260,000

$257,000
$292,000
$210,000

What was the mean selling price of the five houses?

Solution: You can compute the mean with pencil and paper or use the following calculator keystroke sequence:

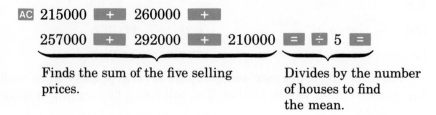

Finds the sum of the five selling prices.

Divides by the number of houses to find the mean.

The display should read 246,800.

The mean selling price of the five houses was $246,800. The Santiagos can use the mean to help them determine a selling price for their house.

2.   The Santiagos want to place a classified ad for the sale of their house. Their local newspaper charges $18 for the first three lines and $5 for each additional line. Each ad runs for five days. How much will the Santiagos pay for a seven-line ad that will run for ten days?

Solution: First the Santiagos must find the cost of running their ad for five days.

7	number of lines in ad
− 3	the first three lines
4	number of additional lines
$ 5.00	price of each additional line
× 4	number of additional lines
$20.00	cost of four additional lines
$20.00	cost of four additional lines
+ 18.00	cost of first three lines
$38.00	total cost of ad for five days
$38.00	cost of ad for five days
× 2	number of times ad runs for five days each
$76.00	cost of ad for ten days

The Santiagos will pay $76.00 for the classified ad.

Problems

1. The Kahn family plans to sell their home. Three similar homes on their block recently sold for prices of $176,000, $215,000, and $191,000. What is the mean selling price of these three houses?

√ 2. The Ortiz family wants to sell their lakeside summer cottage. Five similar homes on the lake recently sold for prices of $80,000, $80,000, $90,000, $84,000, and $80,000.

   a. What was the mean selling price of the five homes?

   b. What was the median selling price of the five homes?

   c. What was the mode selling price of the five homes?

3. Kyle is planning to rent an apartment. He looks through the classified ads and finds four apartments that he is interested in. The monthly rents are $700, $750, $660, and $775. What is the difference in price between the highest and lowest of these monthly rents?

√ 4. The *Glen Head Viking* newspaper charges $17 for a two-line classified real-estate ad. Each extra line costs $7.25. The ad runs for three days. How much would a five-line ad cost to run for six days?

5. The Jacobson family hopes to rent their house for the months of June, July, and August. They are charging $500 per month in rent. How much rent will they receive for these three months?

6. Gina is planning to rent an apartment. She looks through the classified ads and finds an apartment she is interested in. The monthly rent is $850. What is the annual rent for this apartment?

7. The Watsons are looking for a new house. They were interested in one that was selling for $205,000 but then a similar house was listed for $190,000. The owner of the $205,000 house has agreed to lower the price by 12%. Is this new selling price lower than $190,000? Explain your answer.

√ **8.** A real-estate broker lists eight houses for sale at the following prices:

$412,000 $ 80,000
$181,000 $250,000
$215,000 $200,000
$170,000 $200,000

Find the median listing price of these eight houses.

9. The *Locust Valley Legend* charges $8 for each line in a classified ad. In the last edition of the newspaper there were 13 four-line ads and one-dozen five-line ads.
  a. What is the cost of a four-line ad?
  b. What is the cost of a five-line ad?
  c. How much money did the *Locust Valley Legend* collect as payment for the classified ads in its last issue?

10. Four different styles of homes were advertised in last week's *Daily Times*. The circle graph in Figure 11.1 gives information about the 200 classified ads that were run in this newspaper last week. The problems in **a** through **g** relate to Figure 11.1.

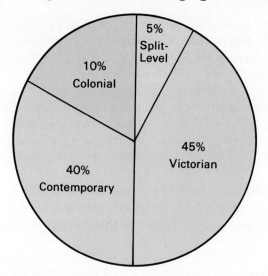

Figure 11.1 Styles of the 200 Homes Advertised in the Daily Times Last Week

  a. How many colonial homes were advertised?
  b. Fifty-five percent of the colonial homes advertised were not sold. How many colonial homes were not sold?

c. How many colonial homes *were* sold?

d. How many more Victorian homes were advertised than contemporary homes?

e. All of the split-level homes that were advertised were sold. How many split-level homes were sold?

f. Half of the contemporary homes that were advertised were sold. How many contemporary homes were sold?

g. None of the advertised Victorian houses was sold. How many of the 200 advertised houses from last week's *Daily Times* were sold?

SECTION 2 • READING A FLOOR PLAN

When you begin to look for a house or an apartment, price is not the only factor you should consider. In Section 1 you learned that other things should be examined before making a choice. One important consideration is room size and the arrangement of the rooms. This information can be found by reading a **floor plan**. A floor plan is a drawing of the layout and the dimensions of rooms in a dwelling. Study the apartment floor plan in Figure 11.2.

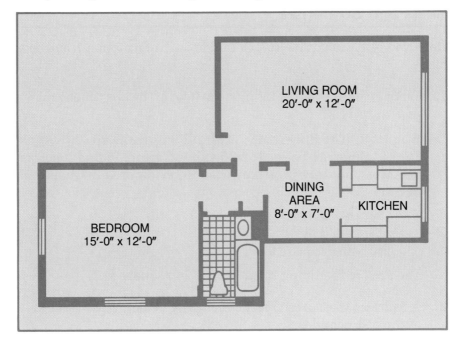

Figure 11.2 Apartment Floor Plan

Here is some of the information that the floor plan in Figure 11.2 gives you:

- The apartment has a kitchen, a dining area, a living room, a bedroom, and a bathroom.

- The bathroom has a sink, a toilet, a bathtub, and one window.

- The bedroom measures 15 feet by 12 feet, and it has two windows and one doorway.

- The living room measures 20 feet by 12 feet, and it has one large window and three entrances.

- The dining area measures 8 feet by 7 feet, and it has three entrances and no windows.

- The kitchen is complete with cabinets, one window, and one entrance.

- The entrance to this apartment is shown by the arrow in the living-room entrance.

Examining a floor plan allows you to make intelligent decisions before you take the step to move in.

Skills and Strategies

Here you will learn how to get important information from floor plans.

1.   What is the area of the living room floor of the apartment shown in Figure 11.2?

Solution: The dimensions of the living room are $20' - 0'' \times 12' - 0''$. This can be read "20 feet by 12 feet." To find the area, you must multiply. (You may wish to review area in Chapter 2, Section 7.)

$$
\begin{array}{r}
20 \quad \text{length (feet)} \\
\times\ 12 \quad \text{width (feet)} \\
\hline
240 \quad \text{area (square feet)}
\end{array}
$$

The area of the living room floor is 240 square feet.

2.   A bedroom measures 17 feet 5 inches by 14 feet. What is the area of the bedroom floor?

Solution: First, make a sketch as shown at the top of page 425.

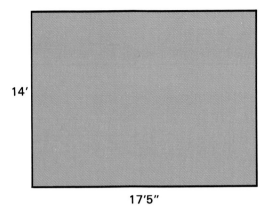

14'

17'5"

Before finding the area, convert 17 feet 5 inches to feet. Since 12 inches = 1 foot, you can say that 1 inch = $\frac{1}{12}$ foot and 5 inches = $\frac{5}{12}$ foot. To find the area, multiply the length by the width. You will need to use your skills in multiplying fractions.

$17\frac{5}{12} \times 14 =$

$$\frac{209}{12} \times \frac{\cancel{14}^{\,1}}{1} = \frac{1463}{6} = 243\frac{5}{6}$$

The area of the bedroom is $243\frac{5}{6}$ square feet.

3. Find the length of Wall A and the length of Wall B from the layout of an L-shaped room in Figure 11.3.

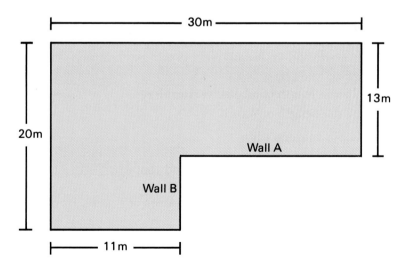

Figure 11.3 Floor Plan of an L-shaped Room

Solution: To find the length of Wall A, focus your attention on the horizontal lines only.

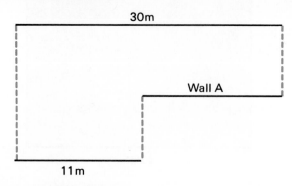

30 m   length of room
− 11 m   length of labeled horizontal line
19 m   length of Wall A

Wall A is 19 meters long.

To find the length of Wall B, focus your attention on the vertical lines only.

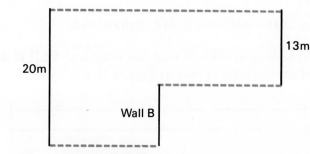

20 m   length of room
− 13 m   length of labeled vertical line
7 m   length of Wall B

Wall B is 7 meters wide.

4. Find the perimeter of the L-shaped room in Figure 11.3.

    Solution: You must add the measures of the walls, or sides.

Note that the L-shaped room has 6 sides. Don't forget to add *all* the sides!

20 + 30 + 13 + 19 + 7 + 11 = 100

The perimeter is 100 meters.

5. Find the area of the L-shaped room in Figure 11.3.

Solution: Create two rectangles by drawing a dashed line as shown:

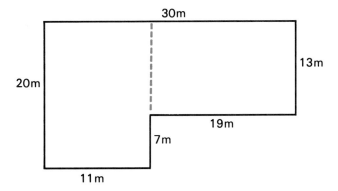

Then draw two identical but separate rectangles as shown:

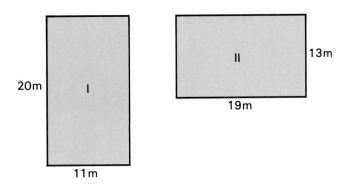

Find the area of each rectangle and add the areas together.

$$\begin{array}{rl} 20 \text{ m} & \text{length of rectangle I} \\ \times\ 11 \text{ m} & \text{width of rectangle I} \\ \hline 220 \text{ m}^2 & \text{area of rectangle I} \end{array}$$

$$\begin{array}{rl} 19 \text{ m} & \text{length of rectangle II} \\ \times\ 13 \text{ m} & \text{width of rectangle II} \\ \hline 247 \text{ m}^2 & \text{area of rectangle II} \end{array}$$

$$
\begin{array}{ll}
220 \text{ m}^2 & \text{area of rectangle I} \\
+\ 247 \text{ m}^2 & \text{area of rectangle II} \\
\hline
467 \text{ m}^2 & \text{total area}
\end{array}
$$

The area of the L-shaped room is 467 square meters.

Problems

✓**1.** Express the following measurements in feet.
   a. 6 inches   **b.** 3 inches   **c.** 4 inches   **d.** 9 inches
   e. 12 inches   **f.** 1 inch   **g.** 7 inches   **h.** 11 inches
   i. 5 inches   **j.** 18 inches

2. Find the area of a rectangle that has dimensions of $6\frac{1}{2}$ feet by 18 feet.

✓**3.** Find the area of a square with each side measuring 30 meters.

4. Find the perimeter of a rectangle with dimensions of 20.2 m by 19 m.

Use the floor plan in Figure 11.4 to answer questions 5–7.

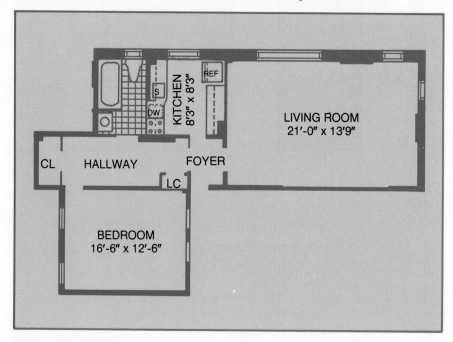

Figure 11.4 Floor Plan

5. a. Express the dimensions of the kitchen in feet.
   b. What is the area of the kitchen?
   c. What is the perimeter of the kitchen?

√**6. a.** Express the dimensions of the living room in feet.

   b. What is the perimeter of the living room?
   c. What is the area of the living room?
   d. How many windows does the living room have?

7. a. Express the dimensions of the bedroom in feet.

   b. What is the area of the bedroom?
   c. How many windows does the bedroom have?
   d. What is the perimeter of the bedroom?

8. Examine the floor plan for an L-shaped room in Figure 11.5.

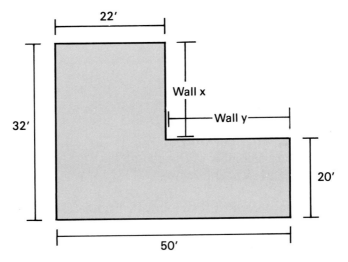

Figure 11.5 Floor Plan

   a. Find the length of Wall X.
   b. Find the length of Wall Y.
   c. Find the perimeter of the room.
   d. Find the area of the room.

9.   Examine the floor plan in Figure 11.6.

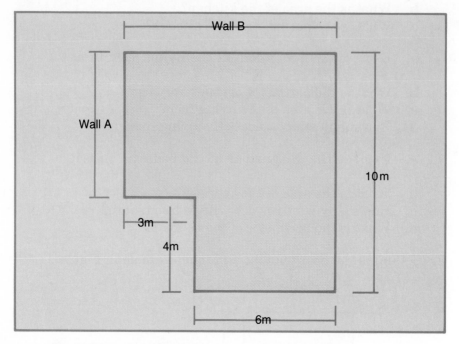

Figure 11.6   Floor Plan

    a.   Find the length of Wall A.
    b.   Find the length of Wall B.
    c.   Find the perimeter of the room.
    d.   Find the area of the room.

✓ **10.**   Examine the backyard floor plan in Figure 11.7 at the top of page 431.

    a.   What are the dimensions of the pool?
    b.   How many square feet of canvas would be needed to cover the top of the pool?
    c.   What are the dimensions of the patio?
    d.   What is the area of the patio?

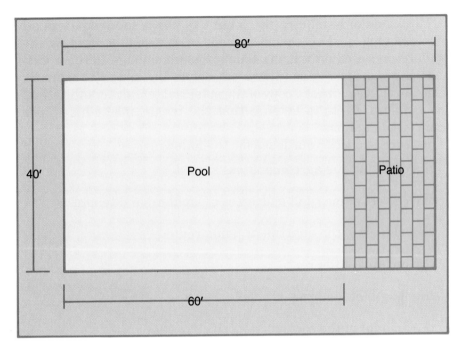

Figure 11.7 Backyard Floor Plan

SECTION 3 • RENTING AN APARTMENT

Your first experience of independent living will probably be in a rented apartment. When you rent an apartment, you are the **tenant,** and the owner of the property is your **landlord.** As you look through the classified ads, you will see **furnished** and **unfurnished** apartments for rent. The cost of renting a furnished apartment includes the use of the landlord's furniture in that apartment. You must provide your own furniture when you rent an unfurnished apartment.

Before you can move into an apartment, you usually sign a **lease.** A lease is a written agreement between the tenant and the landlord. The lease states the amount of rent that you must pay and the length of time that you will rent the apartment. The lease states the rules and regulations that must be followed by the tenant and the landlord. After a lease has expired, the tenant may sign a new lease covering a new period of time. The new lease may include a rent increase.

Most landlords require the tenant to pay a **security deposit** before moving in. This money is kept in a special account by the landlord and used only if the tenant causes damage to the apartment or breaks the lease (moves out before the lease has expired). Some landlords request a copy of the potential tenant's credit rating. The landlord wants to be sure that the tenant meets his or her financial obligations.

Be sure to check your lease for the following:

- the date that the agreement was signed

- the correct names and addresses of landlord and tenant

- the address of the apartment being rented

- the amount of the rent

- the length of the lease

- the amount of the security deposit

- any clauses about rent increases

- any rules about pet ownership

- any rules about apartment maintenance

A lease is a legal commitment. Be sure to read any lease carefully before signing it!

Skills and Strategies

Here you will learn to compute a security deposit, a rent increase, and a finder's fee.

1. Jane is going to rent an apartment for $650 per month. The lease requires her to pay a security deposit equal to two months' rent when she pays her first month's rent. How much must Jane pay the landlord before moving into the apartment?

   Solution: Compute the security deposit and the first month's rent.

$$
\begin{array}{rl}
\$650 & \text{monthly rent} \\
\underline{\times\ 2} & \text{security deposit (equal to two months of rent)} \\
\$1,300 & \text{amount of security deposit}
\end{array}
$$

$1,300   amount of security deposit
+ 650   first month's rent
$1,950   total

Jane must pay her landlord $1,950 before moving into the apartment. Note that this doesn't include any other living expenses, such as gas, water, electricity, food, and so on. These living expenses will be discussed in Chapter 12.

2. Ed pays $600 per month to rent his apartment. He recently signed a two-year lease. The lease states that for the second year his rent may be increased a maximum of 9.5%. What is the most Ed could be required to pay for monthly rent during the second year of his lease?

Solution:

$600   monthly rent during first year of lease
× .095   9.5% expressed as a decimal
$57.00   maximum increase per month

$600   monthly rent during first year of lease
+ 57   maximum increase
$657   maximum monthly rent during second year

Ed's rent could be raised to a maximum of $657 during the second year of his lease.

Ed could have used the following calculator keystroke sequence:

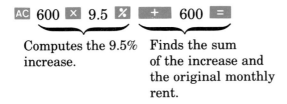

AC 600 × 9.5 % + 600 =

Computes the 9.5% increase.   Finds the sum of the increase and the original monthly rent.

The display should read 657.

3. Joel is moving out of his $500-per-month apartment because the lease has expired. Joel paid a security deposit equal to two months' rent when he signed his lease. Damage to the apartment during a party amounted to $75. Joel never repaired the damage. How much of his security deposit will be returned to him?

Solution:

$ 500   monthly rent
× 2   security deposit (equal to two months of rent)
$1,000   amount of security deposit

$1,000   amount of security deposit
− 75   value of apartment damage
$ 925   amount of security deposit refunded

Joel will receive $925 of his security deposit.

4.   Rachel visited a real-estate broker to look for an apartment. The broker charges 15% of the first month's rent to find an apartment for a client. This is called a **finder's fee.** The apartment that the broker finds for Rachel rents for $725 per month. What is the finder's fee?

Solution: Use the following keystroke sequence:

AC 725 × 15 %

The display should read 108.75.

Rachel must pay a finder's fee of $108.75.

Problems

1.   Robert is going to rent an apartment for $520 per month. He must pay a security deposit equal to three months' rent. How much does Robert have to pay as a security deposit?

✓ 2.   Jan's lease requires her to pay $740 per month rent and a security deposit equal to $1\frac{1}{2}$ months' rent. How much security deposit must Jan pay?

3.   Paul pays $475 per month rent. He paid a security deposit equal to two months' rent when he signed his lease last year. During the year damage to the landlord's kitchen appliances amounted to $300. Paul did not have the damage repaired, and he is moving out this month.
   a.   How much security deposit did Paul pay?
   b.   How much of the security deposit will Paul receive when he moves out?

✓**4.** Joan paid a $600 security deposit when she moved into her apartment. During the year, her fishtank leaked and damaged the carpeting in the amount of $475, which Joan never paid or replaced. How much of her security deposit will she receive when she moves if this is the only damage she caused?

5. Lenore needed help finding an apartment, so she visited the Home-Sweet-Home Real Estate Agency. The broker charges 20% of the first month's rent as a finder's fee. The broker found Lenore an apartment at $640 per month. How much is the finder's fee?

6. The Fast Finders Real Estate Agency found an apartment for Harvey Schuster that rents for $750 per month. The agency charged a 12% finder's fee, and the landlord required a security deposit equal to two months of rent.
   a. How much is the finder's fee?
   b. How much is the security deposit?
   c. How much money must Schuster spend on the finder's fee, the security deposit, and the first month's rent before he can move in?
   d. Schuster's lease is for two years. The second year's rent can be increased a maximum of 10% according to the lease. What is the maximum rent he could pay during the second year of his lease?

✓**7.** Sue rents a one-bedroom apartment for $590 per month. Her lease expires next month. Her landlord informed her that a new lease would feature a 14% rent increase. What is the rent Sue would have to pay if she signed the new lease?

8. Janet and Chrissy are moving into an apartment near the college they attend. They plan to divide all costs equally. Through a broker who charges a 20% finder's fee, they get an apartment that rents for $440 per month. The landlord requires a security deposit equal to $1\frac{1}{2}$ months' rent.
   a. What is the finder's fee?
   b. How much of the finder's fee must each young woman pay?

   c. How much is the security deposit?
   d. What is Janet's share of the security deposit?
   e. What is the annual rent for this apartment?

✓**9.** Nancy's rent is $500 per month. Her lease lasts for three years. The second year's rent can be increased a maximum of 8%, and the third year's rent can be increased a maximum of 9% above the second year's rent.

    a. What is the maximum monthly rent during the second year of Nancy's lease?

    b. What is the maximum monthly rent during the third year of Nancy's lease?

    c. Could Nancy's landlord charge her $550 per month rent during the second year?

10. Tom broke his lease and moved out of his apartment three months before the lease expired. Tom paid $640 per month in rent, and he left a security deposit equal to $1\frac{1}{2}$ months' rent when he signed his lease. His landlord could not find a new tenant to replace Tom during the last three months of the lease. The landlord kept Tom's security deposit but did not receive Tom's last three rent payments.

    a. How much money did Tom pay as a security deposit?

    b. How much did the landlord lose as a result of Tom's breaking the lease?

SECTION 4 • PURCHASING YOUR OWN HOME

What does your dream house look like? Buying a house is an exciting experience that takes careful planning. However, you should ask many questions before purchasing a house:

- What is the cost of the house?

- What is the **down payment?**

- Where is the house located?

- How many rooms does the house have?

- What is the size of the property?

- What type of condition is the house in?

- Does the house have a garage?

- Does the house have a basement?

- Is the house close to shops?

- Is the house near major highways and public transportation?

- Is the house air-conditioned?

- What type of heating system does the house have?

- What is the approximate cost of running the house (electricity, gas, and so on)?

These are only some of the questions that you must investigate thoroughly before purchasing a house.

For most people the biggest concern is financial. Buying a house is probably the most expensive investment you will make during your lifetime. In addition to the purchase price, many homeowners pay **property taxes.** Property taxes are based on the value of the house and the property. Money collected in property taxes from homeowners helps pay for certain government services, such as schools, libraries, and a police force. Property taxes are sometimes called **real estate taxes.** (Property taxes should not be confused with sales taxes or income taxes.) The **market value** is the amount of money the house could be sold for. The **assessed value** is an amount used to determine the property taxes. The assessed value may not be the same as the market value. Property taxes are usually paid monthly or semiannually, and they are most often considered tax-deductible expenses for income-tax purposes.

After making the required down payment, most people take out a loan to pay the balance owed on their new home. These loans are called **mortgages.** Mortgages are available from many of the lending institutions discussed in Chapter 7. Because interest rates on mortgages differ from one lending institution to another, shopping for a mortgage can be as important as shopping for a home. (Review the key terms on page 314 in Chapter 7 to refresh your memory about basic loans.) You should become familiar with the following mortgage vocabulary.

Binder — money paid to the seller by an interested buyer to show that the buyer is serious about buying the house. Sellers want to make sure that people are not "just looking."

Attorney — the lawyer who represents the seller or the buyer.

Origination fee — money paid to the lending institution for the paperwork involved in the loan-application process.

Title — legal claim of property ownership.

Deed — a legal document that specifies the title transfer from seller to buyer.

Title search — a procedure used to make sure that the seller does hold title to the property.

Closing — a meeting attended by the buyer, the seller, their attorneys, and a representative of the lending institution. The official sale and transfer of title take place at the closing.

Points — an extra fee charged by the lending institution for the use of their money.

Fixed-rate mortgage — a type of mortgage in which the monthly payment and APR remain the same throughout the entire loan.

Variable-rate mortgage — a type of mortgage in which the monthly payment and APR may change, as specified in the promissory note.

Foreclosure — the takeover of the property by the lending institution if the borrower fails to meet mortgage payment obligations.

These key terms will give you the foundation to become a knowledgeable home buyer. Most mortgage loans are repaid over a period of 15 to 30 years, and so a home buyer is taking on a long-term financial responsibility.

Skills and Strategies

Here you will compute mortgage payments, finance charges, points, closing costs, and property taxes.

1. Calvin and Rita Flemington have applied for a $175,000, 30-year mortgage to buy a home. Their bank offers them a 12.5% APR. What is the monthly payment for this mortgage?

    Solution: Use Figure 11.8.

12% APR

Principal	25 Years	30 Years
45000	473.96	462.88
50000	526.62	514.31
60000	631.94	617.17
75000	789.92	771.46
100000	1053.23	1028.62
125000	1316.54	1285.77
150000	1579.84	1542.92
175000	1843.15	1800.08
200000	2106.45	2057.23
250000	2633.07	2571.54

13% APR

Principal	25 Years	30 Years
45000	507.53	497.79
50000	563.92	553.10
60000	676.71	663.72
75000	845.88	829.65
100000	1127.84	1106.20
125000	1409.80	1382.75
150000	1691.76	1659.30
175000	1973.72	1935.85
200000	2255.68	2212.40
250000	2819.59	2765.50

12.5% APR

Principal	25 Years	30 Years
45000	490.66	480.27
50000	545.18	533.63
60000	654.22	640.36
75000	817.77	800.45
100000	1090.36	1067.26
125000	1362.95	1334.08
150000	1635.54	1600.89
175000	1908.12	1867.71
200000	2180.71	2134.52
250000	2725.89	2668.15

13.5% APR

Principal	25 Years	30 Years
45000	524.55	515.44
50000	582.83	572.71
60000	699.39	687.25
75000	874.24	859.06
100000	1165.65	1145.42
125000	1457.06	1431.77
150000	1748.47	1718.12
175000	2039.88	2004.48
200000	2331.29	2290.83
250000	2914.12	2863.54

Figure 11.8   Sample Monthly Mortgage Payments

Look at the 12.5% APR table at the top of page 440 for the "principal of $175,000" line. Then look to the right where this line intersects the 30-year column.

	12.5% APR	
Principal	**25 Years**	**30 Years**
45000	490.66	480.27
50000	545.18	533.63
60000	654.22	640.36
75000	817.77	800.45
100000	1090.36	1067.26
125000	1362.95	1334.08
150000	1635.54	1600.89
→175000	1908.12	⟨1867.71⟩
200000	2180.71	2134.52
250000	2725.89	2668.15

The Flemingtons' monthly mortgage payment would be $1,867.71.

2. The Epstein family took out a $100,000, 25-year fixed rate mortgage at an APR of 13%. What is the finance charge (interest) on this loan?

Solution:

$1,127.84	monthly payment
× 12	number of months in a year
$13,534.08	annual payment

$13,534.08	annual payment
× 25	length of mortgage
$338,352.00	total of all monthly payments

$338,352	total of all monthly payments
− 100,000	principal (amount borrowed)
$238,352	finance charge (interest)

The finance charge on this loan is $238,352. The Epsteins could have used the following calculator keystroke sequence to calculate the finance charge on this loan.

AC 1127.84 ⊠ 12 ⊠ 25 🟰 ⊟ 100000 🟰

Computes the   Computes   Subtracts
annual payment.   payments   principal.
                for 25 years.

The display should read 238,352.

3. The Mendelsons' bank has agreed to lend them $87,000 and charges a fee of 3 points. Each point is equal to 1% of the principal. How much will the Mendelsons pay in points at the closing?

Solution: The fee of 3 points is 3% of the principal.

$$
\begin{array}{ll}
\$87,000 & \text{principal} \\
\underline{\times\ .03} & \text{3\% expressed as a decimal} \\
\$2,610.00 & \text{fee for points}
\end{array}
$$

The Mendelsons must pay $2,610 in points at the closing. They could have used the following calculator keystroke sequence:

AC 87,000 ⊠ 3 %

The display should read 2,610.

4. The Langston family will close on a new house today. At the closing they will have to make the following payments:

Points, $795
Attorney, $800
Title search, $100
Title insurance, $75
Credit check, $150

How much money will the Langston family pay at the closing?

Solution: The Langstons use the following calculator keystroke sequence:

AC 795 ➕ 800 ➕ 100 ➕ 75 ➕ 150 🟰

The display should read 1,920.

The Langstons will pay $1,920 at the closing.

5. The Johnsons are considering buying a house with a market value of $250,000. The assessed value of the house is $120,000. The annual property tax is $1.16 per $100 of assessed value. What is the property tax on this house?

Solution:

$$\frac{1{,}200}{100)\overline{120{,}000}} \leftarrow \text{number of 100s in \$120{,}000}$$
$$\phantom{100)\overline{120{,}000}} \leftarrow \text{assessed value}$$

$$
\begin{array}{rl}
1{,}200 & \text{number of 100s in \$120{,}000} \\
\underline{\times\ 1.16} & \text{property tax rate per \$100 of assessed value} \\
\$1{,}392.00 & \text{property tax}
\end{array}
$$

The property tax on the home is $1,392. The property tax could also be computed by using the following calculator keystroke sequence.

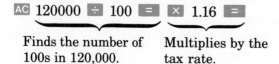

| Finds the number of 100s in 120,000. | Multiplies by the tax rate. |

The display should read 1,392.

Problems

Refer to Figure 11.8, page 439, to solve Problems 1–4, 9–12, and 14.

✓ **1.** Determine the monthly payments for each of the following mortgages.
    a. $75,000, 30 years, APR 13%
    b. $250,000, 25 years, APR 12.5%
    c. $125,000, 25 years, APR 12.5%
    d. $45,000, 30 years, APR 13.5%

2. The Smiths took out a $125,000, 30-year mortgage at an APR of 13%.
    a. What is the monthly payment?
    b. How many monthly payments will be made during the 30 years?
    c. What is the total of all the monthly payments?
    d. What is the finance charge?

✓ **3.** The Axelrod family took out a $150,000, 25-year mortgage at an APR of 12%. What is the finance charge for this mortgage?

4. What is the finance charge on a $200,000, 25-year mortgage at an APR of 12.5%?

5. The Wagner family paid a fee of 2 points at the closing for their new house. Each point is 1% of the principal. The Wagners borrowed $112,000 to buy the house. How much did they pay in points at the closing?

✓6. The Ross family made a $70,000 down payment on their new $200,000 home. They must pay 3 points at the closing. Each point is 1% of the principal.
   a. How much money must they borrow?
   b. How much do they pay in points?

7. The assessed value of the Weber family's house is $86,000. The annual property tax rate is $2.15 per $100 of assessed value. What is the property tax on the Webers' house?

✓8. The market value of the Donaldsons' home is $215,000. The assessed value is $103,000. The annual property tax rate is $12.50 per $1,000 of assessed value.
   a. What is the annual property tax on the Donaldsons' home?

   b. How much do the Donaldsons pay monthly toward property taxes? (Round your answer to the nearest cent.)

9. The Joseph family took out a $175,000, 25-year mortgage at an APR of 12%. The assessed value of their house is $120,000. The annual property tax rate is $1.90 per $100 of assessed value.
   a. What is the monthly mortgage payment?
   b. What is the annual property tax on the Josephs' home?

   c. What is the monthly property tax?
   d. What is the total monthly amount the Josephs pay for their mortgage and property taxes?

10. Jim is taking out a $100,000 mortgage. His bank offers him an APR of 13%. He wants to compare the monthly payments and finance charges of the 25-year loan and the 30-year loan.
   a. What is the monthly payment for the 25-year loan?

   b. What is the finance charge for the 25-year loan?
   c. What is the monthly payment for the 30-year loan?

   d. What is the finance charge for the 30-year loan?
   e. What is the difference in the monthly payments of these two loans?

f.   What is the difference in the finance charges of these two loans?

11.   The Salem National Bank offers variable-rate mortgages. Nancy borrowed $150,000 for 30 years from this bank. For the first year of the loan, the APR was 12%. For the second year, the monthly payment increased to $1,659.
   a.   What was Nancy's monthly payment during the first year?

   b.   What was the total of Nancy's monthly payments during the second year?
   c.   How much was the increase in Nancy's monthly payment from the first year to the second year?

√ **12.**   The Bank of Auburndale offers variable-rate mortgages. Ray Peterson borrowed $200,000 for 25 years from this bank. The APR for the first year was 12.5%. The monthly payment for the second year was $2,255. How much was the increase in Ray's monthly payment from the first year to the second?

13.   At the closing on her new house, Mrs. Philips had to pay the following closing fees:

   Attorney,
   Title search,
   Architect's survey,
   Town fees,
   Fire insurance,

What was the total that Mrs. Philips paid in closing costs?

√ **14.**   Ten years ago the Harrisons took out a $45,000, 25-year fixed-rate loan at an APR of 12.5%. How much money must they pay throughout the remainder of the loan?

15.   Henry wants to buy a $270,000 house. He will need to get a $250,000 loan to make the purchase. Russelville Trust offers a 35-year mortgage with an APR of 14.25%. The monthly mortgage payment would be $2,989.76. The house has an assessed value of $110,000. The annual real-estate tax is $1.02 per $100 of assessed value. Russelville Trust collects monthly mortgage payments and the monthly property tax payments. What would be the total amount that Henry would send to the bank each month?

SECTION 5 • CONDOMINIUMS AND COOPERATIVE RESIDENCES

Maintaining your own house requires time as well as money. Mowing lawns, shoveling snow, and making repairs keep the average homeowner very busy. Some people prefer not to be responsible for these chores. What housing options are open to them?

These people can rent an apartment, but remember that tenants do not *own* the apartments they occupy. Tenants cannot deduct property taxes on their income tax forms, and they can't make a profit from the sale of their homes. For these reasons, many people would rather own a home than pay rent.

There are types of homes other than private houses that people can purchase. A **condominium** is a group of apartments in which each apartment is individually owned. (Sometimes each individual apartment is called a condominium, or a "condo.") Condominiums can be bought and sold just as private homes are bought and sold. There are deeds, closing costs, property taxes, points, mortgage payments, and so on.

Condominium owners are responsible for the maintenance of their own apartments. They are also responsible for the maintenance of the common areas such as the lobby, lawn, roof, and sidewalks of the condominium. Condominium owners are charged a monthly **maintenance fee,** which is used to hire workers to maintain these common areas. (Condominium owners themselves do not mow lawns or shovel snow.)

A "co-op" apartment or **cooperative residence** is another form of home ownership. A cooperative is a corporation that owns a group of apartments. The corporation takes out a mortgage to buy the entire apartment complex. Investors purchase shares in the co-op, and these shares allow them to occupy apartments. Co-op owners do not own their individual apartments; they own a portion of the entire cooperative development. They can sell their shares of ownership and keep any profit from the sale. Co-op owners pay a monthly maintenance fee that covers their share of the maintenance of the apartment complex. Part of this maintenance fee covers the payments that the cooperative corporation must make toward the mortgage loan each month. Condominiums and cooperatives usually have a board of directors to manage certain business matters. Condo and co-op owners often vote on major issues concerning their apartments.

There are advantages and disadvantages that characterize all types of independent living: rental apartments, private homes, condominiums, and co-ops. You must decide which type best suits your life-style and financial situation.

Skills and Strategies

Here you will compute property taxes and determine an individual's share in a cooperative.

1. Last year Burt paid a monthly condominium maintenance fee of $412. Fifteen percent of this fee covered his monthly property taxes. How much did Burt pay last year in property taxes on his condominium?

   Solution:

   $$
   \begin{array}{ll}
   \$\ \ 412 & \text{monthly maintenance fee} \\
   \underline{\times\ .15} & \text{15\% expressed as a decimal} \\
   \$61.80 & \text{monthly property tax payment}
   \end{array}
   $$

   $$
   \begin{array}{ll}
   \$\ \ 61.80 & \text{monthly property tax payment} \\
   \underline{\times\ 12} & \text{number of months in a year} \\
   \$741.60 & \text{annual property taxes}
   \end{array}
   $$

   Burt paid $741.60 in property taxes last year.

Remember, property taxes are tax deductible, and they may change from year to year.

Burt could also use the following calculator keystroke sequence:

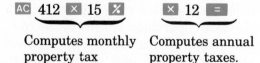

Computes monthly property tax payment.   Computes annual property taxes.

The display should read 741.6.

2. The Seaford Cove Cooperative is owned by many shareholders. The ownership of the entire cooperative is represented by 50,000 shares. Janet has an apartment at Seaford Cove and owns 550 shares of the cooperative. What percentage of the Seaford Cove Cooperative does Janet own?

Solution: First, express Janet's shares as a fraction of the total number of shares.

Janet owns $\frac{550}{50,000}$ of the cooperative.

Use the following calculator keystroke sequence to express the fraction as a percent.

AC 550 ÷ 50000 %

The display should read 1.1.

Janet owns 1.1% of the Seaford Cove Cooperative.

Problems

1. Three years ago, Jerry purchased a condominium. This year his monthly maintenance fee is $397. Twenty percent of this maintenance fee pays for Jerry's property taxes. How much will Jerry pay this year in property taxes?

2. Last year one-third of Anna's $420 co-op maintenance fee went toward paying property taxes.
   a. How much property tax did Anna pay each month?
   b. How much property tax did Anna pay last year?

✓ 3. The Pinelawn Cooperative is raising its monthly maintenance fee by 8% next year. The fee this year is $300 for a two-bedroom co-op and $400 for a three-bedroom co-op.
   a. What is the difference in monthly fees between the two- and three-bedroom apartments this year?
   b. What will the difference in fees between these two apartments be next year?

4. Ron has a co-op in the Fairview Cooperative development. The cooperative ownership is represented by 40,000 shares. Ron owns 500 shares. What percentage of the co-op corporation does Ron own?

✓ 5. The Johnsons owned a condominium in Bethpage Acres. They bought it for $130,000 two years ago and sold it last week for $195,000. Who keeps the profit from this sale?

6. Ethel rented an apartment from a landlord in Sullivan County. Her rent was $600 per month, until she moved out last week. The new tenants pay $700 per month.

    a. Represent the rent increase as a fraction of $600.
    b. Represent the rent increase as a percent.
    c. Who receives the extra money from the rent increase?

7. The board of directors of Tulip Hills Cooperative Residences issued 8,000 shares of stock when their corporation was formed. Lisa has a cooperative apartment at Tulip Hills and owns 80 shares of the corporation. What percentage of the Tulip Hills Cooperative does Lisa own?

✓ **8.** When Carroll Gardens Cooperative Apartments first opened, 3,000 shares in the corporation were issued. Mary Hartmann has a Carroll Gardens co-op and owns 15 shares of the corporation. What percent of the Carroll Gardens Cooperative does Mary Hartmann own?

9. Jean took out a $125,000, 25-year fixed-rate mortgage at an APR of 13% to purchase a condominium.
    a. Use Figure 11.8 to find her monthly payment.
    b. What is Jean's yearly mortgage payment?
    c. What is the finance charge for Jean's condominium mortgage?

✓ **10.** Linda wants to purchase a Leisure Heights condominium apartment. She will borrow $100,000 from the Milford Savings Bank. The bank presently offers a 30-year fixed rate mortgage with an APR of 12.5%. Her monthly maintenance fee will be $280 on this apartment.
    a. Use Figure 11.8 to determine Linda's monthly mortgage payment.
    b. What will Linda's combined monthly mortgage and maintenance payments be?

11. The Krasilovsky family want to take out a mortgage to purchase a co-op apartment. They must borrow $150,000. Their bank offers them an APR of 13%.
    a. What is the monthly payment for the 25-year loan? (Use Figure 11.8.)
    b. What is the monthly payment for the 30-year loan?
    c. What is the difference in finance charges for these two loans?

12. The Martino family will go on vacation this June, July, and August. They have a co-op and pay a monthly mortgage payment of $712 and a monthly maintenance fee of $300. The Martinos get approval from the co-op board of directors to **sublet** their apartment. This means they will continue to make all the payments, but they will rent their co-op apartment to a tenant for the three months they are away. The Martinos are charging $850 per month in rent.

a. What is the total of three months' mortgage payments and maintenance fee?

b. How much rent will the Martinos receive if they sublet their apartment?

c. Will the rent cover the monthly fees that the Martinos must pay?

d. What is the difference between the rent the Martinos will collect if they sublet and their monthly payments for the three months?

√ **13.** Brian needs to borrow $200,000 to purchase shares in the Winter Valley Cooperative Corporation. His bank offers a 25-year mortgage with an APR of 13%. His monthly maintenance fee on the co-op will be $205.

a. Use Figure 11.8 to determine Brian's monthly mortgage payment.

b. What is the combined total of Brian's monthly mortgage and maintenance payments?

14. Laura owns a condominium. Her monthly mortgage payment is $412.50, and her monthly maintenance fee is $275. Laura is planning to spend the next 12 months traveling in Europe. She places a classified ad in the local newspaper to find someone who would be willing to rent her apartment for these 12 months. She is asking $750 per month in rent.

a. What is the combined total of Laura's monthly mortgage and maintenance payments?

b. Will the monthly rent of $750 cover her mortgage and maintenance payments? Explain your answer.

c. What is the difference between Laura's annual mortgage and maintenance expenses and the amount of rent that she will collect over the 12-month period?

15. Linda thinks that her $900 monthly rent is too high. She would rather purchase a co-op in her neighborhood. She needs to borrow $75,000, and her bank offers her a 25-year loan at an

APR of 13%. The monthly maintenance fee on the co-op she wants is $217.25.

a. What is the monthly payment on the mortgage Linda would need? (Use Figure 11.8.)

b. Would $900 per month cover Linda's mortgage and maintenance fee?

SECTION 6 • INTERIOR DESIGN

Once you have found a place to live, you'll be eager to decorate. Before you start, you need to ask yourself these questions:

• How much money should I set aside for decorating?

• What color scheme do I want?

• Do I want to paint or hang wallpaper?

• What kinds of floor covering do I want?

• What pieces of furniture do I need?

• Where should I position the furniture?

Buying furniture takes planning. Imagine buying a piano, waiting eight weeks for delivery, and finding out that it doesn't fit into the space you thought it would! Before you purchase furniture, you should take very careful measurements. It is impractical to buy furniture without knowing your floor plan and the furniture's dimensions.

Professional **interior designers** can be hired to decorate your home. Interior designers combine an artistic sense with mathematics to create a functional, attractive living space. Interior designers charge money for these services. You may not be able to hire a designer, but you can learn some basic techniques of interior design.

An interior designer begins by drawing a room plan. It is drawn to **scale** — each room dimension is proportionately reduced so it can fit onto a sheet of graph paper. This **scale drawing** is used in making decisions about buying furniture.

Designers use scale drawings of furniture with the room plans. These scale drawings allow a decorator to investigate different room arrangements without actually moving furniture. Figure 11.9 shows a room plan drawn on graph paper. Note that each box represents one square foot.

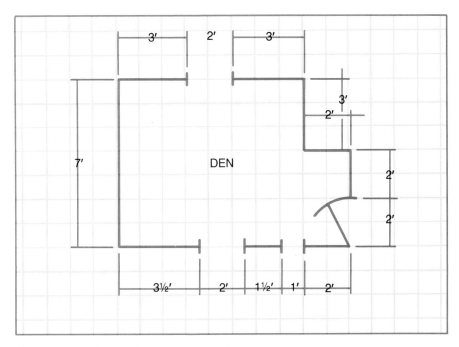

Figure 11.9 Room Plan Drawn to Scale

The photograph shows a decorator and a homeowner experimenting with room arrangements. Note how the pieces of furniture are represented by flat scale models. These paper models are called **templates.**

Some interior designers move these paper cutouts around on a room plan to try out different arrangements.

Some art stores sell plastic furniture stencils that are used to draw the furniture in quarter-inch scale.

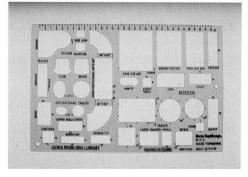

Each of the pieces of furniture is represented by a template.

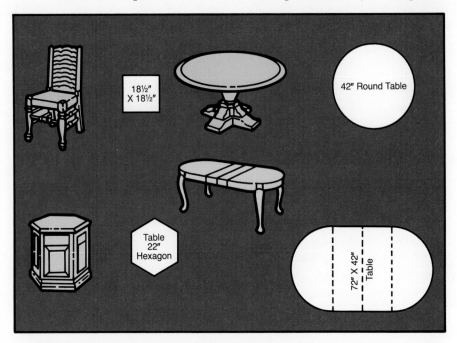

18½" X 18½"

42" Round Table

Table 22" Hexagon

72" X 42" Table

Topic 6 Enhance/Advance will give you a chance to design a room and make a scale drawing. As you can see, all it takes is a ruler, graph paper, and a little imagination!

Skills and Strategies

Most interior designers use a common scale called a quarter-inch scale. They let one-quarter inch on their scale drawings represent one foot of the actual dimensions. Sometimes this is written as

$$\tfrac{1}{4}'' = 1'$$

Keep in mind that the equals sign (=) here means "represents"; $\tfrac{1}{4}$ *represents* 1'. Designers often use one-quarter-inch graph paper to draw room plans. The lines on quarter-inch graph paper are one-quarter-inch apart, and each quarter-inch represents one foot.

1.   A wall of a room measures 22 feet long. A designer wants to represent this wall using a quarter-inch scale. How long should the wall be in the room plan?

   Solution: Since 1 foot is represented by a quarter-inch, 22 feet can be represented by 22 quarter-inches.

" $\dfrac{2\cancel{2}}{1} \times \dfrac{1}{\cancel{4}_2} = \dfrac{11}{2} = 5\dfrac{1}{2}$

The 22-foot wall can be represented by a $5\frac{1}{2}$-inch wall in the room plan.

2. Janine lives in Boston, Massachusetts. She has a summer home in Port St. Lucie, Florida. She wants to purchase a couch that must fit between two windows in the living room. Janine has a quarter-inch-scale floor plan of her summer house. She measures the distance between the windows in the room plan and finds that they are $3\frac{1}{2}$ inches apart. What is the actual distance between these two windows?

Solution: Each quarter-inch represents one foot. Janine must determine the number of quarter-inches in $3\frac{1}{2}$ inches. Janine should divide:

$3\dfrac{1}{2} \div \dfrac{1}{4} =$

$\dfrac{7}{2} \div \dfrac{1}{4} =$

$\dfrac{7}{2} \times \dfrac{4}{1} = \dfrac{14}{1}$

The actual distance between the two windows is 14 feet.

3. Carpeting is sold by the square yard. How many square feet are equal to one square yard?

Solution: One yard is equal to 3 feet.

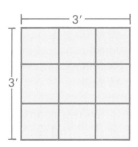

$$\begin{array}{r} 3 \\ \times\,3 \\ \hline 9 \end{array} \quad \begin{array}{l} \text{number of feet in one yard} \\ \text{number of feet in one yard} \\ \text{number of square feet in one square yard} \end{array}$$

Nine square feet are equal to one square yard.

4. Ronna's living room measures 12 feet × 15 feet. Ronna needs to know the area of her living room in square yards before she can purchase carpeting. What is the area of her living room in square yards?

Solution:

$$\begin{array}{r} 12 \\ \times\ 15 \\ \hline 180 \end{array}$$

12   width of room in feet
× 15 length of room in feet
180   area of room in square feet

$$\begin{array}{r} 20 \\ 9{\overline{\smash{)}\,180}} \end{array}$$

20 ←area of room in square yards
9)180 ←area of room in square feet

↗
Number of square
feet in one square yard

Ronna's living room has an area of 20 square yards. Ronna could have used the following calculator keystroke sequence:

AC 12 × 15 = ÷ 9 =

Finds area of   Finds area of
room in square   room in square
feet.   yards.

The display should read 20.

Problems

✓ 1. Express each of the following lengths in quarter-inch scale.
  a. 12 feet   f. 17 feet
  b. 16 feet   g. 27 feet
  c. 9 feet   h. 28 feet
  d. 32 feet   i. 29 feet
  e. 41 feet   j. 30 feet

✓ 2. The following room plan measurements are given in quarter-inch scale. Find the actual measurement in feet that each scale measurement represents.
  a. 3 inches   f. 7 inches
  b. 7 inches   g. $7\frac{1}{4}$ inches
  c. $4\frac{1}{2}$ inches   h. $7\frac{1}{2}$ inches
  d. $3\frac{1}{4}$ inches   i. $7\frac{3}{4}$ inches
  e. $5\frac{3}{4}$ inches   j. 8 inches

3. Sylvia's den measures 21 feet by 15 feet. Express the dimensions in quarter-inch scale.

4. Arthur's garage measures 9 feet by 20 feet.
   a. What is the area of the garage?
   b. Express the dimensions of the garage in quarter-inch scale.

✓ 5. Rosemary wants to have a small ski house built in Vermont. A builder draws up plans in quarter-inch scale. The kitchen in the plans measures $2\frac{1}{2}$ inches by 3 inches.
   a. What are the actual dimensions of the kitchen?

   b. What is the area of the kitchen?
   c. What is the perimeter of the kitchen?

6. Examine the room plan in Figure 11.10.

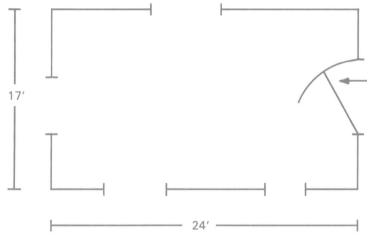

Figure 11.10 Room Plan

   a. Find the area of the room in square feet.
   b. Find the perimeter of the room.
   c. How many windows are in the room?
   d. Represent the length of the room in quarter-inch scale.
   e. Represent the width of the room in quarter-inch scale.

✓ 7. Ellie needs 27 square yards of carpeting for her den. The carpeting she picks out costs $21.90 per square yard. What is the total cost of Ellie's carpeting, including a sales tax of 7%? (Round your answer to the nearest cent.)

8. Andy's bedroom measures 12 feet by 14 feet.
   a. What is the area in square feet?
   b. What is the area in square yards? (Round your answer to the nearest square yard.)
   c. Would 18 square yards of carpeting be enough to carpet this room?
   d. Would 19 square yards of carpeting be enough to cover the floor?
   e. Represent the bedroom's dimensions in quarter-inch scale.

9. Julia is having a summer cottage built on a lake in Maine. The builder draws up plans in quarter-inch scale. Julia's patio measures $4\frac{1}{4}$ inches by $5\frac{3}{4}$ inches on the plans.
   a. What are the actual dimensions of the patio in feet?

   b. What is the area of the patio in square feet?
   c. What is the area of the patio in square yards? (Round your answer to the nearest square yard.)

✓ 10. A piano measures 5 feet, 6 inches by 2 feet.
   a. Represent the length of the piano in feet.
   b. Represent the length of the piano in quarter-inch scale.

   c. Represent the width of the piano in quarter-inch scale.
   d. Would the piano fit lengthwise between two windows that measure $1\frac{1}{2}$ inches apart on a quarter-inch scale room plan? Explain.

11. A certain style of carpet tiles is sold only in packages of two-dozen tiles. The tiles measure 1 foot by 1 foot. Mark needs to buy enough tiles to carpet his den, which measures 14 feet by $15\frac{1}{2}$ feet.
   a. What is the area of the den in square feet?
   b. How many tiles come in a box of two-dozen tiles?
   c. How many boxes of tiles does Mark need?
   d. How many tiles will Mark have left over?

In Problems 12–15, *you* become the interior designer. You will need quarter-inch graph paper and a ruler. Draw a quarter-inch-scale room plan for each of the rooms in Problems 12 through 15 which appear at the top of the next page. Label each dimension.

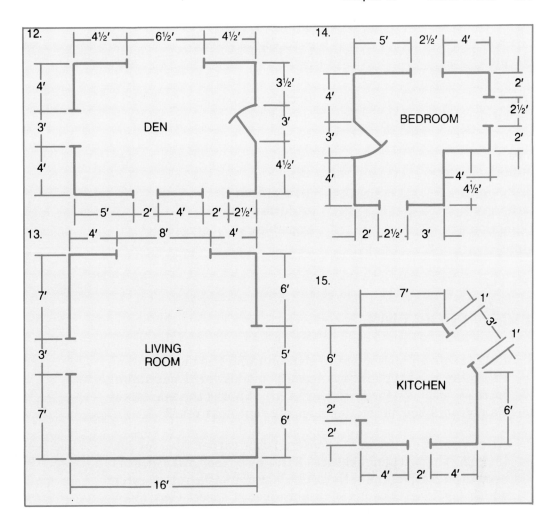

12.
DEN

13.
LIVING
ROOM

14.
BEDROOM

15.
KITCHEN

● KEY TERMS

To find the definition of any term introduced in the chapter, refer to the Glossary in the back of this book.

assessed value	condominium
attorney	cooperative residence
binder	deed
closing	down payment

finder's fee

fixed-rate mortgage

floor plan

foreclosure

furnished

interior designers

landlord

lease

maintenance fee

market value

mortgages

origination fee

points

property taxes

real estate taxes

scale

scale drawing

security deposit

sublet

templates

tenant

title

title search

unfurnished

variable-rate mortgage

• REVIEW PROBLEMS

1. Ralph rents an apartment in Bensonhurst. His monthly rent this year is $740, and his lease provides for a maximum increase of 11.3% for next year's rent. What is the maximum Ralph could be charged for monthly rent next year?

2. Alice wants to purchase 1-foot-by-1-foot carpet tiles for her kitchen. The kitchen measures 8 feet by $9\frac{1}{2}$ feet. Alice doesn't need to put carpet under the counter or under the refrigerator, which together take up 27 square feet of space. How many carpet tiles does Alice need?

3. Mr. Furley owns a building that contains six similar apartments. The rents are different because of the different periods of time the occupants have lived in their apartments. The monthly rents are $720, $510, $930, $520, $590, and $600. What is the mean monthly rent in Mr. Furley's building?

4. Chrissy pays $720 per month for rent. She is filling out her federal income tax form, and she hopes that her refund will be enough to pay one month's rent. Her employer withheld $2,421.61 last year, and her tax liability was $1,731.19. Will Chrissy's refund be enough to pay one month's rent? Explain.

5. A local real-estate agent advertises a house for $172,000. The agent makes a 7% commission if the house is sold. Rich wants to buy the house, but he thinks that the price of the house has been increased so that the sellers can pay the agent. Rich will buy the house only if the price is reduced by 7%. What is the most Rich would pay for this house?

6. Bob and Cathy Carlson are applying for a $75,000 mortgage at the Bank of Blair City. The bank offers a 25-year mortgage with an APR of 13%. Use Figure 11.8 to compute the Carlsons' finance charge over the life of the loan.

7. Katie is purchasing a new home. She was approved for a $200,000 mortgage from her local bank. Her closing costs are as follows:

    3 points (each point equals 1% of the principal)
    Appraisal fee, $150.00
    Service fee, $50.00
    Server tax, $87.50
    Attorney fee, $790.00
    Fire insurance, $92.80

    What are Katie's total closing costs?

8. The McNamaras are interested in buying a condominium. They will need to borrow $125,000 at an APR of 12.5% for 25 years. (Use Figure 11.8.) The monthly maintenance charge will be $382.90. What is the combined total of their monthly mortgage and maintenance payments?

9. Tom will be closing on his new co-op apartment next week. He wants to purchase curtains for the picture window in the living room before he moves in. He uses the quarter-inch-scale drawing of the room plan and finds that the window width is $1\frac{1}{2}$ inches. What is the actual width of Tom's picture window?

10. The sun porch in the Maple Landing Condominium complex measures $18\frac{1}{2}$ feet by 12 feet. What are the quarter-inch-scale dimensions of the sun porch?

CHAPTER *12*

EXPENSES FOR YOUR BUDGET

SECTION 1 • UTILITY BILLS

How much electricity do you use each day? You probably don't know the exact amount, but it is recorded in your home by a device called a **meter.** Once a month, an employee of the electric company comes to read this meter in order to determine how much electricity you have used. Consumers are charged on a monthly basis for natural gas, water, heating oil, electricity, and telephone usage. These services are called **utilities.**

You are charged only for the services you actually use. Your telephone company keeps track of the long distance calls you make and charges you for each call, plus a monthly service charge. Natural gas, water, oil, and electricity use are measured by meters. Apartments, co-ops, condominiums, and private homes all have meters to measure the occupants' use of these services. These meters are read at regular intervals, usually monthly. The company then sends a bill based on how much of the utility the consumer has used.

Skills and Strategies

Here you will learn how your use of natural gas, water, and electricity are measured and how to read utility bills.

Natural Gas and Water

Natural gas and water are sold by the amount of space they occupy, not by their weight. Remember, the amount of space inside a three-dimensional container is called the **volume** of the container. Examine this cube:

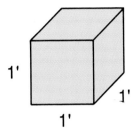

The volume of the container shown above is 1 **cubic foot.** A cubic foot is a measurement of volume. Now examine this rectangular container:

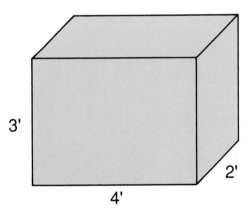

Here's how the rectangular container can be divided into cubic feet:

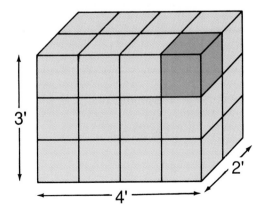

There are 24 cubic feet in this rectangular container. Its volume is 24 cubic feet. This container could hold 24 cubic feet of water, natural gas, flour, topsoil, or any other product.

To find the volume of a rectangular container, you can use the formula:

---

volume = length × width × depth

Volume is always expressed in cubic units.

1. Find the volume of a rectangular solid that has a length of 7 feet, a width of 3 feet, and a depth of 4 feet.

    Solution: First, draw a diagram.

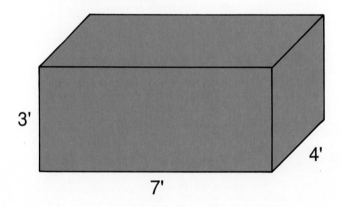

    Next, use the formula to find volume.

---

volume = length × width × depth

Volume = 7' × 3' × 4' = 84 cubic feet

The volume of this solid is 84 cubic feet.

2. Gas and water bills use the symbol **ccf** to represent 100 cubic feet. Last month the Skroy family used 28,600 cubic feet of natural gas. How many ccf of natural gas did they use?

Solution:

$$286 \leftarrow \text{number of ccf used}$$
$$100\overline{)28{,}600} \leftarrow \text{number of cubic feet used}$$

each ccf represents
100 cubic feet

The Skroys used 286 ccf of natural gas last month.

3. The Appletons used 400 cubic feet of water last month. They are charged $1.86 for each ccf of water used. How much should they pay for water service?

   Solution: First convert their water usage into ccf.

   $$4 \leftarrow \text{number of ccf of water used}$$
   $$100\overline{)400} \leftarrow \text{number of cubic feet of water used}$$

   each ccf represents
   100 cubic feet

   Next multiply by cost per ccf.

   $$\begin{array}{rl} \$1.86 & \text{cost per ccf of water used} \\ \underline{\times\ 4} & \text{number of ccf of water used} \\ \$7.44 & \text{water service charge} \end{array}$$

   The Appletons should receive a bill for $7.44 for last month's water usage. You could also use the following calculator keystroke sequence:

   AC 400 ÷ 100 = × 1.86 =

   Calculates the   Multiplies the number
   number of ccf   of ccf by the unit
   used.   cost of one ccf.

   The display should read 7.44.

4. Tom's October water bill listed two meter readings, one for the beginning of the service period (called the previous reading) and one for the end (called the present reading). The previous reading was 3,128 and the present reading is 3,141. How much water did Tom's household consume during the October service period?

Solution:

$$
\begin{array}{rl}
3{,}141 & \text{present reading in ccf} \\
-\ 3{,}128 & \text{previous reading in ccf} \\
\hline
13 & \text{number of ccf used}
\end{array}
$$

Tom's household used 13 ccf (1,300 cubic feet) of water during the October service period.

5. How many ccf of natural gas are represented by the dials on this gas meter?

Solution: Notice where the arrow points on each dial. The correct reading is the *lower* of the two numbers closest to the arrow, with one exception: if the arrow points between 0 and 9, this is read as 9. The gas meter shows a reading of 3,359 ccf of natural gas.

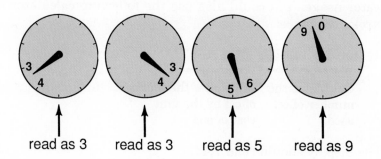

read as 3   read as 3   read as 5   read as 9

Electricity

Every electrical appliance requires a certain amount of electricity to perform. This amount is measured in **watts.** The longer an appliance is on, the more electricity it uses. The amount of electricity *used* is measured in **watt-hours.** For example, a 60-watt light bulb burning for two hours uses 120 watt-hours of electricity.

Today's consumers use thousands of watt-hours of electricity every day. Electric companies install meters that measure electricity usage in **kilowatt-hours (kwh).** Each kilowatt-hour is equivalent to 1,000 watt-hours of electricity.

6. How many kwh of electricity are represented by the dials on this electric meter?

Solution: Read the electric meter in the same way you read a gas meter. The meter shows a reading of 8,551 kwh of electricity.

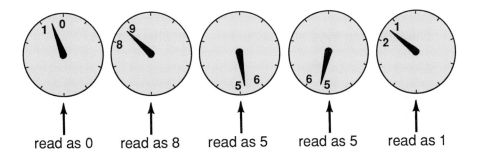

read as 0   read as 8   read as 5   read as 5   read as 1

Utility Bills

Natural gas, water, and electricity bills are usually presented in a similar manner. Two meter readings (previous and present) are listed, as well as an amount due. Read the information on a utility bill carefully.

7. The Hillsdale Water Service Corporation sent Henry Robear the bill at the top of the next page. What did the company charge for one ccf of water?

```
HILLSDALE WATER SERVICE CORPORATION
```

ACCOUNT NUMBER	SERVICE FROM	TO	METER READINGS PREVIOUS	PRESENT	CONSUMPTION IN 100 CU. FT.
23800	10/1	11/2	2078	2090	12

CHARGE DESCRIPTION	
WATER USAGE FEE	
AMOUNT DUE $23.52	HENRY ROBEAR 3 GLEN WAY SEAVILLE, NY

Solution: Find the amount due and the consumption boxes on the bill.

$$\begin{array}{r} \$1.96 \leftarrow \text{cost of one ccf of water} \\ 12\overline{)\$23.52} \leftarrow \text{amount due} \end{array}$$

↑
ccfs of water used (consumption)

Hillsdale charged $1.96 for each ccf of water.

The following keystroke sequence could also be used:

[AC] 23.52 [÷] 12 [=]

The display should read 1.96.

8. Look at the bill below. How much did the American Lighting Corporation charge Lloyd Harbor per kilowatt-hour during the service period shown?

```
AMERICAN LIGHTING CORPORATION
```

FOR SERVICE TO:	LLOYD HARBOR 8 LEWIS RD LINCOLN, NEBRASKA	ACCOUNT NUMBER	1234-5
		BILL DATE	JUNE 5

SERVICE	SERVICE PERIOD FROM	TO	METER READINGS PREVIOUS	PRESENT	USE	$ AMOUNT
ELECTRIC	MAY 5	JUNE 5	15782	17171	1389	125.01

Solution: Find the number of kilowatt-hours used.

$$
\begin{array}{rl}
17{,}171 & \text{present reading in kwh} \\
- \ 15{,}782 & \text{previous reading in kwh} \\
\hline
1{,}389 & \text{kilowatt-hours used}
\end{array}
$$

Then, divide to find the cost per kilowatt-hour.

$$
\text{kilowatt-hours used} \rightarrow 1{,}389 \overline{)\$125.01} \ \leftarrow \text{total amount charged}
$$
$.09 \leftarrow$ charge per kilowatt hour

The company charged $.09 per kilowatt-hour.

9. Last month John earned $2,400. His expenses for utilities were:

   Telephone, $77.30
   Gas, $75.00
   Water, $38.00
   Oil, $121.00
   Electricity, $192.70

   What percentage of John's monthly salary was spent on utilities?

   Solution: Use the following calculator keystroke sequence:

   AC 77.30 + 75 + 38 + 121 + 192.70 = ÷ 2400 %

   The display should read 21.

   John spent 21% of his last month's income on utilities.

Problems

1. Find the volume of a rectangular solid with length 7 feet, width 4 feet, and depth $6\frac{1}{2}$ feet. Draw and label its diagram.

✓ 2. Find the volume of a rectangular solid with length 14.2 meters, width 7.1 meters, and depth 12.7 meters. Draw and label its diagram.

✓ 3. Represent the following gas and water usage in ccf.
   a. 31,600 cubic feet, gas
   b. 7,000 cubic feet, gas
   c. 20,000 cubic feet, water

    d. 19,100 cubic feet, gas

    e. 12,120 cubic feet, water

4. Here is Kerry's last bill from the Glendale Water Corporation. What did Glendale charge for each ccf of water?

GLENDALE WATER CORPORATION					
ACCOUNT NUMBER	SERVICE		METER READINGS		CONSUMPTION IN 100 CU. FT.
	FROM	TO	PREVIOUS	PRESENT	
736-12A	MAY 30	JUNE 26	3271	3302	

CHARGE DESCRIPTION	
WATER USAGE FEE	
	KERRY FAMIGLIETTI 23 CONDLIN COURT FROST POND, NE
AMOUNT DUE $22.32	

✓**5.** Emily's last water bill listed a previous reading of 7,123 ccf and a present reading of 7,171 ccf. Her water company charges $.73 per ccf of water. What should Emily have been charged on her last water bill?

✓**6.** What is the meter reading (in ccf) indicated by each of the gas meters shown at the top of the next page?

    a.   **b.**

    c.   **d.**

7. Bill Heckle's last electric bill is at the bottom of the next page.

    a. What was the previous reading?

    b. What is the present reading?

    c. How many kwh of electricity did Bill Heckle use during the service period shown?

    d. What did Wattco charge per kwh of electricity?

    e. How many days were covered by the above bill? (Do not include August 4.)

    f. What was Bill Heckle's average daily expense for electricity during the service period shown? (Round your answer to the nearest cent.)

WATTCO LIGHTING CORPORATION						
FOR SERVICE TO: BILL HECKLE 12 CAVERN ST. LIVERPOOL, N.Y.			ACCOUNT NUMBER		3761-21	
			BILL DATE	AUG 11		
SERVICE	SERVICE PERIOD		METER READINGS		USE	$ AMOUNT
	FROM	TO	PREVIOUS	PRESENT		
ELECTRIC	JULY 3	AUG 4	21,780	24,100	2320	$255.20

√**8.** Ron Sargeant earned $3,100 last July. His expenses for utilities were:

Telephone, $63.11
Gas, $79.10
Electricity, $199.70
Water, $30.09

a. What was the total amount Ron spent on utilities last July?

b. What percentage of Ron's monthly income was spent on utilities last July?

c. How many days are in July?

d. What was Ron's average daily expense for utilities last July?

9. Home heating oil is sold by the gallon. Last winter, the Romano family used 370 gallons of oil at a price of $1.19 per gallon. What did they spend on oil last winter?

10. Arlene examined her last phone bill and found the following charges:

Monthly service fee, $3.60
Local usage, $25.90
Long distance, $32.00

a. What is the sum of these charges?

b. The monthly service fee remains the same throughout the year. What is the annual service fee?

c. A new phone company claimed that it could cut Arlene's long distance expenses by 45%. How much does this company claim it could have saved Arlene on her last phone bill?

√**11.** The Reed family installed a new phone in their son Carl's room last month. Carl's parents were unhappy because the phone bill they received today was very high. Their last month's bill was $70 and today's bill was $100.

a. How much did the bill increase?

b. Represent the increase as a percent of $70. (Round your answer to the nearest percent.)

c. Mr. Reed claims that Carl's phone habits raised the bill by 50%. Is he correct? Explain.

12. The Zwerling family installed central air-conditioning in their house this summer. They are comparing the electric bills of this summer and last. Here are the data:

Month	This Summer	Last Summer
June	$211.20	$ 79.90
July	$300.65	$103.40
August	$202.50	$101.00

a. What was the total electric bill this summer?
b. What was the total electric bill last summer?
c. How much did the electric bill increase?
d. Represent the increase as a percent of last summer's total. (Round your answer to the nearest percent.)

✓ **13.** A local power company charges $.20 per kwh of electricity. The company has asked the government to allow a 15% increase in this charge. What would the new charge be per kwh if the government approves the increase?

14. Last winter, Ann and Bill Roberts were charged $838.35 for the use of 9,315 kwh of electricity during a 90-day service period.

a. How much were the Roberts charged per kwh of electricity used?
b. What was the average number of kilowatt-hours of electricity used per day during the 90-day service period?

c. What was the average daily cost of electricity during the service period? (Round your answer to the nearest cent.)

✓ **15.** Maria received the list of long-distance calls in her last phone bill shown in Figure 12.1.

NO	DATE	TIME		PLACE		RATE APPLIED	MIN	AMOUNT
1	MAR 23	554PM	TO	FLEMINGTON	NJ	DIALED EVENING	7	1.02
2	MAR 29	405PM	TO	FLEMINGTON	NJ	DIALED NIGHT	5	.60
3	MAR 30	701PM	TO	CAMBRIDGE	NY	DIALED EVENING	3	.69
4	MAR 31	1020AM	TO	AUSTIN	TX	DIALED DAY	3	.99
5	MAR 31	553PM	TO	ALBANY	NY	DIALED EVENING	13	2.45
6	APR 1	944AM	TO	VIENNA	VA	DIALED DAY	3	.85
7	APR 1	636PM	TO	FLEMINGTON	NJ	DIALED EVENING	11	1.69
8	APR 6	741PM	TO	FLEMINGTON	NJ	DIALED EVENING	4	.65
9	APR 7	600PM	TO	FLEMINGTON	NJ	DIALED EVENING	10	1.50
10	APR 8	1250PM	TO	BINGHAMTON	NY	DIALED DAY	2	.63
11	APR 8	211PM	TO	BALTIMORE	MD	DIALED DAY	8	2.15

Figure 12.1 Long Distance Phone Bill

Her phone company offers to register her for a special long-distance-call plan in which she would pay an extra fee of $5 per billing period and receive a 20% discount on all calls that were "dialed evening."

a. What is the total of Maria's long-distance charges as listed in Figure 12.1?

b. What is the total of Maria's calls that were "dialed evening"?

c. What would Maria be charged for the evening calls with the 20% discount if she joined the plan?

d. What would Maria's long-distance bill be if she joined the plan?

e. On the basis of this month's bill, should Maria join the plan? Explain your answer.

SECTION 2 • HOMEOWNER'S INSURANCE

What do you think your single largest expense will be when you are living on your own? For many people, it is their home. A large portion of your income will be spent on purchasing or renting, maintaining, and furnishing your home. It is easy to imagine spending many thousands of dollars on housing during a lifetime.

Your home is obviously important to you as a place to live. It is also important financially. Your investment in a home could be lost because of fire, theft, vandalism, flooding, lightning, or other catastrophe. How can you protect yourself against these financial losses? Most homeowners do so by purchasing insurance. A prepared consumer should understand the possible risks of home owning or renting, as well as the kinds of insurance protection available.

Owners of co-ops, condominiums, and private homes can purchase **homeowner's insurance.** Tenants can purchase **renter's insurance.** As you learned earlier, the amount paid for insurance is called a *premium*. Payment of each premium on time guarantees that you will be covered under the conditions of the written policy. Insurance policies are often difficult for the consumer to read because they are legal documents that must be phrased in technical terms to be precise. Homeowner's insurance can be divided into four basic types of coverage.

1. **Protection for the building.** Your home, porch, and garage are covered against damage due to fire, lightning, smoke, vandalism, explosion, hail, windstorm and other occurrences as specified in your policy.

2. **Protection for the contents.** Your personal property inside the home is covered against damage due to many of the hazards mentioned above.

3. **Protection against theft.** Your personal property is protected in case it is stolen from your home. In some policies, this coverage extends to personal property that is stolen from your car, or when you are away on vacation.

4. **Protection against liability losses.** If someone is injured on your property, you may be held responsible. In the event that you are sued and found liable for damages, you are protected.

Some insurance companies offer extra insurance to their customers who wish to insure special items, such as jewelry, furs, watches, cameras, and musical instruments.

If there is damage to your home or property, you must file a request for payment from your insurance company. This request is called a **claim.** The money you receive from the insurance company is called a **settlement.** Most insurance policies are sold on a **deductible** basis. (In Chapter 3, you learned about deductible automobile insurance policies.) The deductible is a portion of the damages that must be paid for by the person who is insured. For example, if you have a $200 deductible homeowner's policy, you must pay for the first $200 worth of damages for each claim.

When you find a home of your own, be sure to talk to an insurance agent to find out what insurance coverage is available to you.

Skills and Strategies

Here you will learn how much insurance coverage to buy and how to calculate insurance settlements.

1. Linda owns a condominium in Princeton and has condominium insurance. Her personal property is covered up to $25,000. Last week her condo was burglarized. Her color television set, worth

$350, was stolen. Linda has a $100 deductible homeowner's coverage against theft. How much should the insurance company pay her for this loss?

Solution:

$350   value of item stolen
− 100   deductible amount
$250   amount paid to Linda

Linda should receive $250 as settlement of her claim.

2.   Many homeowner's insurance policies include an **80% clause.** This clause states that only homeowners who insure their homes for at least 80% of the replacement cost will receive full payment for damage claims. Homeowners who insure their homes for less than 80% of the replacement cost do not receive full payment for damages claimed. For example, the replacement cost of a certain house is $100,000. The insurance policy for this house contains an 80% clause. What is the minimum amount that the house should be insured for if the owner wants to cover the entire replacement cost of the house?

Solution:

$100,000   replacement cost of house
× .80   80% expressed as a decimal
$ 80,000   80% of replacement cost

The owner should purchase at least $80,000 worth of homeowner's insurance to cover the entire replacement cost of the house.

3.   Mary Ellen's house has a replacement cost of $180,000. The house is insured for $160,000, and the policy contains an 80% clause. Last week, a fire caused $13,000 worth of damages. Mary Ellen filed a claim for $13,000. How much of a settlement should she receive?

Solution: Determine whether or not Mary Ellen's house is covered for at least 80% of its replacement cost.

$180,000   replacement cost
× .80   80% expressed as a decimal
$144,000   80% of replacement cost

Since Mary Ellen's house is insured for more than $144,000, and the claim is less than the replacement cost, the insurance settlement should be $13,000.

4. Mabel's house has a replacement cost of $150,000. The house is insured for $90,000, and the policy contains an 80% clause. Last month, a windstorm caused $12,000 worth of damages to Mabel's home. Mabel filed a claim for $11,000. How much of a settlement should she receive?

    Solution: Determine whether or not Mabel's house is covered for at least 80% of its replacement cost.

$150,000	replacement cost
× .80	80% expressed as a decimal
$120,000	80% of replacement cost

    Since Mabel's house is insured for less than $120,000, the insurance settlement will be a fraction of the claim, not the entire $11,000. Insurance companies compute the settlement in the following way:

$ 90,000	amount of coverage purchased
$120,000	80% of replacement cost

    This fraction represents the portion of the $11,000 claim that the insurance company will pay. The payment can be computed using the following calculator keystroke sequence:

    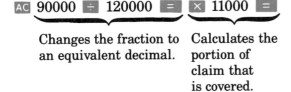

Changes the fraction to an equivalent decimal.	Calculates the portion of claim that is covered.

    The display should read 8,250.

    Mabel's settlement should be $8,250.

Problems

1. Last year, Kyle paid $370 in homeowner's insurance premiums. This year, his premium is going to be increased 11%. What is this year's premium?

✓**2.**   Randi pays a $250 annual premium for renter's insurance. She makes quarterly payments.
   a.   How many payments does Randi make annually?
   b.   How much is each quarterly payment?

3.   Jonathan's condo insurance is paid semiannually. His current annual premium is $180, but this will increase by 9% next year.
   a.   What is this year's semiannual premium?
   b.   What is next year's annual premium?
   c.   What is next year's semiannual premium?

✓**4.**   Ted has insured the contents of his co-op apartment against theft. His co-op insurance policy includes a $200 deductible for theft claims. Last month, Ted's apartment was burglarized and a typewriter valued at $690 was stolen. How much should Ted receive from his insurance company for this loss?

5.   Cheryl's home has a replacement cost of $90,000. She insured the house for $70,000. Is Cheryl's home insured for at least 80% of its replacement cost? Explain your answer.

6.   Courtney's home has a replacement cost of $210,000. She insured her home for $180,000, and her policy has an 80% clause. Last month, a fire caused $19,500 worth of damage to Courtney's attic. Courtney filed a claim with her insurance company.
   a.   Is Courtney's home insured for at least 80% of its replacement value? Explain your answer.
   b.   How much of a settlement should Courtney receive for the damages?

✓**7.**   Garren's home was completely destroyed by fire yesterday. The home's replacement cost is $175,000. Garren insured the home for $100,000. His policy has an 80% clause.
   a.   Is Garren's home insured for at least 80% of its replacement value?
   b.   How much of a settlement should Garren receive for this $175,000 loss? (Round to the nearest dollar.)

8. Kate purchased a house that had a replacement cost of $70,000 and insured it for $60,000. Due to rising prices in the construction industry, the replacement cost has increased to $90,000. Kate must decide if she should increase her homeowner's insurance. Does Kate have her house covered for at least 80% of its replacement cost?

9. Last month, an electrical fire did $22,000 worth of damage to the Cordez family's home. The home's replacement cost is $162,000 and it was insured for $110,000. The policy contains an 80% clause. How much of a settlement should the Cordez family receive for the fire damage? (Round your answer to the nearest cent.)

✓ 10. Ronald's home was damaged by a recent flood. The home's replacement cost is $244,000, it was insured for $170,000, and the policy has an 80% clause. Flood damage amounted to $14,000. How much of a settlement should Ronald receive? (Round your answer to the nearest cent.)

11. Jeanette pays her homeowner's insurance quarterly. Her annual premium is $390. She is hoping that her income tax refund will be enough to cover her next quarterly payment. Her tax liability was $1,514 and her employer withheld $1,599 in income taxes.
   a. What is her quarterly insurance payment?
   b. How much of an income tax refund should Jeanette receive?
   c. Will Jeanette's refund be enough to cover her quarterly insurance payment? Explain your answer.

12. Martin's house was destroyed by a fire last month. The builder who is reconstructing the house has suggested that Martin should include a new kitchen with twice the area of the old one, which measured 9 feet by 10 feet. What is the area of the new kitchen suggested by the builder?

✓ 13. A flood destroyed the carpeting in Sally's basement. Before submitting a claim, Sally needed to determine the replacement cost of new carpeting. The basement measures 27 feet by 30 feet.

    a. Express the area of the basement in square feet.
    b. Express the area of the basement in square yards.
    c. New carpeting will cost Sally $18 per square yard. What is the entire cost of new carpeting, including 4% sales tax?

14. Last year Barbara's condo insurance premium was $240. This year the premium is $300.
    a. How much did the premium increase?
    b. Represent the increase as a fraction of 240.
    c. Represent the increase as a percent.

15. Nina's co-op insurance company will give her a 5% discount on her premium if she installs a smoke detector in her home. Her current annual premium is $191. What will her premium be if she installs a smoke detector?

SECTION 3 • HEALTH INSURANCE AND GENERIC DRUGS

Can you afford to have an accident? Of course, no one wants to have an accident, but it is important to be prepared in case one occurs. Could you pay for all of your medical bills in a time of illness? The cost of health care is on the rise. Checkups, allergy shots, dental treatments, and other routine care can be extremely expensive. A short stay in the hospital can cost thousands of dollars. A long illness can use up a lifetime's savings. Few people can pay the costs for major illnesses easily. What is the best way to protect yourself against high medical costs?

    Many people purchase **health insurance.** Health insurance pays all or part of hospital and medical care costs for the policyholder. Some insurance plans cover the policyholder's family as well. Many students in your school are covered by one of these family insurance policies. When you support yourself, *you* will have to make decisions about health insurance. Understanding the types of insurance available will help you make wise decisions.

    To apply for health insurance, you need to supply the insurance company with your personal medical information. The company uses this information to determine the cost of your premium, which is based on the probability that you will make claims on your policy. Settlements of claims can be paid to you or directly to your health-care professional. Often, however, your doctor or hospital requires payment directly from you. You, in turn, file a claim for an insurance settlement, and your insurance company pays the settlement directly to you. This amount is called a **reimbursement.** Be sure to make copies of all of your medical bills before filing claims for reimbursements.

Individuals can purchase insurance for themselves and their families by contacting an insurance company and paying a premium. Some employers provide health insurance for their employees. This is called **group insurance.** When you look for a job, be sure to find out whether or not the employer will provide you with a health insurance plan. Find out the details of the plan as well. These details should be considered before you accept any job. Premiums for group insurance are much lower than premiums purchased by individuals. Many employers pay all or part of the premiums for their employees.

Group insurance is sometimes made available to members of organizations such as colleges, clubs, and credit unions. If you belong to such an organization, find out whether or not health insurance is offered to members.

Before making a final decision about health insurance, be sure to consider all your options. Find out the cost of joining a **Health Maintenance Organization (HMO).** An HMO is a group of doctors and medical professionals who provide many health-care services at a fixed cost. Members pay an annual fee in return for all the medical attention they may need, with certain restrictions. Patients must use a doctor who belongs to their particular HMO; they cannot choose any doctor they want. The annual fee for an HMO is usually less than the premiums for group and individual insurance plans.

The United States government also provides health insurance plans for eligible citizens. **Medicare** is an insurance system that pays a portion of the medical expenses of senior citizens. **Medicaid** pays a portion of the medical expenses of low-income patients, regardless of their age.

Many basic insurance plans place limits on the amount of money the policyholder can collect. You can increase the amount of coverage by purchasing **major medical insurance** as part of your health insurance policy. Major medical insurance is added coverage that you can purchase to insure yourself against expenses not covered by a basic health insurance plan.

Some insurance plans provide payment for part of the cost of prescription medicine, but many do not. Quite often, medical treatment requires a consumer to purchase prescription medication that can be very expensive. As always, you should compare brands and prices before making a purchase. Patients can lower their prescription costs by purchasing **generic drugs.** Generic drugs are sold by their chemical names, and are usually less costly than brand-name drugs. Generic drugs have the same active ingredients as the brand name drugs they replace. You should ask your doctor about generic drugs whenever your treatment requires you to purchase medication.

You can protect yourself and your good health by learning about the cost and availability of medical insurance and generic drugs. Remember to check all your options, read your policy carefully, and ask questions about any sections you don't understand.

Skills and Strategies

Here you will learn how to solve problems involving health care and insurance costs.

1. Sue belongs to an HMO. She pays a monthly fee of $19.50. What is her annual fee?

    Solution:

    $19.50   monthly payment
    × 12   number of monthly payments
    $234.00   annual fee

    Sue pays $234 annually to belong to her HMO.

2. Pat's employer deducts $23.50 per paycheck for group medical insurance. Pat is paid biweekly. What is her annual medical insurance premium?

    Solution: There are 26 biweekly paychecks in a year.

    $23.50   paycheck deduction
    × 26   number of paychecks
    $611.00   annual premium

    Pat pays $611 per year for medical insurance.

3. Ed's medical insurance plan has a $250 deductible per year. Ed receives 80% of all medical claims after he meets the deductible. Last year, Ed submitted $716 worth of medical claims. How much did Ed pay for medical treatment?

Solution: Ed had to pay the deductible and 20% of his claims after the deductible was met.

$716   total of medical claims
– 250   deductible
$466   amount over deductible

$466   amount over deductible
× .20   20% expressed as a decimal
$93.20   Ed's 20% share of medical claim

$250.00   deductible
+ 93.20   Ed's 20% share of medical costs
$343.20   Ed's medical expenses

Ed paid $343.20 for his medical treatment. He will need this information when he files his income tax return. Ed also could have used the following calculator keystroke sequence:

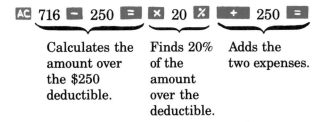

AC 716 − 250 = × 20 % + 250 =

Calculates the amount over the $250 deductible.   Finds 20% of the amount over the deductible.   Adds the two expenses.

The display should read 343.2.

4. Jamie's grandmother takes medication for high blood pressure. She discusses the prescription with her doctor, who allows her to substitute a generic equivalent for the brand-name drug she has been using. The brand-name drug costs $28.50, and the generic equivalent costs $11. What percent savings does the generic equivalent represent?

Solution: Represent the difference in cost as a percent of $28.50.

$28.50   cost of brand-name medication
$\underline{-\ 11.00}$ cost of generic equivalent
$17.50   difference in cost

$\underline{\$17.50}$ difference in cost
$28.50   cost of brand-name medication

Use your calculator and the following keystroke sequence to convert the fraction into a percent:

AC 28.50 — 11 = ÷ 28.50 %

The display should read 61.403508.

The generic equivalent costs approximately 61% less than the brand-name drug.

Problems

1. Paula's family belongs to the Tecumseh Health Center, which is an HMO. The cost is $15 per person per month. There are three people in her family. What is the total annual fee for Paula's family?

2. Mitchell and Kim Simon are married and have two children. Mitchell's employer deducts $21.10 from each of Mitchell's semimonthly paychecks to pay for group medical insurance. Kim's employer deducts $7 from her weekly paychecks. What is the total annual medical insurance cost for the Simon family?

✓3. Lorraine just bought a $200 deductible medical insurance policy. Her only medical expenses this year were payments to a doctor for allergy shots. She has received seven shots so far, each one costing $16.50. How much more does Lorraine have to claim to meet her deductible?

✓4. Alan is filing his income taxes for last year. He spent $9.70 per week for his $300 deductible medical insurance policy. He received $751 worth of medical care last year, and his policy pays for 80% of his claims over the deductible amount.

    a. What is Alan's annual premium?

    b. How much should the insurance company have paid Alan for his $751 worth of claims?

    c. How much did Alan have to pay for his treatment and his insurance?

5. Jane has a $100 deductible medical insurance policy. Her company pays for 80% of her claims after she meets the deductible. How much should her company reimburse her if she submits $1,230 in claims?

6. Mr. Rubin takes medication daily for a heart condition. The brand-name medication costs $27 for a bottle that lasts a week. The generic equivalent costs $19.50 for the same size bottle.

    a. What is the annual cost for the brand-name medication?

    b. What is the annual cost for the generic equivalent?

    c. How much could Mr. Rubin save by using the generic equivalent instead of the brand name-drug?

    d. Represent the generic equivalent's annual savings as a percent of the brand name's annual cost. (Round your answer to the nearest percent.)

✓**7.** At a drugstore in Floral Park, a bottle of 250 brand-name aspirin costs $6.99. At the same drugstore, a bottle of 500 generic-equivalent aspirin costs $3.49. How much can you save by buying the generic equivalent instead of the brand name if you want 500 aspirin tablets?

8. Jake's Pharmacy in Rockville Centre sells a brand-name bottle of medicine for acne for $16.20. The generic equivalent costs 40% less. What is the price of the generic equivalent?

9. Gloria works at Flushing High School. Her employer pays 90% of her $410 group medical insurance premium. How much does Gloria pay toward this premium?

10. Mel was in a serious accident and spent 12 days in a hospital. The total hospital bill was $8,256. What is the mean daily cost of Mel's hospital stay?

✓**11.** At a local drugstore, a popular name-brand cold medicine costs $4.95 for 10 tablets. The generic equivalent costs $2.99 for 12 tablets.

    a. What is the unit price per tablet for the brand-name cold tablet? (Round your answer to the nearest cent.)

    b. What is the unit price per tablet for the generic equivalent? (Round your answer to the nearest cent.)

    c. Represent the difference in the unit prices as a percent of the brand name's unit price.

12. Howard's Pharmacy charges $6.00 for 12 fluid ounces of a popular brand-name cough syrup. The generic equivalent costs $4.40 for 20 fluid ounces.

    a. What is the unit price per fluid ounce of the brand-name cough syrup? (Round your answer to the nearest cent.)

    b. What is the unit price per fluid ounce of the generic equivalent? (Round your answer to the nearest cent.)

    c. Represent the difference in the unit prices as a percent of the brand name's unit price.

13. Janet's medical insurance policy includes a prescription plan. Janet pays just $3 for any prescription that costs more than $3. The insurance company pays the rest. Last year, Janet purchased prescription medicine four times. The regular costs of the prescriptions were as follows: $18.90, $7.70, $16.00, and $9.97. How much did Janet have to pay for the four prescriptions?

✓**14.** Darren's medical insurance policy does not cover checkups. Last year, Darren had these checkups:

    Eye doctor, $70.00

    Physician, $83.00

    Dentist, $75.00

Darren also paid a semiannual medical insurance premium of $230.

    a. What was the total cost of Darren's insurance and medical care last year?

    b. How much of the total cost did Darren have to pay?

15. Construct and label a bar graph based on the information at the top of the next page.

Insurance Expenses for the Santoro Family Last Year

Type of Insurance	Amount of Premium
Automobile Insurance	$1,345.70
Homeowner's Insurance	797.00
Medical Insurance	812.50
Life Insurance	190.90
Dental Insurance	73.00

SECTION 4 ● FOOD AND NUTRITION

A family today can spend hundreds of dollars on food each month. In Chapter 1 you learned about comparison shopping, unit pricing, and finding the better buy. Price is not the only consideration to keep in mind when you buy food. Purchasing the *right* foods at the best price should be the concern of every consumer.

Section 3 introduced you to the many health insurance options that are available so that you and your family can be protected in the event of any illnesses. The thoughtful consumer is aware that maintaining good health is one of the best defenses against unexpected physical problems. Good health is a growing concern of many Americans. Now more than ever, people are exercising, joining health clubs, watching their weight, and eating healthful foods. They want to know the ingredients in the foods they eat because scientists have shown that certain ingredients are good for your health while others should be avoided. These scientists are interested in **nutrition,** which is the study of a well-balanced diet.

A well-balanced diet includes food that contains substances that your body needs to stay healthy. These substances, called **nutrients,** give you energy to help you get through your busy day. Proteins, fats, carbohydrates, vitamins, and minerals are all examples of nutrients, which are contained in different amounts in different foods. **Calories** are used to measure the amount of energy produced by the food you eat.

A government agency called the **Food and Drug Administration (FDA)** supervises the food industry in the United States. The FDA requires most foods to be clearly labeled. These labels must include:

- the name of the product

- the weight of the product

- the name and location of the manufacturer

The FDA also requires most food labels to include a list of ingredients and other nutritional information. It is important that you know how to read nutrition labels.

Skills and Strategies

Here you will learn to interpret nutritional information on the labels of food products. Examine the nutrition label in Figure 12.2.

NUTRITION INFORMATION

SERVING SIZE: 1 OZ. (28.4 g.)
  RICE CEREAL ALONE OR WITH ½ CUP
  VITAMINS A AND D MILK
SERVINGS PER PACKAGE: 19

	CEREAL	WITH MILK
CALORIES	110	190
PROTEIN	2 g	6 g
CARBOHYDRATE	25 g	31 g
FAT	0 g	7 g
CHOLESTEROL	0 mg	10 mg
SODIUM	290 mg	350 mg
POTASSIUM	35 mg	240 mg

**PERCENTAGE OF U.S. RECOMMENDED
DAILY ALLOWANCE (USRDA)**

	CEREAL	WITH MILK
PROTEIN	2	10
VITAMIN A	25	30
VITAMIN C	25	25
THIAMIN	25	30
RIBOFLAVIN	25	35
NIACIN	25	25
CALCIUM	**	15
IRON	10	10
VITAMIN D	10	25
VITAMIN B$_6$	25	25

**CONTAINS LESS THAN 2% OF THE USRDA OF THIS NUTRIENT.

INGREDIENTS: RICE, SUGAR, SALT, CORN SYRUP, MALT FLAVORING.

VITAMINS AND IRON: VITAMIN C (SODIUM ASCORBATE AND ASCORBIC ACID), VITAMIN B$_3$ (NIACINAMIDE), IRON, VITAMIN A (PALMITATE), VITAMIN B$_6$ (PYRIDOXINE HYDROCHLORIDE), VITAMIN B$_2$ (RIBOFLAVIN), VITAMIN B$_1$ (THIAMIN HYDROCHLORIDE), FOLIC ACID, AND VITAMIN D.

Figure 12.2 Nutrition Label for Rice Cereal

All nutrition labels include a **serving size,** which is the amount of a single serving of the food. Note in Figure 12.2 that one ounce is considered to be a single serving of this rice cereal. The metric equivalent (28.4 grams) is also shown. The numerical information given on the label is based on one serving of this rice cereal. Note also that this package contains 19 servings.

1. How many calories does one serving of rice cereal with milk contain?

    Solution: Look at the following part from Figure 12.2. One serving of rice cereal with milk contains 190 calories.

	CEREAL	WITH MILK
CALORIES	110	190

2. Lyndsey had two ounces of rice cereal with milk for breakfast this morning. How many grams of protein are contained in this amount of rice cereal?

    Solution: Two ounces represent two servings of this cereal.

6	number of grams of protein per serving
× 2	number of servings
12	number of grams in two servings

    Lyndsey's portion of cereal contained 12 grams of protein.

3. For various nutrients, the United States government recommends the amount that people should have each day. This is called the **U.S. Recommended Daily Allowance (USRDA)** Each serving of a food gives you a percentage of the USRDA. This percentage is listed on most food labels. What percentage of the USRDA of vitamin A does one serving of rice cereal with milk contain?

    Solution: Look at the following part from Figure 12.2 shown at the top of page 488.

PERCENTAGE OF U.S. RECOMMENDED DAILY ALLOWANCE (USRDA)

	CEREAL	WITH MILK
PROTEIN	2	10
VITAMIN A	25	30
VITAMIN C	25	25
THIAMIN	25	30
RIBOFLAVIN	25	35
NIACIN	25	25
CALCIUM	**	15
IRON	10	10
VITAMIN D	10	25
VITAMIN B$_6$	25	25

**CONTAINS LESS THAN 2% OF THE USRDA OF THIS NUTRIENT.

One serving of the rice cereal contains 30% of the U.S. Recommended Daily Allowance of vitamin A.

4. The ingredients listed on a food label are given in descending (highest to lowest) order, according to their weight. Does this box of rice cereal contain more salt or sugar?

   Solution: Look at the following part from Figure 12.2.

   INGREDIENTS: RICE, SUGAR, SALT, CORN SYRUP, MALT FLAVORING.

   Sugar appears before salt on the ingredients list: this box of rice cereal contains more sugar than salt.

Problems

The nutrition label in Figure 12.3 on page 489 is from a can of fruit. Use the label to answer Problems 1 through 4.

1. How many ounces make up a single serving?

2. How many calories are contained in a single serving?

✓ 3. What percentage of the USRDA for vitamin C is contained in one serving?

KRAM-MARS
MYSTERY
FRUIT SUPREME

INGREDIENTS: DICED PEACHES, WATER, DICED
PEARS, DICED PINEAPPLE, SUGAR.
NUTRITION INFORMATION—PER 4½ OZ. SERVING
SERVINGS PER CONTAINER—ONE

CALORIES	60	FAT	0g
PROTEIN	0g	SODIUM	5mg
CARBOHYDRATE	14g		

PERCENTAGE OF U.S. RECOMMENDED DAILY
ALLOWANCES (USRDA) PER 4½ OZ. SERVING

PROTEIN	*	RIBOFLAVIN (VIT. B₂)	2
VITAMIN A	4	NIACIN	2
VITAMIN C	6	CALCIUM	*
THIAMINE (VIT. B₁)	*	IRON	2

*CONTAINS LESS THAN 2% OF THE USRDA OF THESE NUTRIENTS.

Figure 12.3 Nutrition Label

4. Which nutrients on the list are supplied in amounts that are less than 2% of the USRDA?

The nutrition label shown below was taken from a bag of almonds. Use the label in Figure 12.4 to answer the questions in Problem 5.

NUTHOUSE
ALMONDS
INGREDIENTS:
Almonds

**NUTRITIONAL INFORMATION
PER SERVING**

SERVING SIZE	1 OZ.
SERVINGS PER CONTAINER	10
CALORIES	150
PROTEIN	7 g
CARBOHYDRATE	5 g
FAT	13 g
SODIUM	less than 5 mg
POTASSIUM	195 mg

**PERCENTAGE OF U.S.
RECOMMENDED DAILY
ALLOWANCES (USRDA)**

PROTEIN	10	RIBOFLAVIN	10
VITAMIN A	*	NIACIN	4
VITAMIN C	*	CALCIUM	8
THIAMINE	4	IRON	6

*CONTAINS LESS THAN 2% OF THE
USRDA OF THESE NUTRIENTS.

Figure 12.4 Nutrition Label

√5.   a.   What is the weight of one serving of almonds?
    b.   How many servings come in this package?
    c.   What is the total weight of the contents of the package?

    d.   How many calories are contained in a two-ounce serving of these almonds?
    e.   How many grams of protein are contained in one serving?

    f.   What percentage of the USRDA for protein is contained in one serving?

6.   A nutrition label from a box of oatmeal states that a serving size is 1.5 ounces and that the package contains 10 servings.
    a.   What is the total weight of the contents of the package?

    b.   Does the oatmeal in this package weigh more than one pound?

√7.   One serving of Krisp-Eez breakfast cereal (with milk) provides 25% of the USRDA for vitamin A. How many servings would you have to eat to get a full day's supply of vitamin A?

8.   One slice of a certain whole-wheat bread contains 70 calories. One serving of peanut butter contains 190 calories, and one serving of jelly contains 180 calories. Approximately how many calories do two peanut butter and jelly sandwiches contain?

9.   Six fluid ounces of grape drink contain 88 calories. One 12-fluid-ounce can of iced tea contains two calories. How many more calories are contained in 12 fluid ounces of grape drink than in the can of iced tea?

√10.   Peter is comparing regular and "light" cheeses. The regular cheese contains 90 calories per serving. The light cheese contains 40% fewer calories than the regular cheese. How many calories does the light cheese contain?

11.   Pierre bought a computerized exercise bicycle last year. He has used the bicycle each week and currently rides for 50 minutes every time he exercises. Yesterday the bicycle's digital display showed that Pierre had used up about 275 calories during his 50-minute exercise period. What was the average number of calories Pierre burned per minute during this workout?

12. The South Shore Health Club charges $400 for an annual membership for one person. A 20% discount is offered to any other person from a member's family who decides to join. What would the total annual membership be for a family of four?

✓ **13.** Craig plays racquetball with his friend Dominic for one hour every Wednesday. The annual club membership fee is $100, and it costs $15 an hour for a member to rent a court. Craig and Dominic share the cost of the court rental.
   a. How much is Craig's share of the hourly court rental?

   b. What does Craig spend yearly for court rentals?
   c. What is Craig's total annual cost for membership fee and court rentals?

14. Table 12.1 shows the approximate number of calories burned per hour by a medium-sized male during several activities.

Approximate Number of Calories Burned Per Hour

Activity	Approximate Number of Calories Burned Per Hour
Bicycling	175
Boxing	798
Driving	63
Playing table tennis	308
Playing a violin	42
Running	490
Swimming (2 m.p.h.)	556
Walking (3 m.p.h.)	140

Table 12.1

Use Table 12.1 to determine how many calories would be burned by each activity.
   a. one hour of running
   b. 30 minutes of running

    c.   15 minutes of walking

    d. $1\frac{1}{4}$ hours of swimming at 2 m.p.h.

    e.   45 minutes of walking at 3 m.p.h.

15.   The substance *calcium* strengthens bones. Many foods provide us with calcium. Construct and label a bar graph showing the calcium content of the following foods and beverages.

Food and Amount	Amount of Calcium
Milk (1 pint)	570 mg
Whole wheat bread (1 slice)	23 mg
Orange juice (8 fl. oz.)	24 mg
One egg	27 mg
Ice cream (1 pint)	185 mg
American cheese (1 oz.)	225 mg

SECTION 5 • LIFE INSURANCE

People work very hard throughout their lives to achieve a comfortable life-style for themselves and their families. If the person who provides the sole or main support for a family dies, the situation can be extremely difficult. Think of the ways that such a death can affect family finances. The family's savings may not be enough to cover expenses. Many people want to provide their families with some protection after they die. For this reason, many people buy life insurance. **Life insurance** provides cash benefits to people chosen by the policyholder. These people are called **beneficiaries.** Their names are listed on the life insurance policy.

    Life insurance can help pay for funeral costs, lawyer's fees, loans, mortgages and other living expenses that dependents might not be able to afford after a breadwinner's death. How can you determine the amount of life insurance coverage you need? You should consider the following estimates when deciding how much coverage to purchase.

- Estimate the amount of income you want to provide for your dependents.

- Estimate death-related expenses, such as medical bills, funeral costs, and lawyer's fees.

- Estimate your dependents' special needs. These could include college education, medical expenses for the handicapped, or trade school.

- Estimate your debts. Include all loans, mortgages and credit-card balances.

It is reasonable to assume that costs will rise in years to come. Be sure to consider these higher costs when choosing your coverage.

Life-insurance premiums are based on a number of factors. One is the age of the policyholder. For each age group, the insurance company estimates the number of people expected to die and the number of years that the remainder will live. These facts are used to compute a death rate for males and females in each age group. The death rates are listed in a **mortality table.** Topic 6 Enhance/Advance Activity 4 will help you learn about mortality tables. The death rate for your age group is a key element in determining your premium. People with a higher probability of death pay higher insurance premiums.

Insurance premiums are also based on the amount of coverage you purchase and the type of policy you buy. The amount of coverage that a policy provides is called the **face value** of the policy. There are four main types of life insurance policies.

1. **Term insurance.** Term insurance covers the policyholder for a specified period of time, usually 5, 10, or 20 years. After that time, the policy is no longer in effect, unless it is renewed for another term. If the policyholder dies during the term of the policy, the beneficiaries collect a settlement from the insurance company.

2. **Straight life insurance.** Straight life insurance covers policyholders for their entire life. The premium is paid until the policyholder's death or until an age specified in the policy. When the policyholder dies, the beneficiaries collect a settlement from the insurance company.

3. **Limited payment life insurance.** Limited payment life insurance covers policyholders for their entire life. The premiums are paid over a specified number of years, usually 20 or 30. After that time, no premiums are paid. If the policyholder dies during or after the premium payment period, the beneficiaries receive a settlement from the insurance company.

4. **Endowment policies.** Endowment policies cover policyholders for their entire lives. The premium is paid over a specified time, usually 20 or 30 years. If the policyholder dies during the premium payment period, the beneficiaries collect a settlement from the insurance company. If not, at the end of the premium payment period, the policyholder receives the value of the policy, and the insurance is no longer in effect.

Term insurance is the least expensive; endowment policies are the most expensive. You should talk to an insurance agent to determine how much life insurance you need and how much you can afford.

Skills and Strategies

Here you will learn how to solve problems involving life insurance. Figure 12.5 at the top of page 495 lists some annual premiums per $1,000 worth of coverage for a certain company's life insurance policies. All premiums are fixed at the time of purchase.

1. Jack is 45 years old. He wants to take out a five-year Sun-Belt term life insurance policy with a face value of $40,000. What is the annual premium for this policy?

   Solution: Figure 12.5 lists rates per $1,000 of coverage, so Jack must determine the number of thousands in 40,000.

$$\begin{array}{r} 40 \leftarrow\text{number of thousands} \\ 1{,}000\overline{)40{,}000} \leftarrow\text{face value of policy} \end{array}$$

Sun-Belt Life Insurance Company Annual Premiums for $1,000 of Life Insurance								
Age of Policyholder When Policy is Purchased	5-Year Term Insurance		Straight Life Insurance		20-Year Limited Payment Life Insurance		20-Year Endowment Policy	
	Male	Female	Male	Female	Male	Female	Male	Female
20	$3.10	$2.46	$10.45	$8.36	$17.95	$14.37	$41.80	$37.62
25	$3.35	$2.68	$13.05	$10.45	$20.10	$16.08	$42.10	$37.90
30	$3.80	$3.04	$15.90	$12.70	$23.90	$19.12	$42.75	$38.47
35	$4.45	$3.56	$19.60	$15.68	$28.10	$22.48	$43.65	$39.29
40	$6.20	$4.96	$24.10	$19.28	$33.20	$26.56	$44.70	$40.23
45	$8.00	$7.10	$28.00	$23.10	$39.30	$31.44	$45.30	$40.77
50	$11.90	$10.30	$32.70	$26.16	$47.50	$38.00	$49.90	$41.80

Figure 12.5 Comparison of Premiums for Four Different Types of Life Insurance

Jack must look up his annual premium per $1,000 of insurance in Figure 12.5.

Age of Policyholder When Policy is Purchased	5-Year Term Insurance	
	Male	Female
20	$3.10	$2.46
25	$3.35	$2.68
30	$3.80	$3.04
35	$4.45	$3.56
40	$6.20	$4.96
45	$8.00	$7.10
50	$11.90	$10.30

$8.00   annual premium per $1,000 of coverage
× 40   number of thousands
─────
$320.00   annual premium

Jack's annual premium would be $320.

2. Maria is 35 years old. She just purchased a 20-year, $35,000 limited payment life insurance policy from Sun-Belt Life. What is the total premium Maria will pay for this policy?

Solution:

$$\begin{array}{r} 35 \\ \hline 1{,}000)\overline{35{,}000} \end{array}$$ ←number of thousands
←face value of policy

$22.48   annual premium per $1,000 of coverage
× 35   number of thousands
─────
$786.80   annual premium

$786.80   annual premium
× 20   number of years
─────
$15,736.00   total premium

Maria will pay $15,736 for this policy if she doesn't die before the end of the 20-year payment period. Maria could have used the following calculator keystroke sequence:

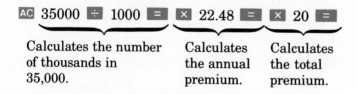

Calculates the number of thousands in 35,000.   Calculates the annual premium.   Calculates the total premium.

The display should read 15,736.

3. Richard is 20 years old. He purchases a $50,000, 20-year endowment policy from Sun-Belt Life. If Richard dies in three years, how much will his beneficiary receive?

Solution: Richard's beneficiary will receive the face value, $50,000.

Problems

Use Figure 12.5 for all problems involving premium costs.

1. Find the annual premiums for $1,000 of the following Sun-Belt life insurance policies.
   a. A straight life insurance policy purchased by a 35-year-old female.
   b. A five-year term policy purchased by a 45-year-old male.

   c. A 20-year limited payment life insurance policy purchased by a 40-year-old male.
   d. A 20-year limited payment life insurance policy purchased by a 40-year-old female.

✓ 2. Find the annual premiums for the following life insurance policies.
   a. A five-year term policy with a face value of $80,000 purchased by a 45-year-old male.
   b. A 20-year endowment policy with a face value of $60,000 purchased by a 30-year-old female.
   c. A 20-year limited payment policy with a face value of $100,000 purchased by a 25-year-old female.
   d. A straight life policy with a face value of $45,000 purchased by a 35-year-old male.

3. Find the total premium for each of the following life insurance policies.
   a. A five-year term policy with a face value of $120,000 purchased by a 25-year-old male.
   b. A five-year term policy with a face value of $20,000 purchased by a 45-year-old male.
   c. A 20-year limited payment policy with a face value of $20,000 purchased by a 35-year-old female.
   d. A 20-year limited payment policy with a face value of $20,000 purchased by a 35-year-old male.

✓ 4. Kyoko and Nu Paltz are a married couple and each is 35 years old. Both of them purchased straight life insurance policies with face values of $50,000. What is the total annual premium the Paltzes pay for their two insurance policies?

✓**5.**   Richard and Laura DeMille are both 40 years old. They are married and have two children. They each want to purchase five-year term policies with face values of $100,000.
   a.   What is the annual premium for Laura's policy?
   b.   What is the total premium for Laura's policy?
   c.   What is the annual premium for Richard's policy?
   d.   What is the total premium for Richard's policy?
   e.   Why is Richard's policy more expensive?

   f.   How much more expensive is Richard's total premium than Laura's?
   g.   What is the total cost of the two policies?
   h.   The DeMilles consider another option. Laura would take a $200,000 policy and Richard would not take any insurance. What is the total cost of a $200,000 five-year term policy for Laura?
   i.   Is Laura's $200,000 policy less expensive than the total of the two $100,000 policies?
   j.   Does Laura's $200,000 policy provide the same coverage as the two $100,000 policies? Explain your answer.

6.   Janet and Dean Wilson are married and have three children. Dean is a carpenter; Janet, his beneficiary, is a homemaker. The Wilsons owe $75,000 to the bank for the purchase of their home. Dean, age 40, is the only source of income for his family. He wants to purchase a $75,000 straight life policy to make sure his family can continue the mortgage payments for the house in the event of his death.
   a.   What is the annual cost of Dean's policy?
   b.   How much will the insurance company pay Dean's beneficiary if he dies?
   c.   How much would Janet owe the bank if Dean died and she used the insurance settlement to pay off the mortgage?

✓**7.**   Denise, age 50, is a single parent. Her daughter Allison enters college next fall, and the approximate cost of Allison's four-year education will be $60,000. Denise wants to purchase a five-year term policy for $60,000 to make sure that Allison will be able to afford college in case of her mother's death. What is the total cost of Denise's policy?

8. Compute the annual premiums for a $50,000 five-year term policy for males ages 20, 25, 30, 35, 40, 45, and 50. Construct and label a bar graph that shows these premiums.

9. Ralph took out a $100,000 straight life policy 11 years ago. He died yesterday at the age of 61. He paid $28 per $1,000 annually.
   a. What was his annual premium during the 11 years?

   b. What was the total premium Ralph paid?
   c. How much will Ralph's beneficiary receive?

10. Six years ago, Melissa Blanck took out a five-year term policy with a face value of $90,000. She did not renew the policy. She died last week. What does her beneficiary receive as a settlement from this policy?

√ 11. Steve, age 45, wants to purchase a five-year term policy to protect his teenage children until they are able to support themselves. Steve can afford to pay about $1,000 per year for this insurance.
   a. What is the cost per $1,000 for a five-year term policy for Steve?
   b. How much insurance could Steve purchase?

12. Jean is comparing the annual premiums per $1,000 of five-year term life insurance for males and females.
   a. What is the difference in cost for males and females age 30 for the five-year term policy?
   b. Express this difference as a percent of the premium for males.

13. Eric, age 35, purchased a 20-year endowment policy with a face value of $70,000.
   a. What is his total premium?
   b. How much will Eric receive if he lives past the 20-year payment period?
   c. What is the difference between Eric's total premium and the benefit he will receive if he lives past the 20-year period?

√**14.** Cathy, age 28, purchased a 20-year, $40,000 endowment policy three years ago, for an annual premium of $1,400. Stu, age 26, purchased a $40,000 five-year term policy last year, for an annual premium of $116. Today, they were both killed in an accident.

   a. What is the total premium paid by Cathy up to her death?

   b. What is the total premium paid by Stu up to his death?

   c. What will Cathy's beneficiary receive as a settlement?

   d. What will Stu's beneficiary receive as a settlement?

15. Explain why a five-year, $200,000 term policy for a 20-year-old male has a lower premium than a five-year, $200,000 term policy for a 50-year-old male.

SECTION 6 • PREPARING A BUDGET

David is a construction worker. He is paid *biweekly*. He takes a bus to work, so he needs money on a *daily* basis. He fills his car's gas tank and does grocery shopping *weekly*. David's mortgage payment is due *monthly;* his homeowner's insurance premium is paid *quarterly*. His auto insurance premium is due *semiannually*. He spends money *annually* for his vacation.

David's paydays do not always fall on the days that he needs money. How can he be sure he will have enough money to meet all of his costs? An itemized spending plan, called a **budget,** will help him balance his income and his expenses.

David's problem is not unusual. Everyone's income limits the amount of money that can be spent. You have learned about many different consumer expenses throughout *Dollars and Sense*. These expenses can get out of hand very quickly if you are not careful. Financial planning can help you manage your income efficiently. Organization, estimation, and good record keeping are needed to prepare a working budget.

Before you can develop a budget, you need to estimate your annual income and your tax liability. You will use this information to estimate your **disposable income**—the amount of money you will have available for spending throughout the year. By budgeting the way you spend your disposable income, you will be able to maintain a good credit rating and avoid financial difficulties.

Skills and Strategies

Martha McCoy is a newspaper reporter. She is single and owns a home in Windmere Falls. She estimates that her annual disposable income is $32,000. Figure 12.6 on page 502 shows Martha's budget for the coming year.

1. What is Martha's estimated annual mortgage expense?

   Solution: Find the *mortgage* line in the household expenses section. The last column on the right lists the estimated annual cost for each expense. Martha's estimated annual mortgage expense is $4,800.

2. In what months will Martha pay her automobile insurance premium?

   Solution: Find the *automobile* line in the insurance section. Notice that a $350 payment is made in January and another in July.

3. What is the total of Martha's estimated household expenses for December?

   Solution: Locate the Household Expenses section. Look to the right and find the column for December. Add the entries in this column that correspond to household expenses. You can use the following calculator keystroke sequence:

   The display should read 800.

   Martha's estimated December household expenses are $800.

4. What are Martha's estimated annual expenses for insurance?

		JAN.	FEB.	MAR.	APR.	MAY	JUNE	JULY	AUG.	SEPT.	OCT.	NOV.	DEC.	Annual Cost
HOUSEHOLD EXPENSES	Rent or Mortgage	400	400	400	400	400	400	400	400	400	400	400	400	4,800
	Property Tax	100	100	100	100	100	100	100	100	100	100	100	100	1,200
	Electric	45	45	45	45	45	45	45	45	45	45	45	45	540
	Natural Gas	40	40	40	40	40	40	40	40	40	40	40	40	480
	Oil	150	150	75							75	75	150	600
	Water													
	Telephone	40	40	40	40	40	40	40	40	40	40	40	40	480
	Pay Television	25	25	25	25	25	25	25	25	25	25	25	25	300
	Maintenance Fee													
INSURANCE	Health		80			80			80			80		320
	Automobile	350						350						700
	Homeowners/Renters										650			650
	Life			45			45			45			45	180
LIVING EXPENSES	Food	300	300	300	300	300	300	300	300	300	300	300	300	3,600
	Clothing				250					350			400	1,000
	Laundering	20	20	20	20	20	20	20	20	20	20	20	20	240
	Entertainment	100	100	100	100	100	100	100	100	100	100	100	100	1,200
	Medical/Dental			200						200				400
	Subscriptions		15			20	10							45
LOANS	Automobile													
	Personal													
	Student	55	55	55	55	55	55	55	55	55	55	55	55	660
TRANSPORTATION	Gasoline	90	90	90	90	90	90	90	90	90	90	90	90	1,080
	Auto Maintenance					50				150				200
	Tolls & Parking													
	Bus & Train Fares	30	30	30	30	30	30	30	30	30	30	30	30	360
MISCELLANEOUS	Contributions													500
	Savings	200	200	200	200	200	200	200	200	200	200	200	200	2,400
	Vacation Expenses						1,800							1,800
	Dues				400									400
	Other (Health Club)								900					900

ESTIMATE OF ANNUAL EXPENSES	25,035
AMOUNT TO BE BUDGETED MONTHLY	2,086
AMOUNT TO BE BUDGETED WEEKLY	481

Figure 12.6   Martha McCoy's Annual Budget

Solution: Locate the Insurance section. Look to the right and find the column labeled Annual Cost. Use the following calculator keystroke sequence to add the four annual insurance premiums:

AC 320 **+** 700 **+** 650 **+** 180 **=**

The display should read 1,850.

Martha's estimated annual expense for insurance is $1,850.

5. Martha puts the disposable income that she does not spend into an emergency fund for unexpected expenses. These expenses could include automobile repairs, home repairs, medical expenses, and other costs. Approximately how much will Martha put into her emergency fund based on her estimated expenses?

Solution:

$32,000   disposable income
− 25,035   estimated annual expenses
$ 6,965   amount for emergency fund

Based on her estimates, Martha will add approximately $6,965 to her emergency fund.

6. Jonathan set up a budget similar to Martha's. Jonathan's estimate of annual expenses is $20,472. How much should Jonathan budget monthly to meet this expense? (Round your answer to the nearest dollar.)

Solution: Use the following calculator keystroke sequence:

AC 20472 **÷** 12 **=**

Divides the annual expense by 12.

The display should read 1,706.

Jonathan should budget $1,706 monthly to meet his expenses.

7. Use the information from Problem 6 to determine how much Jonathan should budget weekly to meet his expenses. Round to the nearest dollar.

Solution: Use the following calculator keystroke sequence:

AC 20472 ÷ 52 =

The display should read 393.6923

Jonathan should budget $394 weekly to meet his expenses.

Problems

For Problems 1 through 10 use Figure 12.6 on page 502.

1. How much does Martha spend monthly to pay back her student loan?

2. How many times per year does Martha pay for her health insurance?

3. In what month is Martha's homeowner's insurance premium due?

✓ 4. Martha sets aside money to have her car tuned up in the spring and winterized in the fall.
    a. What is her total estimated annual cost for these items?

    b. In what months does Martha plan to have her car serviced?

5. Martha's budget shows that in some months she is required to pay more bills than in other months.
    a. Find the total of Martha's estimated expenses for September.
    b. Find the total of Martha's estimated expenses for February.
    c. In what month does Martha not have to pay any insurance premiums?

✓ 6. Martha's health club dues must be paid in August. She wants to save up to make this payment by putting some money into a fund each month for this purpose.
    a. How much are her health club dues?
    b. How much should Martha set aside each month for health club dues?

7. Martha wants to purchase a new car. She is quoted a monthly payment of $191 from her local bank. What would the annual cost of this loan be?

8. In what month are Martha's transportation expenses greatest?

9. Martha wants to cut down on her expenses. She is considering canceling her pay television, magazine and newspaper subscriptions, and reducing her entertainment budget by 20%. How much would this save her annually when compared with her present budget?

✓ 10. Martha has set aside money for contributions to charity. She doesn't plan to make these contributions at any specific time during the year. How much does Martha plan to contribute this year?

11. Keith Fernandez set up a budget and estimated that his total annual expenses would be $17,350.
    a. What is his estimated monthly expense based on this estimate? (Round your answer to the nearest dollar.)
    b. What is his estimated weekly expense based on this estimate? (Round your answer to the nearest dollar.)

✓ 12. Gary Magadan will earn a salary of $33,000 next year. He estimates that his total tax liability will be $6,700. What is his estimated disposable income for next year?

13. Sue is a high-school student. Here is a list of her estimated *monthly* expenses:

    Telephone bill, $10
    Piano lessons, $100
    Entertainment, $50
    Bus fare, $20
    School lunches, $45

    a. Approximately how much does Sue pay yearly for the telephone?
    b. Approximately how much does Sue pay yearly for piano lessons?
    c. Approximately how much does Sue pay annually for entertainment?

    d. Approximately how much does Sue pay for bus fare during the ten months school is in session?

    e. Approximately how much does Sue pay for school lunches during the ten months school is in session?

    f. Sue plans to earn $2,500 as a lifeguard this summer. (The tax liability on $2,500 is zero.) Will this be enough to pay for her total estimated annual expenses? Explain.

√ **14.** Last year Len Backman's property taxes were $1,700. This year they are going to be increased 10%.

    a. How much will Len Backman's property taxes be this year?

    b. How much should Len set aside monthly to meet this property tax expense? (Round your answer to the nearest dollar.)

15. Darryl estimates that his disposable income next year will be $28,000 and his expenses will be $21,000. He will put the difference between these estimates into an emergency fund. What percentage of his disposable income will be put into his emergency fund?

● KEY TERMS

To find the definition of any term introduced in the chapter, refer to the Glossary in the back of this book.

beneficiaries	face value
budget	Food and Drug Administration (FDA)
calories	
ccf	generic drugs
claim	group insurance
cubic foot	health insurance
deductible	Health Maintenance Organization (HMO)
disposable income	
80% clause	homeowner's insurance
endowment policies	kilowatt-hours (kwh)

life insurance

limited payment life
  insurance

major medical insurance

Medicaid

Medicare

meter

mortality table

nutrients

nutrition

policyholder

reimbursement

renter's insurance

serving size

settlement

straight life insurance

term insurance

U.S. Recommended Daily
  Allowance (USRDA)

utilities

volume

watts

watt-hours

• REVIEW PROBLEMS

1. Roy's electric company charges $.14 per kilowatt hour of elec-
    tricity used. Roy's previous meter reading was 4903. How
    much should Roy's electric bill be if the following dials repre-
    sent his present reading?

2. A certain long-distance call costs $.95 for the first three min-
    utes and $.40 for each additional minute. How much would a
    15-minute long-distance call cost?

3. Jason's homeowner's insurance policy contains an 80% clause.
    His house has a replacement cost of $150,000, but is insured
    for $90,000. A fire recently caused $30,000 worth of damage.
    How much of the loss should be covered by Jason's insurance
    company?

4. The label on a 32-ounce box of whole-wheat pancake mix suggests a serving size of 1.6 oz. How many servings are contained in the package?

5. The Healthy-Tyme Yogurt Company offers customers a $1.00 rebate if they purchase a half-dozen containers of blueberry yogurt. Jean bought seven containers at a price of $.79 each. What is the cost of the seven containers after Jean receives her $1.00 rebate?

6. Roger will make the following insurance payments this year:

   • Semiannual payments of $210 for homeowner's insurance

   • Quarterly payments of $47 for life insurance

   • Biweekly payments of $6.10 for medical insurance

   • An annual payment of $790 for automobile insurance

   What is the total annual expense for these insurance policies?

7. Benny has a $300 deductible medical insurance policy. His insurance company pays 80% of his medical bills after he meets the deductible. Benny paid $750 to a doctor yesterday. How much reimbursement should Benny receive from his insurance company?

8. At Fieldstone Pharmacy, 20 fluid ounces of brand-name cough syrup cost $7.20. The generic equivalent costs $4.80 for a 16-fluid-ounce bottle. What is the difference in unit price per fluid ounce of these two cough syrups?

9. Joan, age 35, wants to purchase $75,000 of five-year term life insurance. What is the total premium for this five-year policy? (Use Figure 12.5 on page 495.)

10. Tom Koosman set up a budget and estimated that his total annual expenses would be $21,200. What are his estimated monthly expenses based on this estimate? (Round your answer to the nearest dollar.)

CHAPTER *13*

BANKING

SECTION 1 • SAVINGS ACCOUNTS

Banks today offer many services to their customers. At most banks you can get loans, life insurance policies, safe-deposit boxes, and credit cards, as well as checking accounts and savings accounts. Banks provide these services so that they can attract customers and make a profit. Most Americans use some of these banking services; for this reason, it is important for you to understand the banking process.

People put money in banks for safekeeping and to earn **interest.** Interest is money banks pay their customers for the use of the customers' money. Banks use this money to give loans and to make investments. The money you put into the bank is being used by other people — it is not placed into a special compartment under your name!

Is it possible that you could lose your money while it is in a savings account? What if the bank's loans are not repaid by the borrowers? What if the bank invests your money in stocks and the money is lost? Your account is insured by the **Federal Deposit Insurance Corporation (FDIC),** for up to $100,000. You can be sure that your money is safe in a bank.

One of the most widely used banking services is a **savings account.** A savings account is a service in which the bank agrees to pay interest for the use of the money in the account. Perhaps you have your own savings account, which you opened yourself or which was started for you when you were a small child.

There are many different reasons for opening an account. Here are some:

- saving money for a car and insurance

- saving for a house

- saving for your education

- saving for your child's future

- saving for your retirement

When money is added to the account, a **deposit** has been made. When money is taken out of the account, a **withdrawal** has been made. Only the customer who **opens** (starts) the account can make **transactions** (deposits and withdrawals). Account holders usually receive a **passbook,** which is a written record of all deposits, withdrawals, and interest payments. The amount of money in a savings account at any specific time is called the **balance**.

There are different types of savings accounts available to customers. These accounts include the following:

Individual account. Only one person can make deposits and withdrawals.

Joint account. More than one person can make deposits and withdrawals. The names of the account's holders must be listed on the passbook, and their signatures must be on file with the bank.

Voluntary trust account. This is set up by a person called a **trustee** for a **beneficiary.** The money in the account belongs to the trustee. Upon the trustee's death, the money becomes the property of the beneficiary. The trustee pays income tax on the interest that is earned until the money is transferred to the beneficiary.

Custodian-for-a-minor account. This is set up by an adult, called the **custodian,** for the benefit of a child, called the **minor.** The money belongs to the minor as soon as it is deposited in the account. The minor cannot make deposits or withdrawals. When the minor reaches a certain age (usually 18 to 21 years old), the money is transferred to him or her, and the account is closed. The minor is responsible for paying income taxes on interest earned on this account.

Long-term account. This account is opened by a depositor who agrees not to withdraw money from the account for a long period of time (usually years). It can earn higher interest for the customer than a regular savings account can.

Certificate of Deposit (CD). This is an account in which a bank will pay higher interest to a depositor who agrees not to make withdrawals or deposits for at least six months. Most banks require that the depositor start the certificate of deposit with at least a certain amount of money, usually at least $1,000. This amount is called the **minimum balance.**

Money Market Certificate. This is a savings account that has an interest rate that varies. A minimum balance is required, and depositors are limited to a certain number of withdrawals each month. The interest rate can go higher or lower than the rate that was in effect when the account was opened.

Your bank representative can give you specific information and current interest rates. Be sure to ask whether any of the accounts require a minimum balance. With certain accounts, a penalty is charged for each month the balance falls below the required minimum balance. Some banks do not pay interest on accounts that have balances below a certain minimum. The interest that is earned is taxable income and must be reported on your income tax return.

You should discuss your financial goals with a bank representative to decide what type of savings account you should open. A savings account can be your first step toward financial independence.

Skills and Strategies

Here you will learn how to responsibly handle the money in your savings account and to be on the alert for the highest interest rates. Read each example carefully.

1. Bill wants to deposit $5,000 in a long-term account for a period of two years. He is comparing the interest rates quoted by these three banks:

   First State Bank, $8\frac{3}{8}\%$
   Johnson City Trust, 8.1%
   Land Savings Bank, $8\frac{1}{4}\%$

   Which bank offers the highest interest rate?

   Solution: Convert the percents to decimals.

   $$8\tfrac{3}{8}\% \;=\; 8.375\% \;=\; .08375 \;=\; .08375$$
   $$8.1\% \;=\; 8.1\% \;\;\;=\; .081 \;\;\;\;=\; .08100$$
   $$8\tfrac{1}{4}\% \;=\; 8.25\% \;\;=\; .0825 \;\;\;=\; .08250$$

   Compare the five-place decimals in the column on the right. The highest interest rate is $8\frac{3}{8}\%$.

   First State Bank offers the highest interest rate.

2. Kyoko went to her bank to cash her $371.52 paycheck. She received the following bills and coins from the teller:

   15 twenty-dollar bills
   6 ten-dollar bills
   2 five-dollar bills
   1 one-dollar bill
   2 quarters
   2 pennies

   Did Kyoko receive the correct amount of cash?

   Solution: Do the following multiplication exercises.

Number of Bills or Coins		Value of Bill or Coins		Amount Received
15	×	$20.00	=	$300.00
6	×	10.00	=	60.00
2	×	5.00	=	10.00
1	×	1.00	=	1.00
2	×	.25	=	.50
2	×	.01	=	.02
		total cash received		$371.52

   Kyoko received the correct amount of cash. Always count your money *before* leaving the teller's window.

3. Felix Turner is depositing money in his savings account. He must fill out a **deposit slip** as shown below. Most banks require that each check being deposited must be listed separately on the deposit slip.

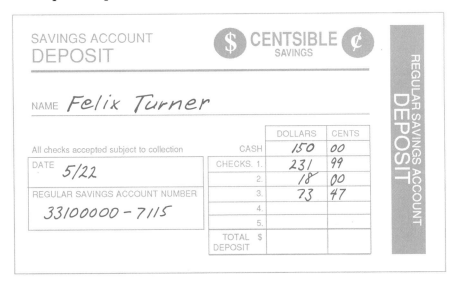

Felix is depositing some cash and three checks. What amount should Felix enter as the total on the deposit slip?

Solution: You can use the following calculator keystroke sequence:

AC 150 **+** 231.99 **+** 18 **+** 73.47 **=**

The display should read 473.46.

Felix should enter $473.46 as the total on the deposit slip. He should check that the passbook entry is correct.

DATE	WITHDRAWALS	DEPOSITS	BALANCE
APR 17	$26.58		$1,487.79
APR 30		$350.00	$1,837.79
MAY 7		$548.37	$2,386.16
MAY 15	$122.50		$2,263.66
MAY 22		$473.46	$2,737.12

4. Cecily Quakere needs to withdraw $270.20 from her savings account to pay for college textbooks. The balance in her account is $4,769.51. What is Cecily's balance after the withdrawal?

Cecily must first fill out a **withdrawal slip** as shown. Notice that the amount of the withdrawal must be written in words and numerals.

Solution: Subtract to find Cecily's balance after the withdrawal.

$4,769.51   balance before the withdrawal
− 270.20   withdrawal ($.20 = twenty cents = $\frac{20}{100}$ dollars)
$4,499.31   balance after the withdrawal

Cecily's correct balance after the withdrawal is $4,499.31. She should check that her passbook entries are correct.

DATE	WITHDRAWALS	DEPOSITS	BALANCE
MAR 30	$135.48		$3,278.29
APR 10		$486.50	$3,764.79
APR 17		$125.00	$3,889.79
APR 21	$75.00		$3,814.79
MAY 9		$256.48	$4071.27
MAY 18		698.24	$4,769.51
MAY 21	$270.20		$4,499.31

5. Gina's bank requires all depositors to keep a minimum balance of $400 in their savings accounts at all times. For each month the balance falls below $400, Gina is charged a fee of $1. Gina had $480 in her account yesterday. She made a $150 withdrawal today. What is her balance after she makes this transaction?

Solution: Subtract Gina's withdrawal from her balance.

$480	balance before the withdrawal
− 150	amount of the withdrawal
$330	balance after the withdrawal

Because her new balance is below $400, you must also subtract the fee of $1.

$330	balance before deduction of fee of $1
− 1	fee
$329	balance after fee

Gina's balance is $329. She will be charged $1 each month her account balance falls below $400.

Problems

√**1.** Express each percent as an equivalent decimal.
   a. 5%
   b. 5.5%
   c. 6.15%
   d. 60.15%
   e. $7\frac{1}{2}\%$
   f. $13\frac{1}{8}\%$

√**2.** Arrange the interest rates in ascending order (from lowest to highest).
   8.29%, $8\frac{1}{2}\%$, $8\frac{1}{4}\%$, 8.2%, $8\frac{3}{8}\%$

3. Pablo is cashing his $426 paycheck. He wants the cash in as few bills as possible, and he wants no bills larger than $50. How many bills should Pablo receive from the teller?

√**4.** Jethro saves quarters in a coffee can in his bedroom. He now has 712 quarters. How much money would Jethro add to his account if he deposited all the quarters?

5. Paula Sorkimmel is depositing a few checks and some cash into her savings account. She lists them on the following deposit slip. What is the total deposit?

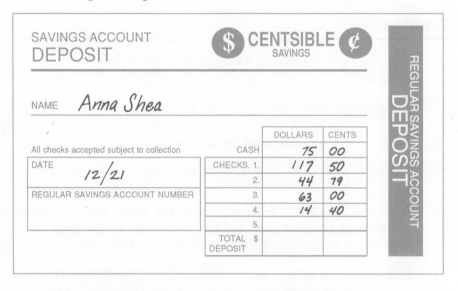

	DOLLARS	CENTS
SAVINGS ACCOUNT DEPOSIT	**CENTSIBLE** SAVINGS	

SAVINGS ACCOUNT
DEPOSIT

$ **CENTSIBLE** ¢
SAVINGS

NAME *Paula Sorkimmel*

All checks accepted subject to collection

		DOLLARS	CENTS
CASH		300	00
CHECKS. 1.		17	50
2.		25	00
3.		1	91
4.		50	00
5.			
TOTAL $ DEPOSIT			

DATE 6/12

REGULAR SAVINGS ACCOUNT NUMBER

REGULAR SAVINGS ACCOUNT
DEPOSIT

✓**6.** Anna Shea has $1,479.11 in her savings account. She plans on making the deposit shown below. What is her balance after making this deposit?

SAVINGS ACCOUNT
DEPOSIT

$ **CENTSIBLE** ¢
SAVINGS

NAME *Anna Shea*

All checks accepted subject to collection

		DOLLARS	CENTS
CASH		75	00
CHECKS. 1.		117	50
2.		44	79
3.		63	00
4.		14	40
5.			
TOTAL $ DEPOSIT			

DATE 12/21

REGULAR SAVINGS ACCOUNT NUMBER

REGULAR SAVINGS ACCOUNT
DEPOSIT

✓**7.** Write each of the dollar amounts in words.
  a. $1,760.43
  b. $1,706.43
  c. $1,072,706.43
  d. $1,270,706.43
  e. $4,370.00
  f. $609.01
  g. $609.10
  h. $600.09

8. Examine the following withdrawal slip. What should be entered on the line labeled "Amount in Words"?

SAVINGS ACCOUNT
WITHDRAWAL

$ CENTSIBLE ¢
SAVINGS

REGULAR SAVINGS ACCOUNT
WITHDRAWAL

NAME   JOSEPH LESTER

AMOUNT
(in words)   DOLLARS

DATE 8/22   SIGNATURE Joseph Lester

ACCOUNT NUMBER   TOTAL WITHDRAWAL
3410000000 $ 3,428   20

9. Examine the following withdrawal slip. What should be entered in the box labeled "Total Withdrawal"?

SAVINGS ACCOUNT
WITHDRAWAL

$ CENTSIBLE ¢
SAVINGS

REGULAR SAVINGS ACCOUNT
WITHDRAWAL

NAME   BARBARA HUXLEY

AMOUNT
(in words) Eight Hundred Five and 60/100   DOLLARS

DATE 4/17   SIGNATURE Barbara Huxley

ACCOUNT NUMBER   TOTAL WITHDRAWAL
300000008

√**10.** Winnie takes a check for $485.25 and a check for $989.91 to her bank. She wants $320 in cash, and she wants to deposit the rest. What is the total amount that will be credited to her account?

11. Melanie has a savings account at the Cliffside Bank. The bank requires that she keep a minimum balance of $150 in the account. If the balance falls below the minimum, a penalty of $3.25 is deducted from her account. On November 2, Melanie had a balance of $490. On November 3, she withdrew $380 from her account. What was Melanie's savings account balance after she made the transaction?

12. Examine the following record of Jacob Stein's savings account deposits and withdrawals.

balance as of October 1, $953.00
deposit on October 2, $3,490.80
deposit on October 9, $4,800.00
withdrawal on October 9, $185.50
withdrawal on October 12, $2,180.55
deposit on October 20, $842.00
withdrawal on October 29, $1,250.90

Assuming that no other transactions were made, what is the balance in Jacob's account on October 31, not including interest?

13. Emma's bank will accept coins for deposit only if they are rolled in coin wrappers. The wrappers hold the following amounts of each type of coin:

pennies, $.50
nickels, $2.00
dimes, $5.00
quarters, $10.00

Emma has 85 quarters, 190 dimes, 48 nickels, and 60 pennies.
a. How many complete rolls of quarters will she be able to wrap?
b. How many complete rolls of dimes will she be able to wrap?
c. How many complete rolls of nickels will she be able to wrap?

    d. How many complete rolls of pennies will she be able to wrap?

    e. What is the total value of the *loose* coins that she will have left?

✓**14.** Rodney had $1,379.59 in his savings account before making a $420 withdrawal. At the time Rodney made this transaction, the bank credited his account with $17.71 in interest earned. What is Rodney's balance after these adjustments?

15. Jerry had not used his bank account for the last 14 months. His balance 14 months ago was $371.15. Jerry's bank charges a one-dollar fee for each month the balance falls below $500. Jerry's account earned $18.19 in interest during the past 14 months. How much is in his account?

SECTION 2 • COMPOUND INTEREST

Most communities have several banks that provide financial services to customers. How should you choose the bank that's right for you? Before opening an account at any bank, ask yourself these questions:

1. Is the bank conveniently located near my home or office?

2. During what hours is the bank open for business?

3. What services does the bank offer?

4. What interest rate does the bank pay for each type of account?

Certainly, the interest rate is a major concern of most consumers. However, it is not enough to know just the interest *rate*. You must also find out *how* the amount of interest is computed. Not all banks compute interest the same way. How the bank computes interest directly affects the amount of interest you will receive. This section will help you understand how a bank computes interest.

Skills and Strategies

The amount of money in an account at any given time is called the **principal.** The principal is used to compute the interest. The principal increases each time interest is added to the account. The interest is called **compound interest.** Compound interest is money you earn on the money you deposited plus previous interest. Interest is compounded annually, semiannually, quarterly, monthly, or daily.

1. How much interest would $1,000 earn in one year at the rate of 6% compounded annually?

   Solution: Use the following calculator keystroke sequence:

   AC 1000 × 6 %

   The display should read 60.

   The account would earn $60 in interest at a rate of 6% compounded annually. Interest compounded annually is sometimes called **simple interest.**

2. Maria deposits $2,500 in a long-term savings account that pays 6% interest compounded annually. What is her balance after one year?

   Solution: Use the following calculator keystroke sequence:

   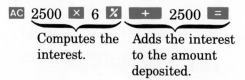

   | Computes the interest. | Adds the interest to the amount deposited. |

   The display should read 2,650.

   Maria's balance is $2,650 at the end of one year.

3. How much interest would $1,000 earn in one year at a rate of 6% compounded semiannually?

   Solution: Accounts that pay interest compounded semiannually have the interest added on twice each year (every six months).

$1,000   amount deposited
× .06   6%, expressed as a decimal
$60.00   annual interest on $1,000

$$30.00 \leftarrow \text{semiannual interest}$$
number of → $2\overline{)60.00}$ ← annual interest
semiannual
interest
periods
per year

$1,000.00   amount deposited
+ 30.00   interest for first six months
$1,030.00   balance after six months

$1,030   balance after six months
× .06   6%, expressed as a decimal
$61.80   annual interest on $1,030

$$30.90 \leftarrow \text{semiannual interest}$$
$2\overline{)61.80}$ ← annual interest on $1,030

$1,030.00   balance after six months
+ 30.90   interest for second six months
$1,060.90   balance after one year

$1,060.90   balance after one year
− 1,000.00   amount deposited
$ 60.90   interest earned after one year

The account would earn $60.90 in interest. Notice that the interest earned on $1,000 at a rate of 6% compounded annually (Problem 1) is *less* than the interest earned on $1,000 at 6% compounded semiannually.

4.   How much interest would $1,000 earn in six months at 6% compounded quarterly?

Solution: There are 12 months in a year and four quarters in a year. Three months represent one quarter of a year.

$1,000   amount deposited
× .06   6%, expressed as a decimal
$60.00   annual interest on $1,000

 15.00 ←interest for first quarter
4)60.00 ←annual interest on $1,000
↑

number of
quarters in
one year

$1,000.00 $\quad$ amount deposited
$\underline{+\ \ 15.00}$ $\quad$ first-quarter interest
$1,015.00 $\quad$ balance after three months

$1,015 $\quad$ balance after three months
$\underline{\times\ .06}$ $\quad$ 6%, expressed as a decimal
$60.90 $\quad$ annual interest on $1,015

 15.23 ←second-quarter interest (rounded to nearest cent)
4)60.90 ←annual interest on $1,015

$1,015.00 $\quad$ first-quarter balance
$\underline{+\ \ 15.23}$ $\quad$ second-quarter interest
$1,030.23 $\quad$ second-quarter balance

$$$1,030.23 $\quad$ second-quarter balance
$\underline{-\ 1,000.00}$ $\quad$ amount deposited
$\$\ \ \ \ 30.23$ $\quad$ interest for six months

The account would earn $30.23 in interest in six months. The balance after six months would be $1,030.23. This number is used to find the interest for the third quarter. This process can be repeated to find the interest for the fourth quarter. At the end of each quarter, the balance increases because of the addition of interest.

5. How much interest would $1,000 earn in two months at a rate of 6% compounded monthly?

Solution: The procedure is similar to quarterly and semiannual compounding, except that there are 12 interest periods per year. Use the following calculator keystroke sequences:

`AC` 1000 `×` 6 `%` `÷` 12 `=`

The display should read 5.

The account would earn $5 in interest the first month. The balance after one month would be $1,005.

⟨AC⟩ 1005 ☒ 6 ⬚% ⬚÷ 12 ⬚=

The display should read 5.025.

The account would earn $5.03 (rounded to the nearest cent) in interest the second month. The total interest for the first two months would be $5 + $5.03 = $10.03. Notice how the interest for the second month is greater than the interest for the first month.

6. How much interest would $1,000 earn in two days at a rate of 6% compounded daily?

   Solution: There are 365 days (interest periods) in one year. Use the following calculator keystroke sequences:

   ⟨AC⟩ 1000 ☒ 6 ⬚% ⬚÷ 365 ⬚=

   The display should read .1643835.

   The account would earn 16 cents (rounded to the nearest cent) in interest the first day. The balance after one day would be $1,000.16.

   ⟨AC⟩ 1000.16 ☒ 6 ⬚% ⬚÷ 365 ⬚=

   The display should read .1644098.

   The account would earn 16 cents (rounded to the nearest cent) in interest the second day. The total interest for the first two days would be $.16 + $.16 = $.32.

7. On May 21, Mary Jean opened a savings account by depositing $2,000. The account pays 7% interest compounded daily. On May 23, she made a $200 deposit. On May 24, she made a $1,320 withdrawal. What was her balance at the end of the day on May 24?

   Solution: Accounts that have interest compounded daily add on interest each day of the year. There are 365 days in a year.

   To find the interest earned on May 21, use the following calculator keystroke sequence:

[AC] 2000 [×] 7 [%] [÷] 365 [=]

The display should read .3835616.

Mary Jean's account earned 38 cents (rounded to the nearest cent) in interest on May 21.

The principal used to compute interest for May 22 was $2,000.38. To find the interest earned on May 22, use the following calculator keystroke sequence:

[AC] 2000.38 [×] 7 [%] [÷] 365 [=]

The display should read .3836345.

Mary Jean's account earned 38 cents (rounded to the nearest cent) in interest on May 22. Her new balance on May 22 was $2,000.76.

The opening balance on May 23 was $2,000.76. The principal used to compute interest on May 23 must include a $200 deposit.

[AC] 2000.76 [+] 200 [=]

The display should read 2,200.76.

The principal of $2,200.76 was used to compute interest on May 23.

Use the following calculator keystroke sequence to find the interest earned on May 23.

[AC] 2200.76 [×] 7 [%] [÷] 365 [=]

The display should read .4220635.

Mary Jean's account earned 42 cents (rounded to the nearest cent) in interest on May 23. Her new balance on May 23 was $2,201.18. The opening balance on May 24 was $2,201.18. The principal used to compute interest on May 24 must include a withdrawal of $1,320.

[AC] 2201.18 [−] 1320 [=]

The display should read 881.18.

The principal of $881.18 was used to compute interest on May 24.

Use the following calculator keystroke sequence to find the interest earned on May 24.

AC 881.18 × 7 % ÷ 365 =

The display should read .1689934.

Mary Jean's account earned 17 cents (rounded to the nearest cent) in interest on May 24. The new balance on May 24 can be found by adding this interest to $881.18. Mary Jean's balance at the end of the day on May 24 was $881.35.

Problems involving interest compounded daily can be summarized in a table. Table 13.1 shows Mary Jean's interest payments and balances from May 21 to May 24.

Compound Interest Calendar

Date	May 21	May 22	May 23	May 24
Opening Balance	- 0 -	$2,000.38	$2,000.76	$2,201.18
Deposit	+ $2,000.00	- 0 -	+ 200.00	- 0 -
Withdrawal	- 0 -	- 0 -	- 0 -	− 1,320.00
Principal	2,000.00	2,000.38	2,200.76	881.18
Interest	+ .38	+ .38	+ .42	+ .17
New Balance	$2,000.38	$2,000.76	$2,201.18	$ 881.35

Table 13.1

Notice that the new balance at the end of each day becomes the opening balance for the following day. Even with a calculator, you can see that this procedure takes time. Banks must compute interest daily for all their customers. Banks use computers to speed up these calculations.

8. Use Table 13.1 to find the total amount of interest that Mary Jean's account earned from May 21 to May 24.

Solution: Add the four entries from the line labeled "Interest."

AC 0.38 + 0.38 + 0.42 + 0.17 =

The display should read 1.35.

Mary Jean's account earned a total of $1.35 in interest from May 21 to May 24.

Problems

Round your answers to the nearest cent.

1. Jerome deposits $3,700 in a long-term savings account that pays $6\frac{1}{2}\%$ interest compounded annually. How much interest does Jerome earn in one year?

✓ 2. Sally deposits $4,000 in a long-term savings account that pays $6\frac{3}{4}\%$ interest compounded annually. What is her balance after one year?

3. Pierre deposits $9,000 in a certificate of deposit that pays 8% interest compounded semiannually.
    a. How much interest does the account earn in the first six months?
    b. What is the balance at the end of the first six months?

✓ 4. Caryl deposits $3,500 in a savings account that pays $7\frac{1}{2}\%$ interest compounded semiannually.
    a. How much interest does the account earn in the first six months?
    b. What is the balance at the end of the first six months?
    c. How much interest does the account earn in the next six months?
    d. What is the balance at the end of one year?
    e. How much interest does the account earn the first year?
    f. How much interest would $3,500 earn in one year at $7\frac{1}{2}\%$ compounded *annually*?
    g. How much more interest does Caryl receive because her account compounds interest semiannually instead of annually?

5. Sarah deposits $3,500 in a savings account that pays $7\frac{1}{2}\%$ interest compounded quarterly.
   a. Find the first quarter's interest.
   b. Find the first quarter's balance.
   c. Find the second quarter's interest.
   d. Find the second quarter's balance.
   e. Find the third quarter's interest.
   f. Find the third quarter's balance.
   g. Find the fourth quarter's interest.
   h. What is the balance at the end of one year?
   i. How much interest does this account earn in the first year?

6. Mike deposits $1,000 in a long-term savings account that pays $8\frac{1}{4}\%$ interest compounded monthly. Write the calculator keystroke sequence that can be used to compute Mike's interest for the first month.

7. Janine opened a savings account with a deposit of $720 on January 7. The account pays 6.5% interest compounded daily. Write the calculator keystroke sequence that can be used to compute Janine's interest for the first day.

✓ 8. Round the following amounts to the nearest cent.
   a. $.7318291
   b. $.7618292
   c. $4.761829
   d. $6.828183
   e. $.0769421
   f. $.0912341
   g. $.4641129
   h. $.4093711

✓ 9. Erik opened a savings account by making a $400 deposit on September 9. The account pays 6% interest compounded daily.
   a. Find the first day's interest.
   b. What was the new balance at the end of the first day?

10. On April 14, Bernadette deposited $900 in a savings account that pays 6% interest compounded daily. On April 16, she made a $75 withdrawal.

    a. How much interest did the account earn on April 14?
    b. What was the new balance at the end of April 14?
    c. How much interest did the account earn on April 15?
    d. What was the new balance on April 15?
    e. Write the calculator keystroke sequence that can be used to compute the interest for April 16.

    f. How much interest did the account earn on April 16?
    g. What was the new balance on April 16?
    h. How much interest did the account earn during these three days?

11. On August 10, Liam Duffy opened a savings account by making a \$4,550 deposit. The account pays $6\frac{1}{2}\%$ interest compounded daily. On August 12, he made a \$250 deposit. On August 14, he made a \$1,000 withdrawal.
    a. Set up a table similar to Table 13.1. Use the dates from August 10 through August 14. Complete the table.

    b. How much interest did the account earn from August 10 through August 14?

✓**12.** Jack and Reva Maniscalco opened a long-term savings account on July 8 with \$7,480 they received in wedding presents. The account pays 9% interest compounded daily. On July 9, they deposited \$490. On July 10, they deposited \$1,200.
    a. Set up a table similar to Table 13.1. Use the dates from July 8 through July 10. Complete the table.

    b. How much interest did the account earn from July 8 through July 10?

13. Dianne Burke invested \$10,000 in a certificate of deposit almost six months ago. The certificate pays $8\frac{7}{8}\%$ interest compounded semiannually. Dianne will collect the interest next week. She plans to use the interest to pay her \$697 mortgage payment next month. She will then invest \$10,000 in another certificate of deposit.
    a. How much interest should Dianne receive?
    b. Will this amount of interest cover the monthly mortgage payment?

√ **14.** Randy Ross inherited $70,000 from his grandfather. Randy plans to invest some of the money in stocks, but until he decides how to invest it, the $70,000 will be put into a savings account that pays $6\frac{1}{2}\%$ interest compounded daily. How much interest will this money earn the first week? (Round your answer to the nearest dollar.)

15. Louise opened a savings account with $800 on March 7. The account pays 6.6% interest compounded daily. There is no interest paid on any day the balance falls below $500. Louise made a $60 withdrawal on March 8 and a $400 withdrawal on March 9.

    a. Set up a table similar to Table 13.1. Use the dates from March 7 through March 9. Complete the table.

    b. How much interest did the account earn on March 8?

    c. How much interest did the account earn on March 9?

SECTION 3 • CHECKING ACCOUNTS

Barry and Carol Watson live in New Jersey. They are on vacation in San Francisco, and they want to purchase tickets to a baseball game. The Watsons did not bring a great deal of cash on their vacation. They plan to pay for most of their expenses using credit cards and their checking account. A **checking account** allows the Watsons to withdraw money from their account and cover an expense simply by writing a check. A **check** is a written request by a person to transfer money from his or her checking account. Mrs. Watson writes out a check payable to the San Francisco Giants Baseball Team for $40. The check shows that Mrs. Watson wants money withdrawn from her account and paid to the baseball team. In this case, Mrs. Watson is the **drawer** and the baseball team is the **payee**. There must be enough money in the Watsons' checking account to pay for the tickets. A clerk for the baseball team will sign or stamp the back of the check. This is called **endorsing the check.** The check will be deposited in the baseball team's bank account. Within a few (three to eight) business days, the check will be processed and then sent back to the bank in New Jersey, where the Watsons have their checking account. If enough money is in the account to pay the $40, the check will **clear.** The check will eventually be mailed back to the Watsons or stored by their bank. These checks are called **canceled checks.** Canceled checks should be saved. They can help you determine when you made certain purchases for warranty, insurance, and income tax purposes.

If the Watsons' account has less than $40 in it, the check will **bounce.** This means that there are **insufficient funds** in the account and the baseball team will not receive its money for the tickets. The Watsons will be charged a fee (usually about $10) for bouncing the check. They may have to issue another check to the baseball team after they deposit money in their checking account. People with acceptable credit ratings can get **overdraft protection,** which means that the bank will lend them money (and charge interest) to cover checks that would otherwise bounce.

All checking account transactions are summarized and sent to drawers on a **monthly statement.** Consumers should save their monthly statements along with their canceled checks.

Checks should be written in nonerasable ink. If the drawer makes an error on a check, the check should not be used. Such a check is called a **voided check.** If checks are lost or stolen, the drawer can go to the bank and put a **stop payment** on each check that is missing. The bank will not clear any checks on which a stop payment order has been made. There is a fee (usually about $10 per check) to make a stop payment.

You should become familiar with the vocabulary of checking accounts before opening your own account. Most banks offer different types of checking accounts.

1. A **special checking account** requires no minimum balance. No interest is earned on the money in the account. Drawers are charged a fee, called the **per check fee,** for each check they write (usually about 25 cents) and a monthly fee (usually under $10).

2. A **regular checking account** requires the drawer to maintain a minimum balance in the account. The requirements vary from bank to bank. No interest is earned on the money in the

account. Because there are no per check fees and no monthly fees, regular checking is sometimes called **free checking.**

3. **Negotiable order of withdrawal (NOW) accounts** are checking accounts that pay interest. A minimum balance is usually required, and the amount varies from bank to bank. Interest is usually compounded daily and entered into the account, or credited, quarterly. Most banks do not charge per check fees or monthly fees on their NOW accounts.

There is a great deal of paperwork involved in maintaining a checking account. Banks deal with thousands of checks and monthly statements each day. In an effort to cut down on paperwork and make transactions more quickly, many banks have started using **electronic funds transfer (EFT).** Electronic funds transfers use today's computer technology in the following ways:

*   **Automatic teller machines (ATMs)** allow 24-hour-a-day deposits and withdrawals. Each customer receives an EFT card and a **personal identification number (PIN).** Users of these machines must have their EFT cards and must know their PINs in order to make deposits and withdrawals.

*   Telephone bill-paying systems allow consumers to use the telephone to instruct their bank to pay bills or transfer money from their savings accounts to their checking accounts. No checks, deposit slips, or withdrawal slips are filled out when consumers pay bills by telephone.

*   Direct deposits or withdrawals allow consumers to have paychecks or social security checks deposited directly in their

accounts. Paychecks do not have to be issued, endorsed, or cashed. Certain bills can be paid automatically each month, without writing a check, with the direct withdrawal service.

- **Debit cards** allow consumers to pay for purchases by having money automatically transferred from their checking accounts to a store's account at the time and place of the sale. A debit card is similar to a credit card except that the money is immediately withdrawn from a customer's account when a debit card is used. (Credit card customers are billed at a later date.)

Banks of the future will become increasingly dependent on electronic banking. In your immediate future you will benefit from knowing how to handle a checking account.

Skills and Strategies

Here you will learn how to manage a checking account: make deposits, write checks, and keep an accurate check register. Read each example carefully.

1. Roseanne is depositing a $425.33 paycheck, a $20 rebate check, and $70 cash in her regular checking account. What is the total amount of her deposit?

   Solution: Roseanne must first fill out a deposit slip, as shown in Figure 13.1. The checks that are being deposited must be listed separately.

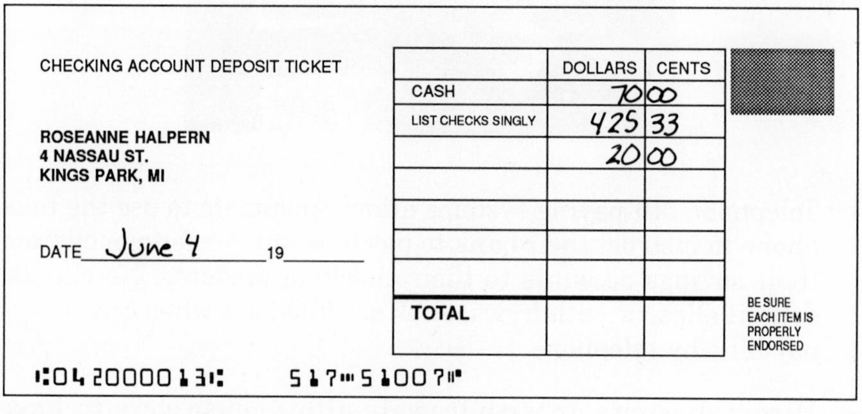
CHECKING ACCOUNT DEPOSIT TICKET

ROSEANNE HALPERN
4 NASSAU ST.
KINGS PARK, MI

DATE June 4 19

	DOLLARS	CENTS
CASH	70	00
LIST CHECKS SINGLY	425	33
	20	00
TOTAL		

BE SURE EACH ITEM IS PROPERLY ENDORSED

⑆042000013⑆ 517⑈5100 7⑈

Figure 13.1 Checking Account Deposit Slip

Use the following calculator keystroke sequence to find the total deposit:

AC 70 + 425.35 + 20 =

The display should read 515.33.

Roseanne is depositing $515.33 in her checking account. The total deposit in checks, $445.33, cannot be drawn on until the checks clear. This could take several business days. Figure 13.2 is the completed deposit slip.

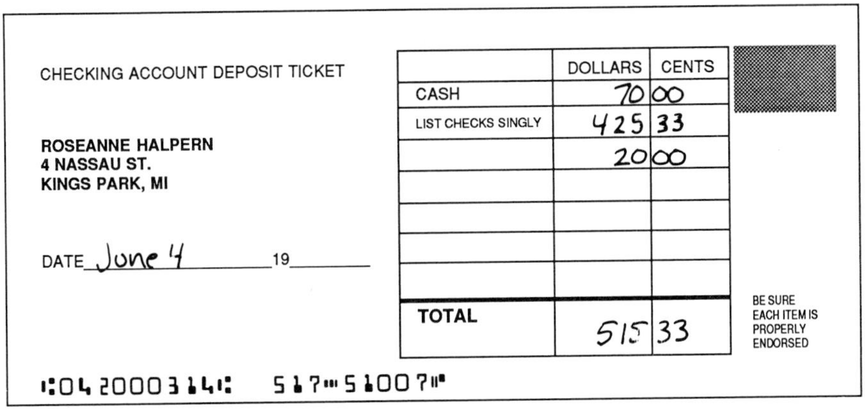

CHECKING ACCOUNT DEPOSIT TICKET

ROSEANNE HALPERN
4 NASSAU ST.
KINGS PARK, MI

DATE June 4 19

	DOLLARS	CENTS
CASH	70	00
LIST CHECKS SINGLY	425	33
	20	00
TOTAL	515	33

BE SURE EACH ITEM IS PROPERLY ENDORSED

⑆0420003114⑆ 517⑈5100 7⑈

Figure 13.2 Completed Deposit Slip

2. Roseanne purchased a bicycle from Papa Wheelie for $197.63 on June 20. What steps did she follow to write the check correctly?

Solution: Here is Roseanne's check.

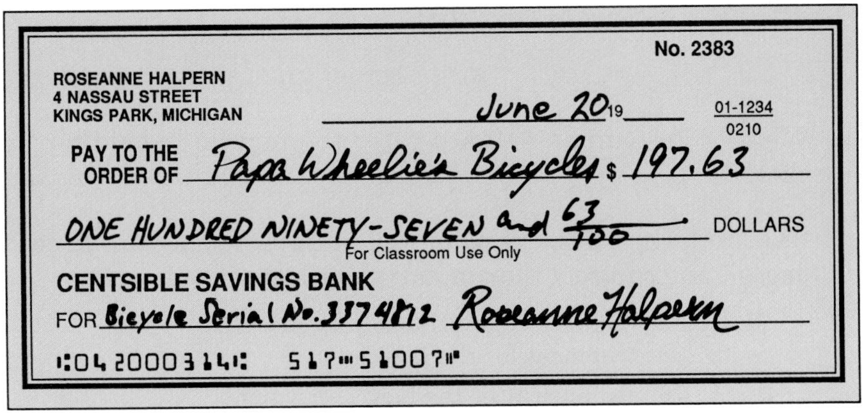

No. 2383

ROSEANNE HALPERN
4 NASSAU STREET
KINGS PARK, MICHIGAN

June 20 19 01-1234 / 0210

PAY TO THE ORDER OF Papa Wheelie's Bicycles $ 197.63

ONE HUNDRED NINETY-SEVEN and 63/100 DOLLARS

For Classroom Use Only

CENTSIBLE SAVINGS BANK

FOR Bicycle Serial No. 3374812 Roseanne Halpern

⑆0420003114⑆ 517⑈5100 7⑈

Follow these steps carefully whenever you fill out a check:

Step 1.   Enter the correct date.

Step 2.   Clearly enter the name of the payee on the line labeled "Pay to the Order Of." Draw a line between the payee's name and the dollar sign.

Step 3.   Write the amount of the check in numbers.

Step 4.   Write the amount of the check in words. Use the word *and* to separate the dollars from the cents. Express the cents as a fraction. Draw a line between the fraction and word *dollars*.

Step 5.   Sign the check.

Step 6.   Use the line in the lower left-hand corner to record information on what the check was written for.

3.   Roseanne has a regular checking account. Here is a page from Roseanne's check register. The **check register** is used to keep track of checks, deposits, and balances.

PLEASE BE SURE TO DEDUCT CHARGES THAT AFFECT YOUR ACCOUNT			SUBTRACTIONS			ADDITIONS	BALANCE FORWARD	
ITEM NO. OR TRANSACTION CODE	DATE	DESCRIPTION OF TRANSACTION	AMOUNT OF PAYMENT OR WITHDRAWAL (-)	✓	OTHER	AMOUNT OF DEPOSIT OR INTEREST (+)	890	00
2382	6/3	TO Safran's Piano Store FOR Piano Tuning	50 00				– 50 840	00 00
	6/4	TO DEPOSIT FOR				515 33	+ 515 1,355	33 33
2383	6/20	TO Papa Wheelie's Bicycles FOR Bicycle Serial No. 3374812	197 63				–197	63
		TO						

What is Roseanne's balance after the bicycle is paid for by check?

Solution: On a check register, you must remember to *add* each deposit and *subtract* the amount of each check you write.

$1,355.33   balance before the bicycle purchase
– 197.63   payment for the bicycle
$1,157.70   balance after the bicycle payment

Roseanne's balance is $1,157.70 after paying for the bicycle. Here is the completed check register entry.

ITEM NO. OR TRANSACTION CODE	DATE	DESCRIPTION OF TRANSACTION	AMOUNT OF PAYMENT OR WITHDRAWAL (-)	✓	OTHER	AMOUNT OF DEPOSIT OR INTEREST (+)	BALANCE FORWARD	
		PLEASE BE SURE TO DEDUCT CHARGES THAT AFFECT YOUR ACCOUNT SUBTRACTIONS ADDITIONS					890	00
2382	6/3	TO Safran's Piano Store FOR Piano Tuning	50 00				− 50 840	00 00
	6/4	TO DEPOSIT FOR				515 33	+ 515 1,355	33 33
2383	6/20	TO Papa Wheelie's Bicycles FOR Bicycle Serial No. 3374812	197 63				− 197 1,157	63 70
		TO						

Since Roseanne has a regular checking account, there is no per check fee. Follow these steps carefully whenever you fill out a check register:

Step 1. Enter the number of the check.

Step 2. Enter the date the check is written.

Step 3. Describe the transaction (to whom the check is written or the word *deposit*).

Step 4. Enter what the payment is for.

Step 5. Enter the amount the check is written for in the column labeled "Subtractions."

Step 6. Enter deposits in the column labeled "Additions."

Step 7. Enter each deposit or withdrawal in the right-hand column before adding or subtracting.

4. Carlos has a special checking account. He must pay 20 cents for each check he writes. A page from his check register is shown at the top of page 536. What is his balance after he enters the amount of the check he wrote for the tune-up?

PLEASE BE SURE TO DEDUCT CHARGES THAT AFFECT YOUR ACCOUNT			SUBTRACTIONS			ADDITIONS	BALANCE FORWARD	
ITEM NO. OR TRANSACTION CODE	DATE	DESCRIPTION OF TRANSACTION	AMOUNT OF PAYMENT OR WITHDRAWAL (-)	✓	OTHER	AMOUNT OF DEPOSIT OR INTEREST (+)	710	00
340	8/10	TO Circle Cruises FOR boat ride	50 00		.20		− 50 659	20 80
341	8/12	TO Royal Ranch Club FOR pool dues	400 00		.20		−400 259	20 60
	8/15	TO DEPOSIT FOR				600 00	+ 600 859	00 60
342	8/17	TO Maple Place Garage FOR Tune-up	75 00		.20			
		TO						

Solution: Remember that each check costs Carlos 20 cents to write.

$75.00   amount of check written for tune-up
+ .20   per check fee
$75.20   amount to be subtracted

$859.60   balance before check number 342
− 75.20   amount to be subtracted
$784.40   balance after check number 342

Carlos's balance is $784.40 after paying for the tune-up. Here is the completed check register entry.

PLEASE BE SURE TO DEDUCT CHARGES THAT AFFECT YOUR ACCOUNT			SUBTRACTIONS			ADDITIONS	BALANCE FORWARD	
ITEM NO. OR TRANSACTION CODE	DATE	DESCRIPTION OF TRANSACTION	AMOUNT OF PAYMENT OR WITHDRAWAL (-)	✓	OTHER	AMOUNT OF DEPOSIT OR INTEREST (+)	710	00
340	8/10	TO Circle Cruises FOR boat ride	50 00		.20		− 50 659	20 80
341	8/12	TO Royal Ranch Club FOR pool dues	400 00		.20		−400 259	20 60
	8/15	TO DEPOSIT FOR				600 00	+ 600 859	00 60
342	8/17	TO Maple Place Garage FOR Tune-up	75 00		.20		75 784	20 40
		TO						

5. Lucy has a special checking account. On the first day of each month, a monthly maintenance fee of $2 is automatically deducted from her account. A page from her check register is shown at the top of page 537. What is her balance after the bank deducts this fee on April 1?

PLEASE BE SURE TO DEDUCT CHARGES THAT AFFECT YOUR ACCOUNT			SUBTRACTIONS			ADDITIONS	BALANCE FORWARD	
ITEM NO. OR TRANSACTION CODE	DATE	DESCRIPTION OF TRANSACTION	AMOUNT OF PAYMENT OR WITHDRAWAL (-)	✓	OTHER	AMOUNT OF DEPOSIT OR INTEREST (+)	993	15
420	3/25	TO Sheldon's Lodge FOR Vacation Weekend	150 00				− 150 843	00 15
421	3/27	TO Glen Oaks Village FOR Rent	600 00				− 600 243	00 15
422	3/31	TO Fred Korahais FOR Music lesson	50 00				− 50 193	00 15
	4/1	TO Bank's FOR Monthly Fee	2 00				− 2	00
		TO FOR						

Solution: Lucy must remember to enter this fee and subtract it.

$193.15   balance on March 31
− 2.00   monthly fee deducted April 1
$191.15   balance after fee has been deducted

Lucy's balance is $191.15 after the monthly maintenance fee has been paid. Here is the completed check register entry.

PLEASE BE SURE TO DEDUCT CHARGES THAT AFFECT YOUR ACCOUNT			SUBTRACTIONS			ADDITIONS	BALANCE FORWARD	
ITEM NO. OR TRANSACTION CODE	DATE	DESCRIPTION OF TRANSACTION	AMOUNT OF PAYMENT OR WITHDRAWAL (-)	✓	OTHER	AMOUNT OF DEPOSIT OR INTEREST (+)	993	15
420	3/25	TO Sheldon's Lodge FOR Vacation Weekend	150 00				− 150 843	00 15
421	3/27	TO Glen Oaks Village FOR Rent	600 00				− 600 243	00 15
422	3/31	TO Fred Korahais FOR Music lesson	50 00				− 50 193	00 15
	4/1	TO Bank's FOR Monthly Fee	2 00				− 2 191	00 15
		TO FOR						

Problems

1. Phyllis is depositing a $762.44 paycheck, a $620 income tax refund check, and $70 in cash in her checking account. What is the total amount of her deposit?

2. For the last few years, Rick's special checking account has charged a monthly fee of $3 and a per check fee of 20 cents. Last

year Rick wrote 73 checks. What was the total fee he paid last year to maintain his checking account?

3. Pete deposited four checks in his checking account today. Approximately how many business days must Pete wait before he can start drawing on this deposit?

✓4. Complete items **a** through **y** from Luke's check register which is shown on page 539.

5. What is the balance forward that will be entered on the top of the next page of Luke's check register, shown in Problem 4?

6. Complete items **a** through **k** for the special checking account shown on page 540. There is a per check fee of 25 cents and a $2.50 monthly fee automatically deducted by the bank on the first day of each month.

✓7. What balance forward will be entered on the next page of the check register shown in Problem 6?

8. Ed has an EFT card which he uses to make nighttime withdrawals from the bank. Ed punched in his PIN and requested a withdrawal of $610. The ATM mistakenly issued Ed nine fifty-dollar bills, six twenty-dollar bills, and one ten-dollar bill. By how much was Ed shortchanged?

9. Can a voided check bounce? Explain your answer.

10. Penny has a regular checking account that requires a minimum balance of $400. A fee of $3 is charged each month that the balance falls below $400. Her account balance was $407 before the cost of 200 new checks was deducted from her account. The new checks cost $8. How much is in Penny's checking account after the new checks were paid for?

ITEM NO. OR TRANSACTION CODE	DATE	DESCRIPTION OF TRANSACTION	AMOUNT OF PAYMENT OR WITHDRAWAL (-)	✓	OTHER	AMOUNT OF DEPOSIT OR INTEREST (+)	BALANCE FORWARD
621	1/3	TO Telephone Co. FOR Dec. bill	d.				1,763 90
							− 71 10
							1,792 80
622	1/7	TO Banner Realty FOR Rent	500 00				e.
a.	1/8	TO Electric Co. FOR Dec. bill	51 12				f.
624	1/10	TO Cathy Santoro FOR Piano Lesson	25 00				g.
							h.
	1/15	TO DEPOSIT FOR				650 00	i.
							j.
625	1/15	TO Don's Day Camp FOR Kids summer camp	200 00				k.
							l.
626	1/15	TO Ed's Sporting Goods FOR Winter Coat	90 00				m.
							n.
627	1/15	TO Maple Place Garage FOR antifreeze & Hose	49 00				o.
							p.
628	1/20	TO Dr. Moe Goldstein FOR Check-up	65 00				q.
							r.
b.	1/21	TO Hicksville H.M.O. FOR yearly premium	300 00				s.
							t.
	1/22	TO DEPOSIT FOR				400 00	u.
							v.
c.	1/23	TO State Ins. Co. FOR Auto Insurance	371 66				w.
		TO					371 66
							x.
							y.

PLEASE BE SURE TO DEDUCT CHARGES THAT AFFECT YOUR ACCOUNT

PLEASE BE SURE TO DEDUCT CHARGES THAT AFFECT YOUR ACCOUNT

ITEM NO. OR TRANSACTION CODE	DATE	DESCRIPTION OF TRANSACTION	SUBTRACTIONS AMOUNT OF PAYMENT OR WITHDRAWAL (-)	✓	OTHER	ADDITIONS AMOUNT OF DEPOSIT OR INTEREST (+)	BALANCE FORWARD
							471 90
444	6/23	TO Ed's Boat Rentals FOR Vacation cruise	75 00		.25		− 75 25
							396 65
445	6/25	TO Flashcard FOR monthly bill	112 60				
446	6/30	TO Glen Head Florist FOR Mom's birthday	27 50		.25		
	7/1	TO Deduction FOR Monthly Maintenance Fee	2 50				− 2 50
	7/4	TO DEPOSIT FOR				612 00	
	7/4	TO Kansas City Royals FOR 4 baseball tickets	34 00		.25		
		TO FOR					

SECTION 4 • RECONCILING A BANK STATEMENT

Michael Vlak is in the twelfth grade and has a part-time job. He opened a regular checking account a few months ago so that he could pay directly for personal expenses. Michael must maintain a minimum balance of $350 in his account. There are no fees, and the account earns no interest.

Michael keeps track of all checks he writes in his check register. He does all the computations by hand and goes over them with a calculator to make sure he is correct. Michael receives a statement and canceled checks from his bank each month. Michael's latest statement is shown in Figure 13.3.

			STARTING BALANCE - - - >	$1,389.54

Michael Vlak
17 Breeze Way
East Williston, NY 11001

ACCOUNT NUMBER 0000000
STATEMENT PERIOD 11/01-11/30

DATE	DESCRIPTION	CHECK NUMBER	TRANSACTION AMOUNT	BALANCE
11/04	W/D	NO.1766	9.00	$1,380.54
11/05	DEPOSIT		35.00	$1,415.54
11/11	DEPOSIT		100.00	$1,515.54
11/13	W/D	NO.1770	158.08	$1,357.46
11/17	W/D	NO.1768	46.50	$1,310.96
11/19	W/D	NO.1769	74.63	$1,236.33
11/27	W/D	NO.1765	19.50	$1,216.83
		ENDING BALANCE - - - >		$1,216.83

Figure 13.3 Michael Vlak's Bank Statement

You should become familiar with the terms used on a bank statement.

Account number. Your account number appears on the lower left-hand portion of your checks. Verify that it is correct on each statement you receive. Michael's account number is 0000000.

Statement period. The bank statement includes deposits and checks received by the bank for a period of approximately one month. Michael's **statement period** is from November 1 through November 30.

Starting balance. The **starting balance** is the amount of money in the checking account at the beginning of the statement period. Michael's starting balance on November 1 was $1,389.54.

Date. This is the date the bank receives a particular deposit or check. Dates listed for checks are usually *not* the date the check was written but the day the check clears. Remember, it usually takes several business days for a check to clear after it has been written.

Description. This column shows all deposits and checks. The symbol W/D stands for withdrawal (a check that has cleared). Michael's statement includes two deposits and five checks.

Check number. This is the number of each check that clears. Remember, check numbers appear in the upper right-hand corner of each check. Note that deposits are not numbered.

Transaction amount. This is the amount that is deposited or withdrawn.

Balance. This is the amount in the checking account after the transaction is entered.

Ending balance. This is the amount in the checking account at the end of the statement period.

Michael wants to make sure the bank's records are correct and that they agree with his own records. This task is not difficult except for one problem: monthly statements do not include checks that were written very recently.

Stores that receive checks take time to deposit them, and it takes a few business days for each check to clear. Checks that are received from out-of-state banks can take even longer to clear. Michael's bank will not necessarily receive his checks in the order that Michael wrote them. In addition, Michael's monthly statement may not include recent deposits to his checking account.

Michael *can* verify the bank's records even though they are not as up to date as his own. This procedure is called **balancing a checkbook** or **reconciling a bank statement.** The reverse side of the statement includes directions for reconciling the bank statement.

Skills and Strategies

Here you will learn how to reconcile a bank statement.

What steps should you follow to reconcile Mike's statement? First compare the entries in his check register (Figure 13.4) with the bank statement (Figure 13.3).

ITEM NO. OR TRANSACTION CODE	DATE	DESCRIPTION OF TRANSACTION	AMOUNT OF PAYMENT OR WITHDRAWAL (-)	✓	OTHER	AMOUNT OF DEPOSIT OR INTEREST (+)	BALANCE FORWARD 748 95
1763	10/13	TO Deepdale Country Club / FOR Swimming lessons	50 00				- 50 00 / 698 95
1764	10/13	TO Joe's Sporting Goods / FOR Tennis Racket	48 00	✓			- 48 00 / 650 95
1765	10/14	TO Ellio's Pizzeria / FOR Pizza Party	19 50	✓			- 19 50 / 631 45
1766	10/15	TO Bethpage Auto Parts / FOR Air Filter	9 00	✓			- 9 00 / 622 45
	10/15	TO Deposit / FOR		✓		100 00	+ 100 00 / 722 45
1767	10/16	TO Maple Place Garage / FOR Inspection	18 00				- 18 00 / 704 45
1768	10/18	TO Ticket Man / FOR Concert Tickets	46 50	✓			- 46 50 / 657 95
1769	10/21	TO Caruso's Restaurant / FOR Dinner	74 63	✓			- 74 63 / 583 32
1770	10/22	TO Nickel's Home Center / FOR Tool Chest	158 08	✓			-158 08 / 425 24
1771	11/4	TO Aunt Bella's Restaurant / FOR dinner	29 10				- 29 10 / 396 14
	11/5	TO DEPOSIT / FOR		✓		35 00	+ 35 00 / 431 14
1772	11/9	TO Living Color Lab / FOR Film Developing	15 00				- 15 00 / 416 14
	11/11	TO DEPOSIT / FOR		✓		100 00	+ 100 00 / 516 14
	12/1	TO DEPOSIT / FOR				125 00	+ 125 00 / 641 14

PLEASE BE SURE TO DEDUCT CHARGES THAT AFFECT YOUR ACCOUNT — SUBTRACTIONS — ADDITIONS

Figure 13.4 Mike's Check Register

Note that some entries from his check register are not on his bank statement. Some of these appeared on a previous month's statement. These are shown with a check mark, ✔.

Solution: Follow these steps carefully.

Step 1. Enter a check mark in the check register for each deposit and check listed on the monthly statement.

Deposits that do not have a check mark are called **outstanding deposits.** List all outstanding deposits.

Step 2. List checks that do not have any check mark, as shown in Figure 13.5. These are called **outstanding checks.**

CHECKS OUTSTANDING	
CHECK NO.	AMOUNT
1763	50 00
1767	18 00
1771	29 10
1772	15 00
TOTAL OF CHECKS OUTSTANDING	$112 10

Figure 13.5 Checks Outstanding

Step 3. Complete the information required in the checking account summary as shown in Figure 13.6 on page 545. Since several transactions took place since the ending balance was entered on the monthly statement, the balance from the checkbook does not equal the ending balance from the statement. On the checking account summary, the outstanding deposits and the outstanding checks are used to revise the ending balance from the statement.

ENDING BALANCE FROM STATEMENT	$ *628.24*
DEPOSITS OUTSTANDING	+ $ *125.00*
TOTAL OF CHECKS OUTSTANDING	– $ *112.10*
REVISED STATEMENT BALANCE	$ *641.14*
BALANCE FROM CHECKBOOK	$ *641.14*

Figure 13.6 Checking Account Summary

Step 4. Use the following calculator keystroke sequence to find Michael's revised statement balance.

AC 628.24 + 125 − 112.10 =

The display should read 641.14.

Step 5. The revised statement balance should equal the last balance in the check register. Michael's revised statement balance, $641.14, does equal his check register balance, so his account is reconciled.

If your own account does not reconcile, go back and recheck all the arithmetic in the check register and on the statement since the last time the account was reconciled. Be sure you remembered to subtract any monthly fees and per check charges on your check register.

Problems

✓ **1.** Elliot filled out the chart on the back of his monthly statement as shown at the top of page 546.

   a. How many checks are outstanding?

   b. What is the total amount of the outstanding checks?

   c. Is check number 2066 outstanding?

CHECKS OUTSTANDING	
CHECK NO.	AMOUNT
2073	265 | 80
2091	13 | 45
2092	868 | 91
2093	14 | 00
2094	127 | 37
TOTAL OF CHECKS OUTSTANDING	

2. Rona filled out the following information on the back of her monthly statement.

ENDING BALANCE FROM STATEMENT	$	725.71
DEPOSITS OUTSTANDING	+ $	610.00
TOTAL OF CHECKS OUTSTANDING	– $	471.19
REVISED STATEMENT BALANCE	$	b.
BALANCE FROM CHECKBOOK	$	864.52

    a. Write the calculator keystroke sequence that could be used to find Rona's revised statement balance.

    b. Find Rona's revised statement balance.

    c. Does Rona's account reconcile?

✓**3.** Ken filled out the following information on the back of his bank statement.

ENDING BALANCE FROM STATEMENT	$	197.10
DEPOSITS OUTSTANDING	+ $	600.00
TOTAL OF CHECKS OUTSTANDING	– $	615.15
REVISED STATEMENT BALANCE	$	a.
BALANCE FROM CHECKBOOK	$	210.10

a. Find Ken's revised statement balance.

b. Is Ken's checking account balanced? Explain.

4. Laurie opened a checking account last month. Today she received her first bank statement. The statement listed 3 deposits and 17 checks that cleared. Laurie's check register shows 5 outstanding checks. How many checks has Laurie written since opening her account?

✓**5.** Jill cannot maintain the $1,000 minimum balance required to keep her regular checking account. She will switch to a special checking account with a per check fee of 20 cents and a $2 monthly maintenance fee. Jill wants to estimate her average fees per month for checking. She lists the following information from her last four monthly statements:

Month	Number of Checks Listed on Statement
May	14
June	19
July	23
August	24

a. What is the mean number of checks Jill wrote out per month during the last four months?

b. Based on the mean, about how much can Jill expect to pay in per check fees each month after she switches to the special account?

    c. Use your answer to item **b** to approximate Jill's total checking account fees for an entire year. Include monthly fees and per check fees.

6. Figure 13.7 shows Tom Weaver's monthly statement. Figure 13.8 is his check register. Use Tom's monthly statement and check register to complete items **a** through **f** related to his checking account summary in Figure 13.9.

Tom Weaver
41 Slider Lane
Greenwich, CT

ACCOUNT NUMBER 76666600A
STATEMENT PERIOD 3/01–3/31

STARTING BALANCE - - - > $871.50

DATE	DESCRIPTION	CHECK NUMBER	TRANSACTION AMOUNT	BALANCE
3/3	W/D	NO. 395	79.00	$792.50
3/4	DEPOSIT		600.00	$1,392.50
3/10	W/D	NO. 396	51.10	$1,341.40
3/14	W/D	NO. 393	12.00	$1,329.40
3/19	W/D	NO. 394	133.81	$1,195.59
3/24	DEPOSIT		250.00	$1,445.59
3/30	W/D	NO. 398	11.40	$1,434.19

ENDING BALANCE - - - -> $1,434.19

Figure 13.7 Tom Weaver's Monthly Statement

ITEM NO. OR TRANSACTION CODE	DATE	DESCRIPTION OF TRANSACTION	AMOUNT OF PAYMENT OR WITHDRAWAL (-)		✓	OTHER	AMOUNT OF DEPOSIT OR INTEREST (+)		BALANCE FORWARD 948 30	
392	2/20	TO Conn Telephone Co. / FOR Telephone Bill	76	80	✓				-76 871	80 50
393	2/21	TO Rod's Bike Shop / FOR TIRE	12	00	✓				-12 859	00 50
394	3/1	TO Windows Restaurant / FOR Dinner	133	81	✓				-133 725	81 69
395	3/2	TO Centsible Bank / FOR Loan	79	00	✓				-79 646	00 69
	3/4	TO DEPOSIT / FOR			✓		600	00	+600 1,246	00 69
396	3/4	TO Spear's Dept. Store / FOR Auto Parts	51	10	✓				-51 1,195	10 59
397	3/15	TO Mary Lewis / FOR Gift	50	00	✓				-50 1,145	00 59
398	3/21	TO Sea Cliff Records / FOR Compact Disc	11	40	✓				-11 1,134	40 19
	3/21	TO DEPOSIT / FOR					250	00	+250 1,384	00 19
399	4/2	TO Ciangiola Motors / FOR Towing car	39	00	✓				-39 1,345	00 19
	4/3	TO DEPOSIT / FOR					700	00	+700 2,045	00 19
		TO								

PLEASE BE SURE TO DEDUCT CHARGES THAT AFFECT YOUR ACCOUNT   SUBTRACTIONS   ADDITIONS

Figure 13.8   Tom's Check Register

ENDING BALANCE FROM STATEMENT		a. $_____
DEPOSITS OUTSTANDING	+	b. $_____
TOTAL OF CHECKS OUTSTANDING	−	c. $_____
REVISED STATEMENT BALANCE		d. $_____
BALANCE FROM CHECKBOOK		e. $_____

Figure 13.9   Tom's Checking Account Summary

f. Is Tom's checking account balanced? (*Hint:* If you find that Tom's account is not balanced, recheck the arithmetic in his check register and on the statement. Also check your own work.)

7. Pictured in Figures 13.10 and 13.11 are Dyna Evalin's most recent statement and a page from her check register. Use the statement and the check register to complete items **a** through **f** about her checking account summary shown in Figure 13.12.

Dyna Evalin
2 Patch Drive
Mortin, WI

ACCOUNT NUMBER 0000000
STATEMENT PERIOD 5/01–5/31

STARTING BALANCE - - - > $1,298.46

DATE	DESCRIPTION	CHECK NUMBER	TRANSACTION AMOUNT	BALANCE
5/1	DEPOSIT		30.00	$1,328.46
5/4	W/D	NO.785	50.00	$1,278.46
5/4	W/D	NO.782	50.00	$1,228.46
5/15	W/D	NO.787	38.00	$1,190.46
5/16	DEPOSIT		1,209.00	$2,399.76
5/26	W/D	NO.788	200.00	$2,199.76

ENDING BALANCE - - - -> $2,199.76

Figure 13.10 Dyna Evalin's Monthly Statement

PLEASE BE SURE TO DEDUCT CHARGES THAT AFFECT YOUR ACCOUNT			SUBTRACTIONS				ADDITIONS		BALANCE FORWARD	
ITEM NO. OR TRANSACTION CODE	DATE	DESCRIPTION OF TRANSACTION	AMOUNT OF PAYMENT OR WITHDRAWAL (-)		✓	OTHER	AMOUNT OF DEPOSIT OR INTEREST (+)		1,298	46
782	4/20	TO Ray Smith FOR Insurance	50	00	✓				-50 00 / 1,248 46	
783	4/22	TO Darian Antiques FOR Table	325	80					-325 80 / 922 66	
784	4/23	TO VOID FOR							— / 922 66	
	5/1	TO DEPOSIT FOR			✓		30	00	+30 00 / 952 66	
785	5/1	TO NEW YORK BOOKS FOR TEXTBOOK	50	00	✓				-50 00 / 902 66	
786	5/11	TO GLENDEN CORP. FOR RENT	625	00					-625 00 / 277 66	
787	5/12	TO MARSHA'S FLOWERS FOR BOUQUET	38	00	✓				-38 00 / 239 66	
788	5/13	TO Taylor's Dept. Store FOR Summer Clothes	200	00	✓				-200 00 / 39 66	
	5/16	TO DEPOSIT FOR			✓		1,209	30	1,209 30 / 1,248 96	

Figure 13.11 Dyna's Check Register

ENDING BALANCE FROM STATEMENT		a. $_____
DEPOSITS OUTSTANDING	+	b. $_____
TOTAL OF CHECKS OUTSTANDING	−	c. $_____
REVISED STATEMENT BALANCE		d. $_____
BALANCE FROM CHECKBOOK		e. $_____

Figure 13.12   Dyna's Checking Account Summary

    f. Is Dyna's checking account balanced? (*Hint:* If you find that Dyna's account is not balanced, recheck the arithmetic in her check register and on the statement. Also check your own work.)

✓ **8.** Pamela opened a special checking account recently. There is a per check fee of 25 cents and a $3 monthly fee. Pamela received her first monthly statement last week. The statement showed that 13 checks cleared. Pamela couldn't get her account reconciled because she forgot to subtract the fees. What was the total of the fees on her monthly statement?

  9. Yesterday, Maura opened a NOW checking account that pays 6% interest compounded daily. She started the account with a deposit of $7,500. What was her first day's interest rounded to the nearest cent?

✓ **10.** Last month Ray opened two accounts at Lewis Savings Bank. His long-term $10,000 savings account pays 6% interest compounded monthly. His checking account has a per check fee of 20 cents and a $4 monthly fee. Last month, 27 of Ray's checks cleared.
    a. How much interest did Ray receive on his savings account the first month?
    b. How much did Ray spend on checking account fees the first month?
    c. Did Ray's savings account earn enough interest to cover his checking account fees the first month?

• KEY TERMS

To find the definition of any term introduced in the chapter, refer to the Glossary in the back of this book.

automatic teller machines (ATM)

balance

balancing a checkbook

beneficiary

bounce

canceled checks

certificate of deposit (CD)

check

checking account

check register

clear

compound interest

custodian

custodian-for-a-minor account

debit card

deposit

deposit slip

drawer

electronic funds transfer (EFT)

endorsing the check

Federal Deposit Insurance Corporation (FDIC)

free checking

individual account

insufficient funds

interest

joint account

long-term account

minimum balance

minor

money market certificate

monthly statement

negotiable order of withdrawal (NOW) account

opens

outstanding checks

outstanding deposits

overdraft protection

passbook

payee

per check fee

personal identification number

principal

reconciling a bank statement

regular checking account

savings account

simple interest

special checking account

starting balance

statement period

stop payment

swatches

transactions

trustee

voided check

voluntary trust account

withdrawal

withdrawal slip

● REVIEW PROBLEMS

Round your answers to the nearest cent.

1. Janet is writing a check for a purchase costing $11,032.71. Write this amount in words.

2. Diane takes four checks to her bank: $371.12, $415.20, $80, and $21.03. She wants $250 in cash, and the rest she wants to deposit in her savings account. What is the total amount that will be credited to her account?

3. Pierre opened a savings account today with a deposit of $1,070. The account pays $6\frac{1}{4}\%$ interest compounded daily. How much interest will Pierre receive the first day?

4. Alice deposited $19,000 in a certificate of deposit that pays $7\frac{3}{4}\%$ interest compounded semiannually. She does not make deposits or withdrawals from this account. The certificate expires in six months, and the bank will write Alice a check for her principal and interest. Write in words the amount Alice will receive.

5. Paul is reconciling his checking account statement. The statement shows an ending balance of $1,718, and Paul has $910 in outstanding deposits and $615 in outstanding checks. What is Paul's revised statement balance?

6. Rachel has a savings account that pays 6% interest compounded daily. Her savings bank requires her to maintain a $500 balance to receive interest. For each month the balance falls below $500, there is a fee of $1. Rachel now has $480 in the account. She will not be making deposits or withdrawals for three months because she is going to Europe. What will Rachel's balance be in three months?

7. Kelly was ripping a check out of her checkbook and by accident she ripped a page of the check register. Shown at the top of page 554 is the ripped page. She cannot read the balance forward. What is Kelly's balance forward?

ITEM NO. OR TRANSACTION CODE	DATE	DESCRIPTION OF TRANSACTION	AMOUNT OF PAYMENT OR WITHDRAWAL (-)	✓	OTHER	AMOUNT OF DEPOSIT OR INTEREST (+)			
4112	6/30	TO Cooperstown Inn FOR Water Ski Rental	87 18					– 87	18
							$	315	00
4113	7/1	TO Zuk Studios FOR Prom Pictures	12 00					– 12	00
							$	303	00
4114	7/6	TO Safran Jeans Store FOR Designer Jeans	59 15					– 59	15
							$	243	85
	7/7	TO DEPOSIT FOR				100 00		+100	00
							$	343	85

Note at top of register: PLEASE BE SURE TO DEDUCT CHARGES THAT AFFECT YOUR ACCOUNT — SUBTRACTIONS — ADDITIONS

8. Alex's special checking account features a $4 monthly fee and a per check fee of 15 cents. Alex writes about 17 checks each month. At this rate, how much would Alex pay in checking fees per year?

9. Barbara is reconciling her bank statement with her check register. Shown below is the checking account summary from the back of her monthly statement.

ENDING BALANCE FROM STATEMENT		$ 726.00
DEPOSITS OUTSTANDING	+	$ 410.00
TOTAL OF CHECKS OUTSTANDING	–	$ 97.50
REVISED STATEMENT BALANCE		$
BALANCE FROM CHECKBOOK		$ 1,044.50

Is Barbara's checking account balanced? Explain.

10. Pictured in Figures 13.13 and 13.14 are Allison Shannon's checking account statement and check register. Use this information to answer questions **a** through **e** on pages 555-556.

Allison Shannon
3 Honey Drive
Flemington, NY

ACCOUNT NUMBER 76666600A
STATEMENT PERIOD 12/01–12/31

STARTING BALANCE - - - > $1,685.91

DATE	DESCRIPTION /	CHECK NUMBER	TRANSACTION AMOUNT	BALANCE
12/8	W/D	NO.1502	147.28	$1,538.63
12/10	W/D	NO.1501	130.00	$1,408.63
12/15	DEPOSIT		749.00	$2,157.63
12/23	W/D	NO.1504	250.00	$1,907.63
12/27	W/D	NO.1503	72.00	$1,835.63
12/29	W/D	NO.1506	26.00	$1,809.63

ENDING BALANCE - - - -> $1,809.63

Figure 13.13 Allison Shannon's Checking Account Statement

			AMOUNT OF PAYMENT OR WITHDRAWAL (-)	✓	OTHER	AMOUNT OF DEPOSIT OR INTEREST (+)	BALANCE FORWARD 1,685 91
DATE	NO.	DESCRIPTION OF TRANSACTION					
11/20	1500	TO Girl Scouts FOR cookies	32 00				− 32 00 / 1,653 91
11/30	1501	TO Bank of Seaford FOR loan payment	130 00	✓			−130 00 / 1,523 91
12/2	1502	TO Macy's Dept Store FOR radio	147 28	✓			−147 28 / 1,376 63
12/11	1503	TO Charge Tix FOR concert tickets	72 00	✓			−72 00 / 1,304 63
12/15		TO DEPOSIT FOR		✓		749 00	+749 00 / 2,053 63
12/16	1504	TO FLASHCARD FOR monthly payment	250 00	✓			−250 00 / 1,803 63
12/17	1505	TO Red Cross FOR donation	100 00				−100 00 / 1,703 63
12/18	1506	TO Daily Newspaper FOR subscription	26 00	✓			−26 00 / 1,677 63
1/5		TO DEPOSIT FOR				150 00	+150 00 / 1,827 63
		TO					

PLEASE BE SURE TO DEDUCT CHARGES THAT AFFECT YOUR ACCOUNT — SUBTRACTIONS — ADDITIONS

Figure 13.14 Allison's Check Register

a. What is the balance in Allison's account at the end of the statement period?

b. What is the total of all outstanding deposits?

    c. What is the total of all outstanding checks?

    d. Use your answers from items **a, b,** and **c** to find Allison's revised statement balance.

    e. Is Allison's checking account balanced? Explain your answer.

TOPIC *6* ENHANCE/ADVANCE

1. Go to the library and find the address of the Food and Drug Administration (FDA) in Washington, D.C. Write a business letter to the FDA requesting pamphlets on food and nutrition labeling. Share this information with your classmates.

2. Make a scale drawing of a house you design. Include bedrooms, bathrooms, a kitchen, a living room, a dining room, a den, and anything else you choose. Use a scale of $\frac{1}{4}$ inch = 1 foot and label all the dimensions in feet.

3. Make a set of furniture templates (as shown on pages 450–454). Arrange the templates in the house you designed in Enhance/Advance Activity 2.

4. Visit an insurance broker who sells life insurance. Ask the broker to show you mortality tables. Find out the annual cost per $1,000 for the following types of $100,000 policies: a 5-year term policy, a straight-life policy, an endowment policy, and a 20-year policy. Compute the total cost of these policies. Prepare a wall chart showing all this information.

5. Write a business letter to:
   Insurance Information Institute
   110 William Street
   New York, NY 10038
   Request information on life and health insurance. Share this information with your teacher and classmates.

6. Write a business letter to:
   American Council of Life Insurance
   1850 K Street, NW
   Washington, DC 20006
   Request information on life insurance. Share this information with your teacher and classmates.

7. Visit a real estate broker. Find out information on homes in your area, including:
   - price range of homes
   - average price of a private house
   - average price of a co-op

- average price of a condominium
- range of property taxes on private homes
- mortgage rates offered by local banks
- required percent of down payment

Ask any other questions about local real estate that you can think of. Prepare a report that includes all your findings.

8. Go to the library and find out the addresses of the gas, water, and electric companies that serve your area. Write a business letter to each company requesting information on how the electric, gas, and water bills are computed. Share this information with your classmates.

9. Visit a local bank. Make a list of the different types of savings accounts offered by the bank and the interest rate that each account currently pays. Be sure to include how often the interest is compounded on each type of account and whether a minimum balance is required. Prepare a wall chart displaying all the information you find.

10. Visit a local bank. Make a list of the different types of checking accounts offered by the bank. Be sure to include per check fees, monthly fees, required minimum balances, and interest rates for each account. Also find out the charges for ordering new checks, making a stop payment order, and bouncing a check. Prepare a wall chart displaying all the information you find.

11. Throughout *Dollars and Sense*, you have been urged to comparison-shop before making any purchase. Too often, it is not practical to comparison-shop funeral costs. Usually, the person planning the funeral is too sad to take time to compare prices. Funerals can be very expensive, however, so you should become familiar with funeral costs. Visit a local funeral parlor and discuss the price of a funeral with a representative. Ask questions. Include all the information in a report.

12. You are going to visit several places to find out the cost of a wedding and a honeymoon:
- catering hall
- photographer
- music agency
- florist
- travel agent

Discuss the cost of the wedding of your choice, and ask for written price estimates from each place you visit. Let the people you speak with know that you are getting the information for a school assignment. Make a scrapbook of the receipts and any pictures, pamphlets, or business cards you receive. Find the total cost of the wedding and honeymoon of your choice. Share this information with your classmates.

13. Do you have an idea of what it costs to purchase a house in your area? Look at the homes-for-sale part of the classified ad section of the newspaper every day for two weeks. Make a wall chart divided into four columns:
   Column 1. Under $100,000
   Column 2. $100,000–$199,999
   Column 3. $200,000–$299,999
   Column 4. $300,000 and over
   Cut out the classified ads, and paste them into each column according to price. Share this information with the class.

14. Visit a local bank, and find out the current interest rate for home mortgages. Also find out the monthly payments for the following mortgages:

Mortgage	APR	Monthly payment
$100,000 for 15 years		
$100,000 for 25 years		
$100,000 for 30 years		
$200,000 for 15 years		
$200,000 for 25 years		
$200,000 for 30 years		

TOPIC *6* MANIPULATIVE ACTIVITY

INTERIOR DESIGN

Interior decorators combine mathematics and their artistic sense to design rooms or entire houses. People usually want to get an idea of what the interior decorators are planning before the room is actually worked on, so interior decorators draw up presentation boards for their clients. In this activity, you are going to combine your math and artistic ability!

Directions: You will need a large piece of white poster board, glue, a piece of quarter-inch graph paper, a tape measure, and samples of the carpeting, wallpaper, and paint you will use. These little samples are called **swatches**.

1. Pick a room. Measure it using the tape measure. Record all the dimensions.

2. Draw the room to quarter-inch scale ($\frac{1}{4}''$ represents $1'$) on the graph paper. Label doors, windows, and dimensions clearly.

3. Find the area and perimeter of the room.

4. Visit a paint store, hardware store, or decorating store. Ask for swatches of the wallpaper and carpeting you would use. Also get a sample of the paint colors you would use. Find out the total cost of purchasing these items for the room you chose by showing your scale drawing to the salesperson.

5. Get a catalog or decorating magazine and cut out pictures of the furnishings you would use. You can include furniture, blinds, curtains, wall hangings, and so forth.

6. Glue the swatches, roomplan, and furniture pictures on to the presentation board.

7. List the area, perimeter, cost of each item, and total cost on the presentation board.

TOPIC *6* COMPUTER APPLICATION

SAVINGS ACCOUNTS

As you have seen, it is fairly simple to determine how much interest a certain principal earns on accounts that are compounded annually and semiannually. These methods of compounding require only a few calculations that can easily be done with paper and pencil. Accounts that are compounded monthly, daily, and even hourly are much more difficult to compute by hand.

By using the *Savings Accounts* program, you will use the computer to compute the amount of interest earned on accounts that are compounded in different ways.

Directions: If necessary, follow the start-up procedures for your computer which are found in Appendix A. Select Topic 6 titled *Savings Accounts* from the Main Menu. Follow the instructions on your computer screen to find the missing information in the following chart. Once this has been completed, run the program again for any principal, for one year, and at any given interest rate. Do not write in this book. Make a similar chart on a piece of paper, then fill in the proper answers as you see them displayed on the screen.

Yearly Interest Earned
When Compounded

Principal	Rate	Annually	Semiannually	Monthly	Daily	Hourly
$50	6%					
$100	7%					
$500	6.5%					
$1,000	7.25%					
$10,000	8.5%					

APPENDIX A

START-UP PROCEDURES FOR COMPUTER APPLICATIONS

Start-Up Procedures for the Apple IIe, Apple IIc, and Apple IIGS

Step 1. Turn on the television/monitor.

Step 2. Open the door to the disk drive. If your microcomputer has more than one drive, be sure to open the door to Drive 1.

Step 3. With your thumb on the diskette label, carefully insert the *Computer Applications* program diskette into Drive 1 with the label facing upwards. The diskette is completely inserted when the label is past the entrance to the drive.

Step 4. Gently close the disk drive door.

Step 5. If the computer is off, reach to the back left side of the machine and turn on the power switch. If your computer is already on, you must boot the diskette. On the Apple IIe, IIc, and IIGS, hold down the CONTROL and OPEN APPLE keys, and at the same time press RESET. The power light on the computer will illuminate. The red IN USE light on the disk drive will come on and you will hear a soft whirring sound. After a few seconds, the title screen will be displayed.

Step 6. Press the RETURN key to continue until you have passed the three opening screens. After the third opening screen, the message LOADING COMPUTER APPLICATIONS will appear. The *Computerized Applications* Main Menu will then come up.

Compiled Start-Up Procedures for the IBM PC, PCjr, and Tandy 1000

Step 1. Carefully insert your copy of the DOS diskette into Drive A with the label facing up. The diskette is completely inserted when the label is past the entrance to the drive.

Step 2.   If the computer is off, turn on the power switch. If the computer is already turned on, hold down the control (Ctrl), alternate (Alt), and the delete (Del) key at the same time. The cursor will appear in the upper left corner of the screen and the red light on Drive A will come on. A prompt message will appear on the screen indicating that the current date should be key-entered.

Step 3.   Key-enter the date or just press the ENTER key. The prompt to key-enter the current time will then be displayed.

Step 4.   Key-enter a new time or just press the ENTER key. You should see the A> displayed on the screen.

Step 5.   Remove the DOS diskette from Drive A.

Step 6.   Insert the *Computerized Applications* program diskette into Drive A.

Step 7.   Key-enter CONTROL and press the ENTER key.

Step 8.   Press the ENTER key to continue through the opening screens. The *Computerized Applications* Main Menu will appear. You are now ready to operate the software.

APPENDIX B

ANSWERS TO SELECTED PROBLEMS

TOPIC 1   LET THE BUYER PREPARE

CHAPTER   *1*   Let the Buyer Beware

Section 1 • Types of Warranties: **2.** no, the warranty expires on July 30 of the following year   **4.** Dec. 26   **6.** Dec. 31   **8.** July 29

Section 2 • The Sales Receipt: 4a. $10 \times 6.5 = 65$ 4b. **AC** 10.2 **×** 6.7 **=**   4c. 68.34   **8.** $535.45   11a. $119.80   11b. $21.80   11c. $24   11d. $38.50   11e. $204.10   13a. $59.97   13b. $10.00   13c. $94.95   13d. $164.92

Section 3 • Discounts and Percents: 1a. 10%   1b. $\frac{10}{100}$ 1c. .10   1d. 60%   2a. .98   2c. .162   2g. .188   2k. .007   4a. .30   4b. .50   4c. yes   4d. no

Section 4 • Sales Tax: 1a. $72.56   1e. $16.42   3c. 3,200,000   3e. $2,440   **5.** $36   7a. $676   7b. $930   7c. $1,146   8a. $15,850

Section 5 • Catalog Shopping: 1h. $14.25   1i. $19.25   1j. $53.90   3a. 4   3b. $46   **6.** $1,361.05   7a. $294.60   7b. 120   7c. 3   7d. $29.85   7e. $324.45   7f. $19.20   7g. $343.65

Section 6 • Understanding Prices: 1d. File Cabinet, Retail Price, $43.30   1e. Rocking Chair, Markup, $50.00   2g. $38.33   2h. $74.83   2k. $172.20   5a. $32.30   5b. $70.30   5c. $281.20   5d. $70.30   5e. $210.90   5f. $16.87   5g. $227.77

Section 7 • Where to Shop: 1a. $69   1b. $1,219   1c. $920   1d. $975.20   1e. $850.50   1f. the damaged couch   **3.** $44   5a. $1.32   5b. $6.96

Section 8 • Supermarket Pricing: 1e. $2.97   1f. $1.86   1g. $2.32   **3.** 1.8 pounds   5d. $1.22   5e. $.89   8a. $.03   8b. $.03125   8c. department store

CHAPTER   2 Measurement

Section 1 • Units of Length: **1.** a   **3.** d   **6.** d   **11a.** 75.3 m
11b. Eiffel Tower

Section 2 • Units of Weight: **1.** b   **4.** b   **7.** a   **10.** a
14a. 90 kg   **14b.** $180.00   **14c.** overcharged by $25.79

Section 3 • Units of Liquid Measure: **1.** a   **4.** a   **5.** c   **9.** a
12. 372 L

Section 4 • Rulers and Tape Measures: **1a.** 2″   **1b.** $2\frac{1}{2}$″
1c. $2\frac{3}{4}$″   **1d.** $3\frac{1}{8}$″   **1e.** $3\frac{3}{16}$″   **4.** AC 8 ÷ 7 =

Section 5 • Perimeter of Polygons: **1a.** 4   **1d.** 6   **1i.** 9   **1l.** 12
2b. $\frac{25}{8}$ **2h.** $\frac{46}{5}$ **2j.** $\frac{40}{7}$ **3b.** $3\frac{4}{5}$ **3d.** $7\frac{1}{3}$ **3h.** $8\frac{2}{6} = 8\frac{1}{3}$
5. $50\frac{1}{2}$ ft   **7a.** 200 ft   **7b.** 100   **7c.** $936   **9.** 35 m

Section 6 • Circumference: **2.** $18\frac{1}{2}$ yds   **4.** AC 8 × 3.14 =
7. AC 20 × 2 × 3.14 =   **10.** 18.84″

Section 7 • Area: **2c.** 93   **2f.** 13   **3c.** 4   **3f.** $5\frac{15}{16}$ **5a.** 105 ft
5b. 50.4 m   **7.** 156.25 sq ft   **10.** 78.5 sq ft   **13.** $9\frac{1}{2}$ ft

---

TOPIC 2   TRAVEL AND TOURISM

CHAPTER   3 The Automobile

Section 1 • Classified Ads: **2.** $67.50   **4.** $40   **7.** $86.50
9. $13.30

Section 2 • Using Statistics: **1b.** 98   **2b.** mean = 49; median =
45   **3b.** mean = 6; median = 5; mode = 2   **6a.** $113
6b. $80   **6c.** median; $265 is extreme   **9.** $4.25

Section 3 • Probability: The Basis of Insurance: **2a.** $\frac{1}{5000}$
2b. $\frac{4999}{5000}$ **2c.** 1:4999   **4b.** 15   **4c.** LB, LW, LT, LG, LM, CB, CW,
CT, CG, CM, VB, VW, VT, VG, VM   **6.** $26 \times 26 \times 26 \times 10 \times 10$
= 1,757,6000   **8.** $6 \times 5 \times 4 \times 3 \times 2 \times 1 = 720$

Section 4 • Automobile Insurance: **2a.** 2   **2b.** $438.15
5a. $392   **5b.** $294   **5c.** $294   **7a.** $10,000   **7b.** $2,000
11a. PD   **11b.** $1,400   **11c.** collision   **11d.** $300

Section 5 • Automobile Maintenance Costs: **3.** $204   **5.** $252   **7.** $5,362   **10.** $.49

Section 6 • Driving Data: **2.** 15.5 hours   **5a.** 518.5 miles   **5b.** $114.07   **8a.** 52 feet   **8b.** 135.2 feet   **8c.** 187.2 feet

Section 7 • Renting a Car: **1.** $308   **4.** $244.10   **6a.** $3,000   **6b.** $1,100   **6c.** $0   **8a.** $206   **8b.** $174   **8c.** Sunshine; $32

Section 8 • Using a Road Map: **2a.** 91 miles   **2b.** 152 miles   **2c.** 254 miles   **2d.** 244 miles   **2e.** 154 miles   **5a.** 57 miles   **5b.** 50 miles   **5c.** 1 hour   **7a.** 310 miles   **7b.** 300   **7c.** 15 gallons   **7d.** No, 15 > 11   **7e.** $20.25   **7f.** 6 hours

CHAPTER   4   Be Your Own Travel Agent

Section 1 • Elapsed Time: **1e.** 11 hrs, 34 min   **1f.** 12 hrs, 5 min   **1g.** 23 hrs, 55 min   **3.** 1 hr, 46 min   **7.** 7:45 PM   **9.** 8 hrs, 15 min

Section 2 • Time Zones: **1b.** mountain   **1d.** eastern   **1g.** Pacific   **2c.** 6:07 PM   **2e.** 4:15 AM   **2f.** 12:23 AM   **4.** 6:30 PM   **7.** 3:30 AM

Section 3 • Purchasing Airline Tickets: **2.** $336   **4.** 197   **7.** $399   **9.** 142 mi

Section 4 • Reading Plane, Train, and Bus Schedules: **1.** 2:46 PM EST   **5.** snack   **8a.** 7:00 AM   **8b.** mountain   **8c.** 12:55 PM   **8d.** central   **8e.** 4 hrs, 55 min   **9.** 11:08 AM PST   **13.** 460 miles   **15.** 8 hrs, 10 min   **19.** 13 hrs, 35 min

Section 5 • Vacation Expenses: **4.** $10.30   **6.** $1,440   **10.** $1,820

TOPIC 3   THE STOCK MARKET

CHAPTER   5   Investing in Stocks and Bonds

Section 1 • Types of Business Organizations: **2.** $3,880,000   **4.** 2%   **7.** $25,000   **9.** 25%

Section 2 • Reading The New York Stock Exchange Ticker Tape: **2.** 600   **4.** $48.50   **6.** $7,475   **12.** IBM, 17,000S42$\frac{3}{8}$

Section 3 • Reading Newspaper Stock Tables: **3.** 12.50   **6.** 58.75   **9.** no change; net change is 0. (....)   **11a.** 31$\frac{1}{2}$ **11b.** 32$\frac{1}{2}$ **11d.** 16$\frac{5}{8}$

Section 4 • Stock Transactions: **2.** −$417   **5.** $176.38   **7.** $3,262.50   **9.** −$3,412.50

Section 5 • Stockbroker Commissions: **2a.** $3,425   **2b.** $34.25   **2c.** $3,459.25   **4a.** $8,100   **4b.** $162   **4c.** $7,938   **7.** $698.40   **10a.** .5   **10b.** .005   **10c.** $\frac{1}{2}$% < 1%   **10d.** no; 50% = .50 and $\frac{1}{2}$% = .005

Section 6 • Dividend Income: **1.** $431.75   **4.** $30   **6a.** $567   **6b.** $189   **6c.** no; 191.68 > 189   **9.** $12   **10a.** $210   **10b.** $4.20

Section 7 • Corporate Bonds: **2a.** .0625   **2b.** $62.50   **2c.** $31.25   **5a.** .0635   **5b.** $63.50   **5c.** $31.75   **5d.** 19   **5e.** $603.25   **6a.** .09   **6b.** $90   **6c.** $45   **6j.** .085   **6k.** $85   **6l.** $42.50

CHAPTER   6   Using Graphs to Display Business Information

Section 1 • Bar Graphs: **1.** 800   **3.** 200   **6a.** 3,050   **6b.** 610   **6c.** 700   **6d.** 700   **9.** 41   **12.** 3

Section 2 • Line Graphs: **1.** 150   **6.** 100   **8.** 15   **10.** 35   **13.** 25

Section 3 • Circle Graphs: **2.** 21   **3.** 15

Section 4 • Pictographs: **4.** 32   **5.** 20%   **7.** 3,500   **8.** 24,000

Section 5 • Graphing Stock Trends: **3.** 64,500   **5.** 43$\frac{3}{4}$ **7a.** 43$\frac{3}{4}$ **7b.** 43$\frac{3}{4}$ **7c.** 0   **9a.** April 19, 20   **9b.** April 13, 14

TOPIC 4   **CONSUMER CREDIT**

CHAPTER   **7   Loans and Installment Buying**

Section 1 • Beginning a Credit History: **1.** 15   **4a.** 20 checks
   4b. 40 weeks   **7.** 14 weeks   **9a.** 24 weeks   **9b.** no

Section 2 • Installment Purchases: **2.** $284   **4a.** $180   **4b.** 12
   4c. $1,416   **4d.** $1,596   **6.** $120   **9a.** 2   **9b.** $120
   9c. $117

Section 3 • Lending Institutions: **1.** Omni Trust   **4a.** .104
   4b. .105   **4c.** Federal Plumbers   **5.** Miller Credit Union, First
   Bank of Hanover, Glenlawn National Bank, Larson County
   Trust   **6.** Emten Consumer Finance Company, Richardsville
   Trust, First Bank of Linden County, The Robert National Bank,
   Lauraton Teachers Credit Union   **9.** yes, 72% of 3,000 = 2,160,
   and 2,160 > 2,000

Section 4 • Borrowing Money: **1a.** $621.95   **1b.** $155.72
   1c. $232.51   **3a.** $160.97   **3b.** $7,726.56   **3c.** $1,726.56
   5. $1,778.88   **8a.** Merit   **8b.** $1,297.76   **8c.** $1,410.08
   8d. $112.32   **10a.** $660   **10b.** $99.85   **10c.** $396.40
   10d. He should borrow the money. The loan's interest, $396.40, is
   less than the installment plan's interest.

CHAPTER   **8   Credit Cards**

Section 1 • Reading a Monthly Statement: **7.** $4,388.35
   8. 1.8%   **10.** It is correct.

Section 2 • Credit Card Finance Charges: **1.** $7.05   **3a.** 2%
   3b. $25   **5.** $0

TOPIC 5   **PERSONAL INCOME**

CHAPTER   **9   Getting a Job**

Section 1 • Looking for Employment: **2.** $461.54   **5a.** $425
   5b. $1,275   **5c.** $510   **7.** $296   **8.** $43.99   **10.** $95.58

Section 2 • Pay Periods: **1.** June 26   **4.** June 8, June 15, June 22,
   June 29, July 6   **9a.** $3,116.67   **9b.** $384.11   **9c.** $2,732.56

Section 3 • Hourly Pay: **2.** $88.80   **3a.** $10.50   **3b.** $63
   6. $301   **8a.** 50   **8b.** $240   **8c.** 10   **8d.** $12   **8e.** $360
   9a. $11.25   **9c.** $7.35   **9e.** $9.83

Section 4 • Commissions and Royalties: **3.** $231   **5.** $1,095
   7. $36,400   **10.** $762.50

Section 5 • Piecework Pay: **2.** $112.20   **4a.** $90.60
   4b. $242.60   **6.** $2,340   **8.** $96.33   **10a.** 317.4
   10b. 390   **10c.** median; 22 is an extreme number   **10d.** 390

Section 6 • Insurance Available to Employees: **2.** $157.44
   4a. $168.03   **4b.** $672.12   **6a.** $61,955   **6b.** $62,560
   6c. $35,933.90   **9a.** $1,129.60   **9b.** $282.40   **10.** $14.01

CHAPTER   *10*   Income Taxes

Section 1 • Social Security: **1a.** .0585   **1c.** .0613   **1e.** .067
   1g. .0715   **5.** $2,002.20   **7a.** $2,000   **7b.** $1,124   **9.** yes,
$33,111 > $32,400

Section 2 • Reading Tax Tables: **1a.** $1,867   **1c.** $3,044
   1e. $2,976   **2b.** $16,132.74   **2d.** $30,464.16   **2f.** $171,886.50
   5. $5,000

Section 3 • Net Pay: **7.** March 10, March 17, March 24   **9.** $364.52
   13. 24   **15.** $22,596.12

Section 4 • Filing Tax Returns: **1.** $29,962.16   **3a.** owe
   3b. $89   **6a.** $22,990.56   **6b.** no   **6c.** $990.56   **8a.** $240
   8b. $464   **8c.** yes, $464 > $240   **8d.** no, $464 < $480.14

Section 5 • Itemized Deductions: **3.** $2,306   **5.** $3,370
   7a. $14,144.20   **7b.** $1,673   **7c.** no   **7d.** $5,267.82
   9a. $21,855   **9b.** $3,535   **9e.** $21,655   **9f.** $3,483
   11c. $47,210   **11d.** $12,154.80   **11i.** $35,210   **11j.** $7,561.20

TOPIC 6   INDEPENDENT LIVING

CHAPTER   *11*   Where to Live

Section 1 • Finding a Place to Live: **2a.** $82,800   **2b.** $80,000
   2c. $80,000   **4.** $77.50   **8.** $200,000

Section 2 • Reading a Floor Plan: 1a. $\frac{1}{2}$ ft   1c. $\frac{1}{3}$ ft   1e. 1 ft
  1g. $\frac{7}{12}$ ft   **3.** 900 m²   **6a.** 21 ft by 13$\frac{3}{4}$ ft   **6b.** 69$\frac{1}{2}$ ft
  6c. 288$\frac{3}{4}$ sq ft   **6d.** 3   **10a.** 60 ft by 40 ft   **10b.** 2,400 sq ft
  10c. 20 ft by 40 ft   **10d.** 800 sq ft

Section 3 • Renting an Apartment: **2.** $1,100   **4.** $125
  7. $672.60   **9a.** $540   **9b.** $588.60   **9c.** no

Section 4 • Purchasing Your Own Home: 1a. $829.65
  1c. $1,362.95   **3.** $323,952   **6a.** $130,000   **6b.** $3,900
  8a. $1,287.50   **8b.** $107.29   **12.** $74.29   **14.** $88,318.80

Section 5 • Condominiums and Cooperative Residences:
  3a. $100   **3b.** $108   **5.** the Johnsons   **8.** 0.5%
  10a. $1,067.26   **10b.** $1,347.26   **13a.** $2,255.68
  13b. $2,460.68

Section 6 • Interior Design: **1b.** 4″   **1e.** 10$\frac{1}{4}$″   **1h.** 7″   **1j.** 7$\frac{1}{2}$″
  2b. 28 ft   **2e.** 23 ft   **2h.** 30 ft   **5a.** 10 ft × 12 ft   **7.** $632.69
  10a. 5$\frac{1}{2}$ ft   **10b.** 1$\frac{3}{8}$ **10c.** $\frac{1}{2}$″   **10d.** yes, 1$\frac{3}{8}$ < 1$\frac{1}{2}$

CHAPTER   *12*   Expenses for Your Budget

Section 1 • Utility Bills: **2.** 1280.414 cubic meters   **3d.** 191
  3e. 121.2   **5.** $35.04   **6b.** 9,416   **8a.** $372   **8b.** 12%
  8c. 31   **8d.** $12   **11a.** $30   **11b.** 43%   **11c.** no, 43% <
  50%   **13.** $.23   **15a.** $13.22

Section 2 • Homeowner's Insurance: **2a.** 4   **2b.** $62.50
  4. $490   **7a.** no   **7b.** $125,000   **10.** $12,192.62   **13a.** 810 sq
  ft   **13b.** 90 sq yd   **13c.** $1,684.80

Section 3 • Health Insurance and Generic Drugs: **3.** $84.50
  4a. $504.40   **4b.** $360.80   **4c.** $894.60   **7.** $10.49
  8. $9.72   **11a.** $.50   **11b.** $.25   **11c.** 50%   **14a.** $688
  14b. $688

Section 4 • Food and Nutrition: **3.** 6%   **5a.** 1 oz   **5b.** 10
  5c. 10 oz   **5d.** 300 calories   **5e.** 7   **5f.** 10   **7.** 4
  10. 54   **13a.** $7.50   **13b.** $390   **13c.** $490

Section 5 • Life Insurance: **2a.** $640   **2b.** $2,308.20
  2c. $1,608   **2d.** $882   **4.** $1,764   **5a.** $496   **5b.** $2,480
  5h. $4,960   **7.** $3,090   **11a.** $8   **11b.** $125,000
  14a. $4,200   **14b.** $116   **14c.** $40,000   **14d.** $40,000

Section 6 • Preparing a Budget: 4a. $200 4b. May, September
 6a. $900 6b. $75 10. $500 12. $26,300
 14a. $1,870 14b. $156

CHAPTER *13* Banking

Section 1 • Savings Accounts: 1a. .05 1e. .075 2. 8.2%, $8\frac{1}{4}$%,
 8.29%, $8\frac{3}{8}$%, $8\frac{1}{2}$% 4. $178 6. $1,793.80 7b. one thousand
 seven hundred six dollars and forty-three cents 7d. one million
 two hundred seventy thousand seven hundred six dollars and forty-
 three cents 7f. six hundred nine dollars and one cent
 10. $1,155.16 14. $977.30

Section 2 • Compound Interest: 2. $4,270 4a. $131.25
 4b. $3,631.25 4c. $136.17 4d. $3,767.42 4e. $267.42
 4f. $262.50 4g. $4.92 8a. $.73 8c. $4.76 8e. $.08
 9a. $.07 9b. $400.07 12b. $6.07 14. $87

Section 3 • Checking Accounts: 4a. 623 4b. 629 4c. 630
 4d. 71.10 4e. −500.00 4f. 1,292.80 4g. −51.12
 4h. 1,241.68 4i. −25.00 4j. 1,216.68 4k. +650.00
 4l. 1,866.68 7. $831.30

Section 4 • Reconciling a Bank Statement: 1a. 5 1b. $1,289.53
 1c. no 3a. $181.95 3b. no; $181.95 ≠ $210.10
 5a. 20 5b. $4.00 5c. $72 8. $6.25 10a. $50
 10b. $9.40 10c. yes

GLOSSARY

Account number

A unique number assigned to identify a credit card or other financial record.

Account type

A term on a statement that identifies the name of the credit card used to make the transactions listed on a bill.

Annual dividend

The profits distributed each year to shareholders of a corporation.

Annual percentage rate (APR)

The interest rate paid, expressed as a percent, calculated on a yearly basis.

Annually

Each year.

Area

The amount of space inside a flat, closed figure.

Arrival time

The time at which a plane, train, or bus gets to its destination.

Arrow diagram

A technique that can be used to show the amount of time that elapses between two given times.

Ascending

An order of arrangement from lowest to highest number, size, and so on.

Assessed value

The dollar amount used to determine property taxes; often called appraised value.

Assets

Anything of value owned by a person or company.

Attorney

Lawyer.

Automatic teller machines (ATM)

Convenient computer-controlled units located outside of a regular bank, which allow 24-hour-a-day deposits and withdrawals.

Automobile insurance

Protection against loss of money for injury or damage having to do with cars.

Automobile insurance policy

A contract between the owner of a car and an insurance company.

Available credit

The difference between the maximum amount a person can owe and the amount a person actually owes.

Average daily balance

The average of the daily amounts owed during the billing cycle.

Axes

The plural of axis.

Axis

A vertical or horizontal line on a graph.

Baggage insurance

A contract that provides protection in case of lost, stolen, or damaged baggage.

Bait and switch

An advertising strategy in which a store advertises an item at a discounted price, and when customers come to the store to ask about that item, they are persuaded to buy a higher-priced item instead.

Bakery thrift stores

Shops that sell bakery goods at a discount.

Balance

The amount of money in a savings account at any specific time.

Balancing a checkbook

Also called *reconciling a bank statement.*

A procedure by which a person verifies his or her own records with a bank's records and monthly statements.

Balloon payment

The last high payment, much larger than earlier required payments, required on a certain type of loan.

Banks

Financial institutions which, among other things, lend money.

Bar graph

A visual aid that uses thick lines or bars to show individual data, often used to compare amounts or sizes.

Basic charge

The rate paid for each day or week a car is rented, regardless of how much it was used.

Beneficiaries

1. Persons who receive the cash benefits of a life insurance policy.
2. In banking, the people who receive benefits or cash from a voluntary trust account upon the trustee's death.

Billing date

The date a bill is made out.

Binder

Money paid to the seller by an interested buyer to show that the buyer is serious about buying a house.

Biweekly

Every two weeks.

Board of directors

Those people elected by shareholders to manage a corporation.

Bodily injury liability (BI)

Insurance that pays medical expenses of anyone injured in a car accident other than the insured.

Bond

A document that proves that money was loaned to a corporation or a government.

Bounce

The refusal by a bank to pay the amount of a check because of insufficient funds in the check-writer's account.

Braking distance

The distance a car travels while braking to a complete stop.

Braking distance formula

A way to approximate the distance it takes to stop a car safely. Stated: $(.1 \times$ car speed$)^2 \times 5$.

Budget

An itemized spending plan.

Bumped

When someone is denied boarding a plane despite having a confirmed reservation.

Calculator keystroke sequence

Pressing certain calculator keys in a particular order.

Calories

The units used to measure the amount of energy produced by the food people eat.

Canceled checks

Those checks that have been paid from an account (cleared) and later usually returned, with the bank statement, to the person who wrote the check to be saved as a record of payment.

Capital

Money used to start or expand a business.

Car pool

A group of people who share the expenses of driving.

Car-rental insurance

Insurance that pays the policyholder part of the cost of a rented car if the policyholder's car is disabled in an accident.

Carrier

A company, such as bus, railroad, or airline, that transports people (or goods) to their destinations.

Catalog shopping

One way consumers can make purchases without going to a store. Consumers can make purchases after selecting from a brochure or booklet that lists and describes products available for order by mail.

Caveat emptor

From Latin, meaning: "Let the buyer beware." A phrase that is often used to warn consumers to be careful and informed shoppers and to know their rights before purchasing.

ccf

The symbol used on gas and water bills to represent 100 cubic feet.

Center

The exact middle; the midpoint of a circle equally distant from every point on the circumference of a circle.

Certificate of deposit (CD)

One type of account in which a bank pays a higher interest rate to a depositor who agrees not to make withdrawals on deposits for at least six months. A minimum deposit is usually required to start the certificate.

Check

A written request by a person to transfer money from his or her checking account.

Check register

A form used to keep track of checks, deposits, and balances.

Checking account

A banking arrangement by which people can withdraw money from their account and cover an expense by writing a check.

Chord

Any line segment that connects two different points on a circle.

Circle

A figure formed by a curved line at all points equally distant from the center.

Circle graph

A visual aid in the form of a circle divided into pie-shaped segments, often used to present data in percentages.

Circumference

The distance around a circle.

Claim

A request for payment from an insurance company due in accordance with an insurance policy.

Classified ads

Notices in a newspaper or magazine that advertise items available for sale, trade, and so on.

Clear

To pass (a check) through the banking system; to pay the amount on a check when there is enough money in the account.

Clearance centers

Places where major stores sell their damaged goods, floor samples, and overstocked items at a substantial discount.

Closing

A meeting attended by the buyer, the sellers, the attorneys, and a representative of the lending institution during which the official sale and transfer of title of a property takes place.

Collateral

Personal property held until a borrower repays a loan.

Collision-damage waiver

Insurance that enables a person who rents a car to be completely protected from financial loss in case of damages caused in an accident.

Collision insurance

Insurance that pays to repair or replace a car if it collides with another car or if it overturns.

Commercial bank

A financial institution that provides banking services required by businesses.

Commission

A stockbroker's fee; money paid to a salesperson or agent based on a percentage of the value of the goods he or she buys or sells.

Commission

Payment to a salesperson based on the total sales made.

Compound interest

The money earned on money deposited plus previous interest.

Comprehensive insurance

Insurance which pays for repairs (or replacement) for a car if it is damaged by natural disasters, vandalism, or is stolen.

Condominium

A group of apartments in which each apartment is individually owned.

Confirmed reservation

A ticket purchased for a certain flight that entitles the ticket holder to several specific benefits.

Consequential damages

Harm or loss following the use of defective goods or services.

Consumer

Anyone who buys goods or services.

Consumer finance company

A lending institution that gives loans to consumers whose credit ratings might not be acceptable to a bank or a credit union.

Cooperative resident

A form of home ownership in which the apartments or dwellings are owned jointly by those people who purchase shares in the co-op. These shares allow them to occupy an apartment and use the facilities.

Coordinates

The letters and numbers used to identify a particular location on a map.

Corporation

A form of business that is owned by one person or a group of people, each of whom invests money in the business and owns shares in the business.

Cosigner

A person who agrees to pay back a loan if the borrower is unable to make the payments.

Coupons

1. Parts of an advertisement which, when detached and redeemed, entitle the purchaser to some extra benefit such as reduced price, free gift, refund, contest entry, and so on.
2. Dated stubs on a bond that can be cashed in for interest payments.

Coverage limit

The maximum amount that an insurance company will reimburse a policyholder for a specific type of insurance policy.

Credit

1. An arrangement to purchase goods and services and pay for them in the future.
2. A payment made to reduce a debt.

Credit card invoice

A receipt used only for customers paying with credit cards.

Credit line

The maximum amount a person can owe at any specific time.

Credit rating

A report of how past financial obligations have been met.

Credit reporting agencies

Business establishments that compile financial records on users of credit.

Credit union

An organization that provides financial services for its members only.

Creditors

Organizations or persons that give or extend credit.

Cubic foot

A measurement of volume.

Custodian

For a bank account, the person who sets up and is in charge of the account for the benefit of a minor (a child).

Custodian-for-a-minor account

A bank account set up by an adult, called the *custodian,* for the benefit of a child, called the *minor.*

Customer scale

Scales that supermarket customers can use to check weights of products before bringing them to the check-out counter.

Data

Numerical facts; numbers; information.

Date of maturity

The date on a bond specifying when the face value of the bond must be paid to the owner.

Date of transaction

On a statement, the month and day when purchases were made or payments received.

Date posted

The month and day when the creditor received a copy of the credit card invoice or payments.

Daylight saving time

The term used when clocks are set ahead one hour in the spring.

Debit

The amount charged to an account.

Debit card

An arrangement, similar to a credit card, except that money for a purchase is immediately withdrawn from the customer's checking account when the debit card is used.

Debtors

Persons who use credit.

Decimal equivalent

A number written as a fraction or percent equal in value to that same number written in decimal form.

Deducted

Subtracted.

Deductible

The amount of money the insured person is responsible to pay; the insurance company is responsible for the remainder up to the insured maximum.

Deduction

Money withheld from a paycheck for taxes, social security, insurance, pension, and so on; also, that part of income that is not taxable. The amount a taxpayer may subtract from gross income when computing taxable income.

Deed

A legal document that specifies the title transfer from seller to buyer.

Denied boarding compensation

Payment given to bumped passengers to compensate for their inconvenience.

Denominator

The bottom number of a fraction; the number below the horizontal line of a fraction.

Dental insurance

A plan that covers eligible costs for dental work.

Departure time

The time at which a plane, train, or bus leaves a location.

Dependent

Any household member (including the taxpayer) who receives at least half of his or her financial support from a taxpayer.

Deposit

Money added to an account.

Deposit slip

A form that is filled out and submitted when money is added to an account.

Descending

An order of arrangement from highest to lowest number, size, etc.

Diameter

The longest chord of any circle; the straight line that passes through the center of a circle connecting two points on the circumference.

Difference

The answer to a subtraction problem.

Disability insurance

Protection that pays benefits to persons who are out of work because of an illness or injury that is not job-related.

Disclaimer

Labeling that informs the customer of the limits of the seller's responsibility.

Discount

A reduction in the regular price of an item.

Discount brokers

Persons who charge low fees to make stock transactions, but who do not give investment advice.

Disposable income

The amount of money available for spending.

Dividend

1. The number being divided.
2. Profit distributed to shareholders.

Dividend income

Money received from dividends.

Divisor

The number used to divide another number.

Down payment

That part of the selling price which the customer must pay at the time of purchase.

Drawer

The person who wants money withdrawn from his or her account to be paid to another (the payee).

Drop-off charge

The cost to return a rental car to a place other than where it was rented.

Durable goods

Any items expected to last for a long time.

Earning power

A person's ability to earn money now and in the future.

80% clause

An insurance provision which states that only homeowners who insure their homes for at least 80% of the replacement cost will receive full payment for damage claims.

Elapsed time

The amount of time that a trip takes.

Electronic funds transfer (EFT)

A system used to speed banking transactions by employing computer technology.

Emergency road service insurance

Insurance that pays for towing or road service repair when a car is disabled.

Employee's withholding allowance certificate

Also called a *Form W-4*. The form used by an employer and the employee for tax purposes.

Employment agency

A business that has lists of job openings, and that charges a fee for placing a person in a job.

Endorsing the check

Signing or stamping the back of a check in order to be credited with the amount written on the front.

Endowment policy

A type of life insurance policy that covers policyholders for their entire lives. Premiums are paid over a specified time, usually 20 or 30 years. At the end of the payment period, the policyholder receives the face value of the policy. Should the policyholder die during the payment period, the beneficiary collects a settlement from the insurance company.

Equal Credit Opportunity Act

The law which requires a creditor to treat a loan applicant fairly, and without discrimination.

Equally likely

A situation in which one event has the same chance to occur as another.

Equivalent

Equal in value.

Estimation

A technique used to determine whether answers are reasonable approximations.

Events

The results of an occurrence or outcome.

Exemption

Each person whom a taxpayer declares as a dependent, allowing the taxpayer to make certain deductions from taxable income.

Expiration date

The last day of warranty coverage.

Express warranty

A written guarantee covering specific conditions of the warranty. It lists any specific parts that are guaranteed, the length of the warranty and any labor charge for warranty repair.

Face value

1. The dollar amount of a loan represented by a bond.
2. The amount of coverage that an insurance policy provides.

Factory outlets

Stores located in the factory where the merchandise is produced.

Fair Credit Billing Act

The law which protects debtors in case there are any errors or disputed amounts on a monthly statement.

Fair Credit Reporting Act

The law which requires that a lending institution provide a loan applicant with a written reason if a loan application is turned down. If the loan has been denied because of a poor credit rating, the lending institution must provide the loan applicant with the name of the credit reporting agency that supplied the credit history.

Fair Debt Collection Practices Act

The law which prohibits a creditor from threatening a debtor or using unfair means to collect the amount owed.

Federal Deposit Insurance Corporation (FDIC)

The federal agency which insures bank deposits (accounts) against loss or bank failure for up to $100,000.

Federal Insurance Contributions Act (FICA)

The law that established social security.

Fee paid

An arrangement in which the employer is willing to pay the employment agency's fee for a prospective employee.

52-week high

The highest price at which a share of a corporation's stock was traded in the past year.

52-week low

The lowest price at which a share of a corporation's stock was traded in the past year.

Filed

Having mailed or submitted a tax return to the government.

Filing status

A description of a person's marital and family status on the last day of the tax year.

Finance charge

The extra cost charged when buying on credit. Another name for *interest*.

Finder's fee

The money charged by a broker to find an apartment for a client.

First quality

Goods sold with no defects.

Fixed-rate mortgage

A type of mortgage in which the monthly payment and APR (annual percentage rate) remain the same throughout the entire loan.

Floor plan

A drawing of the layout and the dimensions of a room.

Floor samples

A product used for demonstration or for advertising display in a store that is sold *as is*.

Fluid ounce

A unit of volume. One sixteenth of a pint.

Food and Drug Administration (FDA)

The government agency that supervises the food and drug industries in the United States.

Foreclosure

A legal procedure by which property can be repossessed by the lending institution if the borrower fails to meet mortgage payment obligations.

Form SS-5: Application for Social Security Number

The form that a person must fill out in order to be issued a social security number.

Form 1040

An Internal Revenue Service long tax form used by people who itemize deductions.

Form 1040A

One of the basic Internal Revenue Service short tax forms.

Form 1040EZ

One of the basic Internal Revenue Service short, simplified tax forms, used by single persons only.

Form 1099

A form used to report income from bank interest, stock dividends, royalties, and prizes.

Form W-4

Also called the *employee's withholding allowance certificate*. The form used by an employer and the employee for tax purposes.

Form W-2

Also called a *Wage and Tax Statement*. The form received by an employee by January 31 for each job held during the previous year. The form lists each employee's income and annual deductions.

Free checking

Sometimes called *regular checking*. An arrangement that requires the drawer to maintain a minimum balance in the account but which does not require a per check fee or monthly fee.

Full warranty

A written guarantee covering the entire product or certain parts of the product for a specified time.

Fundamental counting principle of probability

A formula used to determine the total number of combinations available.

Furnished

Equipped with furniture.

Gas expenses

The cost of gasoline used to make a specific trip.

Generic drugs

Medication that is sold by its chemical name rather than brand name.

Goods

Any items for sale.

Gram

The basic unit of weight in the metric system.

Gross capital gain

The difference between the selling price of shares of stock and the purchase price of the shares.

Gross pay

A person's total wages or income before any deductions are made.

Group insurance

Insurance coverage bought on behalf of a number of people purchasing insurance together, such as through an employer.

Health insurance

Coverage that pays all or part of hospital and medical care costs as provided in the policy.

Health Maintenance Organization (HMO)

A group of doctors and medical professionals who provide many health-care services at a fixed cost to members.

High

The highest price at which a share of stock was traded during a day's trading.

High risks

Having a greater than average chance of having an accident.

Homeowner's insurance

Coverage purchased by private homeowners against damage, theft, loss, or other occurrences as specified in the policy.

Horizontal axis

The line on a graph which is drawn running across (horizontally).

Hourly rate

The amount a person is paid for each hour worked.

Implied warranty

An unwritten guarantee that a product will do what it is supposed to do.

Improper fraction

Any fraction in which the numerator is greater than, or equal to the denominator.

Income taxes

Federal taxes based upon personal income.

Individual account

One type of savings account in which only one person can make deposits or withdrawals.

Installments

Scheduled payments of a debt, usually made on a monthly basis.

Installment plan

A convenient way to pay for merchandise over a scheduled period of time.

Insufficient funds

Not enough money in an account to cover a check.

Interest

1. The cost of borrowing money or using credit. Another name for *finance charge*.
2. The money banks pay their customers for the use of the customers' money.

Interest rate

Interest expressed as a percent.

Interior designers

Professionals who combine an artistic sense with mathematics to create a functional, attractive living space and to decorate a home.

Internal Revenue Service (IRS)

The government office which collects taxes.

Irregular

Goods that are damaged or contain defects.

Itemized deduction

Any expense, or item, that a taxpayer can subtract, or deduct, from gross income to determine taxable income.

Joint account

One type of savings account in which more than one person can make deposits and withdrawals.

Kilowatt-hours (kwh)

Units of electrical energy. Each kilowatt-hour is equivalent to 1,000 watt-hours of electricity.

Landlord

The owner of a property with space or facilities to rent.

Last (close)

The price of a share at the last or final trade of the day.

Late charge

The penalty charged for late payment of a debt.

Lease

A written agreement between a tenant and a landlord.

Lending institutions

Organizations that make loans.

Liable

Responsible.

Life insurance

A contract to pay money to an assigned party upon the death of the policyholder; often required when one secures a loan as guarantee of payment to a creditor in case the borrower dies before payment of a loan is completed.

Life insurance companies

As a loan source, a business that makes loans to their policyholders only. Also, a company that offers contracts which pay cash benefits to a beneficiary(ies) in case of the policyholder's death.

Limited liability

A legal provision that protects corporate shareholders (owners) so that they cannot lose more than they had invested in the business.

Limited payment life insurance

A type of life insurance that covers policyholders for their entire lives. A predetermined number of premiums are paid over a specified number of years, usually 20 or 30. This type of policy has cash value.

Limited warranty

A written guarantee that covers only certain parts of a product for specified lengths of time.

Line graphs

Visual aids used to depict changes over a period of time.

Line segment

A part of a line.

List price

Also *manufacturer's suggested retail price;* the price that the manufacturer suggests the store charge its customers.

Liter

The basic metric unit of liquid measure.

Loan

Money borrowed and paid back with interest.

Long-term account

An account opened by a depositor who agrees not to withdraw money from the account for a long period of time.

Loss leaders

Products priced lower than wholesale (often out-of-season, discontinued, or overstocked merchandise) advertised in order to attract customers to the store with the hope that they will buy other items as well.

Low

The lowest price at which a share of stock was traded during a day's trading.

Lowest common denominator

The smallest number that is divisible by each of the given denominators.

Maintenance fee

An amount that condominium and cooperative owners pay monthly that covers their share of the maintenance of the apartment complex and of the cooperative corporation's mortgage loan.

Major medical insurance

Coverage added to a health insurance policy to insure the policyholder against expenses not covered by a basic health insurance plan.

Manufacturer's suggested retail price

Another term for *list price*.

Map index

The alphabetical list of cities, towns, counties, or other information included on a map.

Map key

another name for *map legend*.

Map legend

The part of the map that explains what the symbols on that map mean.

Market value

The amount of money a property can be sold for.

Markup

The increase that a store charges from the wholesale to the retail price.

Maturity

The date upon which the owner of a bond must be paid the face value of the bond.

Maximum taxable income

The highest annual income subject to social security tax.

Mean

The arithmetic average; the sum of a group of numbers (data) divided by the number of pieces of data in that group.

Median

The middle piece of data; the middle number of a group of numbers when they are arranged in numerical order.

Medicaid

A government-sponsored health insurance program that pays a portion of the medical expenses of low-income patients regardless of their age.

Medical insurance

A plan that covers medical emergencies, hospital and doctor bills, and other health-related expenses.

Medicare

A government-sponsored health insurance program that pays a portion of the medical expenses of senior citizens.

Memory

In a calculator or computer, where information is stored or saved.

M+ (memory add)

The function key of a calculator that adds the number in the display to the number that is stored in the memory.

MC (memory clear)

The function key of a calculator that clears the memory.

MR (memory recall)

The function key of a calculator that recalls or displays the number that is currently in the memory.

Meter

1. The basic unit of length (distance) in the metric system.

2. A device which records utility usage.

Mileage charge

The amount charged per mile driven.

Mileage tables

Charts on a map that show the distance between selected major cities and towns.

Miles per gallon (mpg)

The number of miles a car can run on one gallon of gas.

Minimum balance

The least amount of money required, either to start a certificate of deposit, to open a regular checking account, or for other banking provisions.

Minimum payment

The lowest amount a creditor will accept as payment for the current billing period.

Minimum wage

The lowest hourly rate that can be paid to an employee in the United States.

Minor

A child; a person who has not reached a legal adult age, 18 to 21.

Mixed number

Any number having both a whole number and a fraction, such as $4\frac{3}{8}$.

Mode

The number that occurs most frequently in a group of numbers.

Money market certificate

A savings account that has an interest rate that varies.

Monthly

Each month; twelve times a year.

Monthly periodic rate

The percentage amount used to compute finance charges.

Monthly statement

1. A bill sent each month.
2. The summary of checking account transactions.

Mortality table

A chart, developed by insurance companies, which lists death rates for males and females in each age group.

Mortgages

Legal contracts providing a loan to a person to purchase a home or property.

Negative capital gain

A loss from sale of shares at a price lower than the purchase price.

Negligent

At fault.

Negotiable order of withdrawal (NOW) account

A checking account which pays interest.

Net change (chg.)

The difference between the previous trading day's closing price and the reported day's closing price.

Net pay

Also called *take-home pay*. The amount of money that a person is paid after all deductions have been subtracted from gross pay.

Net proceeds

The amount of money made after fees are deducted.

New balance

The amount a borrower currently owes.

No-fault insurance

Another term for personal injury protection.

Nontaxable item

Merchandise that is not taxed.

Nontransferable

That provision of a warranty that states protection may not be passed on from the original owner to a new owner.

Number of days in billing cycle

The amount of time, in days, covered by the current bill.

Numerator

The top number of a fraction; the number above the horizontal line of a fraction.

Nutrients

Any nourishing substances in a food that the body needs to stay healthy.

Nutrition

Diet; the study of a well-balanced diet.

Odd lot

A stock purchase of less than 100 shares.

Odds

A ratio expressing the probability of an event occurring.

Odometer

The instrument on a car that keeps track of the distance the car has traveled.

Opens

Starts an account.

Origination fee

Money paid to the lending institution for the paperwork involved in the loan-application process.

Outcome

The result of an occurrence or event.

Outstanding checks

Those checks that are not yet recorded on a bank statement.

Outstanding deposits

Those deposits that do not yet appear on a bank statement.

Overbooking

The practice of selling more confirmed reservations than the number of seats available on a flight.

Overdraft protection

An arrangement by which the bank will lend a person money (and charge interest) to cover checks that would otherwise bounce.

Overtime hours

Any extra hours that an employee works beyond the regular number of required hours.

Partnership

A business in which two or more people share ownership.

Passbook

A written record of all deposits, withdrawals, and interest payments for a savings account.

Pawnbrokers

Persons whose business involves lending money while keeping personal property as a guarantee until the borrower repays the loan, with interest.

Payee

The person or group to whom money is paid, or a check is made out.

Payment due date

The date that the monthly payment must be received by the creditor.

Pensions

Benefits paid to a retired employee.

Per check fee

Money charged by a bank for each check written.

Percents

Literally "per hundred." Numbers indicated by a percent sign (%), a decimal point (.), or as a fraction with a denominator of 100.

Perimeter

The distance around a polygon.

Perishable good

A product or item which, once used or consumed, must be repurchased.

Permutation

An arrangement in which order is important.

Personal identification number (PIN)

The individual code required by users of an electronic funds transfer (EFT) card in order to make deposits and withdrawals at an automated teller machine.

Personal injury protection (PIP)

Another name for *no-fault insurance*. Insurance which pays medical expenses resulting from an auto accident no matter who is to blame.

Personally liable

Being individually held legally responsible for a debt, damage, and so on.

Pictograph

A visual aid which presents information through use of illustrations or pictures.

Piecework

Work paid for by the piece or item, not by the hour.

Piecework rate

The amount of money paid for each item or piece completed.

Pieceworkers

Employees paid by the amount of work done rather than the length of time that it takes to do the job.

Planned obsolescence

The change in style and design of goods made by manufacturers to induce customers to buy simply to have the latest fashion, model, or look.

Points

The extra fee charged by a lending institution for the use of their money.

Policyholder

The person who buys an insurance policy.

Polygon

A closed figure with straight sides.

Portfolio

A list of all the shares of stock owned.

Premium

The amount of money paid for an insurance policy.

Prepayment penalty

An agreement that requires borrowers to pay a fee if they wish to pay back an entire loan before the due date.

Prepayment privilege

A loan feature that allows the borrower to make payments before the due date in order to reduce the amount of interest paid.

Previous balance

Any money owed before the current billing period.

Principal

1. The amount of money borrowed.

2. The amount of money in an account at any given time.

Probability

The study of chance.

Product

In multiplication, the answer to a problem.

Profit

The money left over after expenses are paid.

Promissory note

An agreement signed by the borrower that states the conditions of a loan.

Property damage liability (PD)

Insurance that pays for damages to another person's car or property caused by driving carelessly.

Property taxes

Sometimes called *real estate taxes*. Money collected from homeowners and used to pay for certain government services. The amount is based on the value of the house and property.

Proportion

An equation in which two ratios are equal.

Purchases

Debits on a bill.

Quarterly

Four times a year.

Quotient

The answer to a division problem.

Radii

Plural of *radius*.

Radius

A line segment that connects the center of a circle to any part on the circle.

Random

Chance; an accidental occurrence that happens without preplanning.

Ratio

A comparison of two numbers, usually stated as a fraction, a decimal, or a percent; proportion.

Reaction distance

How far a car moves during the reaction time.

Reaction time

The amount of time it takes a driver to switch from the gas pedal to the brake when preparing to stop.

Real estate taxes

Sometimes called *property taxes*.

Rebate

A partial refund of the purchase price of an item sent to the buyer by the manufacturer.

Reconciling a bank statement

Also called *balancing a checkbook*. Verifying bank records with personal records.

Reference number

A number on a statement used to identify specific transactions.

Refund

To return or repay: For example, money returned to the taxpayer from the government for overpayment of taxes.

Regular, 30-day account

One type of credit card account that requires the monthly bills for all purchases to be paid in full.

Regular checking account

Sometimes called *free checking*. An account that requires the drawer to maintain a minimum balance. No interest is paid, but there are no per check fees and no monthly fees.

Regular gross pay

A person's pay or income before deductions are made, and before any overtime is added.

Regular hours

The specific number of hours per week that an employee is required to work.

Reimbursement

The amount of money an insurance company pays back to the policyholder in settlement of a claim.

Renter's insurance

Coverage purchased by tenants against theft, loss, or other occurrences as specified in the policy.

Repossessed

Having been taken back by the creditor something bought on credit because the buyer has not paid money due.

Résumé

A brief account of a person's career or qualifications.

Retail price

The price a store charges for an item.

Retirement insurance

A plan which provides income for employees after they stop working.

Revolving charge accounts

Credit card accounts that do not require purchases to be paid in full, but for which there is a finance charge for each month the bill is not paid in full.

Round

In mathematics, approximating an answer by dropping unwanted digits from the right.

Round down

Approximating an answer by decreasing to the next lowest desired unit or digit.

Round lots

Groups of 100 shares.

Round up

Approximating an answer by increasing to the next highest desired unit or digit.

Royalty

Also called *commission*. Money earned based on a percentage of sales.

Sale price

The discounted price of an item.

Sales 100's

The number of groups of 100 shares of stock that were traded during the day's trading.

Sales receipt

A paper record of a purchase transaction.

Sales tax

Money that state and local governments use to fund the services they provide.

Sample space

The set of every possible outcome; the collection of all possible events.

Savings account

An arrangement in which a bank or savings institution agrees to pay interest for the use of the money in an account.

Savings and loan associations

Financial institutions that accept savings deposits and make loans to consumers.

Savings banks

Financial institutions that provide banking services to consumers.

Scale

The proportional reduction of each actual dimension (of a room, house, apartment, and so on) so it can be shown on paper.

Scale drawing

In interior design, the representation, on paper, of a home or rooms, in a reduced proportion to its actual size.

Schedule A

The tax form on which itemized deductions are listed.

Sectors

A region of a circle divided by radii.

Security deposit

Money paid by a tenant and kept in a special account by the landlord to be used only if the tenant causes damage to the apartment or breaks the lease.

Semiannually

Twice each year.

Semimonthly

Twice each month.

Services

Any tasks that one person does for another person, such as cut hair, prepare taxes, deliver merchandise, etc.

Serving size

The amount of a single serving of a specific food.

Settlement

The money received from an insurance company.

Shares of stock

Units of ownership of a corporation.

Shareholders

Persons who own stock in a corporation.

Simple interest

Interest compounded annually.

Single-payment loans

Loans in which the borrower pays back the entire loan, plus interest, at one time.

Social security

An insurance program, available jointly through an employer and the federal government, which provides some income and medical benefits for people after they retire.

Social security number

A unique identification, one for each individual who requests a number, which records a person's contributions to social security.

Social security percentage

The amount (percentage) of a person's salary taken out of each paycheck for payment of social security tax.

Social security tax

The money taken out of an employee's paycheck and used to pay for the social security program.

Sole proprietorship

A business owned by an individual.

Special checking account

An account that requires no minimum balance, but a per check fee and monthly fees are charged.

Speedometer

The instrument that indicates the rate at which a car is traveling.

Square centimeter (cm²)

The term used when reporting the total area of a figure measured in centimeters.

Square meter (m²)

The term used when reporting the total area of a figure measured in meters.

Square unit

Any figure that measures area by multiplying lengths.

Standby

A traveler waiting for a place that might become available in case of a last-minute cancellation from a fully booked flight.

Starting balance

The amount of money in an account at the beginning of the statement period.

Statement period

A time equal to approximately one month during which bank transactions are recorded.

Statistics

A branch of mathematics that uses numbers to organize, summarize, and interpret data.

Stock

In published stock tables, the column under which you will find the abbreviations of corporations' names.

Stock certificates

Documents that give evidence of ownership of stock.

Stock exchange

A place where brokers meet to trade stocks.

Stockbrokers

Persons licensed to buy or sell stocks.

Stop payment

A request by a drawer to a bank not to clear a specific check.

Straight life insurance

A type of insurance for which the premium is paid until the policyholder's death or until an age specified in the policy.

Sublet

To rent property to someone other than to the holders of the lease.

Subtotal

On a receipt, the sum of goods and services purchased (not including sales tax).

Sum

The result of addition.

Take-home pay

Also called *net pay*. The amount of money that a person is paid after all deductions have been subtracted from gross pay.

Tax liability

The amount of money a person owes the government.

Tax rate

The amount of money per dollar that a government collects.

Tax return

The form used to report taxable income to the government.

Tax schedule

Data used to determine tax liability.

Tax table

Data printed in columns and rows used to determine tax liability.

Tax worksheet

A list of financial records and other important information which must be organized before tax forms can be filled out.

Taxable income

The amount of earned income upon which taxes must be paid; total income minus allowable deductions.

Taxable items

Items subject to sales tax.

Templates

Flat, scale models.

Tenant

A person who pays rent to use or live in property owned by someone else.

Term insurance

Insurance that covers the policyholder for a specified period of time, usually 5, 10, or 20 years. After that time, the policy is no longer in effect, unless it is renewed for another term. Term insurance pays benefits only in case the insured person dies.

Ticker

A machine with either electronic or paper display that records stock transactions.

Ticker tape

The paper used in tickers to print trades.

Time zone

One of 24 divisions of the globe, each area observing a clock time one hour earlier than the zone immediately to the east.

Title

A legal claim of property ownership.

Title search

The procedure used to make sure that a seller does hold clear title to a property.

Trade

An exchange of shares, either bought or sold.

Transaction

1. A stock trade.
2. A deposit or withdrawal; banking or business activity.

Transaction description

The section of a credit card statement that lists where purchases were made and what payments were paid.

Travel accident insurance

Protection that covers medical expenses resulting from accidents that occur while on vacation.

Travel insurance

A contract which provides protection to people while traveling or on vacation.

Traveler's check

A bank check that can be used as cash, but which, unlike cash, can be replaced if lost or stolen. A safe way to carry cash when traveling.

Tree diagram

A simplified drawing or outline which shows all the combinations or possibilities at each decision point, so called because it resembles the branches of a tree.

Trip cancellation insurance

Protection that covers nonrefundable vacation payments if a person is unable to go on a trip because of illness or injury.

Trustee

A person who sets up and manages an account for someone else.

Truth-in-Lending Act

A law that requires lenders to let consumers know the exact terms of any lending agreement.

Unemployment insurance

A plan that provides income to persons who have lost their jobs through no fault of their own.

Unfurnished

Not equipped with furniture.

Uninsured and underinsured motorist protection (UMP)

Insurance which pays for car accident injury caused by a driver without sufficient insurance.

Unit

A general name for any standard of measurement such as inches, yards, or meters.

Unit price

The price of an item per one unit (one pound, one ounce, etc.) of the product.

U.S. Recommended Daily Allowance (USRDA)

The amount of various nutrients that the U.S. government recommends that people should have each day.

Universal Product Code (UPC)

A number on a product indicated by black stripes that can be read by a cashier's scanner linked to a central computer system.

Unlimited free mileage

One car rental option which allows a rental car to be driven for any number of miles without paying an additional fee.

Utilities

Essential public services such as natural gas, water, heating oil, electricity, and telephone service.

Variable-rate mortgage

A type of mortgage in which the monthly payment and annual percentage rate (APR) may change, as specified in the promissory note.

Vertical axis

The line on a graph that is drawn straight up and down (vertically).

Voided check

A check that contains an error and should not be used.

Volume

The amount of space inside a three-dimensional container, given in cubic units.

Voluntary trust account

A savings account set up by a trustee for a beneficiary.

Wage and Tax Statement

Also called a *Form W-2*. A form that employers must supply to employees by January 31, and that must be submitted by employees with their income tax forms. This form summarizes an employee's income and paycheck deductions.

Waiting list

A register of those customers who wish to purchase a ticket for a flight for which all confirmed reservations have been sold.

Warranty

The guarantee of a product's performance.

Watts

Units for measuring electric power.

Watt-hours

Units of measurement of the amount of electricity used.

Wholesale price

The price a manufacturer charges a store for a product. The store's cost for a product.

Withdrawal

Money taken out of an account.

Withdrawal slip

The form used to take money out of an account.

Withholds

Keep back, retain; deduct from a paycheck.

Withholding tax

Another name for *income tax*. That money that the employer deducts (withholds) from an employee's paycheck and sends to the federal government for payment of the employee's taxes.

Workers' compensation

A plan that provides cash payments and medical coverage to employees who are injured on the job.

INDEX

PHOTO ACKNOWLEDGMENTS